GREATEST
ESSAYS

GREATEST ESSAYS

CHARLES DICKENS • **WALT WHITMAN**
• **JOSEPH CONRAD** • THOMAS BURKE
• ELIZABETH TAYLOR • **EDGAR ALLAN POE**
• NATHANIEL HAWTHORNE
• O. HENRY • **WILLIAM T. FOSTER**
• **JANE ADDAMS** • JONATHAN SWIFT
• FRANCIS BACON • **MARK TWAIN**

Published by
Rupa Publications India Pvt. Ltd 2021
7/16, Ansari Road, Daryaganj
New Delhi 110002

Sales centres:
Bengaluru Chennai
Hyderabad Jaipur Kathmandu
Kolkata Mumbai Prayagraj

Edition Copyright © Rupa Publications India Pvt. Ltd 2021

All rights reserved.

No part of this publication may be reproduced, transmitted, or stored in a retrieval system, in any form or by any means, electronic, mechanical, photocopying, recording or otherwise, without the prior permission of the publisher.

P-ISBN: 978-93-89967-91-3
E-ISBN: 978-93-89967-92-0

Fifth impression 2024

10 9 8 7 6 5

Printed in India

This book is sold subject to the condition that it shall not, by way of trade or otherwise, be lent, resold, hired out, or otherwise circulated, without the publisher's prior consent, in any form of binding or cover other than that in which it is published.

CONTENTS

The Long Voyage *Charles Dickens*	1
The Begging-Letter Writer *Charles Dickens*	12
A Child's Dream of a Star *Charles Dickens*	21
A Meditation upon a Broomstick *Jonathan Swift*	25
How to Tell a Story *Mark Twain*	27
The Memorable Assassination *Mark Twain*	33
On Authorship and Style *Arthur Schopenhauer*	44
Of Truth *Francis Bacon*	86
Gifts *Ralph Waldo Emerson*	89
Uses of Great Men *Ralph Waldo Emerson*	93
Preface to *Leaves Of Grass* *Walt Whitman*	112
Buds and Bird-Voices *Nathaniel Hawthorne*	128
The Philosophy of Composition *Edgar Allan Poe*	137
Bread and the Newspaper *Oliver Wendell Holmes*	150

John Bull *Washington Irving*	162
The Mutability of Literature: A Colloquy in Westminster Abbey *Washington Irving*	174
American Literature *John Macy*	185
Anarchism: What it Really Stands For *Emma Goldman*	197
Niagara Falls *Rupert Brooke*	241
The Almost Perfect State *Don Marquis*	247
A Familiar Preface *Joseph Conrad*	253
O. W. Firkins *O. Henry*	261
The Student Life *William Osler*	269
The Russian Quarter *Thomas Burke*	280
A Clergyman *Max Beerbohm*	288
Bed-Books and Night-Lights *H. M. Tomlinson*	294
The Precept of Peace *Louise Imogen Guiney*	300
On Lying Awake at Night *Stewart Edward White*	306
A Woodland Valentine *Marian Storm*	310
The Elements of Poetry *George Santayana*	313

Nocturne — 316
Simeon Strunsky

Beer and Cider — 320
George Saintsbury

Beyond Life — 326
James Branch Cabell

The Fish Reporter — 334
Robert Cortes Holliday

The Fifty-First Dragon — 343
Heywood Broun

Dogs and Men — 352
Henry C. Merwin

The Devil Baby at Hull-House — 369
Jane Addams

Every Man's Natural Desire to be Somebody Else — 387
Samuel McChord Crothers

The Temple's Difficult Door — 399
Robert M. Gay

Exile and Postman — 408
Jean Kenyon Mackenzie

An Indictment of Intercollegiate Athletics — 416
William T. Foster

Car-Window Botany — 435
Lida F. Baldwin

Studies in Solitude — 443
Fannie Stearns Gifford

The Greek Genius — 451
John Jay Chapman

In Praise of Old Ladies — 473
Lucy Martin Donnelly

A Memory of Old Gentlemen — 480
Sharlot M. Hall

Viola's Lovers: A Study in the New Morality   485
   Richard Bowland Kimball

Haunted Lives   493
   Laura Spencer Portor

The Acropolis and Golgotha   511
   Anne C. E. Allinson

The Baptizing of the Baby   524
   Elizabeth Taylor

Worries of a Winter Walk   534
   William Dean Howells

THE LONG VOYAGE

CHARLES DICKENS

When the wind is blowing and the sleet or rain is driving against the dark windows, I love to sit by the fire, thinking of what I have read in books of voyage and travel. Such books have had a strong fascination for my mind from my earliest childhood; and I wonder it should have come to pass that I never have been round the world, never have been shipwrecked, ice-environed, tomahawked, or eaten.

Sitting on my ruddy hearth in the twilight of New Year's Eve, I find incidents of travel rise around me from all the latitudes and longitudes of the globe. They observe no order or sequence, but appear and vanish as they will—'come like shadows, so depart'. Columbus, alone upon the sea with his disaffected crew, looks over the waste of waters from his high station on the poop of his ship, and sees the first uncertain glimmer of the light, 'rising and falling with the waves, like a torch in the bark of some fisherman', which is the shining star of a new world. Bruce is caged in Abyssinia, surrounded by the gory horrors which shall often startle him out of his sleep at home when years have passed away. Franklin, come to the end of his unhappy overland journey—would that it had been his last!—lies perishing of hunger with his brave companions: each emaciated figure stretched upon its miserable bed without the power to rise: all, dividing the weary days between their prayers, their remembrances of the dear ones at home, and conversation on the pleasures of eating; the last-named topic being ever-present to them, likewise, in their dreams. All the African travellers, wayworn, solitary and sad, submit themselves again to drunken, murderous, man-selling despots, of the lowest order of humanity; and Mungo Park, fainting under a tree and succoured by a woman, gratefully remembers how his Good Samaritan has always come to him in woman's shape, the wide world over.

   A shadow on the wall in which my mind's eye can discern some traces of a rocky sea coast, recalls to me a fearful story of travel derived from that unpromising narrator of such stories, a parliamentary blue book. A convict is its chief figure, and this man escapes with other prisoners from a penal settlement. It is an island, and they seize a boat, and get to the main land. Their way is by a rugged and precipitous seashore, and they have no earthly hope of ultimate escape, for the party of soldiers despatched by an easier course to cut them off, must inevitably arrive at their distant bourne long before them, and retake them if by any hazard they survive the horrors of the way. Famine, as they all must have foreseen, besets them early in their course. Some of the party die and are eaten; some are murdered by the rest and eaten. This one awful creature eats his fill, and sustains his strength, and lives on to be recaptured and taken back. The unrelatable experiences through which he has passed have been so tremendous that he is not hanged as he might be, but goes back to his old chained-gang work. A little time, and he tempts one other prisoner away, seizes another boat, and flies once more—necessarily in the old hopeless direction—for he can take no other. He is soon cut off, and met by the pursuing party face to face, upon the beach. He is alone. In his former journey he acquired an inappeasable relish for his dreadful food. He urged the new man away, expressly to kill him and eat him. In the pockets on one side of his coarse convict-dress are portions of the man's body, on which he is regaling; in the pockets on the other side is an untouched store of salted pork (stolen before he left the island) for which he has no appetite. He is taken back, and he is hanged. But I shall never see that sea beach on the wall or in the fire, without him, solitary monster, eating as he prowls along, while the sea rages and rises at him.

   Captain Bligh (a worse man to be entrusted with arbitrary power there could scarcely be) is handed over the side of the Bounty, and turned adrift on the wide ocean in an open boat, by order of Fletcher Christian, one of his officers, at this very minute.

Another flash of my fire, and 'Thursday October Christian', five-and-twenty years of age, son of the dead and gone Fletcher by a savage mother, leaps aboard His Majesty's ship Briton, hove-to off Pitcairn's Island; says his simple grace before eating, in good English; and knows that a pretty little animal on board is called a dog, because in his childhood he had heard of such strange creatures from his father and the other mutineers, grown grey under the shade of the bread-fruit trees, speaking of their lost country far away.

See the Halsewell, East Indiaman outward bound, driving madly on a January night towards the rocks near Seacombe, on the island of Purbeck! The captain's two dear daughters are aboard, and five other ladies. The ship has been driving many hours, has seven feet water in her hold, and her main mast has been cut away. The description of her loss, familiar to me from my early boyhood, seems to be read aloud as she rushes to her destiny.

'About two in the morning of Friday the sixth of January, the ship still driving, and approaching very fast to the shore, Mr Henry Meriton, the second mate, went again into the cuddy, where the captain then was. Another conversation taking place, Captain Pierce expressed extreme anxiety for the preservation of his beloved daughters, and earnestly asked the officer if he could devise any method of saving them. On his answering with great concern, that he feared it would be impossible, but that their only chance would be to wait for morning, the captain lifted up his hands in silent and distressful ejaculation.

'At this dreadful moment, the ship struck, with such violence as to dash the heads of those standing in the cuddy against the deck above them, and the shock was accompanied by a shriek of horror that burst at one instant from every quarter of the ship.

'Many of the seamen, who had been remarkably inattentive and remiss in their duty during the great part of the storm, now poured upon deck, where no exertions of the officers could keep them, while their assistance might have been useful. They had actually skulked in their hammocks, leaving the working of the pumps and other necessary labours to the officers of the ship, and the soldiers, who had made uncommon exertions. Roused by a sense of their danger, the same seamen, at this moment, in frantic exclamations, demanded of heaven and their fellow-sufferers that succour which their own efforts, timely made, might possibly have procured.

'The ship continued to beat on the rocks; and soon bilging, fell with her broadside towards the shore. When she struck, a number of the men climbed up the ensign-staff, under an apprehension of her immediately going to pieces.

'Mr Meriton, at this crisis, offered to these unhappy beings the best advice which could be given; he recommended that all should come to the side of the ship lying lowest on the rocks, and singly to take the opportunities which might then offer, of escaping to the shore.

'Having thus provided, to the utmost of his power, for the safety of the desponding crew, he returned to the round-house, where, by this time, all the passengers and most of the officers had assembled. The latter were employed in offering consolation to the unfortunate ladies; and, with unparalleled magnanimity, suffering their compassion for the fair and amiable companions of their misfortunes to prevail over the sense of their own danger.

'In this charitable work of comfort, Mr Meriton now joined, by assurances of his opinion, that, the ship would hold together till the morning, when all would be safe. Captain Pierce, observing one of the young gentlemen loud in his exclamations of terror, and frequently cry that the ship was parting, cheerfully bid him be quiet, remarking that though the ship should go to pieces, he would not, but would be safe enough.

'It is difficult to convey a correct idea of the scene of this deplorable catastrophe, without describing the place where it happened. The Haleswell struck on the rocks at a part of the shore where the cliff is of vast height, and rises almost perpendicular from its base. But at this particular spot, the foot of the cliff is excavated into a cavern of ten or twelve yards in depth, and of breadth equal to the length of a large ship. The sides of the cavern are so nearly upright, as to be of extremely difficult access; and the bottom is strewed with sharp and uneven rocks, which seem, by some convulsion of the earth, to have been detached from its roof.

'The ship lay with her broadside opposite to the mouth of this cavern, with her whole length stretched almost from side to side of it. But when she struck, it was too dark for the unfortunate persons on board to discover the real magnitude of the danger, and the extreme horror of such a situation.

'In addition to the company already in the round-house, they had admitted three black women and two soldiers' wives; who, with the husband of one of them, had been allowed to come in, though the seamen, who had tumultuously demanded entrance to get the lights, had been opposed and kept out by Mr Rogers and Mr Brimer, the third and fifth mates. The numbers there were, therefore, now increased to near fifty. Captain Pierce sat on a chair, a cot, or some other moveable, with a daughter on each side, whom he alternately pressed to his affectionate breast. The rest of the melancholy assembly were seated on the deck, which was strewed with musical instruments, and the wreck of furniture and other articles.

'Here also Mr Meriton, after having cut several wax-candles in pieces, and stuck them up in various parts of the round-house, and lighted up all the glass lanthorns he could find, took his seat, intending to wait the approach of dawn; and then assist the partners of his dangers to escape. But, observing that the poor ladies appeared parched and exhausted, he brought a basket of oranges and prevailed on some of them to refresh themselves by sucking a little of the juice. At this time they were all tolerably composed, except Miss Mansel, who was in hysteric fits on the floor of the deck of the round-house.

'But on Mr Meriton's return to the company, he perceived a considerable alteration in the appearance of the ship; the sides were visibly giving way, the deck seemed to be lifting, and he discovered other strong indications that she could not hold much longer together. On this account, he attempted to go forward to look out, but immediately saw that the ship had separated in the middle, and that the forepart having changed its position, lay rather further out towards the sea. In such an emergency, when the next moment might plunge him into eternity, he determined to seize the present opportunity, and follow the example of the crew and the soldiers, who were now quitting the ship in numbers, and making their way to the shore, though quite ignorant of its nature and description.

'Among other expedients, the ensign-staff had been unshipped, and attempted to be laid between the ship's side and some of the rocks, but without success, for it snapped asunder before it reached them. However, by the light of a lanthorn, which a seaman handed through the skylight of the round-house to the deck, Mr Meriton discovered a spar which appeared to be laid from the ship's side to the rocks, and on this spar he resolved to attempt his escape.

'Accordingly, lying down upon it, he thrust himself forward; however, he soon found that it had no communication with the rock; he reached the end of it, and then slipped off, receiving a very violent bruise in his fall, and before he could recover his legs, he was washed off by the surge. He now supported himself by swimming, until a returning wave dashed him against the back part of the cavern. Here he laid hold of a small projection in the rock, but was so much benumbed that he was on the point of quitting it, when a seaman, who had already gained a footing, extended his hand, and assisted him until he could secure himself a little on the rock; from which he clambered on a shelf still higher, and out of the reach of the surf.

'Mr Rogers, the third mate, remained with the captain and the unfortunate ladies and their companions nearly twenty minutes after Mr Meriton had quitted the ship. Soon after the latter left the round-house, the captain asked what was become of him, to which Mr Rogers replied that he was gone on deck to see what could be done. After this, a heavy sea breaking over the ship, the ladies exclaimed, 'Oh, poor Meriton! He is drowned; had he stayed with us he would have been safe!' and they all, particularly Miss Mary Pierce, expressed great concern at the apprehension of his loss.

'The sea was now breaking in at the fore part of the ship, and reached as far as the mainmast. Captain Pierce gave Mr Rogers a nod, and they took a lamp and went together into the stern-gallery, where, after viewing the rocks for some time, Captain Pierce asked Mr Rogers if he thought there was any possibility of saving the girls; to which he replied, he feared there was none; for they could only discover the black face of the perpendicular rock, and not the cavern which afforded shelter to those who escaped. They then returned to the round-house, where Mr Rogers hung up the lamp, and Captain Pierce sat down between his two daughters.

'The sea continuing to break in very fast, Mr Macmanus, a midshipman, and Mr Schutz, a passenger, asked Mr Rogers what they could do to escape. 'Follow me,' he replied, and they all went into the stern-gallery, and from thence to the upper-quarter-gallery on the poop. While there, a very heavy sea fell on board, and the round-house gave way; Mr Rogers heard the ladies shriek at intervals, as if the water reached them; the noise of the sea at other times drowning their voices.

'Mr Brimer had followed him to the poop, where they remained together about five minutes, when on the breaking of this heavy sea, they jointly seized a hen-coop. The same wave which proved fatal to some of those below, carried him and his companion to the rock, on which they were violently dashed and miserably bruised.

'Here on the rock were twenty-seven men; but it now being low water, and as they were convinced that on the flowing of the tide all must be washed off, many attempted to get to the back or the sides of the cavern, beyond the reach of the returning sea. Scarcely more than six, besides Mr Rogers and Mr Brimer, succeeded.

'Mr Rogers, on gaining this station, was so nearly exhausted, that had his exertions been protracted only a few minutes longer, he must have sunk under them. He was now prevented from joining Mr Meriton, by at least twenty men between them, none of whom could move, without the imminent peril of his life.

'They found that a very considerable number of the crew, seamen and soldiers, and some petty officers, were in the same situation as themselves, though many who had reached the rocks below, perished in attempting to ascend. They could yet discern some part of the ship, and in their dreary station solaced themselves with the hopes of its remaining entire until daybreak; for, in the midst of their own distress, the sufferings of the females on board affected them with the most poignant anguish; and every sea that broke inspired them with terror for their safety.

'But, alas, their apprehensions were too soon realised! Within a very few minutes of the time that Mr Rogers gained the rock, an universal shriek, which long vibrated in their ears, in which the voice of female distress was lamentably distinguished, announced the dreadful catastrophe. In a few moments all was hushed, except the roaring of the winds and the dashing of the waves; the wreck was buried in the deep, and not an atom of it was ever afterwards seen.'

The most beautiful and affecting incident I know, associated with a shipwreck, succeeds this dismal story for a winter night. The Grosvenor, East Indiaman, homeward bound, goes ashore on the coast of Caffraria. It is resolved that the officers, passengers, and crew, in number one hundred and thirty-five souls, shall endeavour to penetrate on foot, across trackless deserts, infested by wild beasts and cruel savages, to the Dutch settlements at the Cape of Good Hope. With this forlorn object before them, they finally separate into two parties—never more to meet on earth.

There is a solitary child among the passengers—a little boy of seven years old who has no relation there; and when the first party is moving away he cries after some member of it who has been kind to him. The crying of a child might be supposed to be a little thing to men in such great extremity; but it touches them, and he is immediately taken into that detachment.

From which time forth, this child is sublimely made a sacred charge. He is pushed, on a little raft, across broad rivers by the swimming sailors; they carry him by turns through the deep sand and long grass (he is patiently walking at all other times); they share with him such putrid fish as they find to eat; they lie down and wait for him when the rough carpenter, who becomes his especial friend, lags behind. Beset by lions and tigers, by savages, by thirst, by hunger, by death in a crowd of ghastly shapes, they never—O Father of all mankind, thy name be blessed for it!—forget this child. The captain stops exhausted, and his faithful coxswain goes back and is seen to sit down by his side, and neither of the two shall be any more beheld until the great last day; but, as the rest go on for their lives, they take the child with them. The carpenter dies of poisonous berries eaten in starvation; and the steward, succeeding to the command of the party, succeeds to the sacred guardianship of the child.

God knows all he does for the poor baby; how he cheerfully carries him in his arms when he himself is weak and ill; how he feeds him when he himself is griped with want; how he folds his ragged jacket round him, lays his little worn face with a woman's tenderness upon his sunburnt breast, soothes him in his sufferings, sings to him as he limps along, unmindful of his own parched and bleeding feet. Divided for a few days from the rest, they dig a grave in the sand and bury their good friend the cooper—these two companions alone in the wilderness—and then the time comes when they both are ill, and beg their wretched partners in despair, reduced and few in number now, to wait by them one day. They wait by them one day, they wait by them two days. On the morning of the third, they move very softly about, in making their preparations for the resumption of their journey; for, the child is sleeping by the fire, and it is agreed with one consent that he shall not be disturbed until the last moment. The moment comes, the fire is dying—and the child is dead.

His faithful friend, the steward, lingers but a little while behind him. His grief is great, he staggers on for a few days, lies down in the desert, and dies. But he shall be re-united in his immortal spirit—who can doubt it!—with the child, when he and the poor carpenter shall be raised up with the words, 'Inasmuch as ye have done it unto the least of these, ye have done it unto Me.'

As I recall the dispersal and disappearance of nearly all the participators in this once famous shipwreck (a mere handful being recovered at last), and the legends that were long afterwards revived from time to time among the English officers at the Cape, of a white woman with an infant, said to have been seen weeping outside a savage hut far in the interior, who was whisperingly associated with the remembrance of the missing ladies saved from the wrecked vessel, and who was often sought but never found, thoughts of another kind of travel came into my mind.

Thoughts of a voyager unexpectedly summoned from home, who travelled a vast distance, and could never return. Thoughts of this unhappy wayfarer in the depths of his sorrow, in the bitterness of his anguish, in the helplessness of his self-reproach, in the desperation of his desire to set right what he had left wrong, and do what he had left undone.

For, there were many, many things he had neglected. Little matters while he was at home and surrounded by them, but things of mighty moment when he was at an immeasurable distance. There were many many blessings that he had inadequately felt, there were many trivial injuries that he had not forgiven, there was love that he had but poorly returned, there was friendship that he had too lightly prized: there were a million kind words that he might have spoken, a million kind looks that he might have given, uncountable slight easy deeds in which he might have been most truly great and good. O for a day (he would exclaim), for but one day to make amends! But the sun never shone upon that happy day, and out of his remote captivity he never came.

Why does this traveller's fate obscure, on New Year's Eve, the other histories of travellers with which my mind was filled but now, and cast a solemn shadow over me! Must I one day make his journey? Even so. Who shall say, that I may not then be tortured by such late regrets: that I may not then look from my exile on my empty place and undone work? I stand upon a seashore, where the waves are years. They break and fall, and I may little heed them; but, with every wave the sea is rising, and I know that it will float me on this traveller's voyage at last.

THE BEGGING-LETTER WRITER

CHARLES DICKENS

The amount of money he annually diverts from wholesome and useful purposes in the United Kingdom would be a set-off against the Window Tax. He is one of the most shameless frauds and impositions of this time. In his idleness, his mendacity, and the immeasurable harm he does to the deserving, dirtying the stream of true benevolence, and muddling the brains of foolish justices, with inability to distinguish between the base coin of distress, and the true currency we have always among us, he is more worthy of Norfolk Island than three-fourths of the worst characters who are sent there. Under any rational system, he would have been sent there long ago.

I, the writer of this paper, have been, for some time, a chosen receiver of Begging Letters. For fourteen years, my house has been made as regular a Receiving House for such communications as any one of the great branch Post Offices is for general correspondence. I ought to know something of the Begging-Letter Writer. He has besieged my door at all hours of the day and night; he has fought my servant; he has lain in ambush for me, going out and coming in; he has followed me out of town into the country; he has appeared at provincial hotels, where I have been staying for only a few hours; he has written to me from immense distances, when I have been out of England. He has fallen sick; he has died and been buried; he has come to life again, and again departed from this transitory scene: he has been his own son, his own mother, his own baby, his idiot brother, his uncle, his aunt, his aged grandfather. He has wanted a greatcoat, to go to India in; a pound to set him up in life for ever; a pair of boots to take him to the coast of China; a hat to get him into a permanent situation under Government. He has frequently been exactly seven-and-sixpence short of independence. He has had such openings at Liverpool—posts of great trust and confidence in merchants' houses, which nothing but seven-and-sixpence was wanting to him to secure—that I wonder he is not Mayor of that flourishing town at the present moment.

The natural phenomena of which he has been the victim, are of a most astounding nature. He has had two children who have never grown up; who have never had anything to cover them at night; who have been continually driving him mad, by asking in vain for food; who have never come out of fevers and measles (which, I suppose, has accounted for his fuming his letters with tobacco smoke, as a disinfectant); who have never changed in the least degree through fourteen long revolving years. As to his wife, what that suffering woman has undergone, nobody knows. She has always been in an interesting situation through the same long period, and has never been confined yet. His devotion to her has been unceasing. He has never cared for himself; he could have perished—he would rather, in short—but was it not his Christian duty as a man, a husband, and a father, to write begging letters when he looked at her? (He has usually remarked that he would call in the evening for an answer to this question.)

He has been the sport of the strangest misfortunes. What his brother has done to him would have broken anybody else's heart. His brother went into business with him, and ran away with the money; his brother got him to be security for an immense sum and left him to pay it; his brother would have given him employment to the tune of hundreds a year, if he would have consented to write letters on a Sunday; his brother enunciated principles incompatible with his religious views, and he could not (in consequence) permit his brother to provide for him. His landlord has never shown a spark of human feeling. When he put in that execution I don't know, but he has never taken it out. The broker's man has grown grey in possession. They will have to bury him some day.

He has been attached to every conceivable pursuit. He has been in the army, in the navy, in the church, in the law; connected with the press, the fine arts, public institutions, every description and grade of business. He has been brought up as a gentleman; he has been at every college in Oxford and Cambridge; he can quote Latin in his letters (but generally misspells some minor English word); he can tell you what Shakespeare says about begging, better than you know it. It is to be observed, that in the midst of his afflictions he always reads the newspapers; and rounds off his appeal with some allusion, that may be supposed to be in my way, to the popular subject of the hour.

His life presents a series of inconsistencies. Sometimes he has never written such a letter before. He blushes with shame. That is the first time; that shall be the last. Don't answer it, and let it be understood that, then, he will kill himself quietly. Sometimes (and more frequently) he has written a few such letters. Then he encloses the answers, with an intimation that they are of inestimable value to him, and a request that they may be carefully returned. He is fond of enclosing something—verses, letters, pawnbrokers' duplicates, anything to necessitate an answer. He is very severe upon 'the pampered minion of fortune', who refused him the half-sovereign referred to in the enclosure number two—but he knows me better.

He writes in a variety of styles; sometimes in low spirits, sometimes quite jocosely. When he is in low spirits he writes downhill and repeats words—these little indications being expressive of the perturbation of his mind. When he is more vivacious, he is frank with me; he is quite the agreeable rattle. I know what human nature is—who better? Well! He had a little money once, and he ran through it—as many men have done before him. He finds his old friends turn away from him now—many men have done that before him too! Shall he tell me why he writes to me? Because he has no kind of claim upon me. He puts it on that ground plainly; and begs to ask for the loan (as I know human nature) of two sovereigns, to be repaid next Tuesday six weeks, before twelve at noon.

Sometimes, when he is sure that I have found him out, and that there is no chance of money, he writes to inform me that I have got rid of him at last. He has enlisted into the Company's service, and is off directly—but he wants a cheese. He is informed by the sergeant that it is essential to his prospects in the regiment that he should take out a single Gloucester cheese, weighing from twelve to fifteen pounds. Eight or nine shillings would buy it. He does not ask for money, after what has passed; but if he calls at nine, tomorrow morning may he hope to find a cheese? And is there anything he can do to show his gratitude in Bengal?

Once he wrote me a rather special letter, proposing relief in kind. He had got into a little trouble by leaving parcels of mud done up in brown paper, at people's houses, on pretence of being a Railway Porter, in which character he received carriage money. This sportive fancy he expiated in the House of Correction. Not long after his release, and on a Sunday morning, he called with a letter (having first dusted himself all over), in which he gave me to understand that, being resolved to earn an honest livelihood, he had been travelling about the country with a cart of crockery. That he had been doing pretty well until the day before, when his horse had dropped down dead near Chatham, in Kent. That this had reduced him to the unpleasant necessity of getting into the shafts himself, and drawing the cart of crockery to London—a somewhat exhausting pull of thirty miles. That he did not venture to ask again for money; but that if I would have the goodness to leave him out a donkey, he would call for the animal before breakfast!

At another time my friend (I am describing actual experiences) introduced himself as a literary gentleman in the last extremity of distress. He had had a play accepted at a certain Theatre—which was really open; its representation was delayed by the indisposition of a leading actor—who was really ill; and he and his were in a state of absolute starvation. If he made his necessities known to the Manager of the Theatre, he put it to me to say what kind of treatment he might expect? Well! We got over that difficulty to our mutual satisfaction. A little while afterwards he was in some other strait. I think Mrs Southcote, his wife, was in extremity—and we adjusted that point too. A little while afterwards he had taken a new house, and was going headlong to ruin for want of a water-butt. I had my misgivings about the water-butt, and did not reply to that epistle. But a little while afterwards, I had reason to feel penitent for my neglect. He wrote me a few broken-hearted lines, informing me that the dear partner of his sorrows died in his arms last night at nine o'clock!

I despatched a trusty messenger to comfort the bereaved mourner and his poor children; but the messenger went so soon, that the play was not ready to be played out; my friend was not at home, and his wife was in a most delightful state of health. He was taken up by the Mendicity Society (informally it afterwards appeared), and I presented myself at a London Police Office with my testimony against him. The Magistrate was wonderfully struck by his educational acquirements, deeply impressed by the excellence of his letters, exceedingly sorry to see a man of his attainments there, complimented him highly on his powers of composition, and was quite charmed to have the agreeable duty of discharging him. A collection was made for the 'poor fellow', as he was called in the reports, and I left the court with a comfortable sense of being universally regarded as a sort of monster. Next day comes to me a friend of mine, the governor of a large prison. 'Why did you ever go to the Police Office against that man,' says he, 'without coming to me first? I know all about him and his frauds. He lodged in the house of one of my warders, at the very time when he first wrote to you; and then he was eating spring lamb at eighteen pence a pound, and early asparagus at I don't know how much a bundle!' On that very same day, and in that very same hour, my injured gentleman wrote a solemn address to me, demanding to know what compensation I proposed to make him for his having passed the night in a 'loathsome dungeon'. And next morning an Irish gentleman, a member of the same fraternity, who had read the case, and was very well persuaded I should be chary of going to that Police Office again, positively refused to leave my door for less than a sovereign, and resolved to besiege me into compliance, literally 'sat down' before it for ten mortal hours. The garrison being well provisioned, I remained within the walls; and he raised the siege at midnight with a prodigious alarum on the bell.

The Begging-Letter Writer often has an extensive circle of acquaintance. Whole pages of the 'Court Guide' are ready to be references for him. Noblemen and gentlemen write to say there never was such a man for probity and virtue. They have known him time out of mind, and there is nothing they wouldn't do for him. Somehow, they don't give him that one pound ten he stands in need of; but perhaps it is not enough—they want to do more, and his modesty will not allow it. It is to be remarked of his trade that it is a very fascinating one. He never leaves it; and those who are near to him become smitten with a love of it, too, and sooner or later set up for themselves. He employs a messenger—man, woman, or child. That messenger is certain ultimately to become an independent Begging-Letter Writer. His sons and daughters succeed to his calling, and write begging-letters when he is no more. He throws off the infection of begging-letter writing, like the contagion of disease. What Sydney Smith so happily called 'the dangerous luxury of dishonesty' is more tempting, and more catching, it would seem, in this instance than in any other.

He always belongs to a Corresponding-Society of Begging-Letter Writers. Anyone who will may ascertain this fact. Give money today in recognition of a begging-letter—no matter how unlike a common begging-letter—and for the next fortnight you will have a rush of such communications. Steadily refuse to give; and the begging-letters become Angels' visits, until the Society is from some cause or other in a dull way of business, and may as well try you as anybody else. It is of little use inquiring into the Begging-Letter Writer's circumstances. He may be sometimes accidentally found out, as in the case already mentioned (though that was not the first inquiry made); but apparent misery is always a part of his trade, and real misery very often is, in the intervals of spring-lamb and early asparagus. It is naturally an incident of his dissipated and dishonest life.

That the calling is a successful one, and that large sums of money are gained by it, must be evident to anybody who reads the Police Reports of such cases. But prosecutions are of rare occurrence, relatively to the extent to which the trade is carried on. The cause of this is to be found (as no one knows better than the Begging-Letter Writer, for it is a part of his speculation) in the aversion people feel to exhibit themselves as having been imposed upon, or as having weakly gratified their consciences with a lazy, flimsy substitute for the noblest of all virtues. There is a man at large, at the moment when this paper is preparing for the press (on the 29th of April, 1850), and never once taken up yet, who, within these twelve months, has been probably the most audacious and the most successful swindler that even this trade has ever known. There has been something singularly base in this fellow's proceedings; it has been his business to write to all sorts and conditions of people, in the names of persons of high reputation and unblemished honour, professing to be in distress—the general admiration and respect for whom has ensured a ready and generous reply.

Now, in the hope that the results of the real experience of a real person may do something more to induce reflection on this subject than any abstract treatise—and with a personal knowledge of the extent to which the Begging-Letter Trade has been carried on for some time, and has been for some time constantly increasing—the writer of this paper entreats the attention of his readers to a few concluding words. His experience is a type of the experience of many; some on a smaller, some on an infinitely larger scale. All may judge of the soundness or unsoundness of his conclusions from it.

Long doubtful of the efficacy of such assistance in any case whatever, and able to recall but one, within his whole individual knowledge, in which he had the least after-reason to suppose that any good was done by it, he was led, last autumn, into some serious considerations. The begging-letters flying about by every post, made it perfectly manifest that a set of lazy vagabonds were interposed between the general desire to do something to relieve the sickness and misery under which the poor were suffering, and the suffering poor themselves. That many who sought to do some little to repair the social wrongs, inflicted in the way of preventible sickness and death upon the poor, were strengthening those wrongs, however innocently, by wasting money on pestilent knaves cumbering society. That imagination, soberly following one of these knaves into his life of punishment in jail, and comparing it with the life of one of these poor in a cholera-stricken alley, or one of the children of one of these poor, soothed in its dying hour by the late lamented Mr Drouet, contemplated a grim farce, impossible to be presented very much longer before God or man. That the crowning miracle of all the miracles summed up in the New Testament, after the miracle of the blind seeing, and the lame walking, and the restoration of the dead to life, was the miracle that the poor had the Gospel preached to them. That while the poor were unnaturally and unnecessarily cut off by the thousand, in the prematurity of their age, or in the rottenness of their youth—for of flower or blossom such youth has none—the Gospel was *not* preached to them, saving in hollow and unmeaning voices. That of all wrongs, this was the first mighty wrong the Pestilence warned us to set right. And that no Post Office Order to any amount, given to a Begging-Letter Writer for the quieting of an uneasy breast, would be presentable on the Last Great Day as anything towards it.

The poor never write these letters. Nothing could be more unlike their habits. The writers are public robbers; and we who support them are parties to their depredations. They trade upon every circumstance within their knowledge that affects us, public or private, joyful or sorrowful; they pervert the lessons of our lives; they change what ought to be our strength and virtue into weakness, and encouragement of vice. There is a plain remedy, and it is in our own hands. We must resolve, at any sacrifice of feeling, to be deaf to such appeals, and crush the trade.

There are degrees in murder. Life must be held sacred among us in more ways than one—sacred, not merely from the murderous weapon, or the subtle poison, or the cruel blow, but sacred from preventable diseases, distortions, and pains. That is the first great end we have to set against this miserable imposition. Physical life respected, moral life comes next. What will not content a Begging-Letter Writer for a week, would educate a score of children for a year. Let us give all we can; let us give more than ever. Let us do all we can; let us do more than ever. But let us give, and do, with a high purpose; not to endow the scum of the earth, to its own greater corruption, with the offals of our duty.

A CHILD'S DREAM OF A STAR

CHARLES DICKENS

There was once a child, and he strolled about a good deal, and thought of a number of things. He had a sister, who was a child too, and his constant companion. These two used to wonder all day long. They wondered at the beauty of the flowers; they wondered at the height and blueness of the sky; they wondered at the depth of the bright water; they wondered at the goodness and the power of GOD who made the lovely world.

They used to say to one another, sometimes, supposing all the children upon earth were to die, would the flowers, and the water, and the sky be sorry? They believed they would be sorry. For, they said, the buds are the children of the flowers, and the little playful streams that gambol down the hillsides are the children of the water; and the smallest bright specks playing at hide and seek in the sky all night must surely be the children of the stars; and they would all be grieved to see their playmates, the children of men, no more.

There was one clear shining star that used to come out in the sky before the rest, near the church spire, above the graves. It was larger and more beautiful, they thought, than all the others, and every night they watched for it, standing hand in hand at a window. Whoever saw it first cried out, 'I see the star!' And often they cried out both together, knowing so well when it would rise, and where. So they grew to be such friends with it, that, before lying down in their beds, they always looked out once again, to bid it good night; and when they were turning round to sleep, they used to say, 'God bless the star!'

But while she was still very young, oh, very, very young, the sister drooped, and came to be so weak that she could no longer stand in the window at night; and then the child looked sadly out by himself, and when he saw the star, turned round and said to the patient pale face on the bed, 'I see the star!' and then a smile would come upon the face, and a little weak voice used to say, 'God bless my brother and the star!'

And so the time came all too soon! when the child looked out alone, and when there was no face on the bed; and when there was a little grave among the graves, not there before; and when the star made long rays down towards him, as he saw it through his tears.

Now, these rays were so bright, and they seemed to make such a shining way from the earth to Heaven, that when the child went to his solitary bed, he dreamed about the star; and dreamed that, lying where he was, he saw a train of people taken up that sparkling road by angels. And the star, opening, showed him a great world of light, where many more such angels waited to receive them.

All these angels, who were waiting, turned their beaming eyes upon the people who were carried up into the star; and some came out from the long rows in which they stood, and fell upon the people's necks, and kissed them tenderly, and went away with them down avenues of light, and were so happy in their company, that lying in his bed he wept for joy.

But, there were many angels who did not go with them, and among them one he knew. The patient face that once had lain upon the bed was glorified and radiant, but his heart found out his sister among all the host.

His sister's angel lingered near the entrance of the star, and said to the leader among those who had brought the people thither:

'Is my brother come?'

And he said, 'No.'

She was turning hopefully away, when the child stretched out his arms, and cried, 'O, sister, I am here! Take me!' and then she turned her beaming eyes upon him, and it was night; and the star was shining into the room, making long rays down towards him as he saw it through his tears.

From that hour forth, the child looked out upon the star as on the home he was to go to, when his time should come; and he thought that he did not belong to the earth alone, but to the star too, because of his sister's angel gone before.

There was a baby born to be a brother to the child; and while he was so little that he never yet had spoken a word, he stretched his tiny form out on his bed, and died.

Again the child dreamed of the open star, and of the company of angels, and the train of people, and the rows of angels with their beaming eyes all turned upon those people's faces.

Said his sister's angel to the leader:

'Is my brother come?'

And he said, 'Not that one, but another.'

As the child beheld his brother's angel in her arms, he cried, 'O, sister, I am here! Take me!' And she turned and smiled upon him, and the star was shining.

He grew to be a young man, and was busy at his books when an old servant came to him and said:

'Thy mother is no more. I bring her blessing on her darling son!'

Again at night he saw the star, and all that former company. Said his sister's angel to the leader.

'Is my brother come?'

And he said, 'Thy mother!'

A mighty cry of joy went forth through all the star, because the mother was reunited to her two children. And he stretched out his arms and cried, 'O, mother, sister, and brother, I am here! Take me!' And they answered him, 'Not yet,' and the star was shining.

He grew to be a man whose hair was turning grey, and he was sitting in his chair by the fireside, heavy with grief, and with his face bedewed with tears, when the star opened once again.

Said his sister's angel to the leader: 'Is my brother come?'

And he said, 'Nay, but his maiden daughter.'

And the man who had been the child saw his daughter, newly lost to him, a celestial creature among those three, and he said, 'My daughter's head is on my sister's bosom, and her arm is around my mother's neck, and at her feet there is the baby of old time, and I can bear the parting from her, God be praised!'

And the star was shining.

Thus the child came to be an old man, and his once smooth face was wrinkled, and his steps were slow and feeble, and his back was bent. And one night as he lay upon his bed, his children standing around, he cried, as he had cried so long ago:

'I see the star!'

They whispered to one another, 'He is dying.'

And he said, 'I am. My age is falling from me like a garment, and I move towards the star as a child. And O, my Father, now I thank thee that it has so often opened, to receive those dear ones who await me!'

And the star was shining; and it shines upon his grave.

A MEDITATION UPON A BROOMSTICK

JONATHAN SWIFT

*—According to the Style and Manner of the
Hon. Robert Boyle's Meditations*

This single stick, which you now behold ingloriously lying in that neglected corner, I once knew in a flourishing state in a forest. It was full of sap, full of leaves, and full of boughs; but now in vain does the busy art of man pretend to vie with nature, by tying that withered bundle of twigs to its sapless trunk; it is now at best but the reverse of what it was, a tree turned upside-down, the branches on the earth, and the root in the air; it is now handled by every dirty wench, condemned to do her drudgery, and, by a capricious kind of fate, destined to make other things clean, and be nasty itself; at length, worn to the stumps in the service of the maids, it is either thrown out of doors or condemned to the last use—of kindling a fire. When I beheld this I sighed, and said within myself, 'Surely mortal man is a broomstick!' Nature sent him into the world strong and lusty, in a thriving condition, wearing his own hair on his head, the proper branches of this reasoning vegetable, till the axe of intemperance has lopped off his green boughs, and left him a withered trunk; he then flies to art, and puts on a periwig, valuing himself upon an unnatural bundle of hairs, all covered with powder, that never grew on his head; but now should this our broomstick pretend to enter the scene, proud of those birchen spoils it never bore, and all covered with dust, through the sweepings of the finest lady's chamber, we should be apt to ridicule and despise its vanity. Partial judges that we are of our own excellencies, and other men's defaults!

But a broomstick, perhaps you will say, is an emblem of a tree standing on its head; and pray what is a man but a topsy-turvy creature, his animal faculties perpetually mounted on his rational, his head where his heels should be, grovelling on the earth? And yet, with all his faults, he sets up to be a universal reformer and corrector of abuses, a remover of grievances, rakes into every slut's corner of nature, bringing hidden corruptions to light, and raises a mighty dust where there was none before, sharing deeply all the while in the very same pollutions he pretends to sweep away. His last days are spent in slavery to women, and generally the least deserving; till, worn to the stumps, like his brother besom, he is either kicked out of doors, or made use of to kindle flames for others to warm themselves by.

HOW TO TELL A STORY

(The humorous story is an American development. It's different from comic and witty stories.)

MARK TWAIN

I do not claim that I can tell a story as it ought to be told. I only claim to know how a story ought to be told, for I have been almost daily in the company of the most expert storytellers for many years. There are several kinds of stories, but only one difficult kind—the humorous. I will talk mainly about that one. The humorous story is American, the comic story is English, the witty story is French. The humorous story depends for its effect upon the *manner* of the telling; the comic story and the witty story upon the *matter*. The humorous story may be spun out to a great length, and may wander around as much as it pleases, and arrive nowhere in particular; but the comic and witty stories must be brief and end with a point. The humorous story bubbles gently along, the others burst. The humorous story is strictly a work of art—high and delicate art—and only an artist can tell it; but no art is necessary in telling the comic and the witty story; anybody can do it. The art of telling a humorous story—understand, I mean by word of mouth, not print—was created in America, and has remained at home. The humorous story is told gravely; the teller does his best to conceal the fact that he even dimly suspects that there is anything funny about it; but the teller of the comic story tells you beforehand that it is one of the funniest things he has ever heard, then tells it with eager delight, and is the first person to laugh when he gets through. And sometimes, if he has had good success, he is so glad and happy that he will repeat the 'nub' of it and glance around from face to face, collecting applause, and then repeat it again. It is a pathetic thing to see. Very often, of course, the rambling and disjointed humorous story finishes with a nub, point, snapper, or whatever you like to call it. Then the listener must be alert, for in many cases the teller will divert attention from that nub by dropping it in a carefully casual and indifferent way, with the pretense that he does not know it is a nub. Artemus Ward used that trick a good deal; then when the belated audience presently caught the joke he would look up with innocent surprise, as if wondering what they had found to laugh at. Dan Setchell used it before him, Nye and Riley and others use it today. But the teller of the comic story does not slur the nub; he shouts at you—every time. And when he prints it, in England, France, Germany and Italy, he italicises it, puts some whooping exclamation points after it, and sometimes explains it in a parenthesis. All of which is very depressing, and makes one want to renounce joking and lead a better life. Let me set down an instance of the comic method, using an anecdote which has been popular all over the world for twelve or fifteen hundred years. The teller tells it in this way:

THE WOUNDED SOLDIER

In the course of a certain battle a soldier whose leg had been shot off appealed to another soldier who was hurrying by to carry him to the rear, informing him at the same time of the loss which he had sustained; whereupon the generous son of Mars, shouldering the unfortunate, proceeded to carry out his desire. The bullets and cannon-balls were flying in all directions, and presently one of the latter took the wounded man's head off—without, however, his deliverer being aware of it. In no long time he was hailed by an officer, who said: 'Where are you going with that carcass?' 'To the rear, sir—he's lost his leg!' 'His leg, forsooth?' responded the astonished officer. 'You mean his head, you booby.' Whereupon the soldier dispossessed himself of his burden, and stood looking down upon it in great perplexity. At length he said: 'It is true, sir, just as you have said.' Then after a pause he added, '*But he

TOLD *me* IT WAS HIS LEG!!!!!' Here the narrator bursts into explosion after explosion of thunderous horse-laughter, repeating that nub from time to time through his gaspings and shriekings and suffocatings. It takes only a minute and a half to tell that in its comic-story form; and isn't worth the telling, after all. Put into the humorous-story form it takes ten minutes, and is about the funniest thing I have ever listened to—as James Whitcomb Riley tells it. He tells it in the character of a dull-witted old farmer who has just heard it for the first time, thinks it unspeakably funny, and is trying to repeat it to a neighbor. But he can't remember it; so he gets it all mixed up and wanders helplessly round and round, putting in tedious details that don't belong in the tale and only retard it; taking them out conscientiously and putting in others that are just as useless; making minor mistakes now and then and stopping to correct them and explain how he came to make them; remembering things which he forgot to put in in their proper place and going back to put them in there; stopping his narrative a good while in order to try to recall the name of the soldier that was hurt, and finally remembering that the soldier's name was not mentioned, and remarking placidly that the name is of no real importance, after all—and so on, and so on, and so on. The teller is innocent and happy and pleased with himself, and has to stop every little while to hold himself in and keep from laughing outright; and does hold in, but his body quakes in a jelly-like way with interior chuckles; and at the end of the ten minutes the audience have laughed until they are exhausted, and the tears are running down their faces. The simplicity and innocence and sincerity and unconsciousness of the old farmer are perfectly simulated, and the result is a performance which is thoroughly charming and delicious. This is art—and fine and beautiful—and only a master can compass it; but a machine could tell the other story. To string incongruities and absurdities together in a wandering and sometimes purposeless way, and seem innocently unaware that they are absurdities, is the basis of the American art, if my position is correct. Another feature is the slurring of the point. A third is the dropping of a studied remark apparently without knowing it, as if one were thinking aloud. The fourth and last is the pause. Artemus Ward dealt in numbers three and four a good deal. He would begin to tell with great animation something which he seemed to think was wonderful; then lose confidence, and after an apparently absent-minded pause add an incongruous remark in a soliloquizing way; and that was the remark intended to explode the mine—and it did. For instance, he would say eagerly, excitedly, 'I once knew a man in New Zealand who hadn't a tooth in his head,'—here his animation would die out; a silent, reflective pause would follow, then he would say dreamily, and as if to himself, 'and yet that man could beat a drum better than any man I ever saw.' The pause is an exceedingly important feature in any kind of story, and a frequently recurring feature too. It is a dainty thing, and delicate, and also uncertain and treacherous; for it must be exactly the right length—no more and no less—or it fails of its purpose and makes trouble. If the pause is too short, the impressive point is passed, and the audience have had time to divine that a surprise is intended—and then you can't surprise them, of course. On the platform I used to tell a negro ghost story that had a pause in front of the snapper on the end, and that pause was the most important thing in the whole story. If I got the right length precisely, I could spring the finishing ejaculation with effect enough to make some impressionable girl deliver a startled little yelp and jump out of her seat—and that was what I was after. This story was called 'The Golden Arm', and was told in this fashion. You can practise with it yourself—and mind you look out for the pause and get it right.

THE GOLDEN ARM

Once 'pon a time dey wuz a monsus mean man, en he live 'way out in de prairie all 'lone by hisself, 'cep'n he had a wife. En bimeby she died, en he tuck en toted her way out dah in de prairie en buried her. Well, she had a golden arm—all solid gold, fum de shoulder down. He wuz pow'ful mean—pow'ful; en dat night he couldn't sleep, caze he want dat golden arm so bad. When it come midnight he couldn't stan' it no mo'; so he git up, he did, en tuck his lantern en shoved out thoo de storm en dug her up en got de golden arm; en he bent his head down 'gin de win', en plowed en plowed en plowed thoo de snow. Den all on a sudden he stop (make a considerable pause here, and look startled, and take a listening attitude) en say: 'My *lan'*, what's dat!' En he listen—en listen—en de win' say (set your teeth together and imitate the wailing and wheezing singsong of the wind), 'bzzz-z-zzz'—en den, way back yonder what de grave is, he hear a *voice!*—he hear a voice all mix' up in de win'—can't hardly tell 'em 'part—'Bzzz-zzz—W-h-o—g-o-t—m-y—g-o-l-d-e-n—*arm?*—zzz—zzz—W-h-o g-o-t m-y g-o-l-d-e-n *arm?*' (You must begin to shiver violently now.) En he begin to shiver en shake, en say, 'Oh, my! *Oh*, my lan'!' en de win' blow de lantern out, en de snow en sleet blow in his face en mos' choke him, en he start a-plowin' knee-deep toward home mos' dead, he so sk'yerd—en pooty soon he hear de voice agin, en (pause) it 'us comin' *after* him! 'Bzzz—zzz—zzz—W-h-o—g-o-t—m-y g-o-l-d-e-n—*arm?*' When he got to de pasture he hear it agin—closter now, en a-*comin'!*—a-comin' back dah in de dark en de storm—(repeat the wind and the voice). When he git to de house he rush upstairs en jump in de bed en kiver up, head and years, en lay dah shiverin' en shakin'—en den way out dah he hear it *again!*—en a-*comin'!* En bimeby he hear (pause—awed, listening attitude)—pat—pat—pat—*hit's a-comin' upstairs!* Den he hear de latch, en he *know* it's in de room! Den pooty soon he know it's a-*stannin' by de bed!* (Pause.) Den—he know it's a—*bendin' down over him*—en he cain't skasely git his breath! Den—den—he seem to feel someth'n *c-o-l-d*, right down 'most agin his head! (Pause.) Den de voice say, *right at his year* 'W-h-o—g-o-t—m-y—g-o-l-d-e-n *arm?*' (You must wail it out very plaintively and accusingly; then you stare steadily and impressively into the face of the farthest-gone auditor—a girl, preferably—and let that awe-inspiring pause begin to build itself in the deep hush. When it has reached exactly the right length, jump suddenly at that girl and yell, '*You've* got it!' If you've got the *pause* right, she'll fetch a dear little yelp and spring right out of her shoes. But you *must* get the pause right; and you will find it the most troublesome and aggravating and uncertain thing you ever undertook.)—*October 1895*

THE MEMORABLE ASSASSINATION

MARK TWAIN

Note: The assassination of the Empress of Austria at Geneva, 10 September 1898, occurred during Mark Twain's Austrian residence. The news came to him at Kaltenleutgeben, a summer resort a little way out of Vienna. To his friend, the Rev. Jos. H. Twichell, he wrote:

'That good and unoffending lady, the Empress, is killed by a madman, and I am living in the midst of world history again. The Queen's Jubilee last year, the invasion of the Reichsrath by the police, and now this murder, which will still be talked of and described and painted a thousand years from now. To have a personal friend of the wearer of two crowns burst in at the gate in the deep dusk of the evening and say, in a voice broken with tears, 'My God! The Empress is murdered,' and fly toward her home before we can utter a question—why, it brings the giant event home to you, makes you a part of it and personally interested; it is as if your neighbor, Antony, should come flying and say, 'Caesar is butchered—the head of the world is fallen!'

'Of course there is no talk but of this. The mourning is universal and genuine, the consternation is stupefying. The Austrian Empire is being draped with black. Vienna will be a spectacle to see by next Saturday, when the funeral cortege marches.'

He was strongly moved by the tragedy, impelled to write concerning it. He prepared the article which here follows, but did not offer it for publication, perhaps feeling that his own close association with the court circles at the moment prohibited this personal utterance. There appears no such reason for withholding its publication now.

A. B. P.

The more one thinks of the assassination, the more imposing and tremendous the event becomes. The destruction of a city is a large event, but it is one which repeats itself several times in a thousand years; the destruction of a third part of a nation by plague and famine is a large event, but it has happened several times in history; the murder of a king is a large event, but it has been frequent.

The murder of an empress is the largest of all large events. One must go back about two thousand years to find an instance to put with this one. The oldest family of unchallenged descent in Christendom lives in Rome and traces its line back seventeen hundred years, but no member of it has been present in the earth when an empress was murdered, until now. Many a time during these seventeen centuries members of that family have been startled with the news of extraordinary events—the destruction of cities, the fall of thrones, the murder of kings, the wreck of dynasties, the extinction of religions, the birth of new systems of government; and their descendants have been by to hear of it and talk about it when all these things were repeated once, twice, or a dozen times—but to even that family has come news at last which is not staled by use, has no duplicates in the long reach of its memory.

It is an event which confers a curious distinction upon every individual now living in the world: he has stood alive and breathing in the presence of an event such as has not fallen within the experience of any traceable or untraceable ancestor of his for twenty centuries, and it is not likely to fall within the experience of any descendant of his for twenty more.

Time has made some great changes since the Roman days. The murder of an empress then—even the assassination of Caesar himself—could not electrify the world as this murder has electrified it. For one reason, there was then not much of a world to electrify; it was a small world, as to known bulk, and it had rather a thin population, besides; and for another reason, the news traveled so slowly that its tremendous initial thrill wasted away, week by week and month by month, on the journey, and by the time it reached the remoter regions there was but little of it left. It was no longer a fresh event, it was a thing of the far past; it was not properly news, it was history. But the world is enormous now, and prodigiously populated—that is one change; and another is the lightning swiftness of the flight of tidings, good and bad. 'The Empress is murdered!' When those amazing words struck upon my ear in this Austrian village last Saturday, three hours after the disaster, I knew that it was already old news in London, Paris, Berlin, New York, San Francisco, Japan, China, Melbourne, Cape Town, Bombay, Madras, Calcutta, and that the entire globe with a single voice, was cursing the perpetrator of it. Since the telegraph first began to stretch itself wider and wider about the earth, larger and increasingly larger areas of the world have, as time went on, received simultaneously the shock of a great calamity; but this is the first time in history that the entire surface of the globe has been swept in a single instant with the thrill of so gigantic an event.

And who is the miracle-worker who has furnished to the world this spectacle? All the ironies are compacted in the answer. He is at the bottom of the human ladder, as the accepted estimates of degree and value go: a soiled and patched young loafer, without gifts, without talents, without education, without morals, without character, without any born charm or any acquired one that wins or beguiles or attracts; without a single grace of mind or heart or hand that any tramp or prostitute could envy him; an unfaithful private in the ranks, an incompetent stone-cutter, an inefficient lackey; in a word, a mangy, offensive, empty, unwashed, vulgar, gross, mephitic, timid, sneaking, human polecat. And it was within the privileges and powers of this sarcasm upon the human race to reach up—up—up—and strike from its far summit in the social skies the world's accepted ideal of Glory and Might and Splendor and Sacredness! It realizes to us what sorry shows and shadows we are. Without our clothes and our pedestals we are poor things and much of a size; our dignities are not real, our pomps are shams. At our best and stateliest we are not suns, as we pretended, and teach, and believe, but only candles; and any bummer can blow us out.

And now we get realized to us once more another thing which we often forget—or try to: that no man has a wholly undiseased mind; that in one way or another all men are mad. Many are mad for money. When this madness is in a mild form it is harmless and the man passes for sane; but when it develops powerfully and takes possession of the man, it can make him cheat, rob, and kill; and when he has got his fortune and lost it again it can land him in the asylum or the suicide's coffin. Love is a madness; if thwarted it develops fast; it can grow to a frenzy of despair and make an otherwise sane and highly gifted prince, like Rudolph, throw away the crown of an empire and snuff out his own life. All the whole list of desires, predilections, aversions, ambitions, passions, cares, griefs, regrets, remorses, are incipient madness, and ready to grow, spread, and consume, when the occasion comes. There are no healthy minds, and nothing saves any man but accident—the accident of not having his malady put to the supreme test.

One of the commonest forms of madness is the desire to be noticed, the pleasure derived from being noticed. Perhaps it is not merely common, but universal. In its mildest form it doubtless is universal. Every child is pleased at being noticed; many intolerable children put in their whole time in distressing and idiotic effort to attract the attention of visitors; boys are always 'showing off'; apparently all men and women are glad and grateful when they find that they have done a thing which has lifted them for a moment out of obscurity and caused wondering talk. This common madness can develop, by nurture, into a hunger for notoriety in one, for fame in another. It is this madness for being noticed and talked about which has invented kingship and the thousand other dignities, and tricked them out with pretty and showy fineries; it has made kings pick one another's pockets, scramble for one another's crowns and estates, slaughter one another's subjects; it has raised up prize-fighters, and poets, and village mayors, and little and big politicians, and big and little charity-founders, and bicycle champions, and banditti chiefs, and frontier desperadoes, and Napoleons. Anything to get notoriety; anything to set the village, or the township, or the city, or the State, or the nation, or the planet shouting, 'Look—there he goes—that is the man!' And in five minutes' time, at no cost of brain, or labor, or genius this mangy Italian tramp has beaten them all, transcended them all, outstripped them all, for in time their names will perish; but by the friendly help of the insane newspapers and courts and kings and historians, his is safe to live and thunder in the world all down the ages as long as human speech shall endure! Oh, if it were not so tragic, how ludicrous it would be!

She was so blameless, the Empress; and so beautiful, in mind and heart, in person and spirit; and whether with a crown upon her head or without it and nameless, a grace to the human race, and almost a justification of its creation; WOULD be, indeed, but that the animal that struck her down re-establishes the doubt.

In her character was every quality that in woman invites and engages respect, esteem, affection and homage. Her tastes, her instincts and her aspirations were all high and fine and all her life her heart and brain were busy with activities of a noble sort. She had had bitter griefs, but they did not sour her spirit, and she had had the highest honors in the world's gift, but she went her simple way unspoiled. She knew all ranks, and won them all, and made them her friends. An English fisherman's wife said, 'When a body was in trouble she didn't send her help, she brought it herself.' Crowns have adorned others, but she adorned her crowns.

It was a swift celebrity the assassin achieved. And it is marked by some curious contrasts. At noon last Saturday there was no one in the world who would have considered acquaintanceship with him a thing worth claiming or mentioning; no one would have been vain of such an acquaintanceship; the humblest honest bootblack would not have valued the fact that he had met him or seen him at some time or other; he was sunk in abysmal obscurity, he was away beneath the notice of the bottom grades of officialdom. Three hours later he was the one subject of conversation in the world, the gilded generals and admirals and governors were discussing him, all the kings and queens and emperors had put aside their other interests to talk about him. And wherever there was a man, at the summit of the world or the bottom of it, who by chance had at some time or the other come across that creature, he remembered it with a secret satisfaction, and MENTIONED it—for it was a distinction, now! It brings human dignity pretty low, and for a moment the thing is not quite realizable—but it is perfectly true. If there is a king who can remember, now, that he once saw that creature in a time past, he has let that fact out, in a more or less studiedly casual and indifferent way, some dozens of times during the past week. For a king is merely human; the inside of him is exactly like the inside of any other person; and it is human to find satisfaction in being in a kind of personal way connected with amazing events. We are all privately vain of such a thing; we are all alike; a king is a king by accident; the reason the rest of us are not kings is merely due to another accident; we are all made out of the same clay, and it is a sufficiently poor quality.

Below the kings, these remarks are in the air these days; I know it as well as if I were hearing them:

THE COMMANDER: 'He was in my army.'

THE GENERAL: 'He was in my corps.'

THE COLONEL: 'He was in my regiment. A brute. I remember him well.'

THE CAPTAIN: 'He was in my company. A troublesome scoundrel. I remember him well.'

THE SERGEANT: 'Did I know him? As well as I know you. Why, every morning I used to—' ...etc., etc.; a glad, long story, told to devouring ears.

THE LANDLADY: 'Many's the time he boarded with me. I can show you his very room, and the very bed he slept in. And the charcoal mark there on the wall—he made that. My little Johnny saw him do it with his own eyes. Didn't you, Johnny?'

It is easy to see, by the papers, that the magistrate and the constables and the jailer treasure up the assassin's daily remarks and doings as precious things, and as wallowing this week in seas of blissful distinction. The interviewer, too; he tries to let on that he is not vain of his privilege of contact with this man whom few others are allowed to gaze upon, but he is human, like the rest, and can no more keep his vanity corked in than could you or I.

Some think that this murder is a frenzied revolt against the criminal militarism which is impoverishing Europe and driving the starving poor mad. That has many crimes to answer for, but not this one, I think. One may not attribute to this man a generous indignation against the wrongs done the poor; one may not dignify him with a generous impulse of any kind. When he saw his photograph and said, 'I shall be celebrated,' he laid bare the impulse that prompted him. It was a mere hunger for notoriety. There is another confessed case of the kind which is as old as history—the burning of the temple of Ephesus.

Among the inadequate attempts to account for the assassination we must concede high rank to the many which have described it as a 'peculiarly brutal crime' and then added that it was 'ordained from above'. I think this verdict will not be popular 'above'. If the deed was ordained from above, there is no rational way of making this prisoner even partially responsible for it, and the Genevan court cannot condemn him without manifestly committing a crime. Logic is logic, and by disregarding its laws even the most pious and showy theologian may be beguiled into preferring charges which should not be ventured upon except in the shelter of plenty of lightning rods.

I witnessed the funeral procession, in company with friends, from the windows of the Krantz, Vienna's sumptuous new hotel. We came into town in the middle of the forenoon, and I went on foot from the station. Black flags hung down from all the houses; the aspects were Sunday-like; the crowds on the sidewalks were quiet and moved slowly; very few people were smoking; many ladies wore deep mourning, gentlemen were in black as a rule; carriages were speeding in all directions, with footmen and coachmen in black clothes and wearing black cocked hats; the shops were closed; in many windows were pictures of the Empress: as a beautiful young bride of seventeen; as a serene and majestic lady with added years; and finally in deep black and without ornaments—the costume she always wore after the tragic death of her son nine years ago, for her heart broke then, and life lost almost all its value for her. The people stood grouped before these pictures, and now and then one saw women and girls turn away wiping the tears from their eyes.

In front of the Krantz is an open square; over the way was the church where the funeral services would be held. It is small and old and severely plain, plastered outside and whitewashed or painted, and with no ornament but a statue of a monk in a niche over the door, and above that a small black flag. But in its crypt lie several of the great dead of the House of Habsburg, among them Maria Theresa and Napoleon's son, the Duke of Reichstadt. Hereabouts was a Roman camp, once, and in it the Emperor Marcus Aurelius died a thousand years before the first Habsburg ruled in Vienna, which was six hundred years ago and more.

The little church is packed in among great modern stores and houses, and the windows of them were full of people. Behind the vast plate-glass windows of the upper floors of a house on the corner one glimpsed terraced masses of fine-clothed men and women, dim and shimmery, like people under water. Under us the square was noiseless, but it was full of citizens; officials in fine uniforms were flitting about on errands, and in a doorstep sat a figure in the uttermost raggedness of poverty, the feet bare, the head bent humbly down; a youth of eighteen or twenty, he was, and through the field-glass one could see that he was tearing apart and munching riffraff that he had gathered somewhere. Blazing uniforms flashed by him, making a sparkling contrast with his drooping ruin of moldy rags, but he took no notice; he was not there to grieve for a nation's disaster; he had his own cares, and deeper. From two directions two long files of infantry came plowing through the pack and press in silence; there was a low, crisp order and the crowd vanished, the square save the sidewalks was empty, the private mourner was gone. Another order, the soldiers fell apart and enclosed the square in a double-ranked human fence. It was all so swift, noiseless, exact—like a beautifully ordered machine.

It was noon now. Two hours of stillness and waiting followed. Then carriages began to flow past and deliver the two or three hundred court personages and high nobilities privileged to enter the church. Then the square filled up; not with civilians, but with army and navy officers in showy and beautiful uniforms. They filled it compactly, leaving only a narrow carriage path in front of the church, but there was no civilian among them. And it was better so; dull clothes would have marred the radiant spectacle. In the jam in front of the church, on its steps, and on the sidewalk was a bunch of uniforms which made a blazing splotch of color—intense red, gold and white—which dimmed the brilliancies around them; and opposite them on the other side of the path was a bunch of cascaded bright-green plumes above pale-blue shoulders which made another splotch of splendor emphatic and conspicuous in its glowing surroundings. It was a sea of flashing color all about, but these two groups were the high notes. The green plumes were worn by forty or fifty Austrian generals, the group opposite them were chiefly Knights of Malta and knights of a German order. The mass of heads in the square were covered by gilt helmets and by military caps roofed with a mirror-like glaze, and the movements of the wearers caused these things to catch the sun rays, and the effect was fine to see—the square was like a garden of richly colored flowers with a multitude of blinding and flashing little suns distributed over it.

Think of it—it was by command of that Italian loafer yonder on his imperial throne in the Geneva prison that this splendid multitude was assembled there; and the kings and emperors that were entering the church from a side street were there by his will. It is so strange, so unrealizable.

At three o'clock the carriages are still streaming by in single file. At three-five a cardinal arrives with his attendants; later some bishops; then a number of archdeacons—all in striking colors that add to the show. At three-ten a procession of priests passes along, with a crucifix. Another one, presently; after an interval, two more; at three-fifty another one—very long, with many crosses, gold-embroidered robes, and much white lace; also great pictured banners, at intervals, receding into the distance.

A hum of tolling bells makes itself heard, but not sharply. At three-fifty-eight a waiting interval. Presently a long procession of gentlemen in evening dress comes in sight and approaches until it is near to the square, then falls back against the wall of soldiers at the sidewalk, and the white shirt-fronts show like snowflakes and are very conspicuous where so much warm color is all about.

A waiting pause. At four-twelve the head of the funeral procession comes into view at last. First, a body of cavalry, four abreast, to widen the path. Next, a great body of lancers, in blue, with gilt helmets. Next, three six-horse mourning-coaches; outriders and coachmen in black, with cocked hats and white wigs. Next, troops in splendid uniforms, red, gold, and white, exceedingly showy.

Now the multitude uncover. The soldiers present arms; there is a low rumble of drums; the sumptuous great hearse approaches, drawn at a walk by eight black horses plumed with black bunches of nodding ostrich feathers; the coffin is borne into the church, the doors are closed.

The multitude cover their heads, and the rest of the procession moves by; first the Hungarian Guard in their indescribably brilliant and picturesque and beautiful uniform, inherited from the ages of barbaric splendor, and after them other mounted forces, a long and showy array.

Then the shining crown in the square crumbled apart, a

wrecked rainbow, and melted away in radiant streams, and in the turn of a wrist the three dirtiest and raggedest and cheerfulest little slum-girls in Austria were capering about in the spacious vacancy. It was a day of contrasts.

Twice the Empress entered Vienna in state. The first time was in 1854, when she was a bride of seventeen, and then she rode in measureless pomp and with blare of music through a fluttering world of gay flags and decorations, down streets walled on both hands with a press of shouting and welcoming subjects; and the second time was last Wednesday, when she entered the city in her coffin and moved down the same streets in the dead of the night under swaying black flags, between packed human walls again; but everywhere was a deep stillness, now—a stillness emphasized, rather than broken, by the muffled hoofbeats of the long cavalcade over pavements cushioned with sand, and the low sobbing of gray-headed women who had witnessed the first entry forty-four years before, when she and they were young—and unaware!

A character in Baron von Berger's recent fairy drama 'Habsburg' tells about that first coming of the girlish Empress-Queen, and in his history draws a fine picture: I cannot make a close translation of it, but will try to convey the spirit of the verses:

I saw the stately pageant pass: In her high place I saw the Empress-Queen: I could not take my eyes away From that fair vision, spirit-like and pure, That rose serene, sublime, and figured to my sense A noble Alp far lighted in the blue, That in the flood of morning rends its veil of cloud And stands a dream of glory to the gaze Of them that in the Valley toil and plod.

ON AUTHORSHIP AND STYLE

ARTHUR SCHOPENHAUER

There are, first of all, two kinds of authors: those who write for the subject's sake, and those who write for writing's sake. The first kind have had thoughts or experiences which seem to them worth communicating, while the second kind need money and consequently write for money. They think in order to write, and they may be recognised by their spinning out their thoughts to the greatest possible length, and also by the way they work out their thoughts, which are half-true, perverse, forced, and vacillating; then also by their love of evasion, so that they may seem what they are not; and this is why their writing is lacking in definiteness and clearness.

Consequently, it is soon recognised that they write for the sake of filling up the paper, and this is the case sometimes with the best authors; for example, in parts of Lessing's Dramaturgie, and even in many of Jean Paul's romances. As soon as this is perceived the book should be thrown away, for time is precious. As a matter of fact, the author is cheating the reader as soon as he writes for the sake of filling up paper; because his pretext for writing is that he has something to impart. Writing for money and preservation of copyright are, at bottom, the ruin of literature. It is only the man who writes absolutely for the sake of the subject that writes anything worth writing. What an inestimable advantage it would be, if, in every branch of literature, there existed only a few but excellent books! This can never come to pass so long as money is to be made by writing. It seems as if money lay under a curse, for every author deteriorates directly when he writes in any way for the sake of money. The best works of great men all come from the time when they had to write either for nothing or for very little pay. This is confirmed by the Spanish proverb: honra y provecho no caben en un saco (honour and money are not to be found in the same purse). The deplorable condition of the literature of today, both in Germany and other countries, is due to the fact that books are written for the sake of earning money. Everyone who is in want of money sits down and writes a book, and the public is stupid enough to buy it. The secondary effect of this is the ruin of language.

A great number of bad authors eke out their existence entirely by the foolishness of the public, which only will read what has just been printed. I refer to journalists, who have been appropriately so-called. In other words, it would be 'day labourer'.

◆

Again, it may be said that there are three kinds of authors. In the first place, there are those who write without thinking. They write from memory, from reminiscences, or even direct from other people's books. This class is the most numerous. In the second are those who think whilst they are writing. They think in order to write; and they are numerous. In the third place, there are those who have thought before they begin to write. They write solely because they have thought; and they are rare.

Authors of the second class, who postpone their thinking until they begin to write, are like a sportsman who goes out at random—he is not likely to bring home very much. While the writing of an author of the third, the rare class, is like a chase where the game has been captured beforehand and cooped up in some enclosure from which it is afterwards set free, so many at a time, into another enclosure, where it is not possible for it to escape, and the sportsman now has nothing to do but to aim and fire—that is to say, put his thoughts on paper. This is the kind of sport which yields something.

But although the number of those authors who really and seriously think before they write is small, only extremely few of them think about the subject itself; the rest think only about the books written on this subject, and what has been said by others upon it, I mean. In order to think, they must have the more direct and powerful incentive of other people's thoughts. These become their next theme, and therefore they always remain under their influence and are never, strictly speaking, original. On the contrary, the former are roused to thought through the subject itself, hence their thinking is directed immediately to it. It is only among them that we find the authors whose names become immortal. Let it be understood that I am speaking here of writers of the higher branches of literature, and not of writers on the method of distilling brandy.

It is only the writer who takes the material on which he writes direct out of his own head that is worth reading. Book manufacturers, compilers, and the ordinary history writers, and others like them, take their material straight out of books; it passes into their fingers without its having paid transit duty or undergone inspection when it was in their heads, to say nothing of elaboration. (How learned many a man would be if he knew everything that was in his own books!) Hence their talk is often of such a vague nature that one racks one's brains in vain to understand what they are really thinking. They are not thinking at all. The book from which they copy is sometimes composed in the same way: so that writing of this kind is like a plaster cast of a cast of a cast, and so on, until finally all that is left is a scarcely recognisable outline of the face of Antinous. Therefore, compilations should be read as seldom as possible: it is difficult to avoid them entirely, since compendia, which contain in a small space knowledge that has been collected in the course of several centuries, are included in compilations.

No greater mistake can be made than to imagine that what has been written latest is always the more correct; that what is written later on is an improvement on what was written previously; and that every change means progress. Men who think and have correct judgment, and people who treat their subject earnestly, are all exceptions only. Vermin is the rule everywhere in the world: it is always at hand and busily engaged in trying to improve in its own way upon the mature deliberations of the thinkers. So that if a man wishes to improve himself in any subject he must guard against immediately seizing the newest books written upon it, in the assumption that science is always advancing and that the older books have been made use of in the compiling of the new. They have, it is true, been used; but how? The writer often does not thoroughly understand the old books; he will, at the same time, not use their exact words, so that the result is he spoils and bungles what has been said in a much better and clearer way by the old writers; since they wrote from their own lively knowledge of the subject. He often leaves out the best things they have written, their most striking elucidations of the matter, their happiest remarks, because he does not recognise their value or feel how pregnant they are. It is only what is stupid and shallow that appeals to him. An old and excellent book is frequently shelved for new and bad ones; which, written for the sake of money, wear a pretentious air and are much eulogised by the authors' friends. In science, a man who wishes to distinguish himself brings something new to market; this frequently consists in his denouncing some principle that has been previously held as correct, so that he may establish a wrong one of his own. Sometimes his attempt is successful for a short time, when a return is made to the old and correct doctrine. These innovators are serious about nothing else in the world than their own priceless person, and it is with this that they wish to make its mark. They bring this quickly about by beginning a paradox; the sterility of their own heads suggests their taking the path of negation; and truths that have long been recognised are now denied—for instance, the vital power, the sympathetic nervous system, generatio equivoca, Bichat's distinction between the working of the passions and the working of intelligence, or they return to crass atomism, etc., etc. Hence the course of science is often retrogressive.

To this class of writers belong also those translators who, besides translating their author, at the same time correct and alter him, a thing that always seems to me impertinent. Write books yourself which are worth translating and leave the books of other people as they are. One should read, if it is possible, the real authors, the founders and discoverers of things, or at any rate the recognised great masters in every branch of learning, and buy second-hand books rather than read their contents in new ones.

It is true that *inventis aliquid addere facile est*, therefore a man, after having studied the principles of his subject, will have to make himself acquainted with the more recent information written upon it. In general, the following rule holds good here as elsewhere, namely: what is new is seldom good; because a good thing is only new for a short time.

What the address is to a letter the title should be to a book—that is, its immediate aim should be to bring the book to that part of the public that will be interested in its contents. Therefore, the title should be effective, and since it is essentially short, it should be concise, laconic, pregnant, and if possible express the contents in a word. Therefore a title that is prolix, or means nothing at all, or that is indirect or ambiguous, is bad; so is one that is false and misleading: this last may prepare for the book the same fate as that which awaits a wrongly addressed letter. The worst titles are those that are stolen, such titles that is to say that other books already bear; for in the first place they are a plagiarism, and in the second a most convincing proof of an absolute want of originality. A man who has not enough originality to think out a new title for his book will be much less capable of giving it new contents. Akin to these are those titles which have been imitated, in other words, half stolen; for instance, a long time after I had written 'On Will in Nature', Oersted wrote 'On Mind in Nature'.

◆

A book can never be anything more than the impression of its author's thoughts. The value of these thoughts lies either in the matter about which he has thought, or in the form in which he develops his matter—that is to say, what he has thought about it.

The matter of books is very various, as also are the merits

conferred on books on account of their matter. All matter that is the outcome of experience, in other words everything that is founded on fact, whether it be historical or physical, taken by itself and in its widest sense, is included in the term matter. It is the motif that gives its peculiar character to the book, so that a book can be important whoever the author may have been; while with form the peculiar character of a book rests with the author of it. The subjects may be of such a nature as to be accessible and well known to everybody; but the form in which they are expounded, what has been thought about them, gives the book its value, and this depends upon the author. Therefore if a book, from this point of view, is excellent and without a rival, so also is its author. From this it follows that the merit of a writer worth reading is all the greater the less he is dependent on matter—and the better known and worn out this matter, the greater will be his merit. The three great Grecian tragedians, for instance, all worked at the same subject.

So that when a book becomes famous one should carefully distinguish whether it is so on account of its matter or its form.

Quite ordinary and shallow men are able to produce books of very great importance because of their matter, which was accessible to them alone. Take, for instance, books which give descriptions of foreign countries, rare natural phenomena, experiments that have been made, historical events of which they were witnesses, or have spent both time and trouble in inquiring into and specially studying the authorities for them.

On the other hand, it is on form that we are dependent, where the matter is accessible to everyone or very well known; and it is what has been thought about the matter that will give any value to the achievement; it will only be an eminent man who will be able to write anything that is worth reading. For the others will only think what is possible for every other man to think. They give the impress of their own mind; but everyone already possesses the original of this impression.

However, the public is very much more interested in matter

than in form, and it is for this very reason that it is behindhand in any high degree of culture. It is most laughable the way the public reveals its liking for matter in poetic works; it carefully investigates the real events or personal circumstances of the poet's life which served to give the motif of his works; nay, finally, it finds these more interesting than the works themselves; it reads more about Goethe than what has been written by Goethe, and industriously studies the legend of Faust in preference to Goethe's Faust itself. And when Bürger said that 'people would make learned expositions as to who Leonora really was', we see this literally fulfilled in Goethe's case, for we now have many learned expositions on Faust and the Faust legend. They are and will remain of a purely material character. This preference for matter to form is the same as a man ignoring the shape and painting of a fine Etruscan vase in order to make a chemical examination of the clay and colours of which it is made. The attempt to be effective by means of the matter used, thereby ministering to this evil propensity of the public, is absolutely to be censured in branches of writing where the merit must lie expressly in the form; as, for instance, in poetical writing. However, there are numerous bad dramatic authors striving to fill the theatre by means of the matter they are treating. For instance, they place on the stage any kind of celebrated man, however stripped of dramatic incidents his life may have been, nay, sometimes without waiting until the persons who appear with him are dead.

The distinction between matter and form, of which I am here speaking, is true also in regard to conversation. It is chiefly intelligence, judgment, wit and vivacity that enable a man to converse; they give form to the conversation. However, the matter of the conversation must soon come into notice—in other words, that about which one can talk to the man, namely, his knowledge. If this is very small, it will only be his possessing the above-named formal qualities in a quite exceptionally high degree that will make his conversation of any value, for his matter will be restricted to things concerning humanity and nature, which are known generally. It is just the reverse if a man is wanting in these formal qualities, but has, on the other hand, knowledge of such a kind that it lends value to his conversation; this value, however, will then entirely rest on the matter of his conversation, for, according to the Spanish proverb, *mas sabe el necio en su casa, que el sabio en la agena.*

A thought only really lives until it has reached the boundary line of words; it then becomes petrified and dies immediately; yet it is as everlasting as the fossilised animals and plants of former ages. Its existence, which is really momentary, may be compared to a crystal the instant it becomes crystallised.

As soon as a thought has found words it no longer exists in us or is serious in its deepest sense.

When it begins to exist for others it ceases to live in us; just as a child frees itself from its mother when it comes into existence. The poet has also said:

Ihr müsst mich nicht durch Widerspruch verwirren! Sobald man spricht, beginnt man schon zu irren.

The pen is to thought what the stick is to walking, but one walks most easily without a stick, and thinks most perfectly when no pen is at hand. It is only when a man begins to get old that he likes to make use of a stick and his pen.

A hypothesis that has once gained a position in the mind, or been born in it, leads a life resembling that of an organism, in so far as it receives from the outer world matter only that is advantageous and homogeneous to it; on the other hand, matter that is harmful and heterogeneous to it is either rejected, or if it must be received, cast off again entirely.

Abstract and indefinite terms should be employed in satire only as they are in algebra, in place of concrete and specified quantities. Moreover, it should be used as sparingly as the dissecting knife on the body of a living man. At the risk of forfeiting his life it is an unsafe experiment.

For a work to become immortal it must possess so many excellences that it will not be easy to find a man who understands and values them all; so that there will be in all ages men who recognise and appreciate some of these excellences; by this means the credit of the work will be retained throughout the long course of centuries and ever-changing interests, for, as it is appreciated first in this sense, then in that, the interest is never exhausted.

An author like this, in other words, an author who has a claim to live on in posterity, can only be a man who seeks in vain his like among his contemporaries over the wide world, his marked distinction making him a striking contrast to everyone else. Even if he existed through several generations, like the wandering Jew, he would still occupy the same position; in short, he would be, as Ariosto has put it, *lo fece natura, e poi ruppe lo stampo*. If this were not so, one would not be able to understand why his thoughts should not perish like those of other men.

In almost every age, whether it be in literature or art, we find that if a thoroughly wrong idea, or a fashion, or a manner is in vogue, it is admired. Those of ordinary intelligence trouble themselves inordinately to acquire it and put it in practice. An intelligent man sees through it and despises it, consequently he remains out of fashion. Some years later the public sees through it and takes the sham for what it is worth; it now laughs at it, and the much-admired colour of all these works of fashion falls off like the plaster from a badly-built wall: and they are in the same dilapidated condition. We should be glad and not sorry when a fundamentally wrong notion of which we have been secretly conscious for a long time finally gains a footing and is proclaimed both loudly and openly. The falseness of it will soon be felt and eventually proclaimed equally loudly and openly. It is as if an abscess had burst.

The man who publishes and edits an article written by an anonymous critic should be held as immediately responsible for it as if he had written it himself; just as one holds a manager responsible for bad work done by his workmen. In this way the fellow would be treated as he deserves to be—namely, without any ceremony.

An anonymous writer is a literary fraud against whom one should immediately cry out, 'Wretch, if you do not wish to admit what it is you say against other people, hold your slanderous tongue.'

An anonymous criticism carries no more weight than an anonymous letter, and should therefore be looked upon with equal mistrust. Or do we wish to accept the assumed name of a man, who in reality represents a société anonyme, as a guarantee for the veracity of his friends?

The little honesty that exists among authors is discernible in the unconscionable way they misquote from the writings of others. I find whole passages in my works wrongly quoted, and it is only in my appendix, which is absolutely lucid, that an exception is made. The misquotation is frequently due to carelessness, the pen of such people has been used to write down such trivial and banal phrases that it goes on writing them out of force of habit. Sometimes the misquotation is due to impertinence on the part of someone who wants to improve upon my work; but a bad motive only too often prompts the misquotation—it is then horrid baseness and roguery, and, like a man who commits forgery, he loses the character for being an honest man forever.

Style is the physiognomy of the mind. It is a more reliable key to character than the physiognomy of the body. To imitate another person's style is like wearing a mask. However fine the mask, it soon becomes insipid and intolerable because it is without life; so that even the ugliest living face is better. Therefore authors who write in Latin and imitate the style of the old writers essentially wear a mask; one certainly hears what they say, but one cannot watch their physiognomy—that is to say, their style. One observes, however, the style in the Latin writings of men who think for themselves, those who have not deigned to imitate, as, for instance, Scotus Erigena, Petrarch, Bacon, Descartes, Spinoza, etc.

Affectation in style is like making grimaces. The language in which a man writes is the physiognomy of his nation; it establishes a great many differences, beginning from the language of the Greeks down to that of the Caribbean islanders.

We should seek for the faults in the style of another author's works, so that we may avoid committing the same in our own.

In order to get a provisional estimate of the value of an author's Productions, it is not exactly necessary to know the matter on which he has thought or what it is he has thought about—this would compel one to read the whole of his works, but it will be sufficient to know how he has thought. His style is an exact expression of how he has thought, of the essential state and general quality of his thoughts. It shows the formal nature—which must always remain the same—of all the thoughts of a man, whatever the subject on which he has thought or what it is he has said about it. It is the dough out of which all his ideas are kneaded, however various they may be. When Eulenspiegel was asked by a man how long he would have to walk before reaching the next place, and gave the apparently absurd answer Walk, his intention was to judge from the man's walking how far he would go in a given time. And so it is when I have read a few pages of an author, I know about how far he can help me.

In the secret consciousness that this is the condition of things, every mediocre writer tries to mask his own natural style. This instantly necessitates his giving up all idea of being naïve, a privilege which belongs to superior minds sensible of their superiority, and therefore sure of themselves. For instance, it is absolutely impossible for men of ordinary intelligence to make up their minds to write as they think; they resent the idea of their work looking too simple. It would always be of some value, however. If they would only go honestly to work and in a simple way express the few and ordinary ideas they have really thought, they would be readable and even instructive in their own sphere. But instead of that they try to appear to have thought much more deeply than is the case. The result is, they put what they have to say into forced and involved language, create new words and prolix periods which go round the thought and cover it up. They hesitate between the two attempts of communicating the thought and of concealing it. They want to make it look grand so that it has the appearance of being learned and profound, thereby giving one the idea that there is much more in it than one perceives at the moment. Accordingly, they sometimes put down their thoughts in bits, in short, equivocal, and paradoxical sentences which appear to mean much more than they say (a splendid example of this kind of writing is furnished by Schelling's treatises on Natural Philosophy); sometimes they express their thoughts in a crowd of words and the most intolerable diffuseness, as if it were necessary to make a sensation in order to make the profound meaning of their phrases intelligible—while it is quite a simple idea if not a trivial one (examples without number are supplied in Fichte's popular works and in the philosophical pamphlets of a hundred other miserable blockheads that are not worth mentioning), or else they endeavour to use a certain style in writing which it has pleased them to adopt—for example, a style that is so thoroughly Kat' e'xochae'u profound and scientific, where one is tortured to death by the narcotic effect of long-spun periods that are void of all thought (examples of this are specially supplied by those most impertinent of all mortals, the Hegelians in their Hegel newspaper commonly known as Jahrbücher der wissenschaftlichen Literatur); or again, they aim at an intellectual style where it seems then as if they wish to go crazy, and so on. All such efforts whereby they try to postpone the nascetur ridiculus mus make it frequently difficult to understand what they really mean. Moreover, they write down words, nay, whole periods, which mean nothing in themselves, in the hope, however, that someone else will understand something from them. Nothing else is at the bottom of all such endeavours but the inexhaustible attempt which is always venturing on new paths, to sell words for thoughts, and by means of new expressions, or expressions used in a new sense, turns of phrases and combinations of all kinds, to produce the appearance of intellect in order to compensate for the want of it which is so painfully felt. It is amusing to see how, with this aim in view, first this mannerism and then that is tried; these they intend to represent the mask of intellect: this mask may possibly deceive the inexperienced for a while, until it is recognised as being nothing but a dead mask, when it is laughed at and exchanged for another.

We find a writer of this kind sometimes writing in a dithyrambic style, as if he were intoxicated; at other times, nay, on the very next page, he will be high-sounding, severe, and deeply learned, prolix to the last degree of dulness, and cutting everything very small, like the late Christian Wolf, only in a modern garment. The mask of unintelligibility holds out the longest; this is only in Germany, however, where it was introduced by Fichte, perfected by Schelling, and attained its highest climax finally in Hegel, always with the happiest results. And yet nothing is easier than to write so that no one can understand; on the other hand, nothing is more difficult than to express learned ideas so that everyone must understand them. All the arts I have cited above are superfluous if the writer really possesses any intellect, for it allows a man to show himself as he is and verifies for all time what Horace said: Scribendi recte sapere est et principium et fons.

But this class of authors is like certain workers in metal, who try a hundred different compositions to take the place of gold, which is the only metal that can never have a substitute. On the contrary, there is nothing an author should guard against more than the apparent endeavour to show more intellect than he has; because this rouses the suspicion in the reader that he has very little, since a man always affects something, be its nature what it may, that he does not really possess. And this is why it is praise to an author to call him naïve, for it signifies that he may show himself as he is. In general, naïveté attracts, while anything that is unnatural everywhere repels. We also find that every true thinker endeavours to express his thoughts as purely, clearly, definitely, and concisely as ever possible. This is why simplicity has always been looked upon as a token, not only of truth, but also of genius. Style receives its beauty from the thought expressed, while with those writers who only pretend to think it is their thoughts that are said to be fine because of their style. Style is merely the silhouette of thought; and to write in a vague or bad style means a stupid or confused mind.

Hence, the first rule—nay, this in itself is almost sufficient for a good style—is this, that the author should have something to say. Ah! this implies a great deal. The neglect of this rule is a fundamental characteristic of the philosophical, and generally speaking of all the reflective authors in Germany, especially since the time of Fichte. It is obvious that all these writers wish to appear to have something to say, while they have nothing to say. This mannerism was introduced by the pseudo-philosophers of the Universities and may be discerned everywhere, even among the first literary notabilities of the age. It is the mother of that forced and vague style which seems to have two, nay, many meanings, as well as of that prolix and ponderous style, le stile empesé; and of that no less useless bombastic style, and finally of that mode of concealing the most awful poverty of thought under a babble of inexhaustible chatter that resembles a clacking mill and is just as stupefying: one may read for hours together without getting hold of a single clearly defined and definite idea. The Halleschen, afterwards called the Deutschen Jahrbücher, furnishes almost throughout excellent examples of this style of writing. The Germans, by the way, from force of habit read page after page of all kinds of such verbiage without getting any definite idea of what the author really means: they think it all very proper and do not discover that he is writing merely for the sake of writing. On the other hand, a good author who is rich in ideas soon gains the reader's credit of having really and truly something to say; and this gives the intelligent reader patience to follow him attentively. An author of this kind will always express himself in the simplest and most direct manner, for the very reason that he really has something to say; because he wishes to awaken in the reader the same idea he has in his own mind and no other. Accordingly he will be able to say with Boileau—

> Ma pensée au grand jour partout s'offre et s'expose,
> Et mon vers, bien ou mal, dit toujours quelque chose;

while of those previously described writers it may be said, in the words of the same poet, *et qui parlant beaucoup ne disent jamais rien*. It is also a characteristic of such writers to avoid, if it is possible, expressing themselves definitely, so that they may be always able in case of need to get out of a difficulty; this is why they always choose the more abstract expressions: while people of intellect choose the more concrete; because the latter bring the matter closer to view, which is the source of all evidence. This preference for abstract expressions may be confirmed by numerous examples: a specially ridiculous example is the following. Throughout German literature of the last ten years we find 'to condition' almost everywhere used in place of 'to cause' or 'to effect'. Since it is more abstract and indefinite it says less than it implies, and consequently leaves a little back door open to please those whose secret consciousness of their own incapacity inspires them with a continual fear of all definite expressions. While with other people it is merely the effect of that national tendency to immediately imitate everything that is stupid in literature and wicked in life; this is shown in either case by the quick way in which it spreads. The Englishman depends on his own judgment both in what he writes and what he does, but this applies less to the German than to any other nation. In consequence of the state of things referred to, the words 'to cause' and 'to effect' have almost entirely disappeared from the literature of the last ten years, and people everywhere talk of 'to condition'. The fact is worth mentioning because it is characteristically ridiculous. Everyday authors are only half conscious when they write, a fact which accounts for their want of intellect and the tediousness of their writings; they do not really themselves understand the meaning of their own words, because they take ready-made words and learn them. Hence they combine whole phrases more than words—*phrases banales*. This accounts for that obviously characteristic want of clearly defined thought; in fact, they lack the die that stamps their thoughts, they have no clear thought of their own; in place of it we find an indefinite, obscure interweaving of words, current phrases, worn-out terms of speech, and fashionable expressions. The result is that their foggy kind of writing is like print that has been done with old type. On the other hand, intelligent people really speak to us in their writings, and this is why they are able to both move and entertain us. It is only intelligent writers who place individual words together with a full consciousness of their use and select them with deliberation. Hence their style of writing bears the same relation to that of those authors described above, as a picture that is really painted does to one that has been executed with stencil. In the first instance every word, just as every stroke of the brush, has some special significance, while in the other everything is done mechanically. The same distinction may be observed in music. For it is the omnipresence of intellect that always and everywhere characterises the works of the genius; and analogous to this is Lichtenberg's observation, namely, that Garrick's soul was omnipresent in all the muscles of his body. With regard to the tediousness of the writings referred to above, it is to be observed in general that there are two kinds of tediousness—an objective and a subjective. The objective form of tediousness springs from the deficiency of which we have been speaking—that is to say, where the author has no perfectly clear thought or knowledge to communicate. For if a writer possesses any clear thought or knowledge it will be his aim to communicate it, and he will work with this end in view; consequently the ideas he furnishes are everywhere clearly defined, so that he is neither diffuse, unmeaning, nor confused, and consequently not tedious. Even if his fundamental idea is wrong, yet in such a case it will be clearly thought out and well pondered; in other words, it is at least formally correct, and the writing is always of some value. While, for the same reason, a work that is objectively tedious is at all times without value. Again, subjective tediousness is merely relative: this is because the reader is not interested in the subject of the work, and that what he takes an interest in is of a very limited nature. The most excellent work may therefore be tedious subjectively to this or that person, just as, vice versa, the worst work may be subjectively diverting to this or that person: because he is interested in either the subject or the writer of the book.

It would be of general service to German authors if they discerned that while a man should, if possible, think like a great mind, he should speak the same language as every other person. Men should use common words to say uncommon things, but they do the reverse. We find them trying to envelop trivial ideas in grand words and to dress their very ordinary thoughts in the most extraordinary expressions and the most outlandish, artificial, and rarest phrases. Their sentences perpetually stalk about on stilts. With regard to their delight in bombast, and to their writing generally in a grand, puffed-up, unreal, hyperbolical, and acrobatic style, their prototype is Pistol, who was once impatiently requested by Falstaff, his friend, to 'say what you have to say, like a man of this world!'

There is no expression in the German language exactly corresponding to stile empesé; but the thing itself is all the more prevalent. When combined with unnaturalness it is in works what affected gravity, grandness, and unnaturalness are in social intercourse; and it is just as intolerable. Poverty of intellect is fond of wearing this dress; just as stupid people in everyday life are fond of assuming gravity and formality.

A man who writes in this preziös style is like a person who dresses himself up to avoid being mistaken for or confounded with the mob; a danger which a gentleman, even in his worst clothes, does not run. Hence just as a plebeian is recognised by a certain display in his dress and his tiré à quatre épingles, so is an ordinary writer recognised by his style.

If a man has something to say that is worth saying, he need not envelop it in affected expressions, involved phrases, and enigmatical innuendoes; but he may rest assured that by expressing himself in a simple, clear, and naïve manner he will not fail to produce the right effect. A man who makes use of such artifices as have been alluded to betrays his poverty of ideas, mind and knowledge.

Nevertheless, it is a mistake to attempt to write exactly as one speaks. Every style of writing should bear a certain trace of relationship with the monumental style, which is, indeed, the ancestor of all styles; so that to write as one speaks is just as faulty as to do the reverse, that is to say, to try and speak as one writes. This makes the author pedantic, and at the same time difficult to understand.

Obscurity and vagueness of expression are at all times and everywhere a very bad sign. In ninety-nine cases out of a hundred they arise from vagueness of thought, which, in its turn, is almost always fundamentally discordant, inconsistent, and therefore wrong. When a right thought springs up in the mind it strives after clearness of expression, and it soon attains it, for clear thought easily finds its appropriate expression. A man who is capable of thinking can express himself at all times in clear, comprehensible and unambiguous words. Those writers who construct difficult, obscure, involved, and ambiguous phrases most certainly do not rightly know what it is they wish to say: they have only a dull consciousness of it, which is still struggling to put itself into thought; they also often wish to conceal from themselves and other people that in reality they have nothing to say. Like Fichte, Schelling, and Hegel, they wish to appear to know what they do not know, to think what they do not think, and to say what they do not say.

Will a man, then, who has something real to impart endeavour to say it in a clear or an indistinct way? Quintilian has already said, *plerumque accidit ut faciliora sint ad intelligendum et lucidiora multo, quae a doctissimo quoque dicuntur... Erit ergo etiam obscurior, quo quisque deterior.*

A man's way of expressing himself should not be enigmatical, but he should know whether he has something to say or whether he has not. It is an uncertainty of expression which makes German writers so dull. The only exceptional cases are those where a man wishes to express something that is in some respect of an illicit nature. As anything that is far-fetched generally produces the reverse of what the writer has aimed at, so do words serve to make thought comprehensible; but only up to a certain point. If words are piled up beyond this point they make the thought that is being communicated more and more obscure. To hit that point is the problem of style and a matter of discernment; for every superfluous word prevents its purpose being carried out. Voltaire means this when he says: *l'adjectif est l'ennemi du substantif*. (But, truly, many authors try to hide their poverty of thought under a superfluity of words.)

Accordingly, all prolixity and all binding together of unmeaning observations that are not worth reading should be avoided. A writer must be sparing with the reader's time, concentration, and patience; in this way he makes him believe that what he has before him is worth his careful reading, and will repay the trouble he has spent upon it. It is always better to leave out something that is good than to write down something that is not worth saying. Hesiod's πλέον ἥμισυ παντός finds its right application. In fact, not to say everything! *Le secret pour être ennuyeux, c'est de tout dire*. Therefore, if possible, the quintessence only! the chief matter only! nothing that the reader would think for himself. The use of many words in order to express little thought is everywhere the infallible sign of mediocrity; while to clothe much thought in a few words is the infallible sign of distinguished minds.

Truth that is naked is the most beautiful, and the simpler its expression the deeper is the impression it makes; this is partly because it gets unobstructed hold of the hearer's mind without his being distracted by secondary thoughts, and partly because he feels that here he is not being corrupted or deceived by the arts of rhetoric, but that the whole effect is got from the thing itself. For instance, what declamation on the emptiness of human existence could be more impressive than Job's: Homo, natus de muliere, brevi vivit tempore, repletus multis miseriis, qui, tanquam flos, egreditur et conteritur, et fugit velut umbra. It is for this very reason that the naïve poetry of Goethe is so incomparably greater than the rhetorical of Schiller. This is also why many folk-songs have so great an effect upon us. An author should guard against using all unnecessary rhetorical adornment, all useless amplification, and in general, just as in architecture he should guard against an excess of decoration, all superfluity of expression—in other words, he must aim at chastity of style. Everything that is redundant has a harmful effect. The law of simplicity and naïveté applies to all fine art, for it is compatible with what is most sublime.

True brevity of expression consists in a man only saying what is worth saying, while avoiding all diffuse explanations of things which every one can think out for himself; that is, it consists in his correctly distinguishing between what is necessary and what is superfluous. On the other hand, one should never sacrifice clearness, to say nothing of grammar, for the sake of being brief. To impoverish the expression of a thought, or to obscure or spoil the meaning of a period for the sake of using fewer words shows a lamentable want of judgment. And this is precisely what that false brevity nowadays in vogue is trying to do, for writers not only leave out words that are to the purpose, but even grammatical and logical essentials.

Subjectivity, which is an error of style in German literature, is, through the deteriorated condition of literature and neglect of old languages, becoming more common. By subjectivity I mean when a writer thinks it sufficient for himself to know what he means and wants to say, and it is left to the reader to discover what is meant. Without troubling himself about his reader, he writes as if he were holding a monologue; whereas it should be a dialogue, and, moreover, a dialogue in which he must express himself all the more clearly as the questions of the reader cannot be heard. And it is for this very reason that style should not be subjective but objective, and for it to be objective the words must be written in such a way as to directly compel the reader to think precisely the same as the author thought. This will only be the case when the author has borne in mind that thoughts, inasmuch as they follow the law of gravity, pass more easily from head to paper than from paper to head. Therefore the journey from paper to head must be helped by every means at his command. When he does this his words have a purely objective effect, like that of a completed oil painting; while the subjective style is not much more certain in its effect than spots on the wall, and it is only the man whose fantasy is accidentally aroused by them that sees figures; other people only see blurs. The difference referred to applies to every style of writing as a whole, and it is also often met with in particular instances; for example, I read in a book that has just been published: I have not written to increase the number of existing books. This means exactly the opposite of what the writer had in view, and is nonsense into the bargain.

A man who writes carelessly at once proves that he himself puts no great value on his own thoughts. For it is only by being convinced of the truth and importance of our thoughts that there arises in us the inspiration necessary for the inexhaustible patience to discover the clearest, finest, and most powerful expression for them; just as one puts holy relics or priceless works of art in silvern or golden receptacles. It was for this reason that the old writers—whose thoughts, expressed in their own words, have lasted for thousands of years and hence bear the honoured title of classics—wrote with universal care. Plato, indeed, is said to have written the introduction to his *Republic* seven times with different modifications. On the other hand, the Germans are conspicuous above all other nations for neglect of style in writing, as they are for neglect of dress, both kinds of slovenliness which have their source in the German national character. Just as neglect of dress betrays contempt for the society in which a man moves, so does a hasty, careless, and bad style show shocking disrespect for the reader, who then rightly punishes it by not reading the book.

ON NOISE.

Kant has written a treatise on The Vital Powers; but I should like to write a dirge on them, since their lavish use in the form of knocking, hammering, and tumbling things about has made the whole of my life a daily torment. Certainly there are people, nay, very many, who will smile at this, because they are not sensitive to noise; it is precisely these people, however, who are not sensitive to argument, thought, poetry or art, in short, to any kind of intellectual impression: a fact to be assigned to the coarse quality and strong texture of their brain tissues. On the other hand, in the biographies or in other records of the personal utterances of almost all great writers, I find complaints of the pain that noise has occasioned to intellectual men. For example, in the case of Kant, Goethe, Lichtenberg, Jean Paul; and indeed when no mention is made of the matter it is merely because the context did not lead up to it. I should explain the subject we are treating in this way: If a big diamond is cut up into pieces, it immediately loses its value as a whole; or if an army is scattered or divided into small bodies, it loses all its power; and in the same way a great intellect has no more power than an ordinary one as soon as it is interrupted, disturbed, distracted, or diverted; for its superiority entails that it concentrates all its strength on one point and object, just as a concave mirror concentrates all the rays of light thrown upon it. Noisy interruption prevents this concentration. This is why the most eminent intellects have always been strongly averse to any kind of disturbance, interruption and distraction, and above everything to that violent interruption which is caused by noise; other people do not take any particular notice of this sort of thing. The most intelligent of all the European nations has called 'Never interrupt' the eleventh commandment. But noise is the most impertinent of all interruptions, for it not only interrupts our own thoughts but disperses them. Where, however, there is nothing to interrupt, noise naturally will not be felt particularly. Sometimes a trifling but incessant noise torments and disturbs me for a time, and before I become distinctly conscious of it I feel it merely as the effort of thinking becomes more difficult, just as I should feel a weight on my foot; then I realise what it is.

But to pass from genus to species, the truly infernal cracking of whips in the narrow resounding streets of a town must be denounced as the most unwarrantable and disgraceful of all noises. It deprives life of all peace and sensibility. Nothing gives me so clear a grasp of the stupidity and thoughtlessness of mankind as the tolerance of the cracking of whips. This sudden, sharp crack which paralyses the brain, destroys all meditation, and murders thought, must cause pain to any one who has anything like an idea in his head. Hence every crack must disturb a hundred people applying their minds to some activity, however trivial it may be; while it disjoints and renders painful the meditations of the thinker; just like the executioner's axe when it severs the head from the body. No sound cuts so sharply into the brain as this cursed cracking of whips; one feels the prick of the whip-cord in one's brain, which is affected in the same way as the mimosa pudica is by touch, and which lasts the same length of time. With all respect for the most holy doctrine of utility, I do not see why a fellow who is removing a load of sand or manure should obtain the privilege of killing in the bud the thoughts that are springing up in the heads of about ten thousand people successively. (He is only half-an-hour on the road.)

Hammering, the barking of dogs, and the screaming of children are abominable; but it is only the cracking of a whip that is the true murderer of thought. Its object is to destroy every favourable moment that one now and then may have for reflection. If there were no other means of urging on an animal than by making this most disgraceful of all noises, one would forgive its existence. But it is quite the contrary: this cursed cracking of whips is not only unnecessary but even useless. The effect that it is intended to have on the horse mentally becomes quite blunted and ineffective; since the constant abuse of it has accustomed the horse to the crack, he does not quicken his pace for it. This is especially noticeable in the unceasing crack of the whip which comes from an empty vehicle as it is being driven at its slowest rate to pick up a fare.

The slightest touch with the whip would be more effective. Allowing, however, that it were absolutely necessary to remind the horse of the presence of the whip by continually cracking it, a crack that made one hundredth part of the noise would be sufficient. It is well known that animals in regard to hearing and seeing notice the slightest indications, even indications that are scarcely perceptible to ourselves. Trained dogs and canary birds furnish astonishing examples of this. Accordingly, this cracking of whips must be regarded as something purely wanton; nay, as an impudent defiance, on the part of those who work with their hands, offered to those who work with their heads. That such infamy is endured in a town is a piece of barbarity and injustice, the more so as it could be easily removed by a police notice requiring every whip cord to have a knot at the end of it. It would do no harm to draw the proletariat's attention to the classes above him who work with their heads; for he has unbounded fear of any kind of head work. A fellow who rides through the narrow streets of a populous town with unemployed post-horses or cart-horses, unceasingly cracking with all his strength a whip several yards long, instantly deserves to dismount and receive five really good blows with a stick. If all the philanthropists in the world, together with all the legislators, met in order to bring forward their reasons for the total abolition of corporal punishment, I would not be persuaded to the contrary.

But we can see often enough something that is even still worse. I mean a carter walking alone, and without any horses, through the streets incessantly cracking his whip. He has become so accustomed to the crack in consequence of its unwarrantable toleration. Since one looks after one's body and all its needs in a most tender fashion, is the thinking mind to be the only thing that never experiences the slightest consideration or protection, to say nothing of respect? Carters, sack-bearers (porters), messengers, and such-like, are the beasts of burden of humanity; they should be treated absolutely with justice, fairness, forbearance and care, but they ought not to be allowed to thwart the higher exertions of the human race by wantonly making a noise. I should like to know how many great and splendid thoughts these whips have cracked out of the world. If I had any authority, I should soon produce in the heads of these carters an inseparable nexus idearum between cracking a whip and receiving a whipping.

Let us hope that those nations with more intelligence and refined feelings will make a beginning, and then by force of example induce the Germans to do the same. Meanwhile, hear what Thomas Hood says of them (Up the Rhine): 'For a musical people they are the most noisy I ever met with.' That they are so is not due to their being more prone to making a noise than other people, but to their insensibility, which springs from obtuseness; they are not disturbed by it in reading or thinking, because they do not think; they only smoke, which is their substitute for thought. The general toleration of unnecessary noise, for instance, of the clashing of doors, which is so extremely ill-mannered and vulgar, is a direct proof of the dulness and poverty of thought that one meets with everywhere. In Germany it seems as though it were planned that no one should think for noise; take the inane drumming that goes on as an instance. Finally, as far as the literature treated of in this chapter is concerned, I have only one work to recommend, but it is an excellent one: I mean a poetical epistle in terzo rimo by the famous painter Bronzino, entitled 'De' Romori: a Messer Luca Martini'. It describes fully and amusingly the torture to which one is put by the many kinds of noises of a small Italian town. It is written in tragicomic style. This epistle is to be found in Opere burlesche del Berni, Aretino ed altri, vol. ii. p. 258, apparently published in Utrecht in 1771.

The nature of our intellect is such that ideas are said to spring by abstraction from observations, so that the latter are in existence before the former. If this is really what takes place, as is the case with a man who has merely his own experience as his teacher and book, he knows quite well which of his observations belong to and are represented by each of his ideas; he is perfectly acquainted with both, and accordingly he treats everything correctly that comes before his notice. We might call this the natural mode of education.

On the other hand, an artificial education is having one's head crammed full of ideas, derived from hearing others talk, from learning and reading, before one has anything like an extensive knowledge of the world as it is and as one sees it. The observations which produce all these ideas are said to come later on with experience; but until then these ideas are applied wrongly, and accordingly both things and men are judged wrongly, seen wrongly, and treated wrongly. And so it is that education perverts the mind; and this is why, after a long spell of learning and reading, we enter the world, in our youth, with views that are partly simple, partly perverted; consequently we comport ourselves with an air of anxiety at one time, at another of presumption. This is because our head is full of ideas which we are now trying to make use of, but almost always apply wrongly. This is the result of ὕστερον πρότερον (putting the cart before the horse), since we are directly opposing the natural development of our mind by obtaining ideas first and observations last; for teachers, instead of developing in a boy his faculties of discernment and judgment, and of thinking for himself, merely strive to stuff his head full of other people's thoughts. Subsequently, all the opinions that have sprung from misapplied ideas have to be rectified by a lengthy experience; and it is seldom that they are completely rectified. This is why so few men of learning have such sound common sense as is quite common among the illiterate.

♦

From what has been said, the principal point in education is that one's knowledge of the world begins at the right end; and the attainment of which might be designated as the aim of all education. But, as has been pointed out, this depends principally on the observation of each thing preceding the idea one forms of it; further, that narrow ideas precede broader; so that the whole of one's instruction is given in the order that the ideas themselves during formation must have followed. But directly this order is not strictly adhered to, imperfect and subsequently wrong ideas spring up; and finally there arises a perverted view of the world in keeping with the nature of the individual—a view such as almost every one holds for a long time, and most people to the end of their lives. If a man analyses his own character, he will find that it was not until he reached a very ripe age, and in some cases quite unexpectedly, that he was able to rightly and clearly understand many matters of a quite simple nature.

Previously, there had been an obscure point in his knowledge of the world which had arisen through his omitting something in his early education, whether he had been either artificially educated by men or just naturally by his own experience. Therefore one should try to find out the strictly natural course of knowledge, so that by keeping methodically to it children may become acquainted with the affairs of the world, without getting false ideas into their heads, which frequently cannot be driven out again. In carrying this out, one must next take care that children do not use words with which they connect no clear meaning. Even children have, as a rule, that unhappy tendency of being satisfied with words instead of wishing to understand things, and of learning words by heart, so that they may make use of them when they are in a difficulty. This tendency clings to them afterwards, so that the knowledge of many learned men becomes mere verbosity.

However, the principal thing must always be to let one's observations precede one's ideas, and not the reverse as is usually and unfortunately the case; which may be likened to a child coming into the world with its feet foremost, or a rhyme begun before thinking of its reason. While the child's mind has made a very few observations one inculcates it with ideas and opinions, which are, strictly speaking, prejudices. His observations and experience are developed through this ready-made apparatus instead of his ideas being developed out of his own observations. In viewing the world one sees many things from many sides, consequently this is not such a short or quick way of learning as that which makes use of abstract ideas, and quickly comes to a decision about everything; therefore preconceived ideas will not be rectified until late, or it may be they are never rectified. For, when a man's view contradicts his ideas, he will reject at the outset what it renders evident as one-sided, nay, he will deny it and shut his eyes to it, so that his preconceived ideas may remain unaffected. And so it happens that many men go through life full of oddities, caprices, fancies and prejudices, until they finally become fixed ideas. He has never attempted to abstract fundamental ideas from his own observations and experience, because he has got everything ready-made from other people; and it is for this very reason that he and countless others are so insipid and shallow. Instead of such a system, the natural system of education should be employed in educating children. No idea should be impregnated but what has come through the medium of observations, or at any rate been verified by them. A child would have fewer ideas, but they would be well-grounded and correct. It would learn to measure things according to its own standard and not according to another's. It would then never acquire a thousand whims and prejudices which must be eradicated by the greater part of subsequent experience and education. Its mind would henceforth be accustomed to thoroughness and clearness; the child would rely on its own judgment, and be free from prejudices. And, in general, children should not get to know life, in any aspect whatever, from the copy before they have learnt it from the original. Instead, therefore, of hastening to place mere books in their hands, one should make them gradually acquainted with things and the circumstances of human life, and above everything one should take care to guide them to a clear grasp of reality, and to teach them to obtain their ideas directly from the real world, and to form them in keeping with it—but not to get them from elsewhere, as from books, fables, or what others have said—and then later to make use of such ready-made ideas in real life. The result will be that their heads are full of chimeras and that some will have a wrong comprehension of things, and others will fruitlessly endeavour to remodel the world according to those chimeras, and so get on to wrong paths both in theory and practice. For it is incredible how much harm is done by false notions which have been implanted early in life, only to develop later on into prejudices; the later education which we get from the world and real life must be employed in eradicating these early ideas. And this is why, as is related by Diogenes Laertius, Antisthenes gave the following answer: ἐρωτηθεις τι των μαθηματων ἀναγκαιοτατον, ἐφη, 'το κακα ἀπομαθειν.' (*Interrogatus quaenam esset disciplina maxime necessaria, Mala, inquit, dediscere.*)

◆

Children should be kept from all kinds of instruction that may make errors possible until their sixteenth year, that is to say, from philosophy, religion, and general views of every description; because it is the errors that are acquired in early days that remain, as a rule, ineradicable, and because the faculty of judgment is the last to arrive at maturity. They should only be interested in such things that make errors impossible, such as mathematics, in things which are not very dangerous, such as languages, natural science, history, and so forth; in general, the branches of knowledge which are to be taken up at any age must be within reach of the intellect at that age and perfectly comprehensible to it. Childhood and youth are the time for collecting data and getting to know specially and thoroughly individual and particular things. On the other hand, all judgment of a general nature must at that time be suspended, and final explanations left alone. One should leave the faculty of judgment alone, as it only comes with maturity and experience, and also take care that one does not anticipate it by inculcating prejudice, when it will be crippled for ever.

On the contrary, the memory is to be specially exercised, as it has its greatest strength and tenacity in youth; however, what has to be retained must be chosen with the most careful and scrupulous consideration. For as it is what we have learnt well in our youth that lasts, we should take the greatest possible advantage of this precious gift. If we picture to ourselves how deeply engraved on our memory the people are whom we knew during the first twelve years of our life, and how indelibly imprinted are also the events of that time, and most of the things that we then experienced, heard, or learnt, the idea of basing education on this susceptibility and tenacity of the youthful mind will seem natural; in that the mind receives its impressions according to a strict method and a regular system. But because the years of youth that are assigned to man are only few, and the capacity for remembering, in general, is always limited (and still more so the capacity for remembering of the individual), everything depends on the memory being filled with what is most essential and important in any department of knowledge, to the exclusion of everything else. This selection should be made by the most capable minds and masters in every branch of knowledge after the most mature consideration, and the result of it established. Such a selection must be based on a sifting of matters which are necessary and important for a man to know in general, and also for him to know in a particular profession or calling. Knowledge of the first kind would have to be divided into graduated courses, like an encyclopædia, corresponding to the degree of general culture which each man has attained in his external circumstances; from a course restricted to what is necessary for primary instruction up to the matter contained in every branch of the philosophical faculty. Knowledge of the second kind would, however, be reserved for him who had really mastered the selection in all its branches. The whole would give a canon specially devised for intellectual education, which naturally would require revision every ten years. By such an arrangement the youthful power of the memory would be put to the best advantage, and it would furnish the faculty of judgment with excellent material when it appeared later on.

◆

What is meant by maturity of knowledge is that state of perfection to which any one individual is able to bring it, when an exact correspondence has been effected between the whole of his abstract ideas and his own personal observations: whereby each of his ideas rests directly or indirectly on a basis of observation, which alone gives it any real value; and likewise he is able to place every observation that he makes under the right idea corresponding to it.

Maturity of knowledge is the work of experience alone, and consequently of time. For the knowledge we acquire from our own observation is, as a rule, distinct from that we get through abstract ideas; the former is acquired in the natural way, while the latter comes through good and bad instruction and what other people have told to us. Consequently, in youth there is generally little harmony and connection between our ideas, which mere expressions have fixed, and our real knowledge, which has been acquired by observation. Later they both gradually approach and correct each other; but maturity of knowledge does not exist until they have become quite incorporated. This maturity is quite independent of that other kind of perfection, the standard of which may be high or low, I mean the perfection to which the capacities of an individual may be brought; it is not based on a correspondence between the abstract and intuitive knowledge, but on the degree of intensity of each.

The most necessary thing for the practical man is the attainment of an exact and thorough knowledge of what is really going on in the world; but it is also the most irksome, for a man may continue studying until old age without having learnt all that is to be learnt; while one can master the most important things in the sciences in one's youth. In getting such a knowledge of the world, it is as a novice that the boy and youth have the first and most difficult lessons to learn; but frequently even the matured man has still much to learn. The study is of considerable difficulty in itself, but it is made doubly difficult by novels, which depict the ways of the world and of men who do not exist in real life.

But these are accepted with the credulity of youth, and become incorporated with the mind; so that now, in the place of purely negative ignorance, a whole framework of wrong ideas, which are positively wrong, crops up, subsequently confusing the schooling of experience and representing the lesson it teaches in a false light. If the youth was previously in the dark, he will now be led astray by a will-o'-the-wisp: and with a girl this is still more frequently the case. They have been deluded into an absolutely false view of life by reading novels, and expectations have been raised that can never be fulfilled. This generally has the most harmful effect on their whole lives. Those men who had neither time nor opportunity to read novels in their youth, such as those who work with their hands, have decided advantage over them. Few of these novels are exempt from reproach—nay, whose effect is contrary to bad. Before all others, for instance, Gil Blas and the other works of Le Sage (or rather their Spanish originals); further, The Vicar of Wakefield, and to some extent the novels of Walter Scott. Don Quixote may be regarded as a satirical presentation of the error in question.

ON READING AND BOOKS

Ignorance is degrading only when it is found in company with riches. Want and penury restrain the poor man; his employment takes the place of knowledge and occupies his thoughts: while rich men who are ignorant live for their pleasure only, and resemble a beast; as may be seen daily. They are to be reproached also for not having used wealth and leisure for that which lends them their greatest value.

When we read, another person thinks for us: we merely repeat his mental process. It is the same as the pupil, in learning to write, following with his pen the lines that have been pencilled by the teacher. Accordingly, in reading, the work of thinking is, for the greater part, done for us. This is why we are consciously relieved when we turn to reading after being occupied with our own thoughts. But, in reading, our head is, however, really only the arena of someone else's thoughts. And so it happens that the person who reads a great deal—that is to say, almost the whole day, and recreates himself by spending the intervals in thoughtless diversion, gradually loses the ability to think for himself; just as a man who is always riding at last forgets how to walk. Such, however, is the case with many men of learning: they have read themselves stupid. For to read in every spare moment, and to read constantly, is more paralysing to the mind than constant manual work, which, at any rate, allows one to follow one's own thoughts. Just as a spring, through the continual pressure of a foreign body, at last loses its elasticity, so does the mind if it has another person's thoughts continually forced upon it. And just as one spoils the stomach by overfeeding and thereby impairs the whole body, so can one overload and choke the mind by giving it too much nourishment. For the more one reads the fewer are the traces left of what one has read; the mind is like a tablet that has been written over and over. Hence it is impossible to reflect; and it is only by reflection that one can assimilate what one has read if one reads straight ahead without pondering over it later, what has been read does not take root, but is for the most part lost. Indeed, it is the same with mental as with bodily food: scarcely the fifth part of what a man takes is assimilated; the remainder passes off in evaporation, respiration, and the like.

From all this it may be concluded that thoughts put down on paper are nothing more than footprints in the sand: one sees the road the man has taken, but in order to know what he saw on the way, one requires his eyes.

◆

No literary quality can be attained by reading writers who possess it: be it, for example, persuasiveness, imagination, the gift of drawing comparisons, boldness or bitterness, brevity or grace, facility of expression or wit, unexpected contrasts, a laconic manner, naïveté, and the like. But if we are already gifted with these qualities—that is to say, if we possess them potentially—we can call them forth and bring them to consciousness; we can discern to what uses they are to be put; we can be strengthened in our inclination, nay, may have courage, to use them; we can judge by examples the effect of their application and so learn the correct use of them; and it is only after we have accomplished all this that we actually possess these qualities. This is the only way in which reading can form writing, since it teaches us the use to which we can put our own natural gifts; and in order to do this it must be taken for granted that these qualities are in us. Without them we learn nothing from reading but cold, dead mannerisms, and we become mere imitators.

◆

The health officer should, in the interest of one's eyes, see that the smallness of print has a fixed minimum, which must not be exceeded. When I was in Venice in 1818, at which time the genuine Venetian chain was still being made, a goldsmith told me that those who made the catena fina turned blind at thirty.

◆

As the strata of the earth preserve in rows the beings which lived in former times, so do the shelves of a library preserve in a like manner the errors of the past and expositions concerning them. Like those creatures, they too were full of life in their time and made a great deal of noise; but now they are stiff and fossilised, and only of interest to the literary palaeontologist.

◆

According to Herodotus, Xerxes wept at the sight of his army, which was too extensive for him to scan, at the thought that a hundred years hence not one of all these would be alive. Who would not weep at the thought in looking over a big catalogue that of all these books not one will be in existence in ten years' time?

It is the same in literature as in life. Wherever one goes one immediately comes upon the incorrigible mob of humanity. It exists everywhere in legions; crowding, soiling everything, like flies in summer. Hence the numberless bad books, those rank weeds of literature which extract nourishment from the corn and choke it.

They monopolise the time, money, and attention which really belong to good books and their noble aims; they are written merely with a view to making money or procuring places. They are not only useless, but they do positive harm. Nine-tenths of the whole of our present literature aims solely at taking a few shillings out of the public's pocket, and to accomplish this, author, publisher, and reviewer have joined forces.

There is a more cunning and worse trick, albeit a profitable one. Littérateurs, hack-writers, and productive authors have succeeded, contrary to good taste and the true culture of the age, in bringing the world elegante into leading-strings, so that they have been taught to read a tempo and all the same thing—namely, the newest books order that they may have material for conversation in their social circles. Bad novels and similar productions from the pen of writers who were once famous, such as Spindler, Bulwer, Eugène Sue, and so on, serve this purpose. But what can be more miserable than the fate of a reading public of this kind, that feels always impelled to read the latest writings of extremely commonplace authors who write for money only, and therefore exist in numbers? And for the sake of this they merely know by name the works of the rare and superior writers, of all ages and countries.

Literary newspapers, since they print the daily smatterings of commonplace people, are especially a cunning means for robbing from the aesthetic public the time which should be devoted to the genuine productions of art for the furtherance of culture.

Hence, in regard to our subject, the art of not reading is highly important. This consists in not taking a book into one's hand merely because it is interesting the great public at the time—such as political or religious pamphlets, novels, poetry, and the like, which make a noise and reach perhaps several editions in their first and last years of existence. Remember rather that the man who writes for fools always finds a large public: and only read for a limited and definite time exclusively the works of great minds, those who surpass other men of all times and countries, and whom the voice of fame points to as such. These alone really educate and instruct.

One can never read too little of bad, or too much of good books: bad books are intellectual poison; they destroy the mind.

In order to read what is good one must make it a condition never to read what is bad; for life is short, and both time and strength limited.

◆

Books are written sometimes about this, sometimes about that great thinker of former times, and the public reads these books, but not the works of the man himself. This is because it wants to read only what has just been printed, and because similis simili gaudet, and it finds the shallow, insipid gossip of some stupid head of today more homogeneous and agreeable than the thoughts of great minds. I have to thank fate, however, that a fine epigram of A.B. Schlegel, which has since been my guiding star, came before my notice as a youth:

> Leset fleizig die Alten, die wahren eigentlich Alten
> Was die Neuen davon sagen bedeutet nicht viel.

Oh, how like one commonplace mind is to another! How they are all fashioned in one form! How they all think alike under similar circumstances, and never differ! This is why their views are so personal and petty. And a stupid public reads the worthless trash written by these fellows for no other reason than that it has been printed today, while it leaves the works of great thinkers undisturbed on the bookshelves.

Incredible are the folly and perversity of a public that will leave unread writings of the noblest and rarest of minds, of all times and all countries, for the sake of reading the writings of commonplace persons which appear daily, and breed every year in countless numbers like flies; merely because these writings have been printed today and are still wet from the press. It would be better if they were thrown on one side and rejected the day they appeared, as they must be after the lapse of a few years. They will then afford material for laughter as illustrating the follies of a former time.

It is because people will only read what is the newest instead of what is the best of all ages, that writers remain in the narrow circle of prevailing ideas, and that the age sinks deeper and deeper in its own mire.

◆

There are at all times two literatures which, although scarcely known to each other, progress side by side—the one real, the other merely apparent. The former grows into literature that lasts. Pursued by people who live for science or poetry, it goes its way earnestly and quietly, but extremely slowly; and it produces in Europe scarcely a dozen works in a century, which, however, are permanent. The other literature is pursued by people who live on science or poetry; it goes at a gallop amid a great noise and shouting of those taking part, and brings yearly many thousand works into the market. But after a few years one asks, Where are they? Where is their fame, which was so great formerly? This class of literature may be distinguished as fleeting, the other as permanent.

◆

It would be a good thing to buy books if one could also buy the time to read them; but one usually confuses the purchase of books with the acquisition of their contents. To desire that a man should retain everything he has ever read is the same as wishing him to retain in his stomach all that he has ever eaten. He has been bodily nourished on what he has eaten, and mentally on what he has read, and through them become what he is. As the body assimilates what is homogeneous to it, so will a man retain what interests him; in other words, what coincides with his system of thought or suits his ends. Everyone has aims, but very few have anything approaching a system of thought. This is why such people do not take an objective interest in anything, and why they learn nothing from what they read: they remember nothing about it.

Repetitio est mater studiorum. Any kind of important book should immediately be read twice, partly because one grasps the matter in its entirety the second time, and only really understands the beginning when the end is known; and partly because in reading it the second time one's temper and mood are different, so that one gets another impression; it may be that one sees the matter in another light.

Works are the quintessence of a mind, and are therefore always of far greater value than conversation, even if it be the conversation of the greatest mind. In every essential a man's works surpass his conversation and leave it far behind. Even the writings of an ordinary man may be instructive, worth reading, and entertaining, for the simple reason that they are the quintessence of that man's mind—that is to say, the writings are the result and fruit of his whole thought and study; while we should be dissatisfied with his conversation. Accordingly, it is possible to read books written by people whose conversation would give us no satisfaction; so that the mind will only by degrees attain high culture by finding entertainment almost entirely in books, and not in men.

There is nothing that so greatly recreates the mind as the works of the old classic writers. Directly one has been taken up, even if it is only for half an hour, one feels as quickly refreshed, relieved, purified, elevated and strengthened as if one had refreshed oneself at a mountain stream. Is this due to the perfections of the old languages, or to the greatness of the minds whose works have remained unharmed and untouched for centuries? Perhaps to both combined. This I know, directly we stop learning the old languages (as is at present threatening) a new class of literature will spring up, consisting of writing that is more barbaric, stupid and worthless than has ever yet existed; that, in particular, the German language, which possesses some of the beauties of the old languages, will be systematically spoilt and stripped by these worthless contemporary scribblers, until, little by little, it becomes impoverished, crippled and reduced to a miserable jargon.

Half a century is always a considerable time in the history of the universe, for the matter which forms it is always shifting; something is always taking place. But the same length of time in literature often goes for nothing, because nothing has happened; unskilful attempts don't count; so that we are exactly where we were fifty years previously.

To illustrate this: imagine the progress of knowledge among mankind in the form of a planet's course. The false paths the human race soon follows after any important progress has been made represent the epicycles in the Ptolemaic system; after passing through any one of them the planet is just where it was before it entered it. The great minds, however, which really bring the race further on its course, do not accompany it on the epicycles which it makes every time. This explains why posthumous fame is got at the expense of contemporary fame, and vice versa. We have an instance of such an epicycle in the philosophy of Fichte and Schelling, crowned by Hegel's caricature of it. This epicycle issued from the limit to which philosophy had been finally brought by Kant, where I myself took it up again later to carry it further. In the interim the false philosophers I have mentioned, and some others, passed through their epicycle, which has just been terminated; hence the people who accompanied them are conscious of being exactly at the point from which they started.

This condition of things shows why the scientific, literary and artistic spirit of the age is declared bankrupt about every thirty years. During that period the errors have increased to such an extent that they fall under the weight of their absurdity; while at the same time the opposition to them has become stronger. At this point there is a crash, which is followed by an error in the opposite direction. To show the course that is taken in its periodical return would be the true practical subject of the history of literature; little notice is taken of it, however. Moreover, through the comparative shortness of such periods, the data of remote times are with difficulty collected; hence the matter can be most conveniently observed in one's own age. An example of this taken from physical science is found in Werter's Neptunian geology. But let me keep to the example already quoted above, for it is nearest to us. In German philosophy Kant's brilliant period was immediately followed by another period, which aimed at being imposing rather than convincing. Instead of being solid and clear, it aimed at being brilliant and hyperbolical, and, in particular, unintelligible; instead of seeking truth, it intrigued. Under these circumstances philosophy could make no progress. Ultimately the whole school and its method became bankrupt. For the audacious, sophisticated nonsense on the one hand, and the unconscionable praise on the other of Hegel and his fellows, as well as the apparent object of the whole affair, rose to such a pitch that in the end the charlatanry of the thing was obvious to everybody; and when, in consequence of certain revelations, the protection that had been given it by the upper classes was withdrawn, it was talked about by everybody. This most miserable of all the philosophies that have ever existed dragged down with it into the abyss of discredit the systems of Fichte and Schelling, which had preceded it. So that the absolute philosophical futility of the first half of the century following upon Kant in Germany is obvious; and yet the Germans boast of their gift for philosophy compared with foreigners, especially since an English writer, with malicious irony, called them a nation of thinkers.

Those who want an example of the general scheme of epicycles taken from the history of art need only look at the School of Sculpture which flourished in the last century under Bernini, and especially at its further cultivation in France. This school represented commonplace nature instead of antique beauty, and the manners of a French minuet instead of antique simplicity and grace. It became bankrupt when, under Winckelmann's direction, a return was made to the antique school. Another example is supplied in the painting belonging to the first quarter of this century. Art was regarded merely as a means and instrument of mediaeval religious feeling, and consequently ecclesiastical subjects alone were chosen for its themes. These, however, were treated by painters who were wanting in earnestness of faith, and in their delusion they took for examples Francesco Francia, Pietro Perugino, Angelico da Fiesole, and others like them, even holding them in greater esteem than the truly great masters who followed. In view of this error, and because in poetry an analogous effort had at the same time met with favour, Goethe wrote his parable Pfaffenspiel. This school, reputedly capricious, became bankrupt, and was followed by a return to nature, which made itself known in genre pictures and scenes of life of every description, even though it strayed sometimes into vulgarity.

It is the same with the progress of the human mind in the history of literature, which is for the most part like the catalogue of a cabinet of deformities; the spirit in which they keep the longest is pigskin. We do not need to look there for the few who have been born shapely; they are still alive, and we come across them in every part of the world, like immortals whose youth is ever fresh. They alone form what I have distinguished as real literature, the history of which, although poor in persons, we learn from our youth up out of the mouths of educated people, and not first of all from compilations. As a specific against the present prevailing monomania for reading literary histories, so that one may be able to chatter about everything without really knowing anything, let me refer you to a passage from Lichtenberg which is well worth reading (vol. ii. p. 302 of the old edition).

But I wish someone would attempt a tragical history of literature, showing how the greatest writers and artists have been treated during their lives by the various nations which have produced them and whose proudest possessions they are. It would show us the endless fight which the good and genuine works of all periods and countries have had to carry on against the perverse and bad. It would depict the martyrdom of almost all those who truly enlightened humanity, of almost all the great masters in every kind of art; it would show us how they, with few exceptions, were tormented without recognition, without any to share their misery, without followers; how they existed in poverty and misery whilst fame, honour, and riches fell to the lot of the worthless; it would reveal that what happened to them happened to Esau, who, while hunting the deer for his father, was robbed of the blessing by Jacob disguised in his brother's coat; and how through it all the love of their subject kept them up, until at last the trying fight of such a teacher of the human race is ended, the immortal laurel offered to him, and the time come when it can be said of him

Der schwere Panzer wird zum Flügelkleide Kurz ist der Schmerz, unendlich ist die Freude.

OF TRUTH

FRANCIS BACON

What is Truth? said jesting Pilate; and would not stay for an answer. Certainly there be that delight in giddiness; and count it a bondage to fix a belief; affecting free will in thinking, as well as in acting. And though the sects of philosophers of that kind be gone, yet there remain certain discoursing wits which are of the same veins, though there be not so much blood in them as was in those of the ancients. But it is not only the difficulty and labour which men take in finding out of truth; nor again that when it is found it imposeth (impose) upon men's thoughts; that doth bring lies in favour; but a natural though corrupt love of the lie itself. One of the later school of the Grecians examineth the matter, and is at a stand to think what should be in it, that men should love lies, where neither they make for pleasure, as with poets, nor for advantage, as with the merchant; but for the lie's sake. But I cannot tell: this same truth is a naked and open day-light, that doth not shew the masks and mummeries and triumphs of the world, half so stately and daintily as candlelights. Truth may perhaps come to the price of a pearl, that sheweth best by day; but it will not rise to the price of a diamond or carbuncle, that sheweth best in varied lights. A mixture of a lie doth ever add pleasure. Doth any man doubt, that if there were taken out of men's minds vain opinions, flattering hopes, false valuations, imaginations as one would and the like, but it would leave the minds of a number of men poor shrunken things, full of melancholy and indisposition, and unpleasing to themselves? One of the Fathers, in great severity, called poesy *vinum dæmonum* because it filleth the imagination; and yet it is but with the shadow of a lie. But it is not the lie that passeth through the mind, but the lie that sinketh in and settleth in it, that doth the hurt; such as we spake of before. But howsoever these things are thus in men's depraved judgments and affections, yet truth, which only doth judge itself, teacheth that the inquiry of truth, which is the love-making or wooing of it, the knowledge of truth, which is the presence of it, and the belief of truth, which is the enjoying of it, is the sovereign good of human nature. The first creature of God, in the works of the days, was the light of the sense; the last was the light of reason; and his sabbath work ever since, is the illumination of his Spirit. First he breathed light upon the face of the matter or chaos; then he breathed light into the face of man; and still he breatheth and inspireth light into the face of his chosen. The poet that beautified the sect that was otherwise inferior to the rest, saith yet excellently well: *It is a pleasure to stand upon the shore, and to see ships tossed upon the sea; a pleasure to stand in the window of a castle, and to see a battle and the adventures thereof below: but no pleasure is comparable to the standing upon the vantage ground of Truth,* (a hill not to be commanded, and where the air is always clear and serene,) *and to see the errors, and wanderings, and mists, and tempests, in the vale below;* so always that this prospect be with pity, and not with swelling or pride. Certainly, it is heaven upon earth, to have a man's mind move in charity, rest in providence, and turn upon the poles of truth. To pass from theological and philosophical truth, to the truth of civil business; it will be acknowledged even by those that practise it not, that clear and round dealing is the honour of man's nature; and that mixture of falsehood is like allay in coin of gold and silver, which may make the metal work the better, but it embaseth (embrace) it. For these winding and crooked courses are the goings of the serpent; which goeth basely upon the belly, and not upon the feet. There is no vice that doth so cover a man with shame as to be found false and perfidious. And therefore Montaigne saith prettily, when he inquired the reason, why the word of the lie should be such a disgrace and such an odious charge? Saith he, *If it be well weighed, to say that a man lieth, is as much to say, as that he is brave towards God and a coward towards men.* For a lie faces God, and shrinks from man. Surely the wickedness of falsehood and breach of faith cannot possibly be so highly expressed, as in that it shall be the last peal to call the judgments of God upon the generations of men; it being foretold, that when Christ cometh, *he shall not find faith upon the earth.*

GIFTS

RALPH WALDO EMERSON

> Gifts of one who loved me,
> 'Twas high time they came;
> When he ceased to love me,
> Time they stopped for shame.

It is said that the world is in a state of bankruptcy, that the world owes the world more than the world can pay, and ought to go into chancery, and be sold. I do not think this general insolvency, which involves in some sort all the population, to be the reason of the difficulty experienced at Christmas and New Year, and other times, in bestowing gifts; since it is always so pleasant to be generous, though very vexatious to pay debts. But the impediment lies in the choosing. If, at any time, it comes into my head that a present is due from me to somebody, I am puzzled what to give until the opportunity is gone. Flowers and fruits are always fit presents; flowers, because they are a proud assertion that a ray of beauty outvalues all the utilities of the world. These gay natures contrast with the somewhat stern countenance of ordinary nature; they are like music heard out of a workhouse. Nature does not cocker us: we are children, not pets: she is not fond: everything is dealt to us without fear or favor, after severe universal laws. Yet these delicate flowers look like the frolic and interference of love and beauty. Men used to tell us that we love flattery, even though we are not deceived by it, because it shows that we are of importance enough to be courted. Something like that pleasure the flowers give us: what am I to whom these sweet hints are addressed? Fruits are acceptable gifts because they are the flower of commodities, and admit of fantastic values being attached to them. If a man should send to me to come a hundred miles to visit him, and should set before me a basket of fine summer fruit, I should think there was some proportion between the labor and the reward.

For common gifts, necessity makes pertinences and beauty every day, and one is glad when an imperative leaves him no option, since if the man at the door have no shoes, you have not to consider whether you could procure him a paint-box. And as it is always pleasing to see a man eat bread, or drink water, in the house or out of doors, so it is always a great satisfaction to supply these first wants. Necessity does everything well. In our condition of universal dependence, it seems heroic to let the petitioner be the judge of his necessity, and to give all that is asked, though at great inconvenience. If it be a fantastic desire, it is better to leave to others the office of punishing him. I can think of many parts I should prefer playing to that of the Furies. Next to things of necessity, the rule for a gift which one of my friends prescribed is, that we might convey to some person that which properly belonged to his character, and was easily associated with him in thought. But our tokens of compliment and love are for the most part barbarous. Rings and other jewels are not gifts, but apologies for gifts. The only gift is a portion of thyself. Thou must bleed for me. Therefore the poet brings his poem; the shepherd, his lamb; the farmer, corn; the miner, a gem; the sailor, coral and shells; the painter, his picture; the girl, a handkerchief of her own sewing. This is right and pleasing, for it restores society in so far to the primary basis, when a man's biography is conveyed in his gift, and every man's wealth is an index of his merit. But it is a cold, lifeless business when you go to the shops to buy me something, which does not represent your life and talent, but a goldsmith's. This is fit for kings, and rich men who represent kings, and a false state of property, to make presents of gold and silver stuffs, as a kind of symbolical sin-offering, or payment of blackmail.

The law of benefits is a difficult channel, which requires careful sailing, or rude boats. It is not the office of a man to receive gifts. How dare you give them? We wish to be self-sustained. We do not quite forgive a giver. The hand that feeds us is in some danger of being bitten. We can receive anything from love, for that is a way of receiving it from ourselves; but not from anyone who assumes to bestow. We sometimes hate the meat which we eat, because there seems something of degrading dependence in living by it.

'Brother, if Jove to thee a present make, Take heed that from his hands thou nothing take.'

We ask the whole. Nothing less will content us. We arraign society if it do not give us besides earth, and fire, and water, opportunity, love, reverence and objects of veneration.

He is a good man who can receive a gift well. We are either glad or sorry at a gift, and both emotions are unbecoming. Some violence, I think, is done, some degradation borne, when I rejoice or grieve at a gift. I am sorry when my independence is invaded, or when a gift comes from such as do not know my spirit, and so the act is not supported; and if the gift pleases me overmuch, then I should be ashamed that the donor should read my heart, and see that I love his commodity, and not him. The gift, to be true, must be the flowing of the giver unto me, correspondent to my flowing unto him. When the waters are at level, then my goods pass to him, and his to me. All his are mine, all mine his. I say to him, How can you give me this pot of oil, or this flagon of wine, when all your oil and wine is mine, which belief of mine this gift seems to deny? Hence the fitness of beautiful, not useful things for gifts. This giving is flat usurpation, and therefore when the beneficiary is ungrateful, as all beneficiaries hate all Timons, not at all considering the value of the gift, but looking back to the greater store it was taken from, I rather sympathize with the beneficiary than with the anger of my lord Timon. For, the expectation of gratitude is mean, and is continually punished by the total insensibility of the obliged person. It is a great happiness to get off without injury and heart-burning, from one who has had the ill-luck to be served by you. It is a very onerous business, this of being served, and the debtor naturally wishes to give you a slap. A golden text for these gentlemen is that which I so admire in the Buddhist, who never thanks, and who says, 'Do not flatter your benefactors.'

The reason for these discords I conceive to be that there is no commensurability between a man and any gift. You cannot give anything to a magnanimous person. After you have served him he at once puts you in debt by his magnanimity. The service a man renders his friend is trivial and selfish, compared with the service he knows his friend stood in readiness to yield him, alike before he had begun to serve his friend, and now also. Compared with that goodwill I bear my friend, the benefit it is in my power to render him seems small. Besides, our action on each other, good as well as evil, is so incidental and at random, that we can seldom hear the acknowledgments of any person who would thank us for a benefit, without some shame and humiliation. We can rarely strike a direct stroke, but must be content with an oblique one; we seldom have the satisfaction of yielding a direct benefit, which is directly received. But rectitude scatters favors on every side without knowing it, and receives with wonder the thanks of all people.

I fear to breathe any treason against the majesty of love, which is the genius and god of gifts, and to whom we must not affect to prescribe. Let him give kingdoms or flower-leaves indifferently. There are persons from whom we always expect fairy-tokens; let us not cease to expect them. This is prerogative, and not to be limited by our municipal rules. For the rest, I like to see that we cannot be bought and sold. The best of hospitality and of generosity is also not in the will, but in fate. I find that I am not much to you; you do not need me; you do not feel me; then am I thrust out of doors, though you proffer me house and lands. No services are of any value, but only likeness. When I have attempted to join myself to others by services, it proved an intellectual trick, no more. They eat your service like apples, and leave you out. But love them, and they feel you, and delight in you all the time.

USES OF GREAT MEN

RALPH WALDO EMERSON

It is natural to believe in great men. If the companions of our childhood should turn out to be heroes, and their condition regal, it would not surprise us. All mythology opens with demigods, and the circumstance is high and poetic; that is, their genius is paramount. In the legends of the Gautama, the first men ate the earth, and found it deliciously sweet.

Nature seems to exist for the excellent. The world is upheld by the veracity of good men: they make the earth wholesome. They who lived with them found life glad and nutritious. Life is sweet and tolerable only in our belief in such society; and actually or ideally we manage to live with superiors. We call our children and our lands by their names. Their names are wrought into the verbs of language, their works and effigies are in our houses, and every circumstance of the day recalls an anecdote of them.

The search after the great is the dream of youth and the most serious occupation of manhood. We travel into foreign parts to find his works—if possible, to get a glimpse of him. But we are put off with fortune instead. You say the English are practical; the Germans are hospitable; in Valencia the climate is delicious; and in the hills of the Sacramento there is gold for the gathering. Yes, but I do not travel to find comfortable, rich, and hospitable people, or clear sky, or ingots that cost too much. But if there were any magnet that would point to the countries and houses where are the persons who are intrinsically rich and powerful, I would sell all, and buy it, and put myself on the road today.

The race goes with us on their credit. The knowledge that in the city is a man who invented the railroad raises the credit of all the citizens. But enormous populations, if they be beggars, are disgusting, like moving cheese, like hills of ants or of fleas—the more, the worse.

Our religion is the love and cherishing of these patrons. The gods of fable are the shining moments of great men. We run all our vessels into one mould. Our colossal theologies of Judaism, Christism, Buddhism, Mahometism, are the necessary and structural action of the human mind. The student of history is like a man going into a warehouse to buy cloths or carpets. He fancies he has a new article. If he go to the factory, he shall find that his new stuff still repeats the scrolls and rosettes which are found on the interior walls of the pyramids of Thebes. Our theism is the purification of the human mind. Man can paint, or make, or think nothing but man. He believes that the great material elements had their origin from his thought. And our philosophy finds one essence collected or distributed.

If now we proceed to inquire into the kinds of service we derive from others, let us be warned of the danger of modern studies, and begin low enough. We must not contend against love, or deny the substantial existence of other people. I know not what would happen to us. We have social strengths. Our affection towards others creates a sort of vantage or purchase which nothing will supply. I can do that by another which I cannot do alone. I can say to you what I cannot first say to myself. Other men are lenses through which we read our own minds. Each man seeks those of different quality from his own, and such as are good of their kind; that is, he seeks other men, and the otherest. The stronger the nature, the more it is reactive. Let us have the quality pure. A little genius let us leave alone. A main difference betwixt men is, whether they attend their own affair or not. Man is that noble endogenous plant which grows, like the palm, from within outward. His own affair, though impossible to others, he can open with celerity and in sport. It is easy to sugar to be sweet, and to nitre to be salt. We take a great deal of pains to waylay and entrap that which of itself will fall into our hands. I count him a great man who inhabits a higher sphere of thought, into which other men rise with labor and difficulty; he has but to open his eyes to see things in a true light, and in large relations; whilst they must make painful corrections, and keep a vigilant eye on many sources of error. His service to us is of like sort. It costs a beautiful person no exertion to paint her image on our eyes; yet how splendid is that benefit! It costs no more for a wise soul to convey his quality to other men. And everyone can do his best thing easiest. '*Peu de moyens, beaucoup d'effét.*' He is great who is what he is from nature, and who never reminds us of others.

But he must be related to us, and our life receive from him some promise of explanation. I cannot tell what I would know; but I have observed there are persons who, in their character and actions, answer questions which I have not skill to put. One man answers some questions which none of his contemporaries put, and is isolated. The past and passing religions and philosophies answer some other question. Certain men affect us as rich possibilities, but helpless to themselves and to their times, the sport perhaps, of some instinct that rules in the air, they do not speak to our want. But the great are near; we know them at sight. They satisfy expectation, and fall into place. What is good is effective, generative; makes for itself room, food and allies. A sound apple produces seed—a hybrid does not. Is a man in his place, he is constructive, fertile, magnetic, inundating armies with his purpose, which is thus executed. The river makes its own shores, and each legitimate idea makes its own channels and welcome—harvests for food, institutions for expression, weapons to fight with, and disciples to explain it. The true artist has the planet for his pedestal; the adventurer, after years of strife, has nothing broader than his own shoes.

Our common discourse respects two kinds of use or service from superior men. Direct giving is agreeable to the early belief of men; direct giving of material or metaphysical aid, as of health, eternal youth, fine senses, arts of healing, magical power and prophecy. The boy believes there is a teacher who can sell him wisdom. Churches believe in imputed merit. But, in strictness, we are not much cognizant of direct serving. Man is endogenous, and education is his unfolding. The aid we have from others is mechanical, compared with the discoveries of nature in us. What is thus learned is delightful in the doing, and the effect remains. Right ethics are central, and go from the soul outward. Gift is contrary to the law of the universe. Serving others is serving us. I must absolve me to myself. 'Mind thy affair,' says the spirit; 'coxcomb, would you meddle with the skies, or with other people?' Indirect service is left. Men have a pictorial or representative quality, and serve us in the intellect. Behmen and Swedenborg saw that things were representative. Men are also representative; first, of things, and secondly, of ideas.

As plants convert the minerals into food for animals, so each man converts some raw material in nature to human use. The inventors of fire, electricity, magnetism, iron, lead, glass, linen, silk, cotton; the makers of tools; the inventor of decimal notation; the geometer; the engineer; the musician, severally make an easy way for all through unknown and impossible confusions. Each man is, by secret liking, connected with some district of nature, whose agent and interpreter he is, as Linnæus, of plants; Huber, of bees; Fries, of lichens; Van Mons, of pears; Dalton, of atomic forms; Euclid, of lines; Newton, of fluxions.

A man is a center for nature, running out threads of relation through everything, fluid and solid, material and elemental. The earth rolls; every clod and stone comes to the meridian; so every organ, function, acid, crystal, grain of dust, has its relation to the brain. It waits long, but its turn comes. Each plant has its parasite, and each created thing its lover and poet. Justice has already been done to steam, to iron, to wood, to coal, to loadstone, to iodine, to corn and cotton; but how few materials are yet used by our arts! The mass of creatures and of qualities are still hid and expectant. It would seem as if each waited, like the enchanted princess in fairy tales, for a destined human deliverer. Each must be disenchanted, and walk forth to the day in human shape. In the history of discovery, the ripe and latent truth seems to have fashioned a brain for itself. A magnet must be made man, in some

Gilbert, or Swedenborg, or Oersted, before the general mind can come to entertain its powers.

If we limit ourselves to the first advantages: a sober grace adheres to the mineral and botanic kingdoms, which in the highest moments comes up as the charm of nature, the glitter of the spar, the sureness of affinity, the veracity of angles. Light and darkness, heat and cold, hunger and food, sweet and sour, solid, liquid, and gas, circle us round in a wreath of pleasures, and, by their agreeable quarrel, beguile the day of life. The eye repeats every day the first eulogy on things—'He saw that they were good.' We know where to find them; and these performers are relished all the more after a little experience of the pretending races. We are entitled, also, to higher advantages. Something is wanting to science, until it has been humanized. The table of logarithms is one thing, and its vital play, in botany, music, optics, and architecture, another. There are advancements to numbers, anatomy, architecture, astronomy, little suspected at first, when, by union with intellect and will, they ascend into the life, and reappear in conversation, character and politics.

But this comes later. We speak now only of our acquaintance with them in their own sphere, and the way in which they seem to fascinate and draw to them some genius who occupies himself with one thing all his life long. The possibility of interpretation lies in the identity of the observer with the observed. Each material thing has its celestial side; has its translation, through humanity, into the spiritual and necessary sphere, where it plays a part as indestructible as any other. And to these, their ends, all things continually ascend. The gases gather to the solid firmament; the chemic lump arrives at the plant, and grows; arrives at the quadruped, and walks; arrives at the man, and thinks. But also the constituency determines the vote of the representative. He is not only representative, but participant. Like can only be known by like. The reason why he knows about them is, that he is of them; he has just come out of nature, or from being a part of that thing. Animated chlorine knows of chlorine, and incarnate zinc, of zinc. Their quality makes his career; and he can variously publish their virtues, because they compose him. Man, made of the dust of the world, does not forget his origin; and all that is yet inanimate will one day speak and reason. Unpublished nature will have its whole secret told. Shall we say that quartz mountains will pulverize into innumerable Werners, Von Buchs and Beaumonts; and the laboratory of the atmosphere holds in solution I know not what Berzeliuses and Davys?

Thus we sit by the fire, and take hold on the poles of the earth. This quasi omnipresence supplies the imbecility of our condition. In one of those celestial days, when heaven and earth meet and adorn each other, it seems a poverty that we can only spend it once: we wish for a thousand heads, a thousand bodies, that we might celebrate its immense beauty in many ways and places. Is this fancy? Well, in good faith, we are multiplied by our proxies. How easily we adopt their labors. Every ship that comes to America got its chart from Columbus. Every novel is a debtor to Homer. Every carpenter who shaves with a foreplane borrows the genius of a forgotten inventor. Life is girt all round with a zodiac of sciences, the contributions of men who have perished to add their point of light to our sky. Engineer, broker, jurist, physician, moralist, theologian, and every man, inasmuch as he has any science, is a definer and map-maker of the latitudes and longitudes of our condition. These road-makers on every hand enrich us. We must extend the area of life, and multiply our relations. We are as much gainers by finding a new property in the old earth as by acquiring a new planet.

We are too passive in the reception of these material or semi-material aids. We must not be sacks and stomachs. To ascend one step—we are better served through our sympathy. Activity is contagious. Looking where others look, and conversing with the same things, we catch the charm which lured them. Napoleon said, 'You must not fight too often with one enemy, or you will teach him all your art of war.' Talk much with any man of vigorous mind, and we acquire very fast the habit of looking at things in the same light, and, on each occurrence, we anticipate his thought.

Men are helpful through the intellect and the affections. Other help, I find a false appearance. If you affect to give me bread and fire, I perceive that I pay for it the full price, and at last it leaves me as it found me, neither better nor worse; but all mental and moral force is a positive good. It goes out from you, whether you will or not, and profits me whom you never thought of. I cannot even hear of personal vigor of any kind, great power of performance, without fresh resolution. We are emulous of all that man can do. Cecil's saying of Sir Walter Raleigh, 'I know that he can toil terribly', is an electric touch. So are Clarendon's portraits—of Hampden: 'who was of an industry and vigilance not to be tired out or wearied by the most laborious, and of parts not to be imposed on by the most subtle and sharp, and of a personal courage equal to his best parts;' of Falkland: 'who was so severe an adorer of truth that he could as easily have given himself leave to steal as to dissemble'. We cannot read Plutarch without a tingling of the blood; and I accept the saying of the Chinese Mencius: 'A sage is the instructor of a hundred ages. When the manners of Loo are heard of, the stupid become intelligent, and the wavering, determined.'

This is the moral of biography; yet it is hard for departed men to touch the quick like our own companions, whose names may not last as long. What is he whom I never think of? Whilst in every solitude are those who succor our genius, and stimulate us in wonderful manners. There is a power in love to divine another's destiny better than that other can, and, by heroic encouragements, hold him to his task. What has friendship so signal as its sublime attraction to whatever virtue is in us? We will never more think cheaply of ourselves, or of life. We are piqued to some purpose, and the industry of the diggers on the railroad will not again shame us.

Under this head, too, falls that homage, very pure, as I think, which all ranks pay to the hero of the day, from Coriolanus and Gracchus, down to Pitt, Lafayette, Wellington, Webster,

Lamartine. Hear the shouts in the street! The people cannot see him enough. They delight in a man. Here is a head and a trunk! What a front! What eyes! Atlantean shoulders, and the whole carriage heroic, with equal inward force to guide the great machine! This pleasure of full expression to that which, in their private experience, is usually cramped and obstructed, runs, also, much higher, and is the secret of the reader's joy in literary genius. Nothing is kept back. There is fire enough to fuse the mountain of ore. Shakespeare's principal merit may be conveyed in saying that he, of all men, best understands the English language, and can say what he will. Yet these unchoked channels and floodgates of expression are only health or fortunate constitution. Shakespeare's name suggests other and purely intellectual benefits.

Senates and sovereigns have no compliment, with their medals, swords, and armorial coats, like the addressing to a human being thoughts out of a certain height, and presupposing his intelligence. This honor, which is possible in personal intercourse scarcely twice in a lifetime, genius perpetually pays; contented, if now and then, in a century, the proffer is accepted. The indicators of the values of matter are degraded to a sort of cooks and confectioners, on the appearance of the indicators of ideas. Genius is the naturalist or geographer of the supersensible regions, and draws their map; and, by acquainting us with new fields of activity, cools our affection for the old. These are at once accepted as the reality, of which the world we have conversed with is the show.

We go to the gymnasium and the swimming-school to see the power and beauty of the body; there is the like pleasure, and higher benefit, from witnessing intellectual feats of all kinds; as feats of memory, of mathematical combination, great power of abstraction, the transmutings of the imagination, even versatility and concentration, as these acts expose the invisible organs and members of the mind, which respond, member for member, to the parts of the body. For we thus enter a new gymnasium, and learn to choose men by their truest marks, taught, with Plato, 'to choose those who can, without aid from the eyes or any other sense, proceed to truth and to being'. Foremost among these activities are the summersaults, spells, and resurrections wrought by the imagination. When this wakes, a man seems to multiply ten times or a thousand times his force. It opens the delicious sense of indeterminate size, and inspires an audacious mental habit. We are as elastic as the gas of gunpowder, and a sentence in a book or a word dropped in conversation sets free our fancy, and instantly our heads are bathed with galaxies, and our feet tread the floor of the pit. And this benefit is real, because we are entitled to these enlargements, and, once having passed the bounds, shall never again be quite the miserable pedants we were.

The high functions of the intellect are so allied that some imaginative power usually appears in all eminent minds, even in arithmeticians of the first class, but especially in meditative men of an intuitive habit of thought. This class serve us, so that they have the perception of identity and the perception of reaction. The eyes of Plato, Shakespeare, Swedenborg, Goethe, never shut on either of these laws. The perception of these laws is a kind of meter of the mind. Little minds are little, through failure to see them.

Even these feasts have their surfeit. Our delight in reason degenerates into idolatry of the herald. Especially when a mind of powerful method has instructed men, we find the examples of oppression. The dominion of Aristotle, the Ptolemaic astronomy, the credit of Luther, of Bacon, of Locke—in religion, the history of hierarchies, of saints, and the sects which have taken the name of each founder—are in point. Alas! every man is such a victim. The imbecility of men is always inviting the impudence of power. It is the delight of vulgar talent to dazzle and to blind the beholder. But true genius seeks to defend us from itself. True genius will not impoverish, but will liberate, and add new senses. If a wise man should appear in our village, he would create, in those who conversed with him, a new consciousness of wealth, by opening their eyes to unobserved advantages; he would establish a sense of immovable equality, calm us with assurances that we could not be cheated; as everyone would discern the checks and guaranties of condition. The rich would see their mistakes and poverty, the poor their escapes and their resources.

But nature brings all this about in due time. Rotation is her remedy. The soul is impatient of masters, and eager for change. Housekeepers say of a domestic who has been valuable, 'She had lived with me long enough.' We are tendencies, or rather symptoms, and none of us complete. We touch and go, and sip the foam of many lives. Rotation is the law of nature. When nature removes a great man, people explore the horizon for a successor; but none comes, and none will. His class is extinguished with him. In some other and quite different field, the next man will appear; not Jefferson, not Franklin, but now a great salesman; than a road-contractor; then a student of fishes; then a buffalo-hunting explorer, or a semi-savage Western general. Thus we make a stand against our rougher masters; but against the best there is a finer remedy. The power which they communicate is not theirs. When we are exalted by ideas, we do not owe this to Plato, but to the idea, to which, also, Plato was debtor.

I must not forget that we have a special debt to a single class. Life is a scale of degrees. Between rank and rank of our great men are wide intervals. Mankind have, in all ages, attached themselves to a few persons, who, either by the quality of that idea they embodied, or by the largeness of their reception, were entitled to the position of leaders and law-givers. These teach us the qualities of primary nature—admit us to the constitution of things. We swim, day by day, on a river of delusions, and are effectually amused with houses and towns in the air, of which the men about us are dupes. But life is a sincerity. In lucid intervals we say, 'Let there be an entrance opened for me into realties; I have worn the fool's cap too long.' We will know the meaning of our economies and politics. Give us the cipher, and, if persons and things are scores of a celestial music, let us read off the strains. We have been cheated of our reason; yet there have been sane men who enjoyed a rich and related existence. What they know they know for us. With each new mind, a new secret of nature transpires; nor can the Bible be closed until the last great man is born. These men correct the delirium of the animal spirits, make us considerate, and engage us to new aims and powers. The veneration of mankind selects these for the highest place. Witness the multitude of statues, pictures, and memorials which recall their genius in every city, village, house, and ship:

> Ever their phantoms arise before us,
> Our loftier brothers, but one in blood;
> At bed and table they lord it o'er us,
> With looks of beauty, and words of good.

How to illustrate the distinctive benefit of ideas, the service rendered by those who introduce moral truths into the general mind? I am plagued, in all my living, with a perpetual tariff of prices. If I work in my garden and prune an apple-tree, I am well enough entertained, and could continue indefinitely in the like occupation. But it comes to mind that a day is gone, and I have got this precious nothing done. I go to Boston or New York, and run up and down on my affairs: they are sped, but so is the day. I am vexed by the recollection of this price I have paid for a trifling advantage. I remember the peau d'âne, on which whoso sat should have his desire, but a piece of the skin was gone for every wish. I go to a convention of philanthropists. Do what I can, I cannot keep my eyes off the clock. But if there should appear in the company some gentle soul who knows little of persons or parties, of Carolina or Cuba, but who announces a law that disposes these particulars, and so certifies me of the equity which checkmates every false player, bankrupts every self-seeker, and apprises me of my independence on any conditions of country, or time, or human body, that man liberates me; I forget the clock. I pass out of the sore relation to persons. I am healed of my hurts. I am made immortal by apprehending my possession of incorruptible goods. Here is great competition of rich and poor. We live in a market, where is only so much wheat, or wool, or land; and if I have so much more, every other must have so much less. I seem to have no good, without breach of good manners. Nobody is glad in the gladness of another, and our system is one of war, of an injurious superiority. Every child of the Saxon race is educated to wish to be first. It is our system; and a man comes to measure his greatness by the regrets, envies, and hatreds of his competitors. But in these new fields there is room: here are no self-esteems, no exclusions.

I admire great men of all classes, those who stand for facts and for thoughts; I like rough and smooth, 'scourges of God' and 'darlings of the human race'. I like the first Cæsar; and Charles V, of Spain; and Charles XII, of Sweden; Richard Plantagenet; and Bonaparte, in France. I applaud a sufficient man, an officer equal to his office; captains, ministers, senators. I like a master standing firm on legs of iron, well-born, rich, handsome, eloquent, loaded with advantages, drawing all men by fascination into tributaries and supports of his power. Sword and staff, or talents sword-like or staff-like, carry on the work of the world. But I find him greater when he can abolish himself, and all heroes, by letting in this element of reason, irrespective of persons; this subtilizer, and irresistible upward force, into our thought, destroying individualism; the power so great that the potentate is nothing. Then he is a monarch who gives a constitution to his people; a pontiff who preaches the equality of souls, and releases his servants from their barbarous homages; an emperor who can spare his empire.

But I intended to specify, with a little minuteness, two or three points of service. Nature never spares the opium or nepenthe; but, wherever she mars her creature with some deformity or defect, lays her poppies plentifully on the bruise, and the sufferer goes joyfully through life, ignorant of the ruin, and incapable of seeing it, though all the world point their finger at it every day. The worthless and offensive members of society, whose existence is a social pest, invariably think themselves the most ill-used people alive, and never get over their astonishment at the ingratitude and selfishness of their contemporaries. Our globe discovers its hidden virtues, not only in heroes and archangels, but in gossips and nurses. Is it not a rare contrivance that lodged the due inertia in every creature, the conserving, resisting energy, the anger at being waked or changed? Altogether independent of the intellectual force in each is the pride of opinion, the security that we are right. Not the feeblest grandame, not a mowing idiot, but uses what spark of perception and faculty is left, to chuckle and triumph in his or her opinion over the absurdities of all the rest. Difference from me is the measure of absurdity. Not one has a misgiving of being wrong. Was it not a bright thought that made things cohere with this bitumen, fastest of cements? But, in the midst of this chuckle of self-gratulation, some figure goes by which Thersites too can love and admire. This is he that should marshal us the way we were going. There is no end to his aid. Without Plato, we should almost lose our faith in the possibility of a reasonable book. We seem to want but one, but we want one. We love to associate with heroic persons, since our receptivity is unlimited; and, with the great, our thoughts and manners easily become great. We are all wise in capacity, though so few in energy. There needs but one wise man in a company, and all are wise, so rapid is the contagion.

Great men are thus a collyrium to clear our eyes from egotism, and enable us to see other people and their works. But there are vices and follies incident to whole populations and ages. Men resemble their contemporaries, even more than their progenitors. It is observed in old couples, or in persons who have been housemates for a course of years, that they grow like; and if they should live long enough, we should not be able to know them apart. Nature abhors these complaisances, which threaten to melt the world into a lump, and hastens to break up such maudlin agglutinations. The like assimilation goes on between men of one town, of one sect, of one political party; and the ideas of the time are in the air, and infect all who breathe it. Viewed from any high point, this city of New York, yonder city of London, the western civilization, would seem a bundle of insanities. We keep each other in countenance, and exasperate by emulation the frenzy of the time. The shield against the stingings of conscience is the universal practice, or our contemporaries. Again: it is very easy to be as wise and good as your companions. We learn of our contemporaries what they know, without effort, and almost through the pores of the skin. We catch it by sympathy, or as a wife arrives at the intellectual and moral elevations of her husband. But we stop where they stop. Very hardly can we take another step. The great, or such as hold of nature, and transcend fashions, by their fidelity to universal ideas, are saviors from these federal errors, and defend us from our contemporaries. They are the exceptions which we want, where all grows alike. A foreign greatness is the antidote for cabalism.

Thus we feed on genius, and refresh ourselves from too much conversation with our mates, and exult in the depth of nature in that direction in which he leads us. What indemnification is one great man for populations of pygmies! Every mother wishes one son a genius, though all the rest should be mediocre. But a new danger appears in the excess of influence of the great man. His attractions warp us from our place. We have become underlings and intellectual suicides. Ah! Yonder in the horizon is our help: other great men, new qualities, counterweights and checks on each other. We cloy of the honey of each peculiar greatness. Every hero becomes a bore at last. Perhaps Voltaire was not bad-hearted, yet he said of the good Jesus, even, 'I pray you, let me never hear that man's name again.' They cry up the virtues of George Washington—' Damn George Washington!' is the poor Jacobin's whole speech and confutation. But it is human nature's indispensable defense. The centripetence augments the centrifugence. We balance one man with his opposite, and the health of the State depends on the seesaw.

There is, however, a speedy limit to the use of heroes. Every genius is defended from approach by quantities of unavailableness. They are very attractive, and seem at a distance our own; but we are hindered on all sides from approach. The more we are drawn, the more we are repelled. There is something not solid in the good that is done for us. The best discovery the discoverer makes for himself. It has something unreal for his companion, until he too has substantiated it. It seems as if the Deity dressed each soul which he sends into nature in certain virtues and powers not communicable to other men, and, sending it to perform one more turn through the circle of beings, wrote, 'Not transferable,' and 'Good for this trip only,' on these garments of the soul. There is somewhat deceptive about the intercourse of minds. The boundaries are invisible, but they are never crossed. There is such good will to impart, and such good will to receive, that each threatens to become the other; but the law of individuality collects its secret strength: you are you, and I am I, and so we remain.

For Nature wishes everything to remain itself; and whilst every individual strives to grow and exclude, and to exclude and grow, to the extremities of the universe, and to impose the law of its being on every other creature, Nature steadily aims to protect each against every other. Each is self-defended. Nothing is more marked than the power by which individuals are guarded from individuals, in a world where every benefactor becomes so easily a malefactor, only by continuation of his activity into places where it is not due; where children seem so much at the mercy of their foolish parents, and where almost all men are too social and interfering. We rightly speak of the guardian angels of children. How superior in their security from infusions of evil persons, from vulgarity and second thought! They shed their own abundant beauty on the objects they behold. Therefore, they are not at the mercy of such poor educators as we adults. If we huff and chide them, they soon come not to mind it, and get a self-reliance; and if we indulge them to folly, they learn the limitation elsewhere.

We need not fear excessive influence. A more generous trust is permitted. Serve the great. Stick at no humiliation. Grudge no office thou canst render. Be the limb of their body, the breath of their mouth. Compromise thy egotism. Who cares for that, so thou gain aught wider and nobler? Never mind the taunt of Boswellism: the devotion may easily be greater than the wretched pride which is guarding its own skirts. Be another—not thyself, but a Platonist; not a soul, but a Christian; not a naturalist, but a Cartesian; not a poet, but a Shakespearean. In vain; the wheels of tendency will not stop, nor will all the forces of inertia, fear, or of love itself, hold thee there. On, and forever onward! The microscope observes a monad or wheel-insect among the infusories circulating in water. Presently a dot appears on the animal, which enlarges to a slit, and it becomes two perfect animals. The ever-proceeding detachment appears not less in all thought, and in society. Children think they cannot live without their parents. But long before they are aware of it, the black dot has appeared, and the detachment taken place. Any accident will now reveal to them their independence.

But great men—the word is injurious. Is there caste? Is there fate? What becomes of the promise to virtue? The thoughtful youth laments the superfœtation of nature. 'Generous and handsome,' he says, 'is your hero; but look at yonder poor Paddy, whose country is his wheelbarrow; look at his whole nation of Paddies.' Why are the masses, from the dawn of history down, food for knives and powder? The idea dignifies a few leaders, who have sentiment, opinion, love, self-devotion; and they make war and death sacred; but what for the wretches whom they hire and kill? The cheapness of man is every day's tragedy. It is as real a loss that others should be low as that we should be low; for we must have society.

Is it a reply to these suggestions, to say society is a Pestalozzian school; all are teachers and pupils in turn. We are equally served by receiving and by imparting. Men who know the same things are not long the best company for each other. But bring to each an intelligent person of another experience, and it is as if you let off water from a lake, by cutting a lower basin. It seems a mechanical advantage, and great benefit it is to each speaker, as he can now paint out his thought to himself. We pass very fast, in our personal moods, from dignity to dependence. And if any appear never to assume the chair, but always to stand and serve, it is because we do not see the company in a sufficiently long period for the whole rotation of parts to come about. As to what we call the masses and common men—there are no common men. All men are at last of a size; and true art is only possible on the conviction that every talent has its apotheosis somewhere. Fair play, and an open field, and freshest laurels to all who have won them! But heaven reserves an equal scope for every creature. Each is uneasy until he has produced his private ray unto the concave sphere, and beheld his talent also in its last nobility and exaltation.

The heroes of the hour are relatively great—of a faster growth; or they are such, in whom, at the moment of success, a quality is ripe which is then in request. Other days will demand other qualities. Some rays escape the common observer, and want a finely adapted eye. Ask the great man if there be none greater. His companions are; and not the less great, but the more, that society cannot see them. Nature never sends a great man into the planet without confiding the secret to another soul.

One gracious fact emerges from these studies—that there is true ascension in our love. The reputations of the nineteenth century will one day be quoted to prove its barbarism. The genius of humanity is the real subject whose biography is written in our annals. We must infer much, and supply many chasms in the record. The history of the universe is symptomatic, and life is mnemonical. No man, in all the procession of famous men, is reason or illumination, or that essence we were looking for, but is an exhibition, in some quarter, of new possibilities. Could we one day complete the immense figure which these flagrant points compose! The study of many individuals leads us to an elemental region wherein the individual is lost, or wherein all touch by their summits. Thought and feeling, that break out there, cannot be impounded by any fence of personality. This is the key to the power of the greatest men—their spirit diffuses itself. A new quality of mind travels by night and by day, in concentric circles from its origin, and publishes itself by unknown methods; the union of all minds appears intimate; what gets admission to one cannot be kept out of any other; the smallest acquisition of truth or of energy, in any quarter, is so much good to the commonwealth of souls. If the disparities of talent and position vanish when the individuals are seen in the duration which is necessary to complete the career of each, even more swiftly the seeming injustice disappears when we ascend to the central identity of all the individuals, and know that they are made of the substance which ordaineth and doeth.

The genius of humanity is the right point of view of history. The qualities abide; the men who exhibit them have now more, now less, and pass away; the qualities remain on another brow. No experience is more familiar. Once you saw phœnixes: they are gone; the world is not therefore disenchanted. The vessels on which you read sacred emblems turn out to be common pottery; but the sense of the pictures is sacred, and you may still read them transferred to the walls of the world. For a time our teachers serve us personally, as meters or milestones of progress. Once they were angels of knowledge, and their figures touched the sky. Then we drew near, saw their means, culture, and limits; and they yielded their place to other geniuses. Happy, if a few names remain so high that we have not been able to read them nearer, and age and comparison have not robbed them of a ray. But, at last, we shall cease to look in men for completeness, and shall content ourselves with their social and delegated quality. All that respects the individual is temporary and prospective, like the individual himself, who is ascending out of his limits into a catholic existence. We have never come at the true and best benefit of any genius, so long as we believe him an original force. In the moment when he ceases to help us as a cause, he begins to help us more as an effect. Then he appears as an exponent of a vaster mind and will. The opaque self becomes transparent with the light of the First Cause.

Yet, within the limits of human education and agency, we may say great men exist that there may be greater men. The destiny of organized nature is amelioration, and who can tell its limits? It is for man to tame the chaos; on every side, whilst he lives, to scatter the seeds of science and of song, that climate, corn, animals, men, may be milder, and the germs of love and benefit may be multiplied.

PREFACE TO *LEAVES OF GRASS*
1855

WALT WHITMAN

America does not repel the past, or what the past has produced under its forms, or amid other politics, or the idea of castes, or the old religions—accepts the lesson with calmness—is not impatient because the slough still sticks to opinions and manners in literature, while the life which served its requirements has passed into the new life of the new forms—perceives that the corpse is slowly borne from the eating and sleeping rooms of the house—perceives that it waits a little while in the door—that it was fittest for its days—that its action has descended to the stalwart and well-shaped heir who approaches—and that he shall be fittest for his days.

The Americans of all nations at any time upon the earth, have probably the fullest poetical nature. The United States themselves are essentially the greatest poem. In the history of the earth hitherto, the largest and most stirring appear tame and orderly to their ampler largeness and stir. Here at last is something in the doings of man that corresponds with the broadcast doings of the day and night. Here is action untied from strings, necessarily blind to particulars and details, magnificently moving in masses. Here is the hospitality which for ever indicates heroes. Here the performance, disdaining the trivial, unapproach'd in the tremendous audacity of its crowds and groupings, and the push of its perspective, spreads with crampless and flowing breadth, and showers its prolific and splendid extravagance. One sees it must indeed own the riches of the summer and winter, and need never be bankrupt while corn grows from the ground, or the orchards drop apples, or the bays contain fish, or men beget children upon women.

Other states indicate themselves in their deputies—but the genius of the United States is not best or most in its executives or legislatures, nor in its ambassadors or authors, or colleges or churches or parlors, nor even in its newspapers or inventors—but always most in the common people, south, north, west, east, in all its States, through all its mighty amplitude. The largeness of the nation, however, were monstrous without a corresponding largeness and generosity of the spirit of the citizen. Not swarming states, nor streets and steamships, nor prosperous business, nor farms, nor capital, nor learning, may suffice for the ideal of man—nor suffice the poet. No reminiscences may suffice either. A live nation can always cut a deep mark, and can have the best authority the cheapest—namely, from its own soul. This is the sum of the profitable uses of individuals or states, and of present action and grandeur, and of the subjects of poets. (As if it were necessary to trot back generation after generation to the eastern records! As if the beauty and sacredness of the demonstrable must fall behind that of the mythical! As if men do not make their mark out of any times! As if the opening of the western continent by discovery, and what has transpired in North and South America, were less than the small theater of the antique, or the aimless sleep-walking of the middle ages!) The pride of the United States leaves the wealth and finesse of the cities, and all returns of commerce and agriculture, and all the magnitude of geography or shows of exterior victory, to enjoy the sight and realization of full-sized men, or one full-sized man unconquerable and simple.

The American poets are to inclose old and new, for America is the race of races. The expression of the American poet is to be transcendent and new. It is to be indirect, and not direct or descriptive or epic. Its quality goes through these to much more. Let the age and wars of other nations be chanted, and their eras and characters be illustrated, and that finish the verse. Not so the great psalm of the republic. Here the theme is creative, and has vista. Whatever stagnates in the flat of custom or obedience or legislation, the great poet never stagnates. Obedience does not master him, he masters it. High up out of reach he stands, turning a concentrated light—he turns the pivot with his finger—he baffles the swiftest runners as he stands, and easily overtakes and envelopes them. The time straying toward infidelity and confections and persiflage he withholds by steady faith. Faith is the antiseptic of the soul—it pervades the common people and preserves them—they never give up believing and expecting and trusting. There is that indescribable freshness and unconsciousness about an illiterate person, that humbles and mocks the power of the noblest expressive genius. The poet sees for a certainty how one not a great artist may be just as sacred and perfect as the greatest artist.

The power to destroy or remould is freely used by the greatest poet, but seldom the power of attack. What is past is past. If he does not expose superior models, and prove himself by every step he takes, he is not what is wanted. The presence of the great poet conquers—not parleying, or struggling, or any prepared attempts. Now he has passed that way, see after him! There is not left any vestige of despair, or misanthropy, or cunning, or exclusiveness, or the ignominy of a nativity or color, or delusion of hell or the necessity of hell—and no man thenceforward shall be degraded for ignorance or weakness or sin. The greatest poet hardly knows pettiness or triviality. If he breathes into anything that was before thought small, it dilates with the grandeur and life of the universe. He is a seer—he is individual—he is complete in himself—the others are as good as he, only he sees it, and they do not. He is not one of the chorus—he does not stop for any regulation—he is the president of regulation. What the eyesight does to the rest, he does to the rest. Who knows the curious mystery of the eyesight? The other senses corroborate themselves, but this is removed from any proof but its own, and foreruns the identities of the spiritual world. A single glance of it mocks all the investigations of man, and all the instruments and books of the earth, and all reasoning. What is marvelous? What is unlikely? What is impossible or baseless or vague—after you have once just open'd the space of a peach-pit, and given audience to far and near, and to the sunset, and had all things enter with electric swiftness, softly and duly, without confusion or jostling or jam?

The land and sea, the animals, fishes and birds, the sky of heaven and the orbs, the forests, mountains and rivers, are not small themes—but folks expect of the poet to indicate more than the beauty and dignity which always attach to dumb real objects—they expect him to indicate the path between reality and their souls. Men and women perceive the beauty well enough—probably as well as he. The passionate tenacity of hunters, woodmen, early risers, cultivators of gardens and orchards and fields, the love of healthy women for the manly form, seafaring persons, drivers of horses, the passion for light and the open air, all is an old varied sign of the unfailing perception of beauty, and of a residence of the poetic in out-door people. They can never be assisted by poets to perceive—some may, but they never can. The poetic quality is not marshal'd in rhyme or uniformity, or abstract addresses to things, nor in melancholy complaints or good precepts, but is the life of these and much else, and is in the soul. The profit of rhyme is that it drops seeds of a sweeter and more luxuriant rhyme, and of uniformity that it conveys itself into its own roots in the ground out of sight. The rhyme and uniformity of perfect poems show the free growth of metrical laws, and bud from them as unerringly and loosely as lilacs and roses on a bush, and take shapes as compact as the shapes of chestnuts and oranges, and melons and pears, and shed the perfume impalpable to form. The fluency and ornaments of the finest poems or music or orations or recitations, are not independent but dependent. All beauty comes from beautiful blood and a beautiful brain. If the greatnesses are in conjunction in a man or woman, it is enough—the fact will prevail through the universe; but the gaggery and gilt of a million years will not prevail. Who troubles himself about his ornaments or fluency is lost. This is what you shall do: Love the earth and sun and the animals, despise riches, give alms to everyone that asks, stand up for the stupid and crazy, devote your income and labor to others, hate tyrants, argue not concerning God, have patience and indulgence toward the people, take off your hat to nothing known or unknown, or to any man or number of men—go freely with powerful uneducated persons, and with the young, and with the mothers of families—re-examine all you have been told in school or church or in any book, and dismiss whatever insults your own soul; and your very flesh shall be a great poem, and have the richest fluency, not only in its words, but in the silent lines of its lips and face, and between the lashes of your eyes, and in every motion and joint of your body. The poet shall not spend his time in unneeded work. He shall know that the ground is already plow'd and manured; others may not know it, but he shall. He shall go directly to the creation. His trust shall master the trust of everything he touches—and shall master all attachment.

The known universe has one complete lover, and that is the greatest poet. He consumes an eternal passion, and is indifferent which chance happens, and which possible contingency of fortune or misfortune, and persuades daily and hourly his delicious pay. What balks or breaks others is fuel for his burning progress to contact and amorous joy. Other proportions of the reception of pleasure dwindle to nothing to his proportions. All expected from heaven or from the highest, he is rapport within the sight of the daybreak, or the scenes of the winter woods, or the presence of children playing, or with his arm round the neck of a man or woman. His love above all love has leisure and expanse—he leaves room ahead of himself. He is no irresolute or suspicious lover—he is sure—he scorns intervals. His experience and the showers and thrills are not for nothing. Nothing can jar him—suffering and darkness cannot—death and fear cannot. To him complaint and jealousy and envy are corpses buried and rotten in the earth—he saw them buried. The sea is not surer of the shore, or the shore of the sea, than he is of the fruition of his love, and of all perfection and beauty.

The fruition of beauty is no chance of miss or hit—it is as

inevitable as life—it is exact and plumb as gravitation. From the eyesight proceeds another eyesight, and from the hearing proceeds another hearing, and from the voice proceeds another voice, eternally curious of the harmony of things with man. These understand the law of perfection in masses and floods—that it is profuse and impartial—that there is not a minute of the light or dark, nor an acre of the earth and sea, without it—nor any direction of the sky, nor any trade or employment, nor any turn of events. This is the reason that about the proper expression of beauty there is precision and balance. One part does not need to be thrust above another. The best singer is not the one who has the most lithe and powerful organ. The pleasure of poems is not in them that take the handsomest measure and sound.

Without effort, and without exposing in the least how it is done, the greatest poet brings the spirit of any or all events and passions and scenes and persons, some more and some less, to bear on your individual character as you hear or read. To do this well is to compete with the laws that pursue and follow Time. What is the purpose must surely be there, and the clew of it must be there—and the faintest indication is the indication of the best, and then becomes the clearest indication. Past and present and future are not disjoin'd but join'd. The greatest poet forms the consistence of what is to be, from what has been and is. He drags the dead out of their coffins and stands them again on their feet. He says to the past, Rise and walk before me that I may realize you. He learns the lesson—he places himself where the future becomes present. The greatest poet does not only dazzle his rays over character and scenes and passions—he finally ascends, and finishes all—he exhibits the pinnacles that no man can tell what they are for, or what is beyond—he glows a moment on the extremest verge. He is most wonderful in his last half-hidden smile or frown; by that flash of the moment of parting the one that sees it shall be encouraged or terrified afterward for many years. The greatest poet does not moralize or make applications of morals—he knows the soul. The soul has that measureless pride which consists in never acknowledging any lessons or deductions but its own. But it has sympathy as measureless as its pride, and the one balances the other, and neither can stretch too far while it stretches in company with the other. The inmost secrets of art sleep with the twain. The greatest poet has lain close betwixt both, and they are vital in his style and thoughts.

The art of art, the glory of expression and the sunshine of the light of letters, is simplicity. Nothing is better than simplicity— nothing can make up for excess, or for the lack of definiteness. To carry on the heave of impulse and pierce intellectual depths and give all subjects their articulations, are powers neither common nor very uncommon. But to speak in literature with the perfect rectitude and insouciance of the movements of animals, and the unimpeachableness of the sentiment of trees in the woods and grass by the roadside, is the flawless triumph of art. If you have look'd on him who has achiev'd it you have look'd on one of the masters of the artists of all nations and times. You shall not contemplate the flight of the gray gull over the bay, or the mettlesome action of the blood horse, or the tall leaning of sunflowers on their stalk, or the appearance of the sun journeying through heaven, or the appearance of the moon afterward, with any more satisfaction than you shall contemplate him. The great poet has less a mark'd style, and is more the channel of thoughts and things without increase or diminution, and is the free channel of himself. He swears to his art, I will not be meddlesome, I will not have in my writing any elegance, or effect, or originality, to hang in the way between me and the rest like curtains. I will have nothing hang in the way, not the richest curtains. What I tell I tell for precisely what it is. Let who may exalt or startle or fascinate or soothe, I will have purposes as health or heat or snow has, and be as regardless of observation. What I experience or portray shall go from my composition without a shred of my composition. You shall stand by my side and look in the mirror with me.

The old red blood and stainless gentility of great poets will be proved by their unconstraint. A heroic person walks at his ease through and out of that custom or precedent or authority that suits him not. Of the traits of the brotherhood of first-class writers, savans, musicians, inventors and artists, nothing is finer than silent defiance advancing from new free forms. In the need of poems, philosophy, politics, mechanism, science, behavior, the craft of art, an appropriate native grand opera, shipcraft, or any craft, he is greatest for ever and ever who contributes the greatest original practical example. The cleanest expression is that which finds no sphere worthy of itself, and makes one.

The messages of great poems to each man and woman are, Come to us on equal terms, only then can you understand us. We are no better than you, what we inclose you inclose, what we enjoy you may enjoy. Did you suppose there could be only one Supreme? We affirm there can be unnumber'd Supremes, and that one does not countervail another any more than one eyesight countervails another—and that men can be good or grand only of the consciousness of their supremacy within them. What do you think is the grandeur of storms and dismemberments, and the deadliest battles and wrecks, and the wildest fury of the elements, and the power of the sea, and the motion of Nature, and the throes of human desires, and dignity and hate and love? It is that something in the soul which says, Rage on, whirl on, I tread master here and everywhere—Master of the spasms of the sky and of the shatter of the sea, Master of nature and passion and death, and of all terror and all pain.

The American bards shall be mark'd for generosity and affection, and for encouraging competitors. They shall be Kosmos, without monopoly or secrecy, glad to pass anything to anyone—hungry for equals night and day. They shall not be careful of riches and privilege—they shall be riches and privilege—they shall perceive who the most affluent man is. The most affluent man is he that confronts all the shows he sees by equivalents out of the stronger wealth of himself. The American bard shall delineate no class of persons, nor one or two out of the strata of interests, nor love most nor truth most, nor the soul most, nor the body most—and not be for the Eastern States more than the Western, or the Northern States more than the Southern.

Exact science and its practical movements are no checks on the greatest poet, but always his encouragement and support. The outset and remembrance are there—there the arms that lifted him first, and braced him best—there he returns after all his goings and comings. The sailor and traveler—the anatomist, chemist, astronomer, geologist, phrenologist, spiritualist, mathematician, historian, and lexicographer, are not poets, but they are the lawgivers of poets, and their construction underlies the structure of every perfect poem. No matter what rises or is utter'd, they sent the seed of the conception of it—of them and by them stand the visible proofs of souls. If there shall be love and content between the father and the son, and if the greatness of the son is the exuding of the greatness of the father, there shall be love between the poet and the man of demonstrable science. In the beauty of poems are henceforth the tuft and final applause of science.

Great is the faith of the flush of knowledge, and of the investigation of the depths of qualities and things. Cleaving and circling here swells the soul of the poet, yet is president of itself always. The depths are fathomless, and therefore calm. The innocence and nakedness are resumed—they are neither modest nor immodest. The whole theory of the supernatural, and all that was twined with it or educed out of it, departs as a dream. What has ever happen'd—what happens, and whatever may or shall happen, the vital laws inclose all. They are sufficient for any case and for all cases—none to be hurried or retarded—any special miracle of affairs or persons inadmissible in the vast clear scheme where every motion and every spear of grass, and the frames and spirits of men and women and all that concerns them, are unspeakably perfect miracles, all referring to all, and each distinct and in its place. It is also not consistent with the reality of the soul to admit that there is anything in the known universe more divine than men and women.

Men and women, and the earth and all upon it, are to be

taken as they are, and the investigation of their past and present and future shall be unintermitted, and shall be done with perfect candor. Upon this basis philosophy speculates, ever looking towards the poet, ever regarding the eternal tendencies of all toward happiness, never inconsistent with what is clear to the senses and to the soul. For the eternal tendencies of all toward happiness make the only point of sane philosophy. Whatever comprehends less than that—whatever is less than the laws of light and of astronomical motion—or less than the laws that follow the thief, the liar, the glutton and the drunkard, through this life and doubtless afterward—or less than vast stretches of time, or the slow formation of density, or the patient upheaving of strata—is of no account. Whatever would put God in a poem or system of philosophy as contending against some being or influence, is also of no account. Sanity and ensemble characterize the great master—spoilt in one principle, all is spoilt. The great master has nothing to do with miracles. He sees health for himself in being one of the mass—he sees the hiatus in singular eminence. To the perfect shape comes common ground. To be under the general law is great, for that is to correspond with it. The master knows that he is unspeakably great, and that all are unspeakably great—that nothing, for instance, is greater than to conceive children, and bring them up well—that to be is just as great as to perceive or tell.

In the make of the great masters the idea of political liberty is indispensable. Liberty takes the adherence of heroes wherever man and woman exist—but never takes any adherence or welcome from the rest more than from poets. They are the voice and exposition of liberty. They out of ages are worthy the grand idea—to them it is confided, and they must sustain it. Nothing has precedence of it, and nothing can warp or degrade it.

As the attributes of the poets of the kosmos concenter in the real body, and in the pleasure of things, they possess the superiority of genuineness over all fiction and romance. As they emit themselves, facts are shower'd over with light—the daylight is lit with more volatile light—the deep between the setting and rising sun goes deeper many fold. Each precise object or condition or combination or process exhibits a beauty—the multiplication table—old age—the carpenter's trade—the grand opera—the huge-hull'd clean-shap'd New York clipper at sea under steam or full sail gleams with unmatch'd beauty—the American circles and large harmonies of government gleam with theirs—and the commonest definite intentions and actions with theirs. The poets of the kosmos advance through all interpositions and coverings and turmoils and stratagems to first principles. They are of use—they dissolve poverty from its need, and riches from its conceit. You large proprietor, they say, shall not realize or perceive more than anyone else. The owner of the library is not he who holds a legal title to it, having bought and paid for it. Anyone and everyone is owner of the library (indeed he or she alone is owner), who can read the same through all the varieties of tongues and subjects and styles, and in whom they enter with ease, and make supple and powerful and rich and large.

These American States, strong and healthy and accomplish'd, shall receive no pleasure from violations of natural models, and must not permit them. In paintings or mouldings or carvings in mineral or wood, or in the illustrations of books or newspapers, or in the patterns of woven stuffs, or anything to beautify rooms or furniture or costumes, or to put upon cornices or monuments, or on the prows or sterns of ships, or to put anywhere before the human eye indoors or out, that which distorts honest shapes, or which creates unearthly beings or places or contingencies, is a nuisance and revolt. Of the human form especially, it is so great it must never be made ridiculous. Of ornaments to a work nothing outre can be allow'd—but those ornaments can be allow'd that conform to the perfect facts of the open air, and that flow out of the nature of the work, and come irrepressibly from it, and are necessary to the completion of the work. Most works are most beautiful without ornament. Exaggerations will be revenged in human physiology. Clean and vigorous children are jetted and conceiv'd only in those communities where the models of natural forms are public every day. Great genius and the people of these States must never be demean'd to romances. As soon as histories are properly told, no more need of romances.

The great poets are to be known by the absence in them of tricks, and by the justification of perfect personal candor. All faults may be forgiven of him who has perfect candor. Henceforth let no man of us lie, for we have seen that openness wins the inner and outer world, and that there is no single exception, and that never since our earth gather'd itself in a mass have deceit or subterfuge or prevarication attracted its smallest particle or the faintest tinge of a shade—and that through the enveloping wealth and rank of a state, or the whole republic of states, a sneak or sly person shall be discover'd and despised—and that the soul has never once been fool'd and never can be fool'd—and thrift without the loving nod of the soul is only a fœtid puff—and there never grew up in any of the continents of the globe, nor upon any planet or satellite, nor in that condition which precedes the birth of babes, nor at any time during the changes of life, nor in any stretch of abeyance or action of vitality, nor in any process of formation or reformation anywhere, a being whose instinct hated the truth.

Extreme caution or prudence, the soundest organic health, large hope and comparison and fondness for women and children, large alimentiveness and destructiveness and causality, with a perfect sense of the oneness of nature, and the propriety of the same spirit applied to human affairs, are called up of the float of the brain of the world to be parts of the greatest poet from his birth out of his mother's womb, and from her birth out of her mother's. Caution seldom goes far enough. It has been thought that the prudent citizen was the citizen who applied himself to solid gains, and did well for himself and for his family, and completed a lawful life without debt or crime. The greatest poet sees and admits these economies as he sees the economies of food and sleep, but has higher notions of prudence than to think he gives much when he gives a few slight attentions at the latch of the gate. The premises of the prudence of life are not the hospitality of it, or the ripeness and harvest of it. Beyond the independence of a little sum laid aside for burial-money, and of a few clapboards around and shingles overhead on a lot of American soil owned, and the easy dollars that supply the year's plain clothing and meals, the melancholy prudence of the abandonment of such a great being as a man is, to the toss and pallor of years of money-making, with all their scorching days and icy nights, and all their stifling deceits and underhand dodgings, or infinitesimals of parlors, or shameless stuffing while others starve, and all the loss of the bloom and odor of the earth, and of the flowers and atmosphere, and of the sea, and of the true taste of the women and men you pass or have to do with in youth or middle age, and the issuing sickness and desperate revolt at the close of a life without elevation or naïveté, (even if you have achieved a secure 10,000 a year, or election to Congress or the Governorship,) and the ghastly chatter of a death without serenity or majesty, is the great fraud upon modern civilization and forethought, blotching the surface and system which civilization undeniably drafts, and moistening with tears the immense features it spreads and spreads with such velocity before the reach'd kisses of the soul.

Ever the right explanation remains to be made about prudence. The prudence of the mere wealth and respectability of the most esteem'd life appears too faint for the eye to observe at all, when little and large alike drop quietly aside at the thought of the prudence suitable for immortality. What is the wisdom that fills the thinness of a year, or seventy or eighty years—to the wisdom spaced out by ages, and coming back at a certain time with strong reinforcements and rich presents, and the clear faces of wedding-guests as far as you can look, in every direction, running gayly toward you? Only the soul is of itself—all else has reference to what ensues. All that a person does or thinks is of consequence. Nor can the push of charity or personal force ever be anything else than the profoundest reason, whether it brings argument to hand or no. No specification is necessary—to add or subtract or divide is in vain. Little or big, learn'd or unlearn'd, white or black, legal or illegal, sick or well, from the first inspiration down the windpipe to the last expiration out of it, all that a male or female does that is vigorous and benevolent and clean is so much sure profit to him or her in the unshakable order of the universe, and through the whole scope of it forever. The prudence of the greatest poet answers at last the craving and glut of the soul, puts off nothing, permits no let-up for its own case or any case, has no particular Sabbath or judgment day, divides not the living from the dead, or the righteous from the unrighteous, is satisfied with the present, matches every thought or act by its correlative, and knows no possible forgiveness or deputed atonement.

The direct trial of him who would be the greatest poet is today. If he does not flood himself with the immediate age as with vast oceanic tides—if he be not himself the age transfigur'd, and if to him is not open'd the eternity which gives similitude to all periods and locations and processes, and animate and inanimate forms, and which is the bond of time, and rises up from its inconceivable vagueness and infiniteness in the swimming shapes of today, and is held by the ductile anchors of life, and makes the present spot the passage from what was to what shall be, and commits itself to the representation of this wave of an hour, and this one of the sixty beautiful children of the wave—let him merge in the general run, and wait his development.

Still the final test of poems, or any character or work, remains. The prescient poet projects himself centuries ahead, and judges performer or performance after the changes of time. Does it live through them? Does it still hold on untired? Will the same style, and the direction of genius to similar points, be satisfactory now? Have the marches of tens and hundreds and thousands of years made willing detours to the right hand and the left hand for his sake? Is he beloved long and long after he is buried? Does the young man think often of him? and the young woman think often of him? and do the middle-aged and the old think of him?

A great poem is for ages and ages in common, and for all degrees and complexions, and all departments and sects, and for a woman as much as a man, and a man as much as a woman. A great poem is no finish to a man or woman, but rather a beginning. Has anyone fancied he could sit at last under some due authority, and rest satisfied with explanations, and realize, and be content and full? To no such terminus does the greatest poet bring—he brings neither cessation nor shelter'd fatness and ease. The touch of him, like Nature, tells in action. Whom he takes he takes with firm sure grasp into live regions previously unattain'd—thenceforward is no rest—they see the space and ineffable sheen that turn the old spots and lights into dead vacuums. Now there shall be a man cohered out of tumult and chaos—the elder encourages the younger and shows him how—they two shall launch off fearlessly together till the new world fits an orbit for itself, and looks unabash'd on the lesser orbits of the stars, and sweeps through the ceaseless rings, and shall never be quiet again.

There will soon be no more priests. Their work is done. A new order shall arise, and they shall be the priests of man, and every man shall be his own priest. They shall find their inspiration in real objects to-day, symptoms of the past and future. They shall not deign to defend immortality or God, or the perfection of things, or liberty, or the exquisite beauty and reality of the soul. They shall arise in America, and be responded to from the remainder of the earth.

The English language befriends the grand American expression—it is brawny enough, and limber and full enough. On the tough stock of a race who through all change of circumstance was never without the idea of political liberty, which is the animus of all liberty, it has attracted the terms of daintier and gayer and subtler and more elegant tongues. It is the powerful language of resistance—it is the dialect of common sense. It is the speech of the proud and melancholy races, and of all who aspire. It is the chosen tongue to express growth, faith, self-esteem, freedom, justice, equality, friendliness, amplitude, prudence, decision, and courage. It is the medium that shall wellnigh express the inexpressible.

No great literature nor any like style of behavior or oratory, or social intercourse or household arrangements, or public institutions, or the treatment by bosses of employ'd people, nor executive detail, or detail of the army and navy, nor spirit of legislation or courts, or police or tuition or architecture, or songs or amusements, can long elude the jealous and passionate instinct of American standards. Whether or not the sign appears from the mouths of the people, it throbs a live interrogation in every freeman's and freewoman's heart, after that which passes by, or this built to remain. Is it uniform with my country? Are its disposals without ignominious distinctions? Is it for the ever-growing communes of brothers and lovers, large, well united, proud, beyond the old models, generous beyond all models? Is it something grown fresh out of the fields, or drawn from the sea for use to me to-day here? I know that what answers for me, an American, in Texas, Ohio, Canada, must answer for any individual or nation that serves for a part of my materials. Does this answer? Is it for the nursing of the young of the republic? Does it solve readily with the sweet milk of the nipples of the breasts of the Mother of Many Children?

America prepares with composure and goodwill for the visitors that have sent word. It is not intellect that is to be their warrant and welcome. The talented, the artist, the ingenious, the editor, the statesman, the erudite, are not unappreciated—they fall in their place and do their work. The soul of the nation also does its work. It rejects none, it permits all. Only toward the like of itself will it advance halfway. An individual is as superb as a nation when he has the qualities which make a superb nation. The soul of the largest and wealthiest and proudest nation may well go halfway to meet that of its poets.

BUDS AND BIRD-VOICES

NATHANIEL HAWTHORNE

Balmy Spring—weeks later than we expected, and months later than we longed for her—comes at last to revive the moss on the roof and walls of our old mansion. She peeps brightly into my study window, inviting me to throw it open and create a summer atmosphere by the intermixture of her genial breath with the black and cheerless comfort of the stove. As the casement ascends, forth into infinite space fly the innumerable forms of thought or fancy that have kept me company in the retirement of this little chamber during the sluggish lapse of wintry weather—visions gay, grotesque and sad, pictures of real life tinted with nature's homely gray and russet, scenes in dreamland bedizened with rainbow-hues which faded before they were well laid on. All these may vanish now, and leave me to mold a fresh existence out of sunshine. Brooding Meditation may flap her dusky wings and take her owl-like flight, blinking amid the cheerfulness of noontide. Such companions befit the season of frosted window-panes and crackling fires, when the blast howls through the black-ash trees of our avenue, and the drifting snowstorm chokes up the wood paths and fills the highway from stone wall to stone wall. In the spring and summer time all somber thoughts should follow the winter northward with the somber and thoughtful crows. The old paradisiacal economy of life is again in force: we live, not to think nor to labor, but for the simple end of being happy; nothing for the present hour is worthy of man's infinite capacity save to imbibe the warm smile of heaven and sympathize with the reviving earth.

The present Spring comes onward with fleeter footsteps because Winter lingered so unconscionably long that with her best diligence she can hardly retrieve half the allotted period of her reign. It is but a fortnight since I stood on the brink of our swollen river and beheld the accumulated ice of four frozen months go down the stream. Except in streaks here and there upon the hillsides, the whole visible universe was then covered with deep snow the nethermost layer of which had been deposited by an early December storm. It was a sight to make the beholder torpid, in the impossibility of imagining how this vast white napkin was to be removed from the face of the corpse-like world in less time than had been required to spread it there. But who can estimate the power of gentle influences, whether amid material desolation or the moral winter of man's heart? There have been no tempestuous rains—even no sultry days—but a constant breath of southern winds, with now a day of kindly sunshine, and now a no less kindly mist, or a soft descent of showers, in which a smile and a blessing seemed to have been steeped. The snow has vanished as if by magic; whatever heaps may be hidden in the woods and deep gorges of the hills, only two solitary specks remain in the landscape, and those I shall almost regret to miss when tomorrow I look for them in vain. Never before, methinks, has spring pressed so closely on the footsteps of retreating winter. Along the roadside the green blades of grass have sprouted on the very edge of the snowdrifts. The pastures and mowing fields have not yet assumed a general aspect of verdure, but neither have they the cheerless brown tint which they wear in later autumn, when vegetation has entirely ceased; there is now a faint shadow of life, gradually brightening into the warm reality. Some tracts in a happy exposure—as, for instance, yonder southwestern slope of an orchard, in front of that old red farmhouse beyond the river—such patches of land already wear a beautiful and tender green to which no future luxuriance can add a charm. It looks unreal—a prophecy, a hope, a transitory effect of some peculiar light, which will vanish with the slightest motion of the eye. But beauty is never a delusion; not these verdant tracts but the dark and barren landscape all around them is a shadow and a dream. Each moment wins some portion of the earth from death to life;

a sudden gleam of verdure brightens along the sunny slope of a bank which an instant ago was brown and bare. You look again, and, behold an apparition of green grass!

The trees in our orchard and elsewhere are as yet naked, but already appear full of life and vegetable blood. It seems as if by one magic touch they might instantaneously burst into full foliage, and that the wind which now sighs through their naked branches might make sudden music amid innumerable leaves. The moss-grown willow tree which for forty years past has overshadowed these western windows will be among the first to put on its green attire. There are some objections to the willow: it is not a dry and cleanly tree, and impresses the beholder with an association of sliminess. No trees, I think, are perfectly agreeable as companions unless they have glossy leaves, dry bark, and a firm and hard texture of trunk and branches. But the willow is almost the earliest to gladden us with the promise and reality of beauty in its graceful and delicate foliage, and the last to scatter its yellow, yet scarcely-withered, leaves upon the ground. All through the winter, too, its yellow twigs give it a sunny aspect which is not without a cheering influence even in the grayest and gloomiest day. Beneath a clouded sky it faithfully remembers the sunshine. Our old house would lose a charm were the willow to be cut down, with its golden crown over the snow-covered roof, and its heap of summer verdure.

The lilac shrubs under my study windows are likewise almost in leaf; in two or three days more I may put forth my hand and pluck the topmost bough in its freshest green. These lilacs are very aged, and have lost the luxuriant foliage of their prime. The heart or the judgment or the moral sense or the taste is dissatisfied with their present aspect. Old age is not venerable when it embodies itself in lilacs, rose-bushes, or any other ornamental shrubs; it seems as if such plants, as they grow only for beauty, ought to flourish only in immortal youth—or, at least, to die before their sad decrepitude. Trees of beauty are trees of paradise, and therefore not subject to decay by their original nature, though they have lost that precious birthright by being transplanted to an earthly soil. There is a kind of ludicrous unfitness in the idea of a time-stricken and grandfatherly lilac-bush. The analogy holds good in human life. Persons who can only be graceful and ornamental—who can give the world nothing but flowers—should die young, and never be seen with gray hair and wrinkles, any more than the flower-shrubs with mossy bark and blighted foliage, like the lilacs under my window. Not that beauty is worthy of less than immortality. No; the beautiful should live forever, and thence, perhaps, the sense of impropriety when we see it triumphed over by time. Apple trees, on the other hand, grow old without reproach. Let them live as long as they may, and contort themselves into whatever perversity of shape they please, and deck their withered limbs with a springtime gaudiness of pink-blossoms, still they are respectable, even if they afford us only an apple or two in a season. Those few apples—or, at all events, the remembrance of apples in bygone years—are the atonement which utilitarianism inexorably demands for the privilege of lengthened life. Human flower shrubs, if they will grow old on earth, should, besides their lovely blossoms, bear some kind of fruit that will satisfy earthly appetites, else neither man nor the decorum of nature will deem it fit that the moss should gather on them.

One of the first things that strikes the attention when the white sheet of winter is withdrawn is the neglect and disarray that lay hidden beneath it. Nature is not cleanly, according to our prejudices. The beauty of preceding years, now transformed to brown and blighted deformity, obstructs the brightening loveliness of the present hour. Our avenue is strewn with the whole crop of autumn's withered leaves. There are quantities of decayed branches which one tempest after another has flung down, black and rotten, and one or two with the ruin of a bird's nest clinging to them. In the garden are the dried bean-vines, the brown stalks of the asparagus-bed, and melancholy old cabbages which were frozen into the soil before their unthrifty cultivator could find time to gather them. How invariable throughout all the forms of life do we find these intermingled memorials of death! On the soil of thought and in the garden of the heart, as well as in the sensual world, lie withered leaves—the ideas and feelings that we have done with. There is no wind strong enough to sweep them away; infinite space will not garner them from our sight. What mean they? Why may we not be permitted to live and enjoy as if this were the first life and our own the primal enjoyment, instead of treading always on these dry bones and mouldering relics from the aged accumulation of which springs all that now appears so young and new? Sweet must have been the spring-time of Eden, when no earlier year had strewn its decay upon the virgin turf, and no former experience had ripened into summer and faded into autumn in the hearts of its inhabitants! That was a world worth living in. Oh, thou murmurer, it is out of the very wantonness of such a life that thou feignest these idle lamentations. There is no decay. Each human soul is the first created inhabitant of its own Eden. We dwell in an old moss-covered mansion and tread in the worn footprints of the past and have a gray clergyman's ghost for our daily and nightly inmate, yet all these outward circumstances are made less than visionary by the renewing power of the spirit. Should the spirit ever lose this power—should the withered leaves and the rotten branches and the moss-covered house and the ghost of the gray past ever become its realities, and the verdure and the freshness merely its faint dream—then let it pray to be released from earth. It will need the air of heaven to revive its pristine energies.

What an unlooked for flight was this from our shadowy avenue of black-ash and balm-of-gilead trees into the infinite! Now we have our feet again upon the turf. Nowhere does the grass spring up so industriously as in this homely yard, along the base of the stone wall and in the sheltered nooks of the buildings, and especially around the southern door-step—a locality which seems particularly favorable to its growth, for it is already tall enough to bend over and wave in the wind. I observe that several weeds—and, most frequently, a plant that stains the fingers with its yellow juice—have survived and retained their freshness and sap throughout the winter. One knows not how they have deserved such an exception from the common lot of their race. They are now the patriarchs of the departed year, and may preach mortality to the present generation of flowers and weeds.

Among the delights of spring, how is it possible to forget the birds? Even the crows were welcome, as the sable harbingers of a brighter and livelier race. They visited us before the snow was off, but seem mostly to have betaken themselves to remote depths of the woods, which they haunt all summer long. Many a time shall I disturb them there, and feel as if I had intruded among a company of silent worshipers as they sit in Sabbath stillness among the treetops. Their voices, when they speak, are in admirable accordance with the tranquil solitude of a summer afternoon, and, resounding so far above the head, their loud clamor increases the religious quiet of the scene instead of breaking it. A crow, however, has no real pretensions to religion, in spite of his gravity of mien and black attire; he is certainly a thief, and probably an infidel. The gulls are far more respectable, in a moral point of view. These denizens of sea-beaten rocks and haunters of the lonely beach come up our inland river at this season, and soar high overhead, flapping their broad wings in the upper sunshine. They are among the most picturesque of birds, because they so float and rest upon the air as to become almost stationary parts of the landscape. The imagination has time to grow acquainted with them; they have not flitted away in a moment. You go up among the clouds and greet these lofty-flighted gulls, and repose confidently with them upon the sustaining atmosphere. Ducks have their haunts along the solitary places of the river, and alight in flocks upon the broad bosom of the overflowed meadows. Their flight is too rapid and determined for the eye to catch enjoyment from it, although it never fails to stir up the heart with the sportsman's ineradicable instinct. They have now gone farther northward, but will visit us again in autumn.

The smaller birds—the little songsters of the woods, and

those that haunt man's dwellings and claim human friendship by building their nests under the sheltering eaves or among the orchard trees—these require a touch more delicate and a gentler heart than mine to do them justice. Their outburst of melody is like a brook let loose from wintry chains. We need not deem it a too high and solemn word to call it a hymn of praise to the Creator, since Nature, who pictures the reviving year in so many sights of beauty, has expressed the sentiment of renewed life in no other sound save the notes of these blessed birds. Their music, however, just now seems to be incidental, and not the result of a set purpose. They are discussing the economy of life and love and the site and architecture of their summer residences, and have no time to sit on a twig and pour forth solemn hymns or overtures, operas, symphonies and waltzes. Anxious questions are asked, grave subjects are settled in quick and animated debate, and only by occasional accident, as from pure ecstasy, does a rich warble roll its tiny waves of golden sound through the atmosphere. Their little bodies are as busy as their voices; they are in a constant flutter and restlessness. Even when two or three retreat to a tree-top to hold council, they wag their tails and heads all the time with the irrepressible activity of their nature, which perhaps renders their brief span of life in reality as long as the patriarchal age of sluggish man. The blackbirds—three species of which consort together—are the noisiest of all our feathered citizens. Great companies of them—more than the famous 'four-and-twenty' whom Mother Goose has immortalized—congregate in contiguous tree-tops and vociferate with all the clamor and confusion of a turbulent political meeting. Politics, certainly, must be the occasion of such tumultuous debates, but still, unlike all other politicians, they instill melody into their individual utterances and produce harmony as a general effect. Of all bird-voices, none are more sweet and cheerful to my ear than those of swallows in the dim, sun-streaked interior of a lofty barn; they address the heart with even a closer sympathy than Robin Redbreast. But, indeed, all these winged people that dwell in the vicinity of homesteads seem to partake of human nature and possess the germ, if not the development, of immortal souls. We hear them saying their melodious prayers at morning's blush and eventide. A little while ago, in the deep of night, there came the lively thrill of a bird's note from a neighboring tree—a real song such as greets the purple dawn or mingles with the yellow sunshine. What could the little bird mean by pouring it forth at midnight? Probably the music gushed out of the midst of a dream in which he fancied himself in paradise with his mate, but suddenly awoke on a cold, leafless bough with a New England mist penetrating through his feathers. That was a sad exchange of imagination for reality.

Insects are among the earliest births of spring. Multitudes, of I know not what species, appeared long ago on the surface of the snow. Clouds of them almost too minute for sight hover in a beam of sunshine, and vanish as if annihilated when they pass into the shade. A mosquito has already been heard to sound the small horror of his bugle-horn. Wasps infest the sunny windows of the house. A bee entered one of the chambers with a prophecy of flowers. Rare butterflies came before the snow was off, flaunting in the chill breeze, and looking forlorn and all astray in spite of the magnificence of their dark velvet cloaks with golden borders.

The fields and wood-paths have as yet few charms to entice the wanderer. In a walk the other day I found no violets nor anemones, nor anything in the likeness of a flower. It was worthwhile, however, to ascend our opposite hill for the sake of gaining a general idea of the advance of spring, which I had hitherto been studying in its minute developments. The river lay round me in a semi-circle, overflowing all the meadows which give it its Indian name, and offering a noble breadth to sparkle in the sunbeams. Along the hither shore a row of trees stood up to their knees in water, and afar off, on the surface of the stream, tufts of bushes thrust up their heads, as it were, to breathe. The most striking objects were great solitary trees here and there with a mile-wide waste of water all around them. The curtailment of the trunk by its immersion in the river quite destroys the fair proportions of the tree, and thus makes us sensible of a regularity and propriety in the usual forms of nature. The flood of the present season, though it never amounts to a freshet on our quiet stream, has encroached farther upon the land than any previous one for at least a score of years. It has overflowed stone fences, and even rendered a portion of the highway navigable for boats. The waters, however, are now gradually subsiding; islands become annexed to the mainland, and other islands emerge like new creations from the watery waste. The scene supplies an admirable image of the receding of the Nile—except that there is no deposit of black slime—or of Noah's flood, only that there is a freshness and novelty in these recovered portions of the continent which give the impression of a world just made rather than of one so polluted that a deluge had been requisite to purify it. These upspringing islands are the greenest spots in the landscape; the first gleam of sunlight suffices to cover them with verdure.

Thank Providence for spring! The earth—and man himself, by sympathy with his birthplace—would be far other than we find them if life toiled wearily onward without this periodical infusion of the primal spirit. Will the world ever be so decayed that spring may not renew its greenness? Can man be so dismally age-stricken that no faintest sunshine of his youth may revisit him once a year? It is impossible. The moss on our time-worn mansion brightens into beauty, the good old pastor who once dwelt here renewed his prime, regained his boyhood, in the genial breezes of his ninetieth spring. Alas for the worn and heavy soul if, whether in youth or age, it have outlived its privilege of springtime sprightliness! From such a soul the world must hope no reformation of its evil—no sympathy with the lofty faith and gallant struggles of those who contend in its behalf. Summer works in the present and thinks not of the future; autumn is a rich conservative; winter has utterly lost its faith, and clings tremulously to the remembrance of what has been; but spring, with its outgushing life, is the true type of the movement.

THE PHILOSOPHY OF COMPOSITION

EDGAR ALLAN POE

Charles Dickens, in a note now lying before me, alluding to an examination I once made of the mechanism of *Barnaby Rudge*, says—'By the way, are you aware that Godwin wrote his *Caleb Williams* backwards? He first involved his hero in a web of difficulties, forming the second volume, and then, for the first, cast about him for some mode of accounting for what had been done.'

I cannot think this precise mode of procedure on the part of Godwin—and indeed what he himself acknowledges, is not altogether in accordance with Mr Dickens' idea—but the author of *Caleb Williams* was too good an artist not to perceive the advantage derivable from at least a somewhat similar process. Nothing is more clear than that every plot, worth the name, must be elaborated to its dénouement before anything be attempted with the pen. It is only with the dénouement constantly in view that we can give a plot its indispensable air of consequence, or causation, by making the incidents, and especially the tone at all points, tend to the development of the intention.

There is a radical error, I think, in the usual mode of constructing a story. Either history affords a thesis—or one is suggested by an incident of the day—or, at best, the author sets himself to work in the combination of striking events to form merely the basis of his narrative—designing, generally, to fill in with description, dialogue, or autorial comment, whatever crevices of fact, or action, may, from page to page, render themselves apparent.

I prefer commencing with the consideration of an effect. Keeping originality always in view—for he is false to himself who ventures to dispense with so obvious and so easily attainable a source of interest—I say to myself, in the first place, 'Of the innumerable effects, or impressions, of which the heart, the intellect, or (more generally) the soul is susceptible, what one shall I, on the present occasion, select?' Having chosen a novel, first, and secondly a vivid effect, I consider whether it can be best wrought by incident or tone—whether by ordinary incidents and peculiar tone, or the converse, or by peculiarity both of incident and tone—afterward looking about me (or rather within) for such combinations of event, or tone, as shall best aid me in the construction of the effect.

I have often thought how interesting a magazine paper might be written by any author who would—that is to say, who could—detail, step by step, the processes by which any one of his compositions attained its ultimate point of completion. Why such a paper has never been given to the world, I am much at a loss to say—but, perhaps, the autorial vanity has had more to do with the omission than any one other cause. Most writers—poets in especial—prefer having it understood that they compose by a species of fine frenzy—an ecstatic intuition—and would positively shudder at letting the public take a peep behind the scenes, at the elaborate and vacillating crudities of thought—at the true purposes seized only at the last moment—at the innumerable glimpses of idea that arrived not at the maturity of full view—at the fully matured fancies discarded in despair as unmanageable—at the cautious selections and rejections—at the painful erasures and interpolations—in a word, at the wheels and pinions—the tackle for scene-shifting—the step-ladders and demon-traps—the cock's feathers, the red paint and the black patches, which, in ninety-nine cases out of hundred, constitute the properties of the literary histrio.

I am aware, on the other hand, that the case is by no means common, in which an author is at all in condition to retrace the steps by which his conclusions have been attained. In general, suggestions, having arisen pell-mell, are pursued and forgotten in a similar manner.

For my own part, I have neither sympathy with the repugnance alluded to, nor, at any time, the least difficulty in recalling to mind the progressive steps of any of my compositions; and, since the interest of an analysis, or reconstruction, such as I have considered a desideratum, is quite independent of any real or fancied interest in the thing analyzed, it will not be regarded as a breach of decorum on my part to show the modus operandi by which someone of my own works was put together. I select 'The Raven,' as the most generally known. It is my design to render it manifest that no one point in its composition is referable either to accident or intuition—that the work proceeded, step by step, to its completion with the precision and rigid consequence of a mathematical problem.

Let us dismiss, as irrelevant to the poem, per se, the circumstance—or say the necessity—which, in the first place, gave rise to the intention of composing a poem that should suit at once the popular and the critical taste.

We commence, then, with this intention.

The initial consideration was that of extent. If any literary work is too long to be read at one sitting, we must be content to dispense with the immensely important effect derivable from unity of impression—for, if two sittings be required, the affairs of the world interfere, and everything like totality is at once destroyed. But since, ceteris paribus, no poet can afford to dispense with anything that may advance his design, it but remains to be seen whether there is, in extent, any advantage to counterbalance the loss of unity which attends it. Here I say no, at once. What we term a long poem is, in fact, merely a succession of brief ones—that is to say, of brief poetical effects. It is needless to demonstrate that a poem is such, only inasmuch as it intensely excites, by elevating, the soul; and all intense excitements are, through a psychal necessity, brief. For this reason, at least one-half of *Paradise Lost* is essentially prose—a succession of poetical excitements interspersed, inevitably, with corresponding depressions—the whole being deprived, through the extremeness of its length, of the vastly important artistic element, totality, or unity, of effect.

It appears evident, then, that there is a distinct limit, as regards length, to all works of literary art—the limit of a single sitting—and that, although in certain classes of prose composition, such as *Robinson Crusoe* (demanding no unity,), this limit may be advantageously overpassed, it can never properly be overpassed in a poem. Within this limit, the extent of a poem may be made to bear mathematical relation to its merit—in other words, to the excitement or elevation—again in other words, to the degree of the true poetical effect which it is capable of inducing; for it is clear that the brevity must be in direct ratio of the intensity of the intended effect—this, with one proviso—that a certain degree of duration is absolutely requisite for the production of any effect at all.

Holding in view these considerations, as well as that degree of excitement which I deemed not above the popular, while not below the critical, taste, I reached at once what I conceived the proper length for my intended poem—a length of about one hundred lines. It is, in fact, a hundred and eight.

My next thought concerned the choice of an impression, or effect, to be conveyed: and here I may as well observe that, throughout the construction, I kept steadily in view the design of rendering the work universally appreciable. I should be carried too far out of my immediate topic were I to demonstrate a point upon which I have repeatedly insisted, and which, with the poetical, stands not in the slightest need of demonstration—the point, I mean, that Beauty is the sole legitimate province of the poem. A few words, however, in elucidation of my real meaning, which some of my friends have evinced a disposition to misrepresent. That pleasure which is at once the most intense, the most elevating, and the most pure, is, I believe, found in the contemplation of the beautiful. When, indeed, men speak of Beauty, they mean, precisely, not a quality, as is supposed, but an effect—they refer, in short, just to that intense and pure elevation of soul—not of intellect, or of heart—upon which I have commented, and which is experienced in consequence of contemplating 'the beautiful'. Now I designate Beauty as the province of the poem, merely because it is an obvious rule of Art that effects should be made to spring from direct causes—that objects should be attained through means best adapted for their attainment—no one as yet having been weak enough to deny that the peculiar elevation alluded to is most readily attained in the poem. Now the object, Truth, or the satisfaction of the intellect, and the object Passion, or the excitement of the heart, are, although attainable, to a certain extent, in poetry, far more readily attainable in prose. Truth, in fact, demands a precision, and Passion, a homeliness (the truly passionate will comprehend me) which are absolutely antagonistic to that Beauty which, I maintain, is the excitement, or pleasurable elevation, of the soul. It by no means follows from anything here said, that passion, or even truth, may not be introduced, and even profitably introduced, into a poem—for they may serve in elucidation, or aid the general effect, as do discords in music, by contrast—but the true artist will always contrive, first, to tone them into proper subservience to the predominant aim, and, secondly, to enveil them, as far as possible, in that Beauty which is the atmosphere and the essence of the poem.

Regarding, then, Beauty as my province, my next question referred to the tone of its highest manifestation—and all experience has shown that this tone is one of sadness. Beauty of whatever kind, in its supreme development, invariably excites the sensitive soul to tears. Melancholy is thus the most legitimate of all the poetical tones.

The length, the province, and the tone, being thus determined, I betook myself to ordinary induction, with the view of obtaining some artistic piquancy which might serve me as a keynote in the construction of the poem—some pivot upon which the whole structure might turn. In carefully thinking over all the usual artistic effects—or more properly, points, in the theatrical sense—I did not fail to perceive immediately that no one had been so universally employed as that of the refrain. The universality of its employment sufficed to assure me of its intrinsic value, and spared me the necessity of submitting it to analysis. I considered it, however, with regard to its susceptibility of improvement, and soon saw it to be in a primitive condition. As commonly used, the refrain, or burden, not only is limited to lyric verse, but depends for its impression upon the force of monotone—both in sound and thought. The pleasure is deduced solely from the sense of identity—of repetition. I resolved to diversify, and so vastly heighten, the effect, by adhering, in general, to the monotone of sound, while I continually varied that of thought: that is to say, I determined to produce continuously novel effects, by the variation of the application of the refrain—the refrain itself remaining, for the most part, unvaried.

These points being settled, I next bethought me of the nature of my refrain. Since its application was to be repeatedly varied, it was clear that the refrain itself must be brief, for there would have been an insurmountable difficulty in frequent variations of application in any sentence of length. In proportion to the brevity of the sentence, would, of course, be the facility of the variation. This led me at once to a single word as the best refrain.

The question now arose as to the character of the word. Having made up my mind to a refrain, the division of the poem into stanzas was, of course, a corollary: the refrain forming the close to each stanza. That such a close, to have force, must be sonorous and susceptible of protracted emphasis, admitted no doubt: and these considerations inevitably led me to the long 'o' as the most sonorous vowel, in connection with 'r' as the most producible consonant.

The sound of the refrain being thus determined, it became necessary to select a word embodying this sound, and at the same time in the fullest possible keeping with that melancholy which I had predetermined as the tone of the poem. In such a search it would have been absolutely impossible to overlook the word 'nevermore'. In fact, it was the very first which presented itself.

The next desideratum was a pretext for the continuous use of the one word 'nevermore'. In observing the difficulty which I at once found in inventing a sufficiently plausible reason for its continuous repetition, I did not fail to perceive that this difficulty arose solely from the pre-assumption that the word was to be so continuously or monotonously spoken by a human being—I did not fail to perceive, in short, that the difficulty lay in the reconciliation of this monotony with the exercise of reason on the part of the creature repeating the word. Here, then, immediately arose the idea of a non-reasoning creature capable of speech; and, very naturally, a parrot, in the first instance, suggested itself, but was superseded forthwith by a Raven, as equally capable of speech, and infinitely more in keeping with the intended tone.

I had now gone so far as the conception of a Raven—the bird of ill omen—monotonously repeating the one word, 'nevermore', at the conclusion of each stanza, in a poem of melancholy tone, and in length about one hundred lines. Now, never losing sight of the object supremeness, or perfection, at all points, I asked myself,—'Of all melancholy topics, what, according to the universal understanding of mankind, is the most melancholy?' Death—was the obvious reply. 'And when,' I said, 'is this most melancholy of topics most poetical?' From what I have already explained at some length, the answer, here also, is obvious—'When it most closely allies itself to Beauty: the death, then, of a beautiful woman is, unquestionably, the most poetical topic in the world—and equally is it beyond doubt that the lips best suited for such topic are those of a bereaved lover.'

I had now to combine the two ideas, of a lover lamenting his deceased mistress and a Raven continuously repeating the word 'Nevermore'—I had to combine these, bearing in mind my design of varying, at every turn, the application of the word repeated; but the only intelligible mode of such combination is that of imagining the Raven employing the word in answer to the queries of the lover. And here it was that I saw at once the opportunity afforded for the effect on which I had been depending—that is to say, the effect of the variation of application. I saw that I could make the first query propounded by the lover—the first query to which the Raven should reply 'nevermore'—that I could make this first query a commonplace one—the second less so—the third still less, and so on—until at length the lover, startled from his original nonchalance by the melancholy character of the word itself—by its frequent repetition—and by a consideration of the ominous reputation of the fowl that uttered it—is at length excited to superstition, and wildly propounds queries of a far different character—queries whose solution he has passionately at heart—propounds them half in superstition and half in that species of despair which delights, in self-torture—propounds them not altogether because he believes in the prophetic or demoniac character of the bird (which, reason assures him, is merely repeating a lesson learned by rote) but because he experiences a frenzied pleasure in so modeling his questions as to receive from the expected 'nevermore' the most delicious because the most intolerable of sorrow. Perceiving the opportunity thus afforded me—or, more strictly, thus forced upon me in the progress of the construction—I first established in mind the climax, or concluding query—that to which 'nevermore' should be in the last place an answer—that in reply to which this word 'nevermore' should involve the utmost conceivable amount of sorrow and despair.

Here then the poem may be said to have its beginning—at the end, where all works of art should begin—for it was here, at this point of my preconsiderations, that I first put pen to paper in the composition of the stanza:

'Prophet,' said I, 'thing of evil! prophet still if bird or devil! By that heaven that bends above us—by that God we both adore, Tell this soul with sorrow laden, if within the distant Aidenn, It shall clasp a sainted maiden whom the angels name Lenore— Clasp a rare and radiant maiden whom the angels name Lenore.' Quoth the raven 'Nevermore.'

I composed this stanza, at this point, first that, by establishing the climax, I might the better vary and graduate, as regards seriousness and importance, the preceding queries of the lover—and, secondly, that I might definitely settle the rhythm, the meter, and the length and general arrangement of the stanza—as well as graduate the stanzas which were to precede, so that none of them might surpass this in rhythmical effect. Had I been able, in the subsequent composition, to construct more vigorous stanzas, I should, without scruple, have purposely enfeebled them, so as not to interfere with the climacteric effect.

And here I may as well say a few words of the versification. My first object (as usual) was originality. The extent to which this has been neglected, in versification, is one of the most unaccountable things in the world. Admitting that there is little possibility of variety in mere rhythm, it is still clear that the possible varieties of meter and stanza are absolutely infinite—and yet, for centuries, no man, in verse, has ever done, or ever seemed to think of doing, an original thing. The fact is, originality (unless in minds of very unusual force) is by no means a matter, as some suppose, of impulse or intuition. In general, to be found, it must be elaborately sought, and although a positive merit of the highest class, demands in its attainment less of invention than negation.

Of course, I pretend to no originality in either the rhythm or meter of the 'Raven'. The former is trochaic—the latter is octameter acatalectic, alternating with heptameter catalectic repeated in the refrain of the fifth verse, and terminating with tetrameter catalectic. Less pedantically—the feet employed throughout (trochees) consist of a long syllable followed by a short: the first line of the stanza consists of eight of these feet—the second of seven and a half (in effect two-thirds)—the third of eight—the fourth of seven and a half—the fifth the same—the sixth three and a half. Now, each of these lines, taken individually, has been employed before, and what originality 'The Raven' has, is in their combination into stanza; nothing even remotely approaching this combination has ever been attempted. The effect of this originality of combination is aided by other unusual, and some altogether novel effects, arising from an extension of the application of the principles of rhyme and alliteration.

The next point to be considered was the mode of bringing

together the lover and the Raven—and the first branch of this consideration was the locale. For this the most natural suggestion might seem to be a forest, or the fields—but it has always appeared to me that a close circumscription of space is absolutely necessary to the effect of insulated incident—it has the force of a frame to a picture. It has an indisputable moral power in keeping concentrated the attention, and, of course, must not be confounded with mere unity of place.

I determined, then, to place the lover in his chamber—in a chamber rendered sacred to him by memories of her who had frequented it. The room is represented as richly furnished—this in mere pursuance of the ideas I have already explained on the subject of Beauty, as the sole true poetical thesis.

The locale being thus determined, I had now to introduce the bird—and the thought of introducing him through the window, was inevitable. The idea of making the lover suppose, in the first instance, that the flapping of the wings of the bird against the shutter, is a 'tapping' at the door, originated in a wish to increase, by prolonging, the reader's curiosity, and in a desire to admit the incidental effect arising from the lover's throwing open the door, finding all dark, and thence adopting the half-fancy that it was the spirit of his mistress that knocked.

I made the night tempestuous, first, to account for the Raven's seeking admission, and secondly, for the effect of contrast with the (physical) serenity within the chamber.

I made the bird alight on the bust of Pallas, also for the effect of contrast between the marble and the plumage—it being understood that the bust was absolutely suggested by the bird—the bust of Pallas being chosen, first, as most in keeping with the scholarship of the lover, and, secondly, for the sonorousness of the word, Pallas, itself.

About the middle of the poem, also, I have availed myself of the force of contrast, with a view of deepening the ultimate impression. For example, an air of the fantastic—approaching as nearly to the ludicrous as was admissible—is given to the Raven's entrance. He comes in 'with many a flirt and flutter'.

Not the least obeisance made he—not a moment stopped or stayed he, But with mien of lord or lady, perched above my chamber door.

In the two stanzas which follow, the design is more obviously carried out:

Then this ebony bird beguiling my sad fancy into smiling By the grave and stern decorum of the countenance it wore, 'Though thy crest be shorn and shaven thou,' I said, 'art sure no craven, Ghastly grim and ancient Raven wandering from the nightly shore— Tell me what thy lordly name is on the Night's Plutonian shore!' Quoth the Raven 'Nevermore'.

Much I marveled this ungainly fowl to hear discourse so plainly, Though its answer little meaning—little relevancy bore; For we cannot help agreeing that no living human being Ever yet was blessed with seeing bird above his chamber door— Bird or beast upon the sculptured bust above his chamber door, With such name as 'Nevermore'.

The effect of the dénouement being thus provided for, I immediately drop the fantastic for a tone of the most profound seriousness—this tone commencing in the stanza directly following the one last quoted, with the line,

'But the Raven, sitting lonely on that placid bust, spoke only,' etc.

From this epoch the lover no longer jests—no longer sees anything even of the fantastic in the Raven's demeanor. He speaks of him as a 'grim, ungainly, ghastly, gaunt, and ominous bird of yore', and feels the 'fiery eyes' burning into his 'bosom's core'. This revolution of thought, or fancy, on the lover's part, is intended to induce a similar one on the part of the reader—to bring the mind into a proper frame for the dénouement—which is now brought about as rapidly and as directly as possible.

With the dénouement proper—with the Raven's reply, 'Nevermore', to the lover's final demand if he shall meet his mistress in another world—the poem, in its obvious phase, that of a simple narrative, may be said to have its completion. So far, everything is within the limits of the accountable—of the real. A raven, having learned by rote the single word 'nevermore', and having escaped from the custody of its owner, is driven at midnight, through the violence of a storm, to seek admission at a window from which a light still gleams—the chamber-window of a student, occupied half in poring over a volume, half in dreaming of a beloved mistress deceased. The casement being thrown open at the fluttering of the bird's wings, the bird itself perches on the most convenient seat out of the immediate reach of the student, who, amused by the incident and the oddity of the visitor's demeanor, demands of it, in jest and without looking for a reply, its name. The raven addressed, answers with its customary word, 'nevermore'—a word which finds immediate echo in the melancholy heart of the student, who, giving utterance aloud to certain thoughts suggested by the occasion, is again startled by the fowl's repetition of 'nevermore'. The student now guesses the state of the case, but is impelled, as I have before explained, by the human thirst for self-torture, and in part by superstition, to propound such queries to the bird as will bring him, the lover, the most of the luxury of sorrow, through the anticipated answer, 'nevermore'. With the indulgence, to the utmost extreme, of this self-torture, the narration, in what I have termed its first or obvious phase, has a natural termination, and so far there has been no overstepping of the limits of the real.

But in subjects so handled, however skillfully, or with however vivid an array of incident, there is always a certain hardness or nakedness, which repels the artistical eye. Two things are invariably required—first, some amount of complexity, or more properly, adaptation; and, secondly, some amount of suggestiveness—some undercurrent, however indefinite, of meaning. It is this latter, in especial, which imparts to a work of art so much of that richness (to borrow from colloquy a forcible term) which we are too fond of confounding with the ideal. It is the excess of the suggested meaning—it is the rendering this the upper instead of the under current of the theme—which turns into prose (and that of the very flattest kind) the so-called poetry of the so-called transcendentalists.

Holding these opinions, I added the two concluding stanzas of the poem—their suggestiveness being thus made to pervade all the narrative which has preceded them. The undercurrent of meaning is rendered first apparent in the lines:

'Take thy beak from out my heart, and take thy form from off my door!' Quoth the Raven 'Nevermore!'

It will be observed that the words, 'from out my heart', involve the first metaphorical expression in the poem. They, with the answer, 'Nevermore', dispose the mind to seek a moral in all that has been previously narrated. The reader begins now to regard the Raven as emblematical—but it is not until the very last line of the very last stanza, that the intention of making him emblematical of Mournful and Never-ending Remembrance is permitted distinctly to be seen:

And the Raven, never flitting, still is sitting, still is sitting, On the pallid bust of Pallas just above my chamber door; And his eyes have all the seeming of a demon's that is dreaming, And the lamplight o'er him streaming throws his shadow on the floor; And my soul from out that shadow that lies floating on the floor Shall be lifted—nevermore.

BREAD AND THE NEWSPAPER

OLIVER WENDELL HOLMES

This is the new version of the Panem et Circenses of the Roman populace. It is our ultimatum, as that was theirs. They must have something to eat, and the circus-shows to look at. We must have something to eat, and the papers to read.

Everything else we can give up. If we are rich, we can lay down our carriages, stay away from Newport or Saratoga, and adjourn the trip to Europe sine die. If we live in a small way, there are at least new dresses and bonnets and everyday luxuries which we can dispense with. If the young Zouave of the family looks smart in his new uniform, its respectable head is content, though he himself grow seedy as a caraway-umbel late in the season. He will cheerfully calm the perturbed nap of his old beaver by patient brushing in place of buying a new one, if only the Lieutenant's jaunty cap is what it should be. We all take a pride in sharing the epidemic economy of the time. Only bread and the newspaper we must have, whatever else we do without.

How this war is simplifying our mode of being! We live on our emotions, as the sick man is said in the common speech to be nourished by his fever. Our ordinary mental food has become distasteful, and what would have been intellectual luxuries at other times, are now absolutely repulsive.

All this change in our manner of existence implies that we have experienced some very profound impression, which will sooner or later betray itself in permanent effects on the minds and bodies of many among us. We cannot forget Corvisart's observation of the frequency with which diseases of the heart were noticed as the consequence of the terrible emotions produced by the scenes of the great French Revolution. Laennec tells the story of a convent, of which he was the medical director, where all the nuns were subjected to the severest penances and schooled in the most painful doctrines. They all became consumptive soon after their entrance, so that, in the course of his ten years' attendance, all the inmates died out two or three times, and were replaced by new ones. He does not hesitate to attribute the disease from which they suffered to those depressing moral influences to which they were subjected.

So far we have noticed little more than disturbances of the nervous system as a consequence of the war excitement in non-combatants. Take the first trifling example which comes to our recollection. A sad disaster to the Federal army was told the other day in the presence of two gentlemen and a lady. Both the gentlemen complained of a sudden feeling at the epigastrium, or, less learnedly, the pit of the stomach, changed color, and confessed to a slight tremor about the knees. The lady had a 'grande révolution', as French patients say, went home, and kept her bed for the rest of the day. Perhaps the reader may smile at the mention of such trivial indispositions, but in more sensitive natures death itself follows in some cases from no more serious cause. An old gentleman fell senseless in fatal apoplexy, on hearing of Napoleon's return from Elba. One of our early friends, who recently died of the same complaint, was thought to have had his attack mainly in consequence of the excitements of the time.

We all know what the war fever is in our young men, what a devouring passion it becomes in those whom it assails. Patriotism is the fire of it, no doubt, but this is fed with fuel of all sorts. The love of adventure, the contagion of example, the fear of losing the chance of participating in the great events of the time, the desire of personal distinction, all help to produce those singular transformations which we often witness, turning the most peaceful of our youth into the most ardent of our soldiers. But something of the same fever in a different form reaches a good many non-combatants, who have no thought of losing a drop of precious blood belonging to themselves or their families. Some of the symptoms we shall mention are almost universal; they are as plain in the people we meet everywhere as the marks of an influenza, when that is prevailing.

The first is a nervous restlessness of a very peculiar character. Men cannot think, or write, or attend to their ordinary business. They stroll up and down the streets, or saunter out upon the public places. We confessed to an illustrious author that we laid down the volume of his work which we were reading when the war broke out. It was as interesting as a romance, but the romance of the past grew pale before the red light of the terrible present. Meeting the same author not long afterwards, he confessed that he had laid down his pen at the same time that we had closed his book. He could not write about the sixteenth century any more than we could read about it, while the nineteenth was in the very agony and bloody sweat of its great sacrifice.

Another most eminent scholar told us in all simplicity that he had fallen into such a state that he would read the same telegraphic dispatches over and over again in different papers, as if they were new, until he felt as if he were an idiot. Who did not do just the same thing, and does not often do it still, now that the first flush of the fever is over? Another person always goes through the side streets on his way for the noon extra, he is so afraid somebody will meet him and tell the news he wishes to read, first on the bulletin-board, and then in the great capitals and leaded type of the newspaper.

When any startling piece of war-news comes, it keeps repeating itself in our minds in spite of all we can do. The same trains of thought go tramping round in circle through the brain, like the supernumeraries that make up the grand army of a stage-show. Now, if a thought goes round through the brain a thousand times in a day, it will have worn as deep a track as one which has passed through it once a week for twenty years. This accounts for the ages we seem to have lived since the twelfth of April last, and, to state it more generally, for that ex post facto operation of a great calamity, or any very powerful impression, which we once illustrated by the image of a stain spreading backwards from the leaf of life open before us through all those which we have already turned.

Blessed are those who can sleep quietly in times like these! Yet, not wholly blessed, either: for what is more painful than the awaking from peaceful unconsciousness to a sense that there is something wrong—we cannot at first think what—and then groping our way about through the twilight of our thoughts until we come full upon the misery, which, like some evil bird, seemed to have flown away, but which sits waiting for us on its perch by our pillow in the gray of the morning?

The converse of this is perhaps still more painful. Many have the feeling in their waking hours that the trouble they are aching with is, after all, only a dream—if they will rub their eyes briskly enough and shake themselves, they will awake out of it, and find all their supposed grief is unreal. This attempt to cajole ourselves out of an ugly fact always reminds us of those unhappy flies who have been indulging in the dangerous sweets of the paper prepared for their especial use.

Watch one of them. He does not feel quite well—at least, he suspects himself of indisposition. Nothing serious—let us just rub our fore-feet together, as the enormous creature who provides for us rubs his hands, and all will be right. He rubs them with that peculiar twisting movement of his, and pauses for the effect. No! All is not quite right yet. Ah! It is our head that is not set on just as it ought to be. Let us settle that where it should be, and then we shall certainly be in good trim again. So he pulls his head about as an old lady adjusts her cap, and passes his fore-paw over it like a kitten washing herself. Poor fellow! It is not a fancy, but a fact, that he has to deal with. If he could read the letters at the head of the sheet, he would see they were Fly-Paper. So with us, when, in our waking misery, we try to think we dream! Perhaps very young persons may not understand this; as we grow older, our waking and dreaming life run more and more into each other.

Another symptom of our excited condition is seen in the breaking up of old habits. The newspaper is as imperious as a

Russian Ukase; it will be had, and it will be read. To this all else must give place. If we must go out at unusual hours to get it, we shall go, in spite of after-dinner nap or evening somnolence. If it finds us in company, it will not stand on ceremony, but cuts short the compliment and the story by the divine right of its telegraphic dispatches.

•

War is a very old story, but it is a new one to this generation of Americans. Our own nearest relation in the ascending line remembers the Revolution well. How should she forget it? Did she not lose her doll, which was left behind, when she was carried out of Boston, about that time growing uncomfortable by reason of cannon-balls dropping in from the neighboring heights at all hours, in token of which see the tower of Brattle Street Church at this very day? War in her memory means '76. As for the brush of 1812, 'we did not think much about that'; and everybody knows that the Mexican business did not concern us much, except in its political relations. No! War is a new thing to all of us who are not in the last quarter of their century. We are learning many strange matters from our fresh experience. And besides, there are new conditions of existence which make war as it is with us very different from war as it has been.

The first and obvious difference consists in the fact that the whole nation is now penetrated by the ramifications of a network of iron nerves which flash sensation and volition backward and forward to and from towns and provinces as if they were organs and limbs of a single living body. The second is the vast system of iron muscles which, as it were, move the limbs of the mighty organism one upon another. What was the railroad-force which put the Sixth Regiment in Baltimore on the 19th of April but a contraction and extension of the arm of Massachusetts with a clenched fist full of bayonets at the end of it?

This perpetual intercommunication, joined to the power of instantaneous action, keeps us always alive with excitement.

It is not a breathless courier who comes back with the report from an army we have lost sight of for a month, nor a single bulletin which tells us all we are to know for a week of some great engagement, but almost hourly paragraphs, laden with truth or falsehood as the case may be, making us restless always for the last fact or rumor they are telling. And so of the movements of our armies. Tonight the stout lumbermen of Maine are encamped under their own fragrant pines. In a score or two of hours they are among the tobacco-fields and the slave-pens of Virginia. The war passion burned like scattered coals of fire in the households of Revolutionary times; now it rushes all through the land like a flame over the prairie. And this instant diffusion of every fact and feeling produces another singular effect in the equalizing and steadying of public opinion. We may not be able to see a month ahead of us; but as to what has passed a week afterwards it is as thoroughly talked out and judged as it would have been in a whole season before our national nervous system was organized.

> As the wild tempest wakes the slumbering sea,
> Thou only teachest all that man can be!

We indulged in the above apostrophe to War in a Phi Beta Kappa poem of long ago, which we liked better before we read Mr Cutler's beautiful prolonged lyric delivered at the recent anniversary of that Society.

Oftentimes, in paroxysms of peace and goodwill towards all mankind, we have felt twinges of conscience about the passage—especially when one of our orators showed us that a ship of war costs as much to build and keep as a college, and that every port-hole we could stop would give us a new professor. Now we begin to think that there was some meaning in our poor couplet. War has taught us, as nothing else could, what we can be and are. It has exalted our manhood and our womanhood, and driven us all back upon our substantial human qualities, for a long time more or less kept out of sight by the spirit of commerce, the love of art, science, or literature, or other qualities not belonging to all of us as men and women.

It is at this very moment doing more to melt away the petty social distinctions which keep generous souls apart from each other, than the preaching of the Beloved Disciple himself would do. We are finding out that not only 'patriotism is eloquence', but that heroism is gentility. All ranks are wonderfully equalized under the fire of a masked battery. The plain artisan or the rough fireman, who faces the lead and iron like a man, is the truest representative we can show of the heroes of Crécy and Agincourt. And if one of our fine gentlemen puts off his straw-colored kids and stands by the other, shoulder to shoulder, or leads him on to the attack, he is as honorable in our eyes and in theirs as if he were ill-dressed and his hands were soiled with labor.

Even our poor 'Brahmins',—whom a critic in ground-glass spectacles (the same who grasps his statistics by the blade and strikes at his supposed antagonist with the handle) oddly confounds with the 'bloated aristocracy', whereas they are very commonly pallid, undervitalized, shy, sensitive creatures, whose only birthright is an aptitude for learning—even these poor New England Brahmins of ours—subvirates—of an organizable base as they often are, count as full men, if their courage is big enough for the uniform which hangs so loosely about their slender figures.

A young man was drowned not very long ago in the river running under our windows. A few days afterwards a field-piece was dragged to the water's edge, and fired many times over the river. We asked a bystander, who looked like a fisherman, what that was for. It was to 'break the gall', he said, and so bring the drowned person to the surface. A strange physiological fancy and a very odd—non sequitur; but that is not our present point. A good many extraordinary objects do really come to the surface when the great guns of war shake the waters, as when they roared over Charleston harbor.

Treason came up, hideous, fit only to be huddled into its dishonorable grave. But the wrecks of precious virtues, which had been covered with the waves of prosperity, came up also.

And all sorts of unexpected and unheard-of things, which had lain unseen during our national life of fourscore years, came up and are coming up daily, shaken from their bed by the concussions of the artillery bellowing around us.

It is a shame to own it, but there were persons otherwise respectable not unwilling to say that they believed the old valor of Revolutionary times had died out from among us. They talked about our own Northern people as the English in the last centuries used to talk about the French—Goldsmith's old soldier, it may be remembered, called one Englishman good for five of them. As Napoleon spoke of the English, again, as a nation of shopkeepers, so these persons affected to consider the multitude of their countrymen as unwarlike artisans,—forgetting that Paul Revere taught himself the value of liberty in working upon gold, and Nathanael Greene fitted himself to shape armies in the labor of forging iron.

These persons have learned better now. The bravery of our free working-people was overlaid, but not smothered; sunken, but not drowned. The hands which had been busy conquering the elements had only to change their weapons and their adversaries, and they were as ready to conquer the masses of living force opposed to them as they had been to build towns, to dam rivers, to hunt whales, to harvest ice, to hammer brute matter into every shape civilization can ask for.

Another great fact came to the surface, and is coming up every day in new shapes—that we are one people. It is easy to say that a man is a man in Maine or Minnesota, but not so easy to feel it, all through our bones and marrow. The camp is deprovincializing us very fast. Brave Winthrop, marching with the city élégants, seems to have been a little startled to find how wonderfully human were the hard-handed men of the Eighth Massachusetts. It takes all the nonsense out of everybody, or ought to do it, to see how fairly the real manhood of a country is distributed over its surface. And then, just as we are beginning to think our own soil has a monopoly of heroes as well as of cotton, up turns a regiment of gallant Irishmen, like the Sixty-ninth, to show us that continental provincialism is as bad as that of Coos County, New Hampshire, or of Broadway, New York.

Here, too, side by side in the same great camp, are half a dozen chaplains, representing half a dozen modes of religious belief. When the masked battery opens, does the 'Baptist' Lieutenant believe in his heart that God takes better care of him than of his 'Congregationalist' Colonel? Does any man really suppose, that, of a score of noble young fellows who have just laid down their lives for their country, the Homoousians are received to the mansions of bliss, and the Homoiousians translated from the battlefield to the abodes of everlasting woe? War not only teaches what man can be, but it teaches also what he must not be. He must not be a bigot and a fool in the presence of that day of judgment proclaimed by the trumpet which calls to battle, and where a man should have but two thoughts: to do his duty, and trust his Maker. Let our brave dead come back from the fields where they have fallen for law and liberty, and if you will follow them to their graves, you will find out what the Broad Church means; the narrow church is sparing of its exclusive formulæ over the coffins wrapped in the flag which the fallen heroes had defended! Very little comparatively do we hear at such times of the dogmas on which men differ; very much of the faith and trust in which all sincere Christians can agree. It is a noble lesson, and nothing less noisy than the voice of cannon can teach it so that it shall be heard over all the angry cries of theological disputants.

Now, too, we have a chance to test the sagacity of our friends, and to get at their principles of judgment. Perhaps most of us will agree that our faith in domestic prophets has been diminished by the experience of the last six months. We had the notable predictions attributed to the Secretary of State, which so unpleasantly refused to fulfill themselves. We were infested at one time with a set of ominous-looking seers, who shook their heads and muttered obscurely about some mighty preparations that were making to substitute the rule of the minority for that of the majority. Organizations were darkly hinted at; some thought our armories would be seized; and there are not wanting ancient women in the neighboring University town who consider that the country was saved by the intrepid band of students who stood guard, night after night, over the G. R. cannon and the pile of balls in the Cambridge Arsenal.

As a general rule, it is safe to say that the best prophecies are those which the sages remember after the event prophesied of has come to pass, and remind us that they have made long ago. Those who are rash enough to predict publicly beforehand commonly give us what they hope, or what they fear, or some conclusion from an abstraction of their own, or some guess founded on private information not half so good as what everybody gets who reads the papers—never—by any possibility a word that we can depend on, simply because there are cobwebs of contingency between every today and tomorrow that no field-glass can penetrate when fifty of them lie woven one over another. Prophesy as much as you like, but always hedge. Say that you think the rebels are weaker than is commonly supposed, but, on the other hand, that they may prove to be even stronger than is anticipated. Say what you like—only don't be too peremptory and dogmatic; we know that wiser men than you have been notoriously deceived in their predictions in this very matter.

'Ibis et redibis nunquam in bello peribis.'

Let that be your model; and remember, on peril of your reputation as a prophet, not to put a stop before or after the nunquam.

There are two or three facts connected with time, besides that already referred to, which strike us very forcibly in their relation to the great events passing around us. We spoke of the long period seeming to have elapsed since this war began. The buds were then swelling which held the leaves that are still green. It seems as old as Time himself. We cannot fail to observe how the mind brings together the scenes of today and those of the old Revolution. We shut up eighty years into each other like the joints of a pocket-telescope. When the young men from Middlesex dropped in Baltimore the other day, it seemed to bring Lexington and the other Nineteenth of April close to us. War has always been the mint in which the world's history has been coined, and now every day or week or month has a new medal for us. It was Warren that the first impression bore in the last great coinage; if it is Ellsworth now, the new face hardly seems fresher than the old. All battlefields are alike in their main features. The young fellows who fell in our earlier struggle seemed like old men to us until within these few months; now we remember they were like these fiery youth we are cheering as they go to the fight; it seems as if the grass of our bloody hillside was crimsoned but yesterday, and the cannon-ball imbedded in the church-tower would feel warm, if we laid our hand upon it.

Nay, in this our quickened life we feel that all the battles from earliest time to our own day, where Right and Wrong have grappled, are but one great battle, varied with brief pauses or hasty bivouacs upon the field of conflict. The issues seem to vary, but it is always a right against a claim, and, however the struggle of the hour may go, a movement onward of the campaign, which uses defeat as well as victory to serve its mighty ends. The very implements of our warfare change less than we think. Our bullets and cannon-balls have lengthened into bolts like those which whistled out of old arbalests. Our soldiers fight with weapons, such as are pictured on the walls of Theban tombs, wearing a newly invented headgear as old as the days of the Pyramids.

Whatever miseries this war brings upon us, it is making us wiser, and, we trust, better. Wiser, for we are learning our weakness, our narrowness, our selfishness, our ignorance, in lessons of sorrow and shame. Better, because all that is noble in men and women is demanded by the time, and our people are rising to the standard the time calls for. For this is the question the hour is putting to each of us: Are you ready, if need be, to sacrifice all that you have and hope for in this world, that the generations to follow you may inherit a whole country whose natural conditions shall be peace, and not a broken province which must live under the perpetual threat, if not in the constant presence, of war and all that war brings with it? If we are all ready for this sacrifice, battles may be lost, but the campaign and its grand object must be won.

Heaven is very kind in its way of putting questions to mortals. We are not abruptly asked to give up all that we most care for, in view of the momentous issues before us. Perhaps we shall never be asked to give up all, but we have already been called upon to part with much that is dear to us, and should be ready to yield the rest as it is called for. The time may come when even the cheap public print shall be a burden our means cannot support, and we can only listen in the square that was once the market-place to the voices of those who proclaim defeat or victory. Then there will be only our daily food left. When we have nothing to read and nothing to eat, it will be a favorable moment to offer a compromise. At present we have all that nature absolutely demands—we can live on bread and the newspaper.

JOHN BULL

WASHINGTON IRVING

An old song, made by an aged old pate,
Of an old worshipful gentleman who had a great estate,
That kept a brave old house at a bountiful rate,
And an old porter to relieve the poor at his gate.
With an old study fill'd full of learned old books,
With an old reverend chaplain, you might know him by his looks,
With an old buttery hatch worn quite off the hooks,
And an old kitchen that maintained half-a-dozen old cooks.
Like an old courtier, etc.

—OLD SONG

There is no species of humor in which the English more excel, than that which consists in caricaturing and giving ludicrous appellations, or nicknames. In this way they have whimsically designated, not merely individuals, but nations; and, in their fondness for pushing a joke, they have not spared even themselves. One would think that, in personifying itself, a nation would be apt to picture something grand, heroic and imposing, but it is characteristic of the peculiar humor of the English, and of their love for what is blunt, comic, and familiar, that they have embodied their national oddities in the figure of a sturdy, corpulent old fellow, with a three-cornered hat, red waistcoat, leather breeches, and stout oaken cudgel. Thus they have taken a singular delight in exhibiting their most private foibles in a laughable point of view; and have been so successful in their delineations, that there is scarcely a being in actual existence more absolutely present to the public mind than that eccentric personage, John Bull.

Perhaps the continual contemplation of the character thus

drawn of them has contributed to fix it upon the nation; and thus to give reality to what at first may have been painted in a great measure from the imagination. Men are apt to acquire peculiarities that are continually ascribed to them. The common orders of English seem wonderfully captivated with the beau ideal which they have formed of John Bull, and endeavor to act up to the broad caricature that is perpetually before their eyes. Unluckily, they sometimes make their boasted Bull-ism an apology for their prejudice or grossness; and this I have especially noticed among those truly homebred and genuine sons of the soil who have never migrated beyond the sound of Bow-bells. If one of these should be a little uncouth in speech, and apt to utter impertinent truths, he confesses that he is a real John Bull, and always speaks his mind. If he now and then flies into an unreasonable burst of passion about trifles, he observes, that John Bull is a choleric old blade, but then his passion is over in a moment, and he bears no malice. If he betrays a coarseness of taste, and an insensibility to foreign refinements, he thanks heaven for his ignorance—he is a plain John Bull, and has no relish for frippery and nicknacks. His very proneness to be gulled by strangers, and to pay extravagantly for absurdities, is excused under the plea of munificence—for John is always more generous than wise.

Thus, under the name of John Bull, he will contrive to argue every fault into a merit, and will frankly convict himself of being the honestest fellow in existence.

However little, therefore, the character may have suited in the first instance, it has gradually adapted itself to the nation, or rather they have adapted themselves to each other; and a stranger who wishes to study English peculiarities, may gather much valuable information from the innumerable portraits of John Bull, as exhibited in the windows of the caricature-shops. Still, however, he is one of those fertile humorists, that are continually throwing out new portraits, and presenting different aspects from different points of view; and, often as he has been described, I cannot resist the temptation to give a slight sketch of him, such as he has met my eye.

John Bull, to all appearance, is a plain downright matter-of-fact fellow, with much less of poetry about him than rich prose. There is little of romance in his nature, but a vast deal of strong natural feeling. He excels in humor more than in wit; is jolly rather than gay; melancholy rather than morose; can easily be moved to a sudden tear, or surprised into a broad laugh; but he loathes sentiment, and has no turn for light pleasantry. He is a boon companion, if you allow him to have his humor, and to talk about himself; and he will stand by a friend in a quarrel, with life and purse, however soundly he may be cudgeled.

In this last respect, to tell the truth, he has a propensity to be somewhat too ready. He is a busy-minded personage, who thinks not merely for himself and family, but for all the country round, and is most generously disposed to be everybody's champion. He is continually volunteering his services to settle his neighbors' affairs, and takes it in great dudgeon if they engage in any matter of consequence without asking his advice; though he seldom engages in any friendly office of the kind without finishing by getting into a squabble with all parties, and then railing bitterly at their ingratitude. He unluckily took lessons in his youth in the noble science of defense, and having accomplished himself in the use of his limbs and his weapons, and become a perfect master at boxing and cudgel-play, he has had a troublesome life of it ever since. He cannot hear of a quarrel between the most distant of his neighbors, but he begins incontinently to fumble with the head of his cudgel, and consider whether his interest or honor does not require that he should meddle in the broil. Indeed he has extended his relations of pride and policy so completely over the whole country, that no event can take place, without infringing some of his finely-spun rights and dignities. Couched in his little domain, with these filaments stretching forth in every direction, he is like some choleric, bottle-bellied old spider, who has woven his web over a whole chamber, so that a fly cannot buzz, nor a breeze blow, without startling his repose, and causing him to sally forth wrathfully from his den.

Though really a good-hearted, good-tempered old fellow at bottom, yet he is singularly fond of being in the midst of contention. It is one of his peculiarities, however, that he only relishes the beginning of an affray; he always goes into a fight with alacrity, but comes out of it grumbling even when victorious; and though no one fights with more obstinacy to carry a contested point, yet, when the battle is over, and he comes to the reconciliation, he is so much taken up with the mere shaking of hands, that he is apt to let his antagonist pocket all that they have been quarreling about. It is not, therefore, fighting that he ought so much to be on his guard against, as making friends. It is difficult to cudgel him out of a farthing; but put him in a good humor, and you may bargain him out of all the money in his pocket. He is like a stout ship, which will weather the roughest storm uninjured, but roll its masts overboard in the succeeding calm.

He is a little fond of playing the magnifico abroad; of pulling out a long purse; flinging his money bravely about at boxing matches, horse races, cock fights, and carrying a high head among 'gentlemen of the fancy': but immediately after one of these fits of extravagance, he will be taken with violent qualms of economy; stop short at the most trivial expenditure; talk desperately of being ruined and brought upon the parish; and, in such moods, will not pay the smallest tradesman's bill, without violent altercation. He is in fact the most punctual and discontented paymaster in the world; drawing his coin out of his breeches pocket with infinite reluctance; paying to the uttermost farthing, but accompanying every guinea with a growl.

With all his talk of economy, however, he is a bountiful provider, and a hospitable housekeeper. His economy is of a whimsical kind, its chief object being to devise how he may afford to be extravagant; for he will begrudge himself a beefsteak and pint of port one day, that he may roast an ox whole, broach a hogshead of ale, and treat all his neighbors on the next.

His domestic establishment is enormously expensive: not

so much from any great outward parade, as from the great consumption of solid beef and pudding; the vast number of followers he feeds and clothes; and his singular disposition to pay hugely for small services. He is a most kind and indulgent master, and, provided his servants humor his peculiarities, flatter his vanity a little now and then, and do not peculate grossly on him before his face, they may manage him to perfection. Everything that lives on him seems to thrive and grow fat. His house-servants are well paid, and pampered, and have little to do. His horses are sleek and lazy, and prance slowly before his state carriage; and his house-dogs sleep quietly about the door, and will hardly bark at a housebreaker.

His family mansion is an old castellated manor-house, gray with age, and of a most venerable, though weather-beaten appearance. It has been built upon no regular plan, but is a vast accumulation of parts, erected in various tastes and ages. The center bears evident traces of Saxon architecture, and is as solid as ponderous stone and old English oak can make it. Like all the relics of that style, it is full of obscure passages, intricate mazes, and dusky chambers; and though these have been partially lighted up in modern days, yet there are many places where you must still grope in the dark. Additions have been made to the original edifice from time to time, and great alterations have taken place; towers and battlements have been erected during wars and tumults: wings built in time of peace; and out-houses, lodges, and offices, run up according to the whim or convenience of different generations, until it has become one of the most spacious, rambling tenements imaginable. An entire wing is taken up with the family chapel, a reverend pile, that must have been exceedingly sumptuous, and, indeed, in spite of having been altered and simplified at various periods, has still a look of solemn religious pomp. Its walls within are stored with the monuments of John's ancestors; and it is snugly fitted up with soft cushions and well-lined chairs, where such of his family as are inclined to church services, may doze comfortably in the discharge of their duties.

To keep up this chapel has cost John much money; but he is stanch in his religion, and piqued in his zeal, from the circumstance that many dissenting chapels have been erected in his vicinity, and several of his neighbors, with whom he has had quarrels, are strong papists.

To do the duties of the chapel he maintains, at a large expense, a pious and portly family chaplain. He is a most learned and decorous personage, and a truly well-bred Christian, who always backs the old gentleman in his opinions, winks discreetly at his little peccadilloes, rebukes the children when refractory, and is of great use in exhorting the tenants to read their Bibles, say their prayers, and, above all, to pay their rents punctually, and without grumbling.

The family apartments are in a very antiquated taste, somewhat heavy, and often inconvenient, but full of the solemn magnificence of former times; fitted up with rich, though faded tapestry, unwieldy furniture, and loads of massy gorgeous old plate. The vast fireplaces, ample kitchens, extensive cellars, and sumptuous banqueting halls, all speak of the roaring hospitality of days of yore, of which the modern festivity at the manor-house is but a shadow. There are, however, complete suites of rooms apparently deserted and time-worn; and towers and turrets that are tottering to decay; so that in high winds there is danger of their tumbling about the ears of the household.

John has frequently been advised to have the old edifice thoroughly overhauled; and to have some of the useless parts pulled down, and the others strengthened with their materials; but the old gentleman always grows testy on this subject. He swears the house is an excellent house—that it is tight and weather proof, and not to be shaken by tempests—that it has stood for several hundred years, and, therefore, is not likely to tumble down now—that as to its being inconvenient, his family is accustomed to the inconveniences, and would not be comfortable without them—that as to its unwieldy size and irregular construction, these result from its being the growth of centuries, and being improved by the wisdom of every generation—that an old family, like his, requires a large house to dwell in; new, upstart families may live in modern cottages and snug boxes; but an old English family should inhabit an old English manor-house. If you point out any part of the building as superfluous, he insists that it is material to the strength or decoration of the rest, and the harmony of the whole; and swears that the parts are so built into each other, that if you pull down one, you run the risk of having the whole about your ears.

The secret of the matter is, that John has a great disposition to protect and patronize. He thinks it indispensable to the dignity of an ancient and honorable family, to be bounteous in its appointments, and to be eaten up by dependents; and so, partly from pride, and partly from kind-heartedness, he makes it a rule always to give shelter and maintenance to his superannuated servants.

The consequence is that, like many other venerable family establishments, his manor is encumbered by old retainers whom he cannot turn off, and an old style which he cannot lay down. His mansion is like a great hospital of invalids, and, with all its magnitude, is not a whit too large for its inhabitants. Not a nook or corner but is of use in housing some useless personage. Groups of veteran beefeaters, gouty pensioners, and retired heroes of the buttery and the larder, are seen lolling about its walls, crawling over its lawns, dozing under its trees, or sunning themselves upon the benches at its doors. Every office and outhouse is garrisoned by these supernumeraries and their families; for they are amazingly prolific, and when they die off, are sure to leave John a legacy of hungry mouths to be provided for. A mattock cannot be struck against the most mouldering tumble-down tower, but out pops, from some cranny or loop-hole, the gray pate of some superannuated hanger-on, who has lived at John's expense all his life, and makes the most grievous outcry at their pulling down the roof from over the head of a worn-out servant of the family. This is an appeal that John's honest heart never can withstand; so that a man, who has faithfully eaten his beef and pudding all his life, is sure to be rewarded with a pipe and tankard in his old days.

A great part of his park, also, is turned into paddocks, where his broken-down chargers are turned loose to graze undisturbed for the remainder of their existence—a worthy example of grateful recollection, which if some of his neighbors were to imitate, would not be to their discredit. Indeed, it is one of his great pleasures to point out these old steeds to his visitors, to dwell on their good qualities, extol their past services, and boast, with some little vainglory, of the perilous adventures and hardy exploits through which they have carried him.

He is given, however, to indulge his veneration for family usages, and family encumbrances, to a whimsical extent. His manor is infested by gangs of gipsies; yet he will not suffer them to be driven off, because they have infested the place time out of mind, and been regular poachers upon every generation of the family. He will scarcely permit a dry branch to be lopped from the great trees that surround the house, lest it should molest the rooks, that have bred there for centuries. Owls have taken possession of the dovecote; but they are hereditary owls, and must not be disturbed. Swallows have nearly choked up every chimney with their nests; martins build in every frieze and cornice; crows flutter about the towers, and perch on every weathercock; and old gray-headed rats may be seen in every quarter of the house, running in and out of their holes undauntedly in broad daylight. In short, John has such a reverence for everything that has been long in the family, that he will not hear even of abuses being reformed, because they are good old family abuses.

All those whims and habits have concurred woefully to drain the old gentleman's purse; and as he prides himself on punctuality in money matters, and wishes to maintain his credit in the neighborhood, they have caused him great perplexity in meeting his engagements. This, too, has been increased by the altercations and heart-burnings which are continually taking place in his family. His children have been brought up to different callings, and are of different ways of thinking; and as they have always been allowed to speak their minds freely, they do not fail to exercise the privilege most clamorously in the present posture of his affairs. Some stand up for the honor of the race, and are clear that the old establishment should be kept up in all its state, whatever may be the cost; others, who are more prudent and considerate, entreat the old gentleman to retrench his expenses, and to put his whole system of housekeeping on a more moderate footing. He has, indeed, at times, seemed inclined to listen to their opinions, but their wholesome advice has been completely defeated by the obstreperous conduct of one of his sons. This is a noisy, rattle-pated fellow, of rather low habits, who neglects his business to frequent ale-houses—is the orator of village clubs, and a complete oracle among the poorest of his father's tenants. No sooner does he hear any of his brothers mention reform or retrenchment, than up he jumps, takes the words out of their mouths, and roars out for an overturn. When his tongue is once going nothing can stop it. He rants about the room; hectors the old man about his spendthrift practices; ridicules his tastes and pursuits; insists that he shall turn the old servants out of doors; give the broken-down horses to the hounds; send the fat chaplain packing, and take a field-preacher in his place—nay, that the whole family mansion shall be leveled with the ground, and a plain one of brick and mortar built in its place. He rails at every social entertainment and family festivity, and skulks away growling to the ale-house whenever an equipage drives up to the door. Though constantly complaining of the emptiness of his purse, yet he scruples not to spend all his pocket-money in these tavern convocations, and even runs up scores for the liquor over which he preaches about his father's extravagance.

It may readily be imagined how little such thwarting agrees with the old cavalier's fiery temperament. He has become so irritable, from repeated crossings, that the mere mention of retrenchment or reform is a signal for a brawl between him and the tavern oracle. As the latter is too sturdy and refractory for paternal discipline, having grown out of all fear of the cudgel, they have frequent scenes of wordy warfare, which at times run so high, that John is fain to call in the aid of his son Tom, an officer who has served abroad, but is at present living at home, on half-pay. This last is sure to stand by the old gentleman, right or wrong; likes nothing so much as a racketing, roystering life; and is ready at a wink or nod, to out saber, and flourish it over the orator's head, if he dares to array himself against paternal authority.

These family dissensions, as usual, have got abroad, and are rare food for scandal in John's neighborhood. People begin to look wise, and shake their heads, whenever his affairs are mentioned. They all 'hope that matters are not so bad with him as represented; but when a man's own children begin to rail at his extravagance, things must be badly managed. They understand he is mortgaged over head and ears, and is continually dabbling with money lenders. He is certainly an open-handed old gentleman, but they fear he has lived too fast; indeed, they never knew any good come of this fondness for hunting, racing, reveling and prize-fighting. In short, Mr Bull's estate is a very fine one, and has been in the family a long time; but, for all that, they have known many finer estates come to the hammer.'

What is worst of all, is the effect which these pecuniary embarrassments and domestic feuds have had on the poor man himself. Instead of that jolly round corporation, and smug rosy face, which he used to present, he has of late become as shriveled and shrunk as a frost-bitten apple. His scarlet gold-laced waistcoat, which bellied out so bravely in those prosperous days when he sailed before the wind, now hangs loosely about him like a mainsail in a calm. His leather breeches are all in folds and wrinkles, and apparently have much ado to hold up the boots that yawn on both sides of his once sturdy legs.

Instead of strutting about as formerly, with his three-cornered hat on one side; flourishing his cudgel, and bringing it down every moment with a hearty thump upon the ground; looking everyone sturdily in the face, and trolling out a stave of a catch or a drinking song; he now goes about whistling thoughtfully to himself, with his head drooping down, his cudgel tucked under his arm, and his hands thrust to the bottom of his breeches pockets, which are evidently empty.

Such is the plight of honest John Bull at present; yet for all this the old fellow's spirit is as tall and as gallant as ever. If you drop the least expression of sympathy or concern, he takes fire in an instant; swears that he is the richest and stoutest fellow in the country; talks of laying out large sums to adorn his house or buy another estate; and with a valiant swagger and grasping of his cudgel, longs exceedingly to have another bout at quarter-staff.

Though there may be something rather whimsical in all this, yet I confess I cannot look upon John's situation without strong feelings of interest. With all his odd humors and obstinate prejudices, he is a sterling-hearted old blade. He may not be so wonderfully fine a fellow as he thinks himself, but he is at least twice as good as his neighbors represent him. His virtues are all his own; all plain, homebred, and unaffected. His very faults smack of the raciness of his good qualities. His extravagance savors of his generosity; his quarrelsomeness of his courage; his credulity of his open faith; his vanity of his pride; and his bluntness of his sincerity. They are all the redundancies of a rich and liberal character. He is like his own oak, rough without, but sound and solid within; whose bark abounds with excrescences in proportion to the growth and grandeur of the timber; and whose branches make a fearful groaning and murmuring in the least storm, from their very magnitude and luxuriance. There is something, too, in the appearance of his old family mansion that is extremely poetical and picturesque; and, as long as it can be rendered comfortably habitable, I should almost tremble to see it meddled with, during the present conflict of tastes and opinions. Some of his advisers are no doubt good architects, that might be of service; but many, I fear, are mere levelers, who, when they had once got to work with their mattocks on this venerable edifice, would never stop until they had brought it to the ground, and perhaps buried themselves among the ruins. All that I wish is, that John's present troubles may teach him more prudence in future. That he may cease to distress his mind about other people's affairs; that he may give up the fruitless attempt to promote the good of his neighbors, and the peace and happiness of the world, by dint of the cudgel; that he may remain quietly at home; gradually get his house into repair; cultivate his rich estate according to his fancy; husband his income—if he thinks proper; bring his unruly children into order—if he can; renew the jovial scenes of ancient prosperity; and long enjoy, on his paternal lands, a green, an honorable, and a merry old age.

THE MUTABILITY OF LITERATURE: A COLLOQUY IN WESTMINSTER ABBEY

WASHINGTON IRVING

I know that all beneath the moon decays,
And what by mortals in this world is brought,
In time's great period shall return to nought.
I know that all the muse's heavenly lays,
With toil of sprite which are so dearly bought,
As idle sounds, of few or none are sought,
That there is nothing lighter than mere praise.

—DRUMMOND OF HAWTHORNDEN

There are certain half-dreaming moods of mind, in which we naturally steal away from noise and glare, and seek some quiet haunt, where we may indulge our reveries and build our air castles undisturbed. In such a mood I was loitering about the old gray cloisters of Westminster Abbey, enjoying that luxury of wandering thought which one is apt to dignify with the name of reflection; when suddenly an interruption of madcap boys from Westminster School, playing at football, broke in upon the monastic stillness of the place, making the vaulted passages and mouldering tombs echo with their merriment. I sought to take refuge from their noise by penetrating still deeper into the solitudes of the pile, and applied to one of the vergers for admission to the library. He conducted me through a portal rich with the crumbling sculpture of former ages, which opened upon a gloomy passage leading to the chapter-house and the chamber in which doomsday book is deposited. Just within the passage is a small door on the left. To this the verger applied a key; it was double locked, and opened with some difficulty, as if seldom used. We now ascended a dark narrow staircase, and, passing through a second door, entered the library.

I found myself in a lofty antique hall, the roof supported by massive joists of old English oak. It was soberly lighted by a row of Gothic windows at a considerable height from the floor, and which apparently opened upon the roofs of the cloisters. An ancient picture of some reverend dignitary of the church in his robes hung over the fireplace. Around the hall and in a small gallery were the books, arranged in carved oaken cases. They consisted principally of old polemical writers, and were much more worn by time than use. In the center of the library was a solitary table with two or three books on it, an inkstand without ink, and a few pens parched by long disuse. The place seemed fitted for quiet study and profound meditation. It was buried deep among the massive walls of the abbey, and shut up from the tumult of the world. I could only hear now and then the shouts of the school-boys faintly swelling from the cloisters, and the sound of a bell tolling for prayers, echoing soberly along the roofs of the abbey. By degrees the shouts of merriment grew fainter and fainter, and at length died away; the bell ceased to toll, and a profound silence reigned through the dusky hall.

I had taken down a little thick quarto, curiously bound in parchment, with brass clasps, and seated myself at the table in a venerable elbow-chair. Instead of reading, however, I was beguiled by the solemn monastic air, and lifeless quiet of the place, into a train of musing. As I looked around upon the old volumes in their mouldering covers, thus ranged on the shelves, and apparently never disturbed in their repose, I could not but consider the library a kind of literary catacomb, where authors, like mummies, are piously entombed, and left to blacken and moulder in dusty oblivion.

How much, thought I, has each of these volumes, now thrust aside with such indifference, cost some aching head! How many weary days! How many sleepless nights! How have their authors buried themselves in the solitude of cells and cloisters; shut themselves up from the face of man, and the still more blessed face of nature; and devoted themselves to painful research and intense reflection! And all for what? To occupy an inch of dusty shelf—to have the title of their works read now and then in a future age, by some drowsy churchman or casual straggler like myself; and in another age to be lost, even to remembrance. Such is the amount of this boasted immortality. A mere temporary rumor, a local sound; like the tone of that bell which has just tolled among these towers, filling the ear for a moment—lingering transiently in echo—and then passing away like a thing that was not.

While I sat half murmuring, half meditating these unprofitable speculations with my head resting on my hand, I was thrumming with the other hand upon the quarto, until I accidentally loosened the clasps; when, to my utter astonishment, the little book gave two or three yawns, like one awaking from a deep sleep; then a husky hem; and at length began to talk. At first its voice was very hoarse and broken, being much troubled by a cobweb which some studious spider had woven across it; and having probably contracted a cold from long exposure to the chills and damps of the abbey. In a short time, however, it became more distinct, and I soon found it an exceedingly fluent conversable little tome. Its language, to be sure, was rather quaint and obsolete, and its pronunciation, what, in the present day, would be deemed barbarous; but I shall endeavor, as far as I am able, to render it in modern parlance.

It began with railings about the neglect of the world—about merit being suffered to languish in obscurity, and other such commonplace topics of literary repining, and complained bitterly that it had not been opened for more than two centuries; that the dean only looked now and then into the library, sometimes took down a volume or two, trifled with them for a few moments, and then returned them to their shelves. 'What a plague do they mean,' said the little quarto, which I began to perceive was somewhat choleric, 'what a plague do they mean by keeping several thousand volumes of us shut up here, and watched by a set of old vergers, like so many beauties in a harem, merely to be looked at now and then by the dean? Books were written to give pleasure and to be enjoyed; and I would have a rule passed that the dean should pay each of us a visit at least once a year; or if he is not equal to the task, let them once in a while turn loose the whole school of Westminster among us, that at any rate we may now and then have an airing.'

'Softly, my worthy friend,' replied I, 'you are not aware how much better you are off than most books of your generation. By being stored away in this ancient library, you are like the treasured remains of those saints and monarchs, which lie enshrined in the adjoining chapels; while the remains of your contemporary mortals, left to the ordinary course of nature, have long since returned to dust.'

'Sir,' said the little tome, ruffling his leaves and looking big, 'I was written for all the world, not for the bookworms of an abbey. I was intended to circulate from hand to hand, like other great contemporary works; but here have I been clasped up for more than two centuries, and might have silently fallen a prey to these worms that are playing the very vengeance with my intestines, if you had not by chance given me an opportunity of uttering a few last words before I go to pieces.'

'My good friend,' rejoined I, 'had you been left to the circulation of which you speak, you would long ere this have been no more. To judge from your physiognomy, you are now well stricken in years: very few of your contemporaries can be at present in existence; and those few owe their longevity to being immured like yourself in old libraries; which, suffer me to add, instead of likening to harems, you might more properly and gratefully have compared to those infirmaries attached to religious establishments, for the benefit of the old and decrepit, and where, by quiet fostering and no employment, they often endure to an amazingly good-for-nothing old age. You talk of your contemporaries as if in circulation—where do we meet with their works? What do we hear of Robert Groteste, of Lincoln?

No one could have toiled harder than he for immortality. He is said to have written nearly two hundred volumes. He built, as it were, a pyramid of books to perpetuate his name: but, alas! The pyramid has long since fallen, and only a few fragments are scattered in various libraries, where they are scarcely disturbed even by the antiquarian. What do we hear of Giraldus Cambrensis, the historian, antiquary, philosopher, theologian, and poet? He declined two bishoprics, that he might shut himself up and write for posterity; but posterity never inquires after his labors. What of Henry of Huntingdon, who, besides a learned history of England, wrote a treatise on the contempt of the world, which the world has revenged by forgetting him? What is quoted of Joseph of Exeter, styled the miracle of his age in classical composition? Of his three great heroic poems one is lost forever, excepting a mere fragment; the others are known only to a few of the curious in literature; and as to his love verses and epigrams, they have entirely disappeared. What is in current use of John Wallis, the Franciscan, who acquired the name of the tree of life? Of William of Malmsbury; of Simeon of Durham; of Benedict of Peterborough; of John Hanvill of St Albans; of—'

'Prithee, friend,' cried the quarto, in a testy tone, 'how old do you think me? You are talking of authors that lived long before my time, and wrote either in Latin or French, so that they in a manner expatriated themselves, and deserved to be forgotten; but I, sir, was ushered into the world from the press of the renowned Wynkyn de Worde. I was written in my own native tongue, at a time when the language had become fixed; and indeed I was considered a model of pure and elegant English.'

(I should observe that these remarks were couched in such intolerably antiquated terms, that I have had infinite difficulty in rendering them into modern phraseology.)

'I cry your mercy,' said I, 'for mistaking your age; but it matters little: almost all the writers of your time have likewise passed into forgetfulness; and De Worde's publications are mere literary rarities among book-collectors. The purity and stability of language, too, on which you found your claims to perpetuity, have been the fallacious dependence of authors of every age, even back to the times of the worthy Robert of Gloucester, who wrote his history in rhymes of mongrel Saxon. Even now many talk of Spenser's 'well of pure English undefiled', as if the language ever sprang from a well or fountain-head, and was not rather a mere confluence of various tongues, perpetually subject to changes and intermixtures. It is this which has made English literature so extremely mutable, and the reputation built upon it so fleeting. Unless thought can be committed to something more permanent and unchangeable than such a medium, even thought must share the fate of everything else, and fall into decay. This should serve as a check upon the vanity and exultation of the most popular writer. He finds the language in which he has embarked his fame gradually altering, and subject to the dilapidations of time and the caprice of fashion. He looks back and beholds the early authors of his country, once the favorites of their day, supplanted by modern writers. A few short ages have covered them with obscurity, and their merits can only be relished by the quaint taste of the bookworm. And such, he anticipates, will be the fate of his own work, which, however it may be admired in its day, and held up as a model of purity, will in the course of years grow antiquated and obsolete; until it shall become almost as unintelligible in its native land as an Egyptian obelisk, or one of those Runic inscriptions said to exist in the deserts of Tartary. I declare,' added I, with some emotion, 'when I contemplate a modern library, filled with new works, in all the bravery of rich gilding and binding, I feel disposed to sit down and weep; like the good Xerxes, when he surveyed his army, pranked out in all the splendor of military array, and reflected that in one hundred years not one of them would be in existence!'

'Ah,' said the little quarto, with a heavy sigh, 'I see how it is; these modern scribblers have superseded all the good old authors. I suppose nothing is read now-a-days but Sir Philip Sydney's *Arcadia*, Sackville's stately plays, and *Mirror for Magistrates*, or the fine-spun euphuisms of the unparalleled John Lyly.'

'There you are again mistaken,' said I; 'the writers whom you suppose in vogue, because they happened to be so when you were last in circulation, have long since had their day. Sir Philip Sydney's *Arcadia*, the immortality of which was so fondly predicted by his admirers, and which, in truth, is full of noble thoughts, delicate images, and graceful turns of language, is now scarcely ever mentioned. Sackville has strutted into obscurity; and even Lyly, though his writings were once the delight of a court, and apparently perpetuated by a proverb, is now scarcely known even by name. A whole crowd of authors who wrote and wrangled at the time, have likewise gone down, with all their writings and their controversies. Wave after wave of succeeding literature has rolled over them, until they are buried so deep, that it is only now and then that some industrious diver after fragments of antiquity brings up a specimen for the gratification of the curious.

'For my part,' I continued, 'I consider this mutability of language a wise precaution of Providence for the benefit of the world at large, and of authors in particular. To reason from analogy, we daily behold the varied and beautiful tribes of vegetables springing up, flourishing, adorning the fields for a short time, and then fading into dust, to make way for their successors. Were not this the case, the fecundity of nature would be a grievance instead of a blessing. The earth would groan with rank and excessive vegetation, and its surface become a tangled wilderness. In like manner the works of genius and learning decline, and make way for subsequent productions. Language gradually varies, and with it fade away the writings of authors who have flourished their allotted time; otherwise, the creative powers of genius would overstock the world, and the mind would be completely bewildered in the endless mazes of literature. Formerly there were some restraints on this excessive multiplication. Works had to be transcribed by hand, which was a slow and laborious operation; they were written either on parchment, which was expensive, so that one work was often erased to make way for another; or on papyrus, which was fragile and extremely perishable. Authorship was a limited and unprofitable craft, pursued chiefly by monks in the leisure and solitude of their cloisters. The accumulation of manuscripts was slow and costly, and confined almost entirely to monasteries. To these circumstances it may, in some measure, be owing that we have not been inundated by the intellect of antiquity; that the fountains of thought have not been broken up, and modern genius drowned in the deluge. But the inventions of paper and the press have put an end to all these restraints. They have made everyone a writer, and enabled every mind to pour itself into print, and diffuse itself over the whole intellectual world. The consequences are alarming. The stream of literature has swollen into a torrent—augmented into a river—expanded into a sea. A few centuries since, five or six hundred manuscripts constituted a great library; but what would you say to libraries such as actually exist, containing three or four hundred thousand volumes; legions of authors at the same time busy; and the press going on with fearfully increasing activity, to double and quadruple the number? Unless some unforeseen mortality should break out among the progeny of the muse, now that she has become so prolific, I tremble for posterity. I fear the mere fluctuation of language will not be sufficient. Criticism may do much. It increases with the increase of literature, and resembles one of those salutary checks on population spoken of by economists. All possible encouragement, therefore, should be given to the growth of critics, good or bad. But I fear all will be in vain; let criticism do what it may, writers will write, printers will print, and the world will inevitably be overstocked with good books. It will soon be the employment of a lifetime merely to learn their names. Many a man of passable information, at the present day, reads scarcely anything but reviews; and before long a man of erudition will be little better than a mere walking catalogue.'

'My very good sir,' said the little quarto, yawning most drearily in my face, 'excuse my interrupting you, but I perceive you are rather given to prose. I would ask the fate of an author who was making some noise just as I left the world. His reputation, however, was considered quite temporary. The learned shook their heads at him, for he was a poor half-educated varlet, that knew little of Latin, and nothing of Greek, and had been obliged to run the country for deer-stealing. I think his name was Shakespeare. I presume he soon sunk into oblivion.'

'On the contrary,' said I, 'it is owing to that very man that the literature of his period has experienced a duration beyond the ordinary term of English literature. There rise authors now and then, who seem proof against the mutability of language, because they have rooted themselves in the unchanging principles of human nature. They are like gigantic trees that we sometimes see on the banks of a stream; which, by their vast and deep roots, penetrating through the mere surface, and laying hold on the very foundations of the earth, preserve the soil around them from being swept away by the ever-flowing current, and hold up many a neighboring plant, and perhaps worthless weed, to perpetuity. Such is the case with Shakespeare, whom we behold defying the encroachments of time, retaining in modern use the language and literature of his day, and giving duration to many an indifferent author, merely from having flourished in his vicinity. But even he, I grieve to say, is gradually assuming the tint of age, and his whole form is overrun by a profusion of commentators, who, like clambering vines and creepers, almost bury the noble plant that upholds them.'

Here the little quarto began to heave his sides and chuckle, until at length he broke out in a plethoric fit of laughter that had well nigh choked him, by reason of his excessive corpulency. 'Mighty well!' cried he, as soon as he could recover breath, 'mighty well! And so you would persuade me that the literature of an age is to be perpetuated by a vagabond deer-stealer! By a man without learning; by a poet, forsooth—a poet!' And here he wheezed forth another fit of laughter.

I confess that I felt somewhat nettled at this rudeness, which, however, I pardoned on account of his having flourished in a less polished age. I determined, nevertheless, not to give up my point.

'Yes,' resumed I, positively, 'a poet; for of all writers he has the best chance for immortality. Others may write from the head, but he writes from the heart, and the heart will always understand him. He is the faithful portrayer of nature, whose features are always the same and always interesting. Prose writers are voluminous and unwieldy; their pages are crowded with commonplaces, and their thoughts expanded into tediousness. But with the true poet everything is terse, touching, or brilliant. He gives the choicest thoughts in the choicest language. He illustrates them by everything that he sees most striking in nature and art. He enriches them by pictures of human life, such as it is passing before him. His writings, therefore, contain the spirit, the aroma, if I may use the phrase, of the age in which he lives. They are caskets which inclose within a small compass the wealth of the language—its family jewels, which are thus transmitted in a portable form to posterity. The setting may occasionally be antiquated, and require now and then to be renewed, as in the case of Chaucer; but the brilliancy and intrinsic value of the gems continue unaltered. Cast a look back over the long reach of literary history. What vast valleys of dullness, filled with monkish legends and academical controversies! What bogs of theological speculations! What dreary wastes of metaphysics! Here and there only do we behold the heaven-illuminated bards, elevated like beacons on their widely-separate heights, to transmit the pure light of poetical intelligence from age to age.' I was just about to launch forth into eulogiums upon the poets of the day, when the sudden opening of the door caused me to turn my head. It was the verger, who came to inform me that it was time to close the library. I sought to have a parting word with the quarto, but the worthy little tome was silent; the clasps were closed: and it looked perfectly unconscious of all that had passed. I have been to the library two or three times since, and have endeavored to draw it into further conversation, but in vain; and whether all this rambling colloquy actually took place, or whether it was another of those odd day-dreams to which I am subject, I have never to this moment been able to discover.

AMERICAN LITERATURE

JOHN MACY

American literature is a branch of English literature, as truly as are English books written in Scotland or South Africa. Our literature lies almost entirely in the nineteenth century when the ideas and books of the western world were freely interchanged among the nations and became accessible to an increasing number of readers. In literature nationality is determined by language rather than by blood or geography. M. Maeterlinck, born a subject of King Leopold, belongs to French literature. Mr Joseph Conrad, born in Poland, is already an English classic. Geography, much less important in the nineteenth century than before, was never, among modern European nations, so important as we sometimes are asked to believe. Of the ancestors of English literature *Beowulf* is scarcely more significant, and rather less graceful, than our tree-inhabiting forebears with prehensile toes; the true progenitors of English literature are Greek, Latin, Hebrew, Italian, and French.

American literature and English literature of the nineteenth century are parallel derivatives from preceding centuries of English literature. Literature is a succession of books from books. Artistic expression springs from life ultimately but not immediately. It may be likened to a river which is swollen throughout its course by new tributaries and by the seepages of its banks; it reflects the life through which it flows, taking color from the shores; the shores modify it, but its power and volume descend from distant headwaters and affluents far up stream. Or it may be likened to the race-life which our food nourishes or impoverishes, which our individual circumstances foster or damage, but which flows on through us, strangely impersonal and beyond our power to kill or create.

It is well for a writer to say: 'Away with books! I will draw my inspiration from life!' For we have too many books that are simply better books diluted by John Smith. At the same time, literature is not born spontaneously out of life. Every book has its literary parentage, and students find it so easy to trace genealogies that much criticism reads like an Old Testament chapter of 'begats'. Every novel was suckled at the breasts of older novels, and great mothers are often prolific of anæmic offspring. The stock falls off and revives, goes a-wandering, and returns like a prodigal. The family records get blurred. But of the main fact of descent there is no doubt.

American literature is English literature made in this country. Its nineteenth-century characteristics are evident and can be analyzed and discussed with some degree of certainty. Its 'American' characteristics—no critic that I know has ever given a good account of them. You can define certain peculiarities of American politics, American agriculture, American public schools, even American religion. But what is uniquely American in American literature? Poe is just as American as Mark Twain; Lanier is just as American as Whittier. The American spirit in literature is a myth, like American valor in war, which is precisely like the valor of Italians and Japanese. The American, deluded by a falsely idealized image which he calls America, can say that the purity of Longfellow represents the purity of American home life. An Irish Englishman, Mr Bernard Shaw, with another falsely idealized image of America, surprised that a face does not fit his image, can ask: 'What is Poe doing in that galley?' There is no answer. You never can tell. Poe could not help it. He was born in Boston, and lived in Richmond, New York, Baltimore, Philadelphia. Professor van Dyke says that Poe was a maker of 'decidedly un-American cameos,' but I do not understand what that means. Facts are uncomfortable consorts of prejudices and emotional generalities; they spoil domestic peace, and when there is a separation they sit solid at home while the other party goes. Irving, a shy, sensitive gentleman, who wrote with fastidious care, said: 'It has been a matter of marvel, to European readers, that a man from the wilds of America should express himself in tolerable English.' It is a matter of marvel, just as it is a marvel that Blake and Keats flowered in the brutal city of London a hundred years ago.

The literary mind is strengthened and nurtured, is influenced and mastered, by the accumulated riches of literature. In the last century the strongest thinkers in our language were Englishmen, and not only the traditional but the contemporary influences on our thinkers and artists were British. This may account for one negative characteristic of American literature—its lack of American quality. True, our records must reflect our life. Our poets, enamored of nightingales and Persian gardens, have not altogether forgotten the mocking-bird and the woods of Maine. Fiction, written by inhabitants of New York, Ohio, and Massachusetts, does tell us something of the ways of life in those mighty commonwealths, just as English fiction written by Lancashire men about Lancashire people is saturated with the dialect, the local habits and scenery of that county. But wherever an English-speaking man of imagination may dwell, in Dorset or Calcutta or Indianapolis, he is subject to the strong arm of the empire of English literature; he cannot escape it; it tears him out of his obscure bed and makes a happy slave of him. He is assigned to the department of the service for which his gifts qualify him, and his special education is undertaken by drill-masters and captains who hail from provinces far from his birthplace.

Dickens, who writes of London, influences Bret Harte, who writes of California, and Bret Harte influences Kipling, who writes of India. Each is intensely local in subject matter. The affinity between them is a matter of temperament, manifested, for example, in the swagger and exaggeration characteristic of all three. California did not 'produce' Bret Harte; the power of Dickens was greater than that of the Sierras and the Golden Gate. Bret Harte created a California that never existed, and Indian gentlemen, Caucasian and Hindoo, tell us that Kipling invented an army and an empire unknown to geographers and war-offices.

The ideas at work among these English men of letters are world-encircling and fly between book and brain. The dominant power is on the British Islands, and the prevailing stream of influence flows west across the Atlantic. Sometimes it turns and runs the other way. Poe influenced Rossetti; Whitman influenced Henley. For a century Cooper has been in command of the British literary marine. Literature is reprehensibly unpatriotic, even though its votaries are, as individual citizens, afflicted with local prides and hostilities. It takes only a dramatic interest in the guns of Yorktown. Its philosophy was nobly uttered by Gaston Paris in the Collège de France in 1870, when the city was beleaguered by the German armies: 'Common studies, pursued in the same spirit, in all civilized countries, form, beyond the restrictions of diverse and often hostile nationalities, a great country which no war profanes, no conqueror menaces, where souls find that refuge and unity which in former times was offered them by the city of God.' The catholicity of English language and literature transcends the temporal boundaries of states.

What, then, of the 'provincialism' of the American province of the empire of British literature? Is it an observable general characteristic, and is it a virtue or a vice? There is a sense in which American literature is not provincial enough. The most provincial of all literature is the Greek. The Greeks knew nothing outside of Greece and needed to know nothing. The Old Testament is tribal in its provinciality; its god is a local god, and its village police and sanitary regulations are erected into eternal laws. If this racial localism is not essential to the greatness of early literatures, it is inseparable from them; we find it there. It is not possible in our cosmopolitan age and there are few traces of it in American books. No American poet has sung of his neighborhood with naïve passion, as if it were all the world to him. Whitman is pugnaciously American, but his sympathies are universal, his vision is cosmic; when he seems to be standing in a city street looking at life, he is in a trance, and his spirit is racing with the winds.

The welcome that we gave Whitman betrays the lack of an

admirable kind of provincialism; it shows us defective in local security of judgment. Some of us have been so anxiously abashed by high standards of European culture that we could not see a poet in our own back yard until European poets and critics told us he was there. This is queerly contradictory to a disposition found in some Americans to disregard world standards and proclaim a third-rate poet as the Milton of Oshkosh or the Shelley of San Francisco. The passage in Lowell's 'Fable for Critics' about 'The American Bulwers, Disraelis and Scotts' is a spoonful of salt in the mouth of that sort of gaping village reverence.

Of dignified and self-respecting provincialism, such as Professor Royce so eloquently advocates, there might well be more in American books. Our poets desert the domestic landscape to write pseudo-Elizabethan dramas and sonnets about Mont Blanc. They set up an artificial Tennyson park on the banks of the Hudson. Beside the shores of Lake Michigan they croon the love affairs of an Arab in the desert and his noble steed. This is not a very grave offence, for poets live among the stars, and it makes no difference from what point of the earth's surface they set forth on their aerial adventures. A Wisconsin poet may write very beautifully about nightingales, and a New England Unitarian may write beautifully about cathedrals; if it is beautiful, it is poetry, and all is well.

The novelists are the worst offenders. There have been few of them; they have not been adequate in numbers or in genius to the task of describing the sections of the country, the varied scenes and habits from New Orleans to the Portlands. And yet, small band as they are, with great domestic opportunities and responsibilities, they have devoted volumes to Paris, which has an able native corps of story-makers, and to Italy, where the home talent is first-rate. In this sense American literature is too globe-trotting, it has too little savor of the soil.

Of provincialism of the narrowest type American writers, like other men of imagination, are not guilty to any reprehensible degree. It is a vice sometimes imputed to them by provincial critics who view literature from the office of a London weekly review or from the lecture rooms of American colleges. Some American writers are parochial, for example, Whittier. Others, like Mr Henry James, are provincial in outlook, but cosmopolitan in experience, and reveal their provinciality by a self-conscious internationalism. Probably English and French writers may be similarly classified as provincial or not. Mr James says that Poe's collection of critical sketches 'is probably the most complete and exquisite specimen of provincialism ever prepared for the edification of men.' It is nothing like that. It is an example of what happens when a hack reviewer's work in local journals is collected into a volume because he turns out to be a genius. The list of Poe's victims is not more remarkable for the number of nonentities it includes than *The Lives of the Poets*' by the great Doctor Johnson, who was hack for a bookseller, and 'introduced' all the poets that the taste of the time encouraged the bookseller to print. Poe was cosmopolitan in spirit; his prejudices were personal and highly original, usually against the prejudices of his moment and milieu. Hawthorne is less provincial, in the derogatory sense, than his charming biographer, Mr James, as will become evident if one compares Hawthorne's American notes on England, written in long ago days of national rancor, with Mr James's British notes on America (*The American Scene*), written in our happy days of spacious vision.

Emerson's ensphering universality overspreads Carlyle like the sky above a volcanic island. Indeed Carlyle (who knew more about American life and about what other people ought to do than any other British writer earlier than Mr Chesterton) justly complains that Emerson is not sufficiently local and concrete; Carlyle longs to see 'some Event, Man's Life, American Forest, or piece of creation which this Emerson loves and wonders at, well Emersonised'. Longfellow would not stay at home and write more about the excellent village blacksmith; he made poetical tours of Europe and translated songs and legends from several languages for the delight of the villagers who remained behind. Lowell was so heartily cosmopolitan that American newspapers accused him of Anglomania—which proves their provincialism but acquits him. Mr Howells has written a better book about Venice than about Ohio. Mark Twain lived in every part of America, from Connecticut to California, he wrote about every country under the sun (and about some countries beyond the sun), he is read by all sorts and conditions of men in the English-speaking world, and he is an adopted hero in Vienna. It is difficult to come to any conclusion about provincialism as a characteristic of American literature.

American literature is on the whole idealistic, sweet, delicate, nicely finished. There is little of it which might not have appeared in the Youth's Companion. The notable exceptions are our most stalwart men of genius, Thoreau, Whitman and Mark Twain. Any child can read American literature, and if it does not make a man of him, it at least will not lead him into forbidden realms. Indeed, American books too seldom come to grips with the problems of life, especially the books cast in artistic forms. The essayists, expounders, and preachers attack life vigorously and wrestle with the meaning of it. The poets are thin, moonshiny, meticulous in technique. Novelists are few and feeble, and dramatists are non-existent. These generalities, subject to exceptions, are confirmed by a reading of the first fifteen volumes of the *Atlantic Monthly*, which are a treasure-house of the richest period of American literary expression. In those volumes one finds a surprising number of vigorous, distinguished papers on politics, philosophy, science, even on literature and art. Many talented men and women, whose names are not well remembered, are clustered there about the half dozen salient men of genius; and the collection gives one a sense that the New England mind (aided by the outlying contributors) was, in its one Age of Thought, an abundant and diversified power. But the poetry is not memorable, except for some verses by the few standard poets. And the fiction is naïve. Edward Everett Hale's 'The Man Without a Country' is almost the only story there that one comes on with a thrill either of recognition or of discovery.

It is hard to explain why the American, except in his exhortatory and passionately argumentative moods, has not struck deep into American life, why his stories and verses are, for the most part, only pretty things, nicely unimportant. Anthony Trollope had a theory that the absence of international copyright threw our market open too unrestrictedly to the British product, that the American novel was an unprotected infant industry; we printed Dickens and the rest without paying royalty and starved the domestic manufacturer. This theory does not explain. For there were many American novelists, published, read, and probably paid for their work. The trouble is that they lacked genius; they dealt with trivial, slight aspects of life; they did not take the novel seriously in the right sense of the word, though no doubt they were in another sense serious enough about their poor productions. *Uncle Tom's Cabin* and *Huckleberry Finn* are colossal exceptions to the prevailing weakness and superficiality of American novels.

Why do American writers turn their backs on life, miss its intensities, its significance? The American Civil War was the most tremendous upheaval in the world after the Napoleonic period. The imaginative reaction on it consists of some fine essays, Lincoln's addresses, Whitman's war poetry, *Uncle Tom's Cabin* (which came before the war but is part of it), one or two passionate hymns by Whittier, the second series of the Biglow Papers, Hale's 'The Man Without a Country'—and what else? The novels laid in war-time are either sanguine melodrama or absurd idyls of maidens whose lovers are at the front—a tragic theme if tragically and not sentimentally conceived. Perhaps the bullet that killed Theodore Winthrop deprived us of our great novelist of the Civil War, for he was on the right road. In a general speculation such a might-have-been is not altogether futile; if Milton had died of whooping cough there would not have been any *Paradise Lost*; the reverse of this is that some geniuses whose works ought inevitably to have been produced by this or that national development may have died too soon. This suggestion, however, need not be gravely argued. The fact is that the American literary imagination after the Civil War was almost sterile. If no books had been written, the failure of that conflict to get itself embodied in some masterpieces would be less disconcerting. But thousands of books were written by people who knew the war at first hand and who had literary ambition and some skill, and from all these books none rises to distinction.

An example of what seems to be the American habit of writing about everything except American life, is the work of General Lew Wallace. Wallace was one of the important secondary generals in the Civil War, distinguished at Fort Donelson and at Shiloh. After the war he wrote *Ben-Hur*, a doubly abominable book, because it is not badly written and it shows a lively imagination. There is nothing in it so valuable, so dramatically significant as a week in Wallace's war experiences. *Ben-Hur*, fit work for a country clergyman with a pretty literary gift, is a ridiculous inanity to come from a man who has seen the things that Wallace saw! It is understandable that the man of experience may not write at all, and, on the other hand, that the man of secluded life may have the imagination to make a military epic. But for a man crammed with experience of the most dramatic sort and discovering the ability and the ambition to write—for him to make spurious oriental romances which achieve an enormous popularity! The case is too grotesque to be typical, yet it is exceptional in degree rather than in kind. The American literary artist has written about everything under the skies except what matters most in his own life. General Grant's plain autobiography, not art and of course not attempting to be, is better literature than most of our books in artistic forms, because of its intellectual integrity and the profound importance of the subject-matter.

Our dreamers have dreamed about many wonderful things, but their faces have been averted from the mightier issues of life. They have been high-minded, fine-grained, eloquent in manner, in odd contrast to the real or reputed vigor and crudeness of the nation. In the hundred years from Irving's first romance to Mr Howells's latest unromantic novel, most of our books are eminent for just those virtues which America is supposed to lack. Their physique is feminine; they are fanciful, dainty, reserved; they are literose, sophisticated in craftsmanship, but innocently unaware of the profound agitations of American life, of life everywhere. Those who strike the deeper notes of reality, Whitman, Thoreau, Mark Twain, Mrs Stowe in her one great book, Whittier, Lowell and Emerson at their best, are a powerful minority. The rest, beautiful and fine in spirit, too seldom show that they are conscious of contemporaneous realities, too seldom vibrate with a tremendous sense of life.

The Jason of western exploration writes as if he had passed his life in a library. The Ulysses of great rivers and perilous seas is a connoisseur of Japanese prints. The warrior of 'Sixty-one rivals Miss Marie Corelli. The mining engineer carves cherry stones. He who is figured as gaunt, hardy and aggressive, conquering the desert with the steam locomotive, sings of a pretty little rose in a pretty little garden. The judge, haggard with experience, who presides over the most tragi-comic divorce court ever devised by man, writes love stories that would have made Jane Austen smile.

Mr Arnold Bennett is reported to have said that if Balzac had seen Pittsburgh, he would have cried: 'Give me a pen!' The truth is, the whole country is crying out for those who will record it, satirize it, chant it. As literary material, it is virgin land, ancient as life and fresh as a wilderness. American literature is one occupation which is not over-crowded, in which, indeed, there is all too little competition for the new-comer to meet. There are signs that some earnest young writers are discovering the fertility of a soil that has scarcely been scratched.

American fiction shows all sorts of merit, but the merits are not assembled, concentrated; the fine is weak, and the strong is crude. The stories of Poe, Hawthorne, Howells, James, Aldrich, Bret Harte, are admirable in manner, but they are thin in substance, not of large vitality. On the other hand, some of the stronger American fictions fail in workmanship; for example, *Uncle Tom's Cabin*, which is still vivid and moving long after its tractarian interest has faded; the novels of Frank Norris, a man of great vision and high purpose, who attempted to put national economics into something like an epic of daily bread; and Herman Melville's *Moby Dick*, a madly eloquent romance of the sea. A few American novelists have felt the meaning of the life they knew and have tried sincerely to set it down, but have for various reasons failed to make first-rate novels; for example, Edward Eggleston, whose stories of early Indiana have the breath of actuality in them; Mr E. W. Howe, author of *The Story of a Country Town*; Harold Frederic, a man of great ability, whose work was growing deeper, more significant when he died; George W. Cable, whose novels are unsteady and sentimental, but who gives a genuine impression of having portrayed a city and its people; and Stephen Crane, who, dead at thirty, had given in *The Red Badge of Courage* and *Maggie* the promise of better work. Of good short stories America has been prolific. Mrs Wilkins-Freeman, Mrs Annie Trumbull Slosson, Sarah Orne Jewett, Rowland Robinson, H. C. Bunner, Edward Everett Hale, Frank Stockton, Joel Chandler Harris, and O. Henry are some of those whose short stories are perfect in their several kinds. But the American novel, which multiplies past counting, remains an inferior production.

On a private shelf of contemporary fiction and drama in the English language are the works of ten British authors, Mr Galsworthy, Mr H. G. Wells, Mr Arnold Bennett, Mr Eden Phillpotts, Mr George Moore, Mr Leonard Merrick, Mr J. C. Snaith, Miss May Sinclair, Mr William De Morgan, Mr Maurice Hewlett, Mr Joseph Conrad, Mr Bernard Shaw, yes, and Mr Rudyard Kipling. Beside them I find but two Americans, Mrs Edith Wharton and Mr Theodore Dreiser. There may be others, for one cannot pretend to know all the living novelists and dramatists. Yet for every American that should be added, I would agree to add four to the British list. However, a contemporary literature that includes Mrs Wharton's *Ethan Frome* and Mr Dreiser's *Jennie Gerhardt* both published last year, are not to be despaired of.

In the course of a century a few Americans have said in memorable words what life meant to them. Their performance, put together, is considerable, if not imposing. Any sense of dissatisfaction that one feels in contemplating it is due to the disproportion between a limited expression and the multifarious immensity of the country. Our literature, judged by the great literatures contemporaneous with it, is insufficient to the opportunity and the need. The American Spirit may be figured as petitioning the Muses for twelve novelists, ten poets, and eight dramatists, to be delivered at the earliest possible moment.

ANARCHISM: WHAT IT REALLY STANDS FOR

EMMA GOLDMAN

Ever reviled, accursed, ne'er understood,
Thou art the grisly terror of our age.
'Wreck of all order,' cry the multitude,
'Art thou, and war and murder's endless rage.'
O, let them cry. To them that ne'er have striven
The truth that lies behind a word to find,
To them the word's right meaning was not given.
They shall continue blind among the blind.
But thou, O word, so clear, so strong, so pure,
Thou sayest all which I for goal have taken.
I give thee to the future! Thine secure
When each at least unto himself shall waken.
Comes it in sunshine? In the tempest's thrill?
I cannot tell—but it the earth shall see! I am an anarchist!
Wherefore I will Not rule, and also ruled I will not be!

—JOHN HENRY MACKAY

The history of human growth and development is at the same time the history of the terrible struggle of every new idea heralding the approach of a brighter dawn. In its tenacious hold on tradition, the Old has never hesitated to make use of the foulest and cruelest means to stay the advent of the New, in whatever form or period the latter may have asserted itself. Nor need we retrace our steps into the distant past to realize the enormity of opposition, difficulties, and hardships placed in the path of every progressive idea. The rack, the thumbscrew, and the knout are still with us; so are the convict's garb and the social wrath, all conspiring against the spirit that is serenely marching on.

Anarchism could not hope to escape the fate of all other ideas of innovation. Indeed, as the most revolutionary and uncompromising innovator, anarchism must needs meet with the combined ignorance and venom of the world it aims to reconstruct.

To deal even remotely with all that is being said and done against anarchism would necessitate the writing of a whole volume. I shall therefore meet only two of the principal objections. In so doing, I shall attempt to elucidate what anarchism really stands for.

The strange phenomenon of the opposition to anarchism is that it brings to light the relation between so-called intelligence and ignorance. And yet this is not so very strange when we consider the relativity of all things. The ignorant mass has in its favor that it makes no pretense of knowledge or tolerance. Acting, as it always does, by mere impulse, its reasons are like those of a child.

'Why?'

'Because.'

Yet the opposition of the uneducated to anarchism deserves the same consideration as that of the intelligent man.

What, then, are the objections? First, anarchism is impractical, though a beautiful ideal. Second, anarchism stands for violence and destruction, hence it must be repudiated as vile and dangerous. Both the intelligent man and the ignorant mass judge not from a thorough knowledge of the subject, but either from hearsay or false interpretation.

A practical scheme, says Oscar Wilde, is either one already in existence, or a scheme that could be carried out under the existing conditions; but it is exactly the existing conditions that one objects to, and any scheme that could accept these conditions is wrong and foolish. The true criterion of the practical, therefore, is not whether the latter can keep intact the wrong or foolish; rather is it whether the scheme has vitality enough to leave the stagnant waters of the old, and build, as well as sustain, new life. In the light of this conception, anarchism is indeed practical. More than any other idea, it is helping to do away with the wrong and foolish; more than any other idea, it is building and sustaining new life.

The emotions of the ignorant man are continuously kept at a pitch by the most blood-curdling stories about anarchism. Not a thing too outrageous to be employed against this philosophy and its exponents. Therefore anarchism represents to the unthinking what the proverbial bad man does to the child—a black monster bent on swallowing everything; in short, destruction and violence.

Destruction and violence! How is the ordinary man to know that the most violent element in society is ignorance; that its power of destruction is the very thing anarchism is combating? Nor is he aware that anarchism, whose roots, as it were, are part of nature's forces, destroys, not healthful tissue, but parasitic growths that feed on the life's essence of society. It is merely clearing the soil from weeds and sagebrush, that it may eventually bear healthy fruit.

Someone has said that it requires less mental effort to condemn than to think. The widespread mental indolence, so prevalent in society, proves this to be only too true. Rather than to go to the bottom of any given idea, to examine into its origin and meaning, most people will either condemn it altogether, or rely on some superficial or prejudicial definition of non-essentials.

Anarchism urges man to think, to investigate, to analyze every proposition; but that the brain capacity of the average reader be not taxed too much, I also shall begin with a definition, and then elaborate on the latter.

Anarchism: The philosophy of a new social order based on liberty unrestricted by man-made law; the theory that all forms of government rest on violence, and are therefore wrong and harmful, as well as unnecessary.

The new social order rests, of course, on the materialistic basis of life; but while all anarchists agree that the main evil today is an economic one, they maintain that the solution of that evil can be brought about only through the consideration of *every phase* of life—individual, as well as the collective; the internal, as well as the external phases.

A thorough perusal of the history of human development will disclose two elements in bitter conflict with each other; elements that are only now beginning to be understood, not as foreign to each other, but as closely related and truly harmonious, if only placed in proper environment: the individual and social instincts. The individual and society have waged a relentless and bloody battle for ages, each striving for supremacy, because each was blind to the value and importance of the other. The individual and social instincts—the one a most potent factor for individual endeavor, for growth, aspiration, self-realization; the other an equally potent factor for mutual helpfulness and social well-being.

The explanation of the storm raging within the individual, and between him and his surroundings, is not far to seek. The primitive man, unable to understand his being, much less the unity of all life, felt himself absolutely dependent on blind, hidden forces ever ready to mock and taunt him. Out of that attitude grew the religious concepts of man as a mere speck of dust dependent on superior powers on high, who can only be appeased by complete surrender. All the early sagas rest on that idea, which continues to be the leitmotif of the biblical tales dealing with the relation of man to God, to the State, to society. Again and again the same motif, *man is nothing, the powers are everything*. Thus Jehovah would only endure man on condition of complete surrender. Man can have all the glories of the earth, but he must not become conscious of himself. The State, society, and moral laws all sing the same refrain: Man can have all the glories of the earth, but he must not become conscious of himself.

Anarchism is the only philosophy which brings to man the consciousness of himself; which maintains that God, the State, and society are non-existent, that their promises are null and void, since they can be fulfilled only through man's subordination. Anarchism is therefore the teacher of the unity of life; not merely in nature, but in man. There is no conflict between the individual and the social instincts, any more than there is between the heart and the lungs: the one the receptacle of a precious life essence, the other the repository of the element that keeps the essence pure and strong. The individual is the heart of society, conserving the essence of social life; society is the lungs which are distributing the element to keep the life essence—that is, the individual—pure and strong.

'The one thing of value in the world,' says Emerson, 'is the active soul; this every man contains within him. The soul active sees absolute truth and utters truth and creates.' In other words, the individual instinct is the thing of value in the world. It is the true soul that sees and creates the truth alive, out of which is to come a still greater truth, the re-born social soul.

Anarchism is the great liberator of man from the phantoms that have held him captive; it is the arbiter and pacifier of the two forces for individual and social harmony. To accomplish that unity, anarchism has declared war on the pernicious influences which have so far prevented the harmonious blending of individual and social instincts, the individual and society.

Religion, the dominion of the human mind; property, the dominion of human needs; and government, the dominion of human conduct, represent the stronghold of man's enslavement and all the horrors it entails. Religion! How it dominates man's mind, how it humiliates and degrades his soul. God is everything, man is nothing, says religion. But out of that nothing God has created a kingdom so despotic, so tyrannical, so cruel, so terribly exacting that naught but gloom and tears and blood have ruled the world since gods began. Anarchism rouses man to rebellion against this black monster. Break your mental fetters, says anarchism to man, for not until you think and judge for yourself will you get rid of the dominion of darkness, the greatest obstacle to all progress.

Property, the dominion of man's needs, the denial of the right to satisfy his needs. Time was when property claimed a divine right, when it came to man with the same refrain, even as religion,

'Sacrifice! Abnegate! Submit!' The spirit of anarchism has lifted man from his prostrate position. He now stands erect, with his face toward the light. He has learned to see the insatiable, devouring, devastating nature of property, and he is preparing to strike the monster dead.

'Property is robbery,' said the great French anarchist, Proudhon. Yes, but without risk and danger to the robber. Monopolizing the accumulated efforts of man, property has robbed him of his birthright, and has turned him loose a pauper and an outcast. Property has not even the time-worn excuse that man does not create enough to satisfy all needs. The A B C student of economics knows that the productivity of labor within the last few decades far exceeds normal demand a hundredfold. But what are normal demands to an abnormal institution? The only demand that property recognizes is its own gluttonous appetite for greater wealth, because wealth means power; the power to subdue, to crush, to exploit, the power to enslave, to outrage, to degrade. America is particularly boastful of her great power, her enormous national wealth. Poor America, of what avail is all her wealth, if the individuals comprising the nation are wretchedly poor? If they live in squalor, in filth, in crime, with hope and joy gone, a homeless, soilless army of human prey.

It is generally conceded that unless the returns of any business venture exceed the cost, bankruptcy is inevitable. But those engaged in the business of producing wealth have not yet learned even this simple lesson. Every year the cost of production in human life is growing larger (50,000 killed, 100,000 wounded in America last year); the returns to the masses, who help to create wealth, are ever getting smaller. Yet America continues to be blind to the inevitable bankruptcy of our business of production. Nor is this the only crime of the latter. Still more fatal is the crime of turning the producer into a mere particle of a machine, with less will and decision than his master of steel and iron. Man is being robbed not merely of the products of his labor, but of the power of free initiative, of originality, and the interest in, or desire for, the things he is making.

Real wealth consists in things of utility and beauty, in things that help to create strong, beautiful bodies and surroundings inspiring to live in. But if man is doomed to wind cotton around a spool, or dig coal, or build roads for thirty years of his life, there can be no talk of wealth. What he gives to the world is only gray and hideous things, reflecting a dull and hideous existence—too weak to live, too cowardly to die. Strange to say, there are people who extol this deadening method of centralized production as the proudest achievement of our age. They fail utterly to realize that if we are to continue in machine subserviency, our slavery is more complete than was our bondage to the king. They do not want to know that centralization is not only the death-knell of liberty, but also of health and beauty, of art and science, all these being impossible in a clock-like, mechanical atmosphere.

Anarchism cannot but repudiate such a method of production: its goal is the freest possible expression of all the latent powers of the individual. Oscar Wilde defines a perfect personality as 'one who develops under perfect conditions, who is not wounded, maimed, or in danger'. A perfect personality, then, is only possible in a state of society where man is free to choose the mode of work, the conditions of work, and the freedom to work. One to whom the making of a table, the building of a house, or the tilling of the soil, is what the painting is to the artist and the discovery to the scientist—the result of inspiration, of intense longing, and deep interest in work as a creative force. That being the ideal of anarchism, its economic arrangements must consist of voluntary productive and distributive associations, gradually developing into free communism, as the best means of producing with the least waste of human energy. Anarchism, however, also recognizes the right of the individual, or numbers of individuals, to arrange at all times for other forms of work, in harmony with their tastes and desires.

Such free display of human energy being possible only under complete individual and social freedom, anarchism directs its forces against the third and greatest foe of all social equality; namely, the State, organized authority, or statutory law—the dominion of human conduct.

Just as religion has fettered the human mind, and as property, or the monopoly of things, has subdued and stifled man's needs, so has the State enslaved his spirit, dictating every phase of conduct. 'All government in essence,' says Emerson, 'is tyranny.' It matters not whether it is government by divine right or majority rule. In every instance its aim is the absolute subordination of the individual.

Referring to the American government, the greatest American anarchist, David Thoreau, said: 'Government, what is it but a tradition, though a recent one, endeavoring to transmit itself unimpaired to posterity, but each instance losing its integrity; it has not the vitality and force of a single living man. Law never made man a whit more just; and by means of their respect for it, even the well disposed are daily made agents of injustice.'

Indeed, the keynote of government is injustice. With the arrogance and self-sufficiency of the king who could do no wrong, governments ordain, judge, condemn, and punish the most insignificant offenses, while maintaining themselves by the greatest of all offenses, the annihilation of individual liberty. Thus Ouida is right when she maintains that 'the State only aims at instilling those qualities in its public by which its demands are obeyed, and its exchequer is filled. Its highest attainment is the reduction of mankind to clockwork. In its atmosphere all those finer and more delicate liberties, which require treatment and spacious expansion, inevitably dry up and perish. The State requires a taxpaying machine in which there is no hitch, an exchequer in which there is never a deficit, and a public, monotonous, obedient, colorless, spiritless, moving humbly like a flock of sheep along a straight high road between two walls.'

Yet even a flock of sheep would resist the chicanery of the State, if it were not for the corruptive, tyrannical, and oppressive methods it employs to serve its purposes. Therefore Bakunin repudiates the State as synonymous with the surrender of the liberty of the individual or small minorities—the destruction of social relationship, the curtailment, or complete denial even, of life itself, for its own aggrandizement. The State is the altar of political freedom and, like the religious altar, it is maintained for the purpose of human sacrifice.

In fact, there is hardly a modern thinker who does not agree that government, organized authority, or the State, is necessary only to maintain or protect property and monopoly. It has proven efficient in that function only.

Even George Bernard Shaw, who hopes for the miraculous from the State under Fabianism, nevertheless admits that 'it is at present a huge machine for robbing and slave-driving of the poor by brute force.' This being the case, it is hard to see why the clever prefacer wishes to uphold the State after poverty shall have ceased to exist.

Unfortunately there are still a number of people who continue in the fatal belief that government rests on natural laws, that it maintains social order and harmony, that it diminishes crime, and that it prevents the lazy man from fleecing his fellows. I shall therefore examine these contentions.

A natural law is that factor in man which asserts itself freely and spontaneously without any external force, in harmony with the requirements of nature. For instance, the demand for nutrition, for sex gratification, for light, air, and exercise, is a natural law. But its expression needs not the machinery of government, needs not the club, the gun, the handcuff, or the prison. To obey such laws, if we may call it obedience, requires only spontaneity and free opportunity. That governments do not maintain themselves through such harmonious factors is proven by the terrible array of violence, force, and coercion all governments use in order to live. Thus Blackstone is right when he says, 'Human laws are invalid, because they are contrary to the laws of nature.'

Unless it be the order of Warsaw after the slaughter of thousands of people, it is difficult to ascribe to governments any capacity for order or social harmony. Order derived through submission and maintained by terror is not much of a safe guaranty; yet that is the only 'order' that governments have ever maintained. True social harmony grows naturally out of solidarity of interests. In a society where those who always work never have anything, while those who never work enjoy everything, solidarity of interests is non-existent; hence social harmony is but a myth. The only way organized authority meets this grave situation is by extending still greater privileges to those who have already monopolized the earth, and by still further enslaving the disinherited masses. Thus the entire arsenal of government—laws, police, soldiers, the courts, legislatures, prisons—is strenuously engaged in 'harmonizing' the most antagonistic elements in society.

The most absurd apology for authority and law is that they serve to diminish crime. Aside from the fact that the State is itself the greatest criminal, breaking every written and natural law, stealing in the form of taxes, killing in the form of war and capital punishment, it has come to an absolute standstill in coping with crime. It has failed utterly to destroy or even minimize the horrible scourge of its own creation.

Crime is naught but misdirected energy. So long as every institution of today, economic, political, social, and moral, conspires to misdirect human energy into wrong channels; so long as most people are out of place doing the things they hate to do, living a life they loathe to live, crime will be inevitable, and all the laws on the statutes can only increase, but never do away with, crime. What does society, as it exists today, know of the process of despair, the poverty, the horrors, the fearful struggle the human soul must pass on its way to crime and degradation. Who that knows this terrible process can fail to see the truth in these words of Peter Kropotkin:

'Those who will hold the balance between the benefits thus attributed to law and punishment and the degrading effect of the latter on humanity; those who will estimate the torrent of depravity poured abroad in human society by the informer, favored by the Judge even, and paid for in clinking cash by governments, under the pretext of aiding to unmask crime; those who will go within prison walls and there see what human beings become when deprived of liberty, when subjected to the care of brutal keepers, to coarse, cruel words, to a thousand stinging, piercing humiliations, will agree with us that the entire apparatus of prison and punishment is an abomination which ought to be brought to an end.'

The deterrent influence of law on the lazy man is too absurd to merit consideration. If society were only relieved of the waste and expense of keeping a lazy class, and the equally great expense of the paraphernalia of protection this lazy class requires, the social tables would contain an abundance for all, including even the occasional lazy individual. Besides, it is well to consider that laziness results either from special privileges, or physical and mental abnormalities. Our present insane system of production fosters both, and the most astounding phenomenon is that people should want to work at all now. Anarchism aims to strip labor of its deadening, dulling aspect, of its gloom and compulsion. It aims to make work an instrument of joy, of strength, of color, of real harmony, so that the poorest sort of a man should find in work both recreation and hope.

To achieve such an arrangement of life, government, with its unjust, arbitrary, repressive measures, must be done away with. At best it has but imposed one single mode of life upon all, without regard to individual and social variations and needs. In destroying government and statutory laws, anarchism proposes to rescue the self-respect and independence of the individual from all restraint and invasion by authority. Only in freedom can man grow to his full stature. Only in freedom will he learn to think and move, and give the very best in him. Only in freedom will he realize the true force of the social bonds which knit men together, and which are the true foundation of a normal social life.

But what about human nature? Can it be changed? And if not, will it endure under anarchism?

Poor human nature, what horrible crimes have been committed in thy name! Every fool, from king to policeman, from the flatheaded parson to the visionless dabbler in science, presumes to speak authoritatively of human nature. The greater the mental charlatan, the more definite his insistence on the wickedness and weaknesses of human nature. Yet, how can anyone speak of it today, with every soul in a prison, with every heart fettered, wounded, and maimed?

John Burroughs has stated that experimental study of animals in captivity is absolutely useless. Their character, their habits, their appetites undergo a complete transformation when torn from their soil in field and forest. With human nature caged in a narrow space, whipped daily into submission, how can we speak of its potentialities?

Freedom, expansion, opportunity, and, above all, peace and repose, alone can teach us the real dominant factors of human nature and all its wonderful possibilities.

Anarchism, then, really stands for the liberation of the human mind from the dominion of religion; the liberation of the human body from the dominion of property; liberation from the shackles and restraint of government. Anarchism stands for a social order based on the free grouping of individuals for the purpose of producing real social wealth; an order that will guarantee to every human being free access to the earth and full enjoyment of the necessities of life, according to individual desires, tastes, and inclinations.

This is not a wild fancy or an aberration of the mind. It is the conclusion arrived at by hosts of intellectual men and women the world over; a conclusion resulting from the close and studious observation of the tendencies of modern society: individual liberty and economic equality, the twin forces for the birth of what is fine and true in man.

As to methods. Anarchism is not, as some may suppose, a theory of the future to be realized through divine inspiration. It is a living force in the affairs of our life, constantly creating new conditions. The methods of anarchism therefore do not comprise an iron-clad program to be carried out under all circumstances. Methods must grow out of the economic needs of each place and clime, and of the intellectual and temperamental requirements of the individual. The serene, calm character of a Tolstoy will wish different methods for social reconstruction than the intense, overflowing personality of a Michael Bakunin or a Peter Kropotkin. Equally so it must be apparent that the economic and political needs of Russia will dictate more drastic measures than would England or America. Anarchism does not stand for military drill and uniformity; it does, however, stand for the spirit of revolt, in whatever form, against everything that hinders human growth. All anarchists agree in that, as they also agree in their opposition to the political machinery as a means of bringing about the great social change.

'All voting,' says Thoreau, 'is a sort of gaming, like checkers, or backgammon, a playing with right and wrong; its obligation never exceeds that of expediency. Even voting for the right thing is doing nothing for it. A wise man will not leave the right to the mercy of chance, nor wish it to prevail through the power of the majority.' A close examination of the machinery of politics and its achievements will bear out the logic of Thoreau.

What does the history of parliamentarism show? Nothing but failure and defeat, not even a single reform to ameliorate the economic and social stress of the people. Laws have been passed and enactments made for the improvement and protection of labor. Thus it was proven only last year that Illinois, with the most rigid laws for mine protection, had the greatest mine disasters. In States where child labor laws prevail, child exploitation is at its highest, and though with us the workers enjoy full political opportunities, capitalism has reached the most brazen zenith.

Even were the workers able to have their own representatives, for which our good socialist politicians are clamoring, what chances are there for their honesty and good faith? One has but to bear in mind the process of politics to realize that its path of good intentions is full of pitfalls: wire-pulling, intriguing, flattering, lying, cheating; in fact, chicanery of every description, whereby the political aspirant can achieve success. Added to that is a complete demoralization of character and conviction, until nothing is left that would make one hope for anything from such a human derelict. Time and time again the people were foolish enough to trust, believe, and support with their last farthing aspiring politicians, only to find themselves betrayed and cheated.

It may be claimed that men of integrity would not become corrupt in the political grinding mill. Perhaps not; but such men would be absolutely helpless to exert the slightest influence in behalf of labor, as indeed has been shown in numerous instances. The State is the economic master of its servants. Good men, if such there be, would either remain true to their political faith and lose their economic support, or they would cling to their economic master and be utterly unable to do the slightest good. The political arena leaves one no alternative, one must either be a dunce or a rogue.

The political superstition is still holding sway over the hearts and minds of the masses, but the true lovers of liberty will have no more to do with it. Instead, they believe with Stirner that man has as much liberty as he is willing to take. Anarchism therefore stands for direct action, the open defiance of, and resistance to, all laws and restrictions, economic, social, and moral. But defiance and resistance are illegal. Therein lies the salvation of man. Everything illegal necessitates integrity, self-reliance, and courage. In short, it calls for free, independent spirits, for 'men who are men, and who have a bone in their backs which you cannot pass your hand through'.

Universal suffrage itself owes its existence to direct action. If not for the spirit of rebellion, of the defiance on the part of the American revolutionary fathers, their posterity would still wear the King's coat. If not for the direct action of a John Brown and his comrades, America would still trade in the flesh of the black man. True, the trade in white flesh is still going on; but that, too, will have to be abolished by direct action. Trade-unionism, the economic arena of the modern gladiator, owes its existence to direct action. It is but recently that law and government have attempted to crush the trade-union movement, and condemned the exponents of man's right to organize to prison as conspirators. Had they sought to assert their cause through begging, pleading, and compromise, trade-unionism would today be a negligible quantity. In France, in Spain, in Italy, in Russia, nay even in England (witness the growing rebellion of English labor unions) direct, revolutionary, economic action has become so strong a force in the battle for industrial liberty as to make the world realize the tremendous importance of labor's power. The General Strike, the supreme expression of the economic consciousness of the workers, was ridiculed in America but a short time ago. Today every great strike, in order to win, must realize the importance of the solidaric general protest.

Direct action, having proven effective along economic lines, is equally potent in the environment of the individual. There a hundred forces encroach upon his being, and only persistent resistance to them will finally set him free. Direct action against the authority in the shop, direct action against the authority of the law, direct action against the invasive, meddlesome authority of our moral code, is the logical, consistent method of anarchism.

Will it not lead to a revolution? Indeed, it will. No real social change has ever come about without a revolution. People are either not familiar with their history, or they have not yet learned that revolution is but thought carried into action.

Anarchism, the great leaven of thought, is today permeating every phase of human endeavor. Science, art, literature, the drama, the effort for economic betterment, in fact every individual and social opposition to the existing disorder of things, is illumined by the spiritual light of Anarchism. It is the philosophy of the sovereignty of the individual. It is the theory of social harmony. It is the great, surging, living truth that is reconstructing the world, and that will usher in the Dawn.

MINORITIES VERSUS MAJORITIES

If I were to give a summary of the tendency of our times, I would say, quantity. The multitude, the mass spirit, dominates everywhere, destroying quality. Our entire life—production, politics, and education—rests on quantity, on numbers. The worker who once took pride in the thoroughness and quality of his work, has been replaced by brainless, incompetent automatons, who turn out enormous quantities of things, valueless to themselves, and generally injurious to the rest of mankind. Thus quantity, instead of adding to life's comforts and peace, has merely increased man's burden.

In politics, naught but quantity counts. In proportion to its increase, however, principles, ideals, justice and uprightness are completely swamped by the array of numbers. In the struggle for supremacy the various political parties outdo each other in trickery, deceit, cunning, and shady machinations, confident that the one who succeeds is sure to be hailed by the majority as the victor. That is the only god—success. As to what expense, what terrible cost to character, is of no moment. We have not far to go in search of proof to verify this sad fact.

Never before did the corruption, the complete rottenness of our government stand so thoroughly exposed; never before were the American people brought face to face with the Judas nature of that political body, which has claimed for years to be absolutely beyond reproach, as the mainstay of our institutions, the true protector of the rights and liberties of the people.

Yet when the crimes of that party became so brazen that even the blind could see them, it needed but to muster up its minions, and its supremacy was assured. Thus the very victims, duped, betrayed, outraged a hundred times, decided, not against, but in favor of the victor. Bewildered, the few asked how could the majority betray the traditions of American liberty? Where was its judgment, its reasoning capacity? That is just it, the majority cannot reason; it has no judgment. Lacking utterly in originality and moral courage, the majority has always placed its destiny in the hands of others. Incapable of standing responsibilities, it has followed its leaders even unto destruction. Dr Stockman was right: 'The most dangerous enemies of truth and justice in our midst are the compact majorities, the damned compact majority.' Without ambition or initiative, the compact mass hates nothing so much as innovation. It has always opposed, condemned, and hounded the innovator, the pioneer of a new truth.

The oft repeated slogan of our time is, among all politicians, the socialists included, that ours is an era of individualism, of the minority. Only those who do not probe beneath the surface might be led to entertain this view. Have not the few accumulated the wealth of the world? Are they not the masters, the absolute kings of the situation? Their success, however, is due not to individualism, but to the inertia, the cravenness, the utter submission of the mass. The latter wants but to be dominated, to be led, to be coerced. As to individualism, at no time in human history did it have less chance of expression, less opportunity to assert itself in a normal, healthy manner.

The individual educator imbued with honesty of purpose, the artist or writer of original ideas, the independent scientist or explorer, the non-compromising pioneers of social changes are daily pushed to the wall by men whose learning and creative ability have become decrepit with age.

Educators of Ferrer's type are nowhere tolerated, while the dietitians of predigested food, a la Professors Eliot and Butler, are the successful perpetuators of an age of nonentities, of automatons. In the literary and dramatic world, the Humphrey Wards and Clyde Fitches are the idols of the mass, while but few know or appreciate the beauty and genius of an Emerson, Thoreau, Whitman; an Ibsen, a Hauptmann, a Butler Yeats, or a Stephen Phillips. They are like solitary stars, far beyond the horizon of the multitude.

Publishers, theatrical managers, and critics ask not for the quality inherent in creative art, but will it meet with a good sale, will it suit the palate of the people? Alas, this palate is like a dumping ground; it relishes anything that needs no mental mastication. As a result, the mediocre, the ordinary, the commonplace represents the chief literary output.

Need I say that in art we are confronted with the same sad facts? One has but to inspect our parks and thoroughfares to realize the hideousness and vulgarity of the art manufacture. Certainly, none but a majority taste would tolerate such an outrage on art. False in conception and barbarous in execution, the statuary that infests American cities has as much relation to true art, as a totem to a Michaelangelo. Yet that is the only art that succeeds. The true artistic genius, who will not cater to accepted notions, who exercises originality, and strives to be true to life, leads an obscure and wretched existence. His work may some day become the fad of the mob, but not until his heart's blood had been exhausted; not until the pathfinder has ceased to be, and a throng of an idealless and visionless mob has done to death the heritage of the master.

It is said that the artist of today cannot create because Prometheus-like he is bound to the rock of economic necessity. This, however, is true of art in all ages. Michael Angelo was dependent on his patron saint, no less than the sculptor or painter of today, except that the art connoisseurs of those days were far away from the madding crowd. They felt honored to be permitted to worship at the shrine of the master.

The art protector of our time knows but one criterion, one value—the dollar. He is not concerned about the quality of any great work, but in the quantity of dollars his purchase implies. Thus the financier in Mirbeau's *Les Affaires Sont Les Affaires* points to some blurred arrangement in colors, saying 'See how great it is; it cost 50,000 francs.' Just like our own parvenues. The fabulous figures paid for their great art discoveries must make up for the poverty of their taste.

The most unpardonable sin in society is independence of thought. That this should be so terribly apparent in a country whose symbol is democracy, is very significant of the tremendous power of the majority.

Wendell Phillips said fifty years ago: 'In our country of absolute democratic equality, public opinion is not only omnipotent, it is omnipresent. There is no refuge from its tyranny, there is no hiding from its reach, and the result is that if you take the old Greek lantern and go about to seek among a hundred, you will not find a single American who has not, or who does not fancy at least he has, something to gain or lose in his ambition, his social life, or business, from the good opinion and the votes of those around him. And the consequence is that instead of being a mass of individuals, each one fearlessly blurting out his own conviction, as a nation compared to other nations we are a mass of cowards. More than any other people we are afraid of each other.' Evidently we have not advanced very far from the condition that confronted Wendell Phillips.

Today, as then, public opinion is the omnipresent tyrant; today, as then, the majority represents a mass of cowards, willing to accept him who mirrors its own soul and mind poverty. That accounts for the unprecedented rise of a man like Roosevelt. He embodies the very worst element of mob psychology. A politician, he knows that the majority cares little for ideals or integrity. What it craves is display. It matters not whether that be a dog show, a prize fight, the lynching of a 'nigger', the rounding up of some petty offender, the marriage exposition of an heiress, or the acrobatic stunts of an ex-president. The more hideous the mental contortions, the greater the delight and bravos of the mass. Thus, poor in ideals and vulgar of soul, Roosevelt continues to be the man of the hour.

On the other hand, men towering high above such political pygmies, men of refinement, of culture, of ability, are jeered into silence as mollycoddles. It is absurd to claim that ours is the era of individualism. Ours is merely a more poignant repetition of the phenomenon of all history: every effort for progress, for enlightenment, for science, for religious, political, and economic liberty, emanates from the minority, and not from the mass.

Today, as ever, the few are misunderstood, hounded, imprisoned, tortured, and killed.

The principle of brotherhood expounded by the agitator of Nazareth preserved the germ of life, of truth and justice, so long as it was the beacon light of the few. The moment the majority seized upon it, that great principle became a shibboleth and harbinger of blood and fire, spreading suffering and disaster. The attack on the omnipotence of Rome was like a sunrise amid the darkness of the night, only so long as it was made by the colossal figures of a Huss, a Calvin, or a Luther. Yet when the mass joined in the procession against the Catholic monster, it was no less cruel, no less bloodthirsty than its enemy. Woe to the heretics, to the minority, who would not bow to its dicta. After infinite zeal, endurance, and sacrifice, the human mind is at last free from the religious phantom; the minority has gone on in pursuit of new conquests, and the majority is lagging behind, handicapped by truth grown false with age.

Politically the human race would still be in the most absolute slavery, were it not for the John Balls, the Wat Tylers, the Tells, the innumerable individual giants who fought inch by inch against the power of kings and tyrants. But for individual pioneers the world would have never been shaken to its very roots by that tremendous wave, the French Revolution. Great events are usually preceded by apparently small things. Thus the eloquence and fire of Camille Desmoulins was like the trumpet before Jericho, razing to the ground that emblem of torture, of abuse, of horror, the Bastille.

Always, at every period, the few were the banner bearers of a great idea, of liberating effort. Not so the mass, the leaden weight of which does not let it move. The truth of this is borne out in Russia with greater force than elsewhere. Thousands of lives have already been consumed by that bloody regime, yet the monster on the throne is not appeased. How is such a thing possible when ideas, culture, literature, when the deepest and finest emotions groan under the iron yoke? The majority, that compact, immobile, drowsy mass, the Russian peasant, after a century of struggle, of sacrifice, of untold misery, still believes that the rope which strangles 'the man with the white hands' brings luck.

In the American struggle for liberty, the majority was no less of a stumbling block. Until this very day the ideas of Jefferson, of Patrick Henry, of Thomas Paine, are denied and sold by their posterity. The mass wants none of them. The greatness and courage worshipped in Lincoln have been forgotten in the men who created the background for the panorama of that time. The true patron saints of the black men were represented in that handful of fighters in Boston, Lloyd Garrison, Wendell Phillips, Thoreau, Margaret Fuller, and Theodore Parker, whose great courage and sturdiness culminated in that somber giant, John Brown. Their untiring zeal, their eloquence and perseverance undermined the stronghold of the Southern lords. Lincoln and his minions followed only when abolition had become a practical issue, recognized as such by all.

About fifty years ago, a meteor-like idea made its appearance on the social horizon of the world, an idea so far-reaching, so revolutionary, so all-embracing as to spread terror in the hearts of tyrants everywhere. On the other hand, that idea was a harbinger of joy, of cheer, of hope to the millions. The pioneers knew the difficulties in their way, they knew the opposition, the persecution, the hardships that would meet them, but proud and unafraid they started on their march onward, ever onward. Now that idea has become a popular slogan. Almost everyone is a socialist today: the rich man, as well as his poor victim; the upholders of law and authority, as well as their unfortunate culprits; the freethinker, as well as the perpetuator of religious falsehoods; the fashionable lady, as well as the shirtwaist girl. Why not? Now that the truth of fifty years ago has become a lie, now that it has been clipped of all its youthful imagination, and been robbed of its vigor, its strength, its revolutionary ideal—why not? Now that it is no longer a beautiful vision, but a 'practical, workable scheme', resting on the will of the majority, why not? With the same political cunning and shrewdness the mass is petted, pampered, cheated daily. Its praise is being sung in many keys: the poor majority, the outraged, the abused, the giant majority, if only it would follow us.

Who has not heard this litany before? Who does not know this never-varying refrain of all politicians? That the mass bleeds, that it is being robbed and exploited, I know as well as our vote-baiters. But I insist that not the handful of parasites, but the mass itself is responsible for this horrible state of affairs. It clings to its masters, loves the whip, and is the first to cry Crucify! the moment a protesting voice is raised against the sacredness of capitalistic authority or any other decayed institution. Yet how long would authority and private property exist, if not for the willingness of the mass to become soldiers, policemen, jailers, and hangmen. The socialist demagogues know that as well as I, but they maintain the myth of the virtues of the majority, because their very scheme of life means the perpetuation of power. And how could the latter be acquired without numbers? Yes, power, authority, coercion, and dependence rest on the mass, but never freedom, never the free unfoldment of the individual, never the birth of a free society.

Not because I do not feel with the oppressed, the disinherited of the earth; not because I do not know the shame, the horror, the indignity of the lives the people lead, do I repudiate the majority as a creative force for good. Oh, no, no! But because I know so well that as a compact mass it has never stood for justice or equality. It has suppressed the human voice, subdued the human spirit, chained the human body. As a mass its aim has always been to make life uniform, gray, and monotonous as the desert. As a mass it will always be the annihilator of individuality, of free initiative, of originality. I therefore believe with Emerson that 'the masses are crude, lame, pernicious in their demands and influence, and need not to be flattered, but to be schooled. I wish not to concede anything to them, but to drill, divide, and break them up, and draw individuals out of them. Masses! The calamity are the masses. I do not wish any mass at all, but honest men only, lovely, sweet, accomplished women only.'

In other words, the living, vital truth of social and economic well-being will become a reality only through the zeal, courage, the non-compromising determination of intelligent minorities, and not through the mass.

THE PSYCHOLOGY OF POLITICAL VIOLENCE

To analyze the psychology of political violence is not only extremely difficult, but also very dangerous. If such acts are treated with understanding, one is immediately accused of eulogizing them. If, on the other hand, human sympathy is expressed with the attentater, one risks being considered a possible accomplice. Yet it is only intelligence and sympathy that can bring us closer to the source of human suffering, and teach us the ultimate way out of it.

The primitive man, ignorant of natural forces, dreaded their approach, hiding from the perils they threatened. As man learned to understand Nature's phenomena, he realized that though these may destroy life and cause great loss, they also bring relief. To the earnest student it must be apparent that the accumulated forces in our social and economic life, culminating in a political act of violence, are similar to the terrors of the atmosphere, manifested in storm and lightning.

To thoroughly appreciate the truth of this view, one must feel intensely the indignity of our social wrongs; one's very being must throb with the pain, the sorrow, the despair millions of people are daily made to endure. Indeed, unless we have become a part of humanity, we cannot even faintly understand the just indignation that accumulates in a human soul, the burning, surging passion that makes the storm inevitable.

The ignorant mass looks upon the man who makes a violent protest against our social and economic iniquities as upon a wild beast, a cruel, heartless monster, whose joy it is to destroy life and bathe in blood; or at best, as upon an irresponsible lunatic. Yet nothing is further from the truth. As a matter of fact, those who have studied the character and personality of these men, or who have come in close contact with them, are agreed that it is their super-sensitiveness to the wrong and injustice surrounding them which compels them to pay the toll of our social crimes. The most noted writers and poets, discussing the psychology of political offenders, have paid them the highest tribute. Could anyone assume that these men had advised violence, or even approved of the acts? Certainly not. Theirs was the attitude of the social student, of the man who knows that beyond every violent act there is a vital cause.

Bjornstjerne Bjornson, in the second part of Beyond Human Power, emphasizes the fact that it is among the anarchists that we must look for the modern martyrs who pay for their faith with their blood, and who welcome death with a smile, because they believe, as truly as Christ did, that their martyrdom will redeem humanity.

Francois Coppee, the French novelist, thus expresses himself regarding the psychology of the attentater:

'The reading of the details of Vaillant's execution left me in a thoughtful mood. I imagined him expanding his chest under the ropes, marching with firm step, stiffening his will, concentrating all his energy, and, with eyes fixed upon the knife, hurling finally at society his cry of malediction. And, in spite of me, another spectacle rose suddenly before my mind. I saw a group of men and women pressing against each other in the middle of the oblong arena of the circus, under the gaze of thousands of eyes, while from all the steps of the immense amphitheatre went up the terrible cry, Ad Leones! And, below, the opening cages of the wild beasts.

'I did not believe the execution would take place. In the first place, no victim had been struck with death, and it had long been the custom not to punish an abortive crime with the last degree of severity. Then, this crime, however terrible in intention, was disinterested, born of an abstract idea. The man's past, his abandoned childhood, his life of hardship, pleaded also in his favor. In the independent press generous voices were raised in his behalf, very loud and eloquent. 'A purely literary current of opinion' some have said, with no little scorn. It is, on the contrary, an honor to the men of art and thought to have expressed once more their disgust at the scaffold.'

Again Zola, in *Germinal* and *Paris*, describes the tenderness and kindness, the deep sympathy with human suffering, of these men who close the chapter of their lives with a violent outbreak against our system.

Last, but not least, the man who probably better than anyone else understands the psychology of the attentater is M. Hamon, the author of the brilliant work, *Une Psychologie Du Militaire Professionel*, who has arrived at these suggestive conclusions:

'The positive method confirmed by the rational method enables us to establish an ideal type of anarchist, whose mentality is the aggregate of common psychic characteristics. Every anarchist partakes sufficiently of this ideal type to make it possible to differentiate him from other men. The typical anarchist, then, may be defined as follows: A man perceptible by the spirit of revolt under one or more of its forms—opposition, investigation, criticism, innovation—endowed with a strong love of liberty, egoistic or individualistic, and possessed of great curiosity, a keen desire to know. These traits are supplemented by an ardent love of others, a highly developed moral sensitiveness, a profound sentiment of justice, and imbued with missionary zeal.'

To the above characteristics, says Alvin F. Sanborn, must be added these sterling qualities: a rare love of animals, surpassing sweetness in all the ordinary relations of life, exceptional sobriety of demeanor, frugality and regularity, austerity, even, of living, and courage beyond compare.

'There is a truism that the man in the street seems always to forget, when he is abusing the anarchists, or whatever party happens to be his bete noire for the moment, as the cause of some outrage just perpetrated. This indisputable fact is that homicidal outrages have, from time immemorial, been the reply of goaded and desperate classes, and goaded and desperate individuals, to wrongs from their fellowmen, which they felt to be intolerable. Such acts are the violent recoil from violence, whether aggressive or repressive; they are the last desperate struggle of outraged and exasperated human nature for breathing space and life. And their cause lies not in any special conviction, but in the depths of that human nature itself. The whole course of history, political and social, is strewn with evidence of this fact. To go no further, take the three most notorious examples of political parties goaded into violence during the last fifty years: the Mazzinians in Italy, the Fenians in Ireland, and the Terrorists in Russia. Were these people anarchists? No. Did they all three even hold the same political opinions? No. The Mazzinians were Republicans, the Fenians political separatists, the Russians Social Democrats or Constitutionalists. But all were driven by desperate circumstances into this terrible form of revolt. And when we turn from parties to individuals who have acted in like manner, we stand appalled by the number of human beings goaded and driven by sheer desperation into conduct obviously violently opposed to their social instincts.

'Now that anarchism has become a living force in society, such deeds have been sometimes committed by anarchists, as well as by others. For no new faith, even the most essentially peaceable and humane the mind of man has yet accepted, but at its first coming has brought upon earth not peace, but a sword; not because of anything violent or anti-social in the doctrine itself; simply because of the ferment any new and creative idea excites in men's minds, whether they accept or reject it. And a conception of anarchism, which, on one hand, threatens every vested interest, and, on the other, holds out a vision of a free and noble life to be won by a struggle against existing wrongs, is certain to rouse the fiercest opposition, and bring the whole repressive force of ancient evil into violent contact with the tumultuous outburst of a new hope.

'Under miserable conditions of life, any vision of the possibility of better things makes the present misery more intolerable, and spurs those who suffer to the most energetic struggles to improve their lot, and if these struggles only immediately result in sharper misery, the outcome is sheer desperation. In our present society, for instance, an exploited wage worker, who catches a glimpse of what work and life might and ought to be, finds the toilsome routine and the squalor of his existence almost intolerable; and even when he has the resolution and courage to continue steadily working his best, and waiting until new ideas have so permeated society as to pave the way for better times, the mere fact that he has such ideas and tries to spread them, brings him into difficulties with his employers. How many thousands of socialists, and above all anarchists, have lost work and even the chance of work, solely on the ground of their opinions. It is only the specially gifted craftsman, who, if he be a zealous propagandist, can hope to retain permanent employment. And what happens to a man with his brain working actively with a ferment of new ideas, with a vision before his eyes of a new hope dawning for toiling and agonizing men, with the knowledge that his suffering and that of his fellows in misery is not caused by the cruelty of fate, but by the injustice of other human beings—what happens to such a man when he sees those dear to him starving, when he himself is starved? Some natures in such a plight, and those by no means the least social or the least sensitive, will become violent, and will even feel that their violence is social and not anti-social, that in striking when and how they can, they are striking, not for themselves, but for human nature, outraged and despoiled in their persons and in those of their fellow sufferers. And are we, who ourselves are not in this horrible predicament, to stand by and coldly condemn these piteous victims of the Furies and Fates? Are we to decry as miscreants these human beings who act with heroic self-devotion, sacrificing their lives in protest, where less social and less energetic natures would lie down and grovel in abject submission to injustice and wrong? Are we to join the ignorant and brutal outcry which stigmatizes such men as monsters of wickedness, gratuitously running amuck in a harmonious and innocently peaceful society? No! We hate murder with a hatred that may seem absurdly exaggerated to apologists for Matabele massacres, to callous acquiescers in hangings and bombardments, but we decline in such cases of homicide, or attempted homicide, as those of which we are treating, to be guilty of the cruel injustice of flinging the whole responsibility of the deed upon the immediate perpetrator. The guilt of these homicides lies upon every man and woman who, intentionally or by cold indifference, helps to keep up social conditions that drive human beings to despair. The man who flings his whole life into the attempt, at the cost of his own life, to protest against the wrongs of his fellow men, is a saint compared to the active and passive upholders of cruelty and injustice, even if his protest destroy other lives besides his own. Let him who is without sin in society cast the first stone at such an one.'

That every act of political violence should nowadays be attributed to anarchists is not at all surprising. Yet it is a fact known to almost everyone familiar with the anarchist movement that a great number of acts, for which anarchists had to suffer, either originated with the capitalist press or were instigated, if not directly perpetrated, by the police.

For a number of years acts of violence had been committed in Spain, for which the anarchists were held responsible, hounded like wild beasts, and thrown into prison. Later it was disclosed that the perpetrators of these acts were not anarchists, but members of the police department. The scandal became so widespread that the conservative Spanish papers demanded the apprehension and punishment of the gang-leader, Juan Rull, who was subsequently condemned to death and executed. The sensational evidence, brought to light during the trial, forced Police Inspector Momento to exonerate completely the anarchists from any connection with the acts committed during a long period. This resulted in the dismissal of a number of police officials, among them Inspector Tressols, who, in revenge, disclosed the fact that behind the gang of police bomb throwers were others of far higher position, who provided them with funds and protected them.

This is one of the many striking examples of how anarchist conspiracies are manufactured.

That the American police can perjure themselves with the same ease, that they are just as merciless, just as brutal and cunning as their European colleagues, has been proven on more than one occasion. We need only recall the tragedy of the eleventh of November, 1887, known as the Haymarket Riot.

No one who is at all familiar with the case can possibly doubt that the anarchists, judicially murdered in Chicago, died as victims of a lying, bloodthirsty press and of a cruel police conspiracy. Has not Judge Gary himself said: 'Not because you have caused the Haymarket bomb, but because you are anarchists, you are on trial.'

The impartial and thorough analysis by Governor Altgeld of that blotch on the American escutcheon verified the brutal frankness of Judge Gary. It was this that induced Altgeld to pardon the three anarchists, thereby earning the lasting esteem of every liberty loving man and woman in the world.

When we approach the tragedy of September sixth, 1901, we are confronted by one of the most striking examples of how little social theories are responsible for an act of political violence. 'Leon Czolgosz, an anarchist, incited to commit the act by Emma Goldman.' To be sure, has she not incited violence even before her birth, and will she not continue to do so beyond death? Everything is possible with the anarchists.

Today, even, nine years after the tragedy, after it was proven a hundred times that Emma Goldman had nothing to do with the event, that no evidence whatsoever exists to indicate that Czolgosz ever called himself an anarchist, we are confronted with the same lie, fabricated by the police and perpetuated by the press. No living soul ever heard Czolgosz make that statement, nor is there a single written word to prove that the boy ever breathed the accusation. Nothing but ignorance and insane hysteria, which have never yet been able to solve the simplest problem of cause and effect.

The President of a free Republic killed! What else can be the cause, except that the attentater must have been insane, or that he was incited to the act.

A free Republic! How a myth will maintain itself, how it will continue to deceive, to dupe, and blind even the comparatively intelligent to its monstrous absurdities. A free Republic! And yet within a little over thirty years a small band of parasites have successfully robbed the American people, and trampled upon the fundamental principles, laid down by the fathers of this country, guaranteeing to every man, woman, and child 'life, liberty, and the pursuit of happiness'. For thirty years they have been increasing their wealth and power at the expense of the vast mass of workers, thereby enlarging the army of the unemployed, the hungry, homeless, and friendless portion of humanity, who are tramping the country from east to west, from north to south, in a vain search for work. For many years the home has been left to the care of the little ones, while the parents are exhausting their life and strength for a mere pittance. For thirty years the sturdy sons of America have been sacrificed on the battlefield of industrial war, and the daughters outraged in corrupt factory surroundings. For long and weary years this process of undermining the nation's health, vigor, and pride, without much protest from the disinherited and oppressed, has been going on. Maddened by success and victory, the money powers of this 'free land of ours' became more and more audacious in their heartless, cruel efforts to compete with the rotten and decayed European tyrannies for supremacy of power.

In vain did a lying press repudiate Leon Czolgosz as a foreigner. The boy was a product of our own free American soil, that lulled him to sleep with,

My country, 'tis of thee, Sweet land of liberty.

Who can tell how many times this American child had gloried in the celebration of the Fourth of July, or of Decoration Day, when he faithfully honored the Nation's dead? Who knows but that he, too, was willing to 'fight for his country and die for her liberty', until it dawned upon him that those he belonged to have no country, because they have been robbed of all that they have produced; until he realized that the liberty and independence of his youthful dreams were but a farce. Poor Leon Czolgosz, your crime consisted of too sensitive a social consciousness. Unlike your idealless and brainless American brothers, your ideals soared above the belly and the bank account. No wonder you impressed the one human being among all the infuriated mob at your trial—a newspaper woman—as a visionary, totally oblivious to your surroundings. Your large, dreamy eyes must have beheld a new and glorious dawn.

Now, to a recent instance of police-manufactured anarchist plots. In that bloodstained city, Chicago, the life of Chief of Police Shippy was attempted by a young man named Averbuch. Immediately the cry was sent to the four corners of the world that Averbuch was an anarchist, and that anarchists were responsible for the act. Everyone who was at all known to entertain anarchist ideas was closely watched, a number of people arrested, the library of an anarchist group confiscated, and all meetings made impossible. It goes without saying that, as on various previous occasions, I must needs be held responsible for the act. Evidently the American police credit me with occult powers. I did not know Averbuch; in fact, had never before heard his name, and the only way I could have possibly 'conspired' with him was in my astral body. But, then, the police are not concerned with logic or justice. What they seek is a target, to mask their absolute ignorance of the cause, of the psychology of a political act. Was Averbuch an anarchist? There is no positive proof of it. He had been but three months in the country, did not know the language, and, as far as I could ascertain, was quite unknown to the anarchists of Chicago.

What led to his act? Averbuch, like most young Russian immigrants, undoubtedly believed in the mythical liberty of America. He received his first baptism by the policeman's club during the brutal dispersement of the unemployed parade. He further experienced American equality and opportunity in the vain efforts to find an economic master. In short, a three months' sojourn in the glorious land brought him face to face with the fact that the disinherited are in the same position the world over. In his native land he probably learned that necessity knows no law—there was no difference between a Russian and an American policeman.

The question to the intelligent social student is not whether the acts of Czolgosz or Averbuch were practical, any more than whether the thunderstorm is practical. The thing that will inevitably impress itself on the thinking and feeling man and woman is that the sight of brutal clubbing of innocent victims in a so-called free Republic, and the degrading, soul-destroying economic struggle, furnish the spark that kindles the dynamic force in the overwrought, outraged souls of men like Czolgosz or Averbuch. No amount of persecution, of hounding, of repression, can stay this social phenomenon.

But, it is often asked, have not acknowledged anarchists committed acts of violence? Certainly they have, always however ready to shoulder the responsibility. My contention is that they were impelled, not by the teachings of anarchism, but by the tremendous pressure of conditions, making life unbearable to their sensitive natures. Obviously, anarchism, or any other social theory, making man a conscious social unit, will act as a leaven for rebellion. This is not a mere assertion, but a fact verified by all experience. A close examination of the circumstances bearing upon this question will further clarify my position.

Let us consider some of the most important anarchist acts within the last two decades. Strange as it may seem, one of the most significant deeds of political violence occurred here in America, in connection with the Homestead strike of 1892.

During that memorable time the Carnegie Steel Company organized a conspiracy to crush the Amalgamated Association of Iron and Steel Workers. Henry Clay Frick, then Chairman of the Company, was intrusted with that democratic task. He lost no time in carrying out the policy of breaking the Union, the policy which he had so successfully practiced during his reign of terror in the coke regions. Secretly, and while peace negotiations were being purposely prolonged, Frick supervised the military preparations, the fortification of the Homestead Steel Works, the erection of a high board fence, capped with barbed wire and provided with loopholes for sharpshooters. And then, in the dead of night, he attempted to smuggle his army of hired Pinkerton thugs into Homestead, which act precipitated the terrible carnage of the steel workers. Not content with the death of eleven victims, killed in the Pinkerton skirmish, Henry Clay Frick, good Christian and free American, straightway began the hounding down of the helpless wives and orphans, by ordering them out of the wretched Company houses.

The whole country was aroused over these inhuman outrages. Hundreds of voices were raised in protest, calling on Frick to desist, not to go too far. Yes, hundreds of people protested—as one objects to annoying flies. Only one there was who actively responded to the outrage at Homestead—Alexander Berkman. Yes, he was an anarchist. He gloried in that fact, because it was the only force that made the discord between his spiritual longing and the world without at all bearable. Yet not anarchism, as such, but the brutal slaughter of the eleven steel workers was the urge for Alexander Berkman's act, his attempt on the life of Henry Clay Frick.

The record of European acts of political violence affords numerous and striking instances of the influence of environment upon sensitive human beings.

The court speech of Vaillant, who, in 1894, exploded a bomb in the Paris Chamber of Deputies, strikes the true keynote of the psychology of such acts:

'Gentlemen, in a few minutes you are to deal your blow, but in receiving your verdict I shall have at least the satisfaction of having wounded the existing society, that cursed society in which one may see a single man spending, uselessly, enough to feed thousands of families; an infamous society which permits a few individuals to monopolize all the social wealth, while there are hundreds of thousands of unfortunates who have not even the bread that is not refused to dogs, and while entire families are committing suicide for want of the necessities of life.

'Ah, gentlemen, if the governing classes could go down among the unfortunates! But no, they prefer to remain deaf to their appeals. It seems that a fatality impels them, like the royalty of the eighteenth century, toward the precipice which will engulf them, for woe be to those who remain deaf to the cries of the starving, woe to those who, believing themselves of superior essence, assume the right to exploit those beneath them! There comes a time when the people no longer reason; they rise like a hurricane, and pass away like a torrent. Then we see bleeding heads impaled on pikes.

'Among the exploited, gentlemen, there are two classes of individuals: Those of one class, not realizing what they are and what they might be, take life as it comes, believe that they are born to be slaves, and content themselves with the little that is given them in exchange for their labor. But there are others, on the contrary, who think, who study, and who, looking about them, discover social iniquities. Is it their fault if they see clearly and suffer at seeing others suffer? Then they throw themselves into the struggle, and make themselves the bearers of the popular claims.

'Gentlemen, I am one of these last. Wherever I have gone, I have seen unfortunates bent beneath the yoke of capital. Everywhere I have seen the same wounds causing tears of blood to flow, even in the remoter parts of the inhabited districts of South America, where I had the right to believe that he who was weary of the pains of civilization might rest in the shade of the palm trees and there study nature. Well, there even, more than elsewhere, I have seen capital come, like a vampire, to suck the last drop of blood of the unfortunate pariahs.

'Then I came back to France, where it was reserved for me to see my family suffer atrociously. This was the last drop in the cup of my sorrow. Tired of leading this life of suffering and cowardice,

I carried this bomb to those who are primarily responsible for social sufferings.

'I am reproached with the wounds of those who were hit by my projectiles. Permit me to point out in passing that, if the bourgeois had not massacred or caused massacres during the Revolution, it is probable that they would still be under the yoke of the nobility. On the other hand, figure up the dead and wounded on Tonquin, Madagascar, Dahomey, adding thereto the thousands, yes, millions of unfortunates who die in the factories, the mines, and wherever the grinding power of capital is felt. Add also those who die of hunger, and all this with the assent of our Deputies. Beside all this, of how little weight are the reproaches now brought against me!

'It is true that one does not efface the other; but, after all, are we not acting on the defensive when we respond to the blows which we receive from above? I know very well that I shall be told that I ought to have confined myself to speech for the vindication of the people's claims. But what can you expect! It takes a loud voice to make the deaf hear. Too long have they answered our voices by imprisonment, the rope, rifle volleys. Make no mistake; the explosion of my bomb is not only the cry of the rebel Vaillant, but the cry of an entire class which vindicates its rights, and which will soon add acts to words. For, be sure of it, in vain will they pass laws. The ideas of the thinkers will not halt; just as, in the last century, all the governmental forces could not prevent the Diderots and the Voltaires from spreading emancipating ideas among the people, so all the existing governmental forces will not prevent the Reclus, the Darwins, the Spencers, the Ibsens, the Mirbeaus, from spreading the ideas of justice and liberty which will annihilate the prejudices that hold the mass in ignorance. And these ideas, welcomed by the unfortunate, will flower in acts of revolt as they have done in me, until the day when the disappearance of authority shall permit all men to organize freely according to their choice, when we shall each be able to enjoy the product of his labor, and when those moral maladies called prejudices shall vanish, permitting human beings to live in harmony, having no other desire than to study the sciences and love their fellows.

'I conclude, gentlemen, by saying that a society in which one sees such social inequalities as we see all about us, in which we see every day suicides caused by poverty, prostitution flaring at every street corner—a society whose principal monuments are barracks and prisons—such a society must be transformed as soon as possible, on pain of being eliminated, and that speedily, from the human race. Hail to him who labors, by no matter what means, for this transformation! It is this idea that has guided me in my duel with authority, but as in this duel I have only wounded my adversary, it is now its turn to strike me.

'Now, gentlemen, to me it matters little what penalty you may inflict, for, looking at this assembly with the eyes of reason, I cannot help smiling to see you, atoms lost in matter, and reasoning only because you possess a prolongation of the spinal marrow, assume the right to judge one of your fellows.

'Ah! Gentlemen, how little a thing is your assembly and your verdict in the history of humanity; and human history, in its turn, is likewise a very little thing in the whirlwind which bears it through immensity, and which is destined to disappear, or at least to be transformed, in order to begin again the same history and the same facts, a veritably perpetual play of cosmic forces renewing and transferring themselves forever.'

Will anyone say that Vaillant was an ignorant, vicious man, or a lunatic? Was not his mind singularly clear, analytic? No wonder that the best intellectual forces of France spoke in his behalf, and signed the petition to President Carnot, asking him to commute Vaillant's death sentence.

Carnot would listen to no entreaty; he insisted on more than a pound of flesh, he wanted Vaillant's life, and then—the inevitable happened: President Carnot was killed. On the handle of the stiletto used by the attentater was engraved, significantly,

Vaillant!

Santa Caserio was an anarchist. He could have gotten away, saved himself; but he remained, he stood the consequences.

His reasons for the act are set forth in so simple, dignified, and childlike manner that one is reminded of the touching tribute paid Caserio by his teacher of the little village school, Ada Negri, the Italian poet, who spoke of him as a sweet, tender plant, of too fine and sensitive texture to stand the cruel strain of the world.

'Gentlemen of the Jury! I do not propose to make a defense, but only an explanation of my deed.

'Since my early youth I began to learn that present society is badly organized, so badly that every day many wretched men commit suicide, leaving women and children in the most terrible distress. Workers, by thousands, seek for work and cannot find it. Poor families beg for food and shiver with cold; they suffer the greatest misery; the little ones ask their miserable mothers for food, and the mothers cannot give them, because they have nothing. The few things which the home contained have already been sold or pawned. All they can do is beg alms; often they are arrested as vagabonds.

'I went away from my native place because I was frequently moved to tears at seeing little girls of eight or ten years obliged to work fifteen hours a day for the paltry pay of twenty centimes. Young women of eighteen or twenty also work fifteen hours daily, for a mockery of remuneration. And that happens not only to my fellow countrymen, but to all the workers, who sweat the whole day long for a crust of bread, while their labor produces wealth in abundance. The workers are obliged to live under the most wretched conditions, and their food consists of a little bread, a few spoonfuls of rice, and water; so by the time they are thirty or forty years old, they are exhausted, and go to die in the hospitals. Besides, in consequence of bad food and overwork, these unhappy creatures are, by hundreds, devoured by pellagra—a disease that, in my country, attacks, as the physicians say, those who are badly fed and lead a life of toil and privation.

'I have observed that there are a great many people who are

hungry, and many children who suffer, whilst bread and clothes abound in the towns. I saw many and large shops full of clothing and woolen stuffs, and I also saw warehouses full of wheat and Indian corn, suitable for those who are in want. And, on the other hand, I saw thousands of people who do not work, who produce nothing and live on the labor of others; who spend every day thousands of francs for their amusement; who debauch the daughters of the workers; who own dwellings of forty or fifty rooms; twenty or thirty horses, many servants; in a word, all the pleasures of life.

'I believed in God; but when I saw so great an inequality between men, I acknowledged that it was not God who created man, but man who created God. And I discovered that those who want their property to be respected, have an interest in preaching the existence of paradise and hell, and in keeping the people in ignorance.

'Not long ago, Vaillant threw a bomb in the Chamber of Deputies, to protest against the present system of society. He killed no one, only wounded some persons; yet bourgeois justice sentenced him to death. And not satisfied with the condemnation of the guilty man, they began to pursue the anarchists, and arrest not only those who had known Vaillant, but even those who had merely been present at any anarchist lecture.

'The government did not think of their wives and children. It did not consider that the men kept in prison were not the only ones who suffered, and that their little ones cried for bread. Bourgeois justice did not trouble itself about these innocent ones, who do not yet know what society is. It is no fault of theirs that their fathers are in prison; they only want to eat.

'The government went on searching private houses, opening private letters, forbidding lectures and meetings, and practicing the most infamous oppressions against us. Even now, hundreds of anarchists are arrested for having written an article in a newspaper, or for having expressed an opinion in public.

'Gentlemen of the Jury, you are representatives of bourgeois society. If you want my head, take it; but do not believe that in so doing you will stop the anarchist propaganda. Take care, for men reap what they have sown.'

During a religious procession in 1896, at Barcelona, a bomb was thrown. Immediately three hundred men and women were arrested. Some were anarchists, but the majority were trade unionists and socialists. They were thrown into that terrible bastille, Montjuich, and subjected to most horrible tortures. After a number had been killed, or had gone insane, their cases were taken up by the liberal press of Europe, resulting in the release of a few survivors.

The man primarily responsible for this revival of the Inquisition was Canovas del Castillo, Prime Minister of Spain. It was he who ordered the torturing of the victims, their flesh burned, their bones crushed, their tongues cut out. Practiced in the art of brutality during his regime in Cuba, Canovas remained absolutely deaf to the appeals and protests of the awakened civilized conscience.

In 1897 Canovas del Castillo was shot to death by a young Italian, Angiolillo. The latter was an editor in his native land, and his bold utterances soon attracted the attention of the authorities. Persecution began, and Angiolillo fled from Italy to Spain, thence to France and Belgium, finally settling in England. While there he found employment as a compositor, and immediately became the friend of all his colleagues. One of the latter thus described Angiolillo: 'His appearance suggested the journalist rather than the disciple of Guttenberg. His delicate hands, moreover, betrayed the fact that he had not grown up at the "case". With his handsome frank face, his soft dark hair, his alert expression, he looked the very type of the vivacious Southerner. Angiolillo spoke Italian, Spanish, and French, but no English; the little French I knew was not sufficient to carry on a prolonged conversation. However, Angiolillo soon began to acquire the English idiom; he learned rapidly, playfully, and it was not long until he became very popular with his fellow compositors. His distinguished and yet modest manner, and his consideration towards his colleagues, won him the hearts of all the boys.'

Angiolillo soon became familiar with the detailed accounts in the press. He read of the great wave of human sympathy with the helpless victims at Montjuich. On Trafalgar Square he saw with his own eyes the results of those atrocities, when the few Spaniards, who escaped Castillo's clutches, came to seek asylum in England. There, at the great meeting, these men opened their shirts and showed the horrible scars of burned flesh. Angiolillo saw, and the effect surpassed a thousand theories; the impetus was beyond words, beyond arguments, beyond himself even.

Senor Antonio Canovas del Castillo, Prime Minister of Spain, sojourned at Santa Agueda. As usual in such cases, all strangers were kept away from his exalted presence. One exception was made, however, in the case of a distinguished looking, elegantly dressed Italian—the representative, it was understood, of an important journal. The distinguished gentleman was—Angiolillo.

Senor Canovas, about to leave his house, stepped on the veranda. Suddenly Angiolillo confronted him. A shot rang out, and Canovas was a corpse.

The wife of the prime minister rushed upon the scene. 'Murderer! Murderer!' she cried, pointing at Angiolillo. The latter bowed. 'Pardon, Madame,' he said, 'I respect you as a lady, but I regret that you were the wife of that man.'

Calmly Angiolillo faced death. Death in its most terrible form—for the man whose soul was as a child's.

He was garroted. His body lay, sun-kissed, till the day hid in twilight. And the people came, and pointing the finger of terror and fear, they said: 'There—the criminal—the cruel murderer.'

How stupid, how cruel is ignorance! It misunderstands always, condemns always.

A remarkable parallel to the case of Angiolillo is to be found in the act of Gaetano Bresci, whose attentat upon King Umberto made an American city famous.

Bresci came to this country, this land of opportunity, where one has but to try to meet with golden success. Yes, he too would try to succeed. He would work hard and faithfully. Work had no terrors for him, if it would only help him to independence, manhood, self-respect.

Thus full of hope and enthusiasm he settled in Paterson, New Jersey, and there found a lucrative job at six dollars per week in one of the weaving mills of the town. Six whole dollars per week was, no doubt, a fortune for Italy, but not enough to breathe on in the new country. He loved his little home. He was a good husband and devoted father to his bambina, Bianca, whom he adored. He worked and worked for a number of years. He actually managed to save one hundred dollars out of his six dollars per week.

Bresci had an ideal. Foolish, I know, for a workingman to have an ideal—the anarchist paper published in Paterson, La Questione Sociale.

Every week, though tired from work, he would help to set up the paper. Until later hours he would assist, and when the little pioneer had exhausted all resources and his comrades were in despair, Bresci brought cheer and hope, one hundred dollars, the entire savings of years. That would keep the paper afloat.

In his native land people were starving. The crops had been poor, and the peasants saw themselves face to face with famine. They appealed to their good King Umberto; he would help. And he did. The wives of the peasants who had gone to the palace of the king, held up in mute silence their emaciated infants. Surely that would move him. And then the soldiers fired and killed those poor fools.

Bresci, at work in the weaving mill at Paterson, read of the horrible massacre. His mental eye beheld the defenceless women and innocent infants of his native land, slaughtered right before the good king. His soul recoiled in horror. At night he heard the groans of the wounded. Some may have been his comrades, his own flesh. Why, why these foul murders?

The little meeting of the Italian anarchist group in Paterson ended almost in a fight. Bresci had demanded his hundred dollars. His comrades begged, implored him to give them a respite. The paper would go down if they were to return him his loan. But Bresci insisted on its return.

How cruel and stupid is ignorance. Bresci got the money, but lost the good will, the confidence of his comrades. They would have nothing more to do with one whose greed was greater than his ideals.

On the twenty-ninth of July, 1900, King Umberto was shot at Monzo. The young Italian weaver of Paterson, Gaetano Bresci, had taken the life of the good king.

Paterson was placed under police surveillance, everyone known as an anarchist hounded and persecuted, and the act of Bresci ascribed to the teachings of anarchism. As if the teachings of anarchism in its extremest form could equal the force of those slain women and infants, who had pilgrimed to the king for aid. As if any spoken word, ever so eloquent, could burn into a human soul with such white heat as the life blood trickling drop by drop from those dying forms. The ordinary man is rarely moved either by word or deed; and those whose social kinship is the greatest living force need no appeal to respond—even as does steel to the magnet—to the wrongs and horrors of society.

If a social theory is a strong factor inducing acts of political violence, how are we to account for the recent violent outbreaks in India, where anarchism has hardly been born. More than any other old philosophy, Hindu teachings have exalted passive resistance, the drifting of life, the Nirvana, as the highest spiritual ideal. Yet the social unrest in India is daily growing, and has only recently resulted in an act of political violence, the killing of Sir Curzon Wyllie by the Hindu, Madar Sol Dhingra.

If such a phenomenon can occur in a country socially and individually permeated for centuries with the spirit of passivity, can one question the tremendous, revolutionizing effect on human character exerted by great social iniquities? Can one doubt the logic, the justice of these words:

'Repression, tyranny, and indiscriminate punishment of innocent men have been the watchwords of the government of the alien domination in India ever since we began the commercial boycott of English goods. The tiger qualities of the British are much in evidence now in India. They think that by the strength of the sword they will keep down India! It is this arrogance that has brought about the bomb, and the more they tyrannize over a helpless and unarmed people, the more terrorism will grow. We may deprecate terrorism as outlandish and foreign to our culture, but it is inevitable as long as this tyranny continues, for it is not the terrorists that are to be blamed, but the tyrants who are responsible for it. It is the only resource for a helpless and unarmed people when brought to the verge of despair. It is never criminal on their part. The crime lies with the tyrant.'

Even conservative scientists are beginning to realize that heredity is not the sole factor moulding human character. Climate, food, occupation; nay, color, light, and sound must be considered in the study of human psychology.

If that be true, how much more correct is the contention that great social abuses will and must influence different minds and temperaments in a different way. And how utterly fallacious the stereotyped notion that the teachings of anarchism, or certain exponents of these teachings, are responsible for the acts of political violence.

Anarchism, more than any other social theory, values human life above things. All anarchists agree with Tolstoy in this fundamental truth: if the production of any commodity necessitates the sacrifice of human life, society should do without that commodity, but it cannot do without that life. That, however, nowise indicates that anarchism teaches submission. How can it, when it knows that all suffering, all misery, all ills, result from the evil of submission?

Has not some American ancestor said, many years ago, that resistance to tyranny is obedience to God? And he was not an anarchist even. I would say that resistance to tyranny is man's highest ideal. So long as tyranny exists, in whatever form, man's deepest aspiration must resist it as inevitably as man must breathe.

Compared with the wholesale violence of capital and government, political acts of violence are but a drop in the ocean. That so few resist is the strongest proof how terrible must be the conflict between their souls and unbearable social iniquities.

High strung, like a violin string, they weep and moan for life, so relentless, so cruel, so terribly inhuman. In a desperate moment the string breaks. Untuned ears hear nothing but discord. But those who feel the agonized cry understand its harmony; they hear in it the fulfillment of the most compelling moment of human nature.

Such is the psychology of political violence.

NIAGARA FALLS

RUPERT BROOKE

Samuel Butler has a lot to answer for. But for him, a modern traveler could spend his time peacefully admiring the scenery instead of feeling himself bound to dog the simple and grotesque of the world for the sake of their too-human comments. It is his fault if a peasant's naïveté has come to outweigh the beauty of rivers, and the remarks of clergymen are more than mountains. It is very restful to give up all effort at observing human nature and drawing social and political deductions from trifles, and to let oneself relapse into wide-mouthed worship of the wonders of nature. And this is very easy at Niagara. Niagara means nothing. It is not leading anywhere. It does not result from anything. It throws no light on the effects of Protection, nor on the Facility for Divorce in America, nor on Corruption in Public Life, nor on Canadian character, nor even on the Navy Bill. It is merely a great deal of water falling over some cliffs. But it is very remarkably that. The human race, apt as a child to destroy what it admires, has done its best to surround the Falls with every distraction, incongruity, and vulgarity. Hotels, powerhouses, bridges, trams, picture post-cards, sham legends, stalls, booths, rifle-galleries, and side-shows frame them about. And there are Touts. Niagara is the central home and breeding-place for all the touts of earth. There are touts insinuating, and touts raucous, greasy touts, brazen touts, and upper-class, refined, gentlemanly, take-you-by-the-arm touts; touts who intimidate and touts who wheedle; professionals, amateurs, and dilettanti, male and female; touts who would photograph you with your arm round a young lady against a faked background of the sublimest cataract, touts who would bully you into cars, char-à-bancs, elevators, or tunnels, or deceive you into a carriage and pair, touts who would sell you picture post-cards, moccasins, sham Indian beadwork, blankets, tee-pees, and crockery, and touts, finally, who have no apparent object in the world, but just purely, simply, merely, incessantly, indefatigably, and ineffugibly to tout. And in the midst of all this, overwhelming it all, are the Falls. He who sees them instantly forgets humanity. They are not very high, but they are overpowering. They are divided by an island into two parts, the Canadian and the American.

Half a mile or so above the Falls, on either side, the water of the great stream begins to run more swiftly and in confusion. It descends with ever-growing speed. It begins chattering and leaping, breaking into a thousand ripples, throwing up joyful fingers of spray. Sometimes it is divided by islands and rocks, sometimes the eye can see nothing but a waste of laughing, springing, foamy waves, turning, crossing, even seeming to stand for an instant erect, but always borne impetuously forward like a crowd of triumphant feasters. Sit close down by it, and you see a fragment of the torrent against the sky, mottled, steely, and foaming, leaping onward in far-flung criss-cross strands of water. Perpetually the eye is on the point of descrying a pattern in this weaving, and perpetually it is cheated by change. In one place part of the flood plunges over a ledge a few feet high and a quarter of a mile or so long, in a uniform and stable curve. It gives an impression of almost military concerted movement, grown suddenly out of confusion. But it is swiftly lost again in the multitudinous tossing merriment. Here and there a rock close to the surface is marked by a white wave that faces backwards and seems to be rushing madly up-stream, but is really stationary in the headlong charge. But for these signs of reluctance, the waters seem to fling themselves on with some foreknowledge of their fate, in an ever wilder frenzy. But it is no Maeterlinckian prescience. They prove, rather, that Greek belief that the great crashes are preceded by a louder merriment and a wilder gaiety. Leaping in the sunlight, careless, entwining, clamorously joyful, the waves riot on towards the verge.

But there they change. As they turn to the sheer descent, the white and blue and slate color, in the heart of the Canadian Falls at least, blend and deepen to a rich, wonderful, luminous green. On the edge of disaster the river seems to gather herself, to pause, to lift a head noble in ruin, and then, with a slow grandeur, to plunge into the eternal thunder and white chaos below. Where the stream runs shallower it is a kind of violet color, but both violet and green fray and frill to white as they fall. The mass of water, striking some ever-hidden base of rock, leaps up the whole two hundred feet again in pinnacles and domes of spray. The spray falls back into the lower river once more; all but a little that fines to foam and white mist, which drifts in layers along the air, graining it, and wanders out on the wind over the trees and gardens and houses, and so vanishes.

The manager of one of the great power-stations on the banks of the river above the Falls told me that the center of the riverbed at the Canadian Falls is deep and of a saucer shape. So it may be possible to fill this up to a uniform depth, and divert a lot of water for the power-houses. And this, he said, would supply the need for more power, which will certainly soon arise, without taking away from the beauty of Niagara. This is a handsome concession of the utilitarians to ordinary sight-seers. Yet, I doubt if we shall be satisfied. The real secret of the beauty and terror of the Falls is not their height or width, but the feeling of colossal power and of unintelligible disaster caused by the plunge of that vast body of water. If that were taken away, there would be little visible change, but the heart would be gone.

The American Falls do not inspire this feeling in the same way as the Canadian. It is because they are less in volume, and because the water does not fall so much into one place. By comparison their beauty is almost delicate and fragile. They are extraordinarily level, one long curtain of lacework and woven foam. Seen from opposite, when the sun is on them, they are blindingly white, and the clouds of spray show dark against them. With both Falls the color of the water is the ever-altering wonder. Greens and blues, purples and whites, melt into one another, fade, and come again, and change with the changing sun. Sometimes they are as richly diaphanous as a precious stone, and glow from within with a deep, inexplicable light. Sometimes the white intricacies of dropping foam become opaque and creamy. And always there are the rainbows. If you come suddenly upon the Falls from above, a great double rainbow, very vivid, spanning the extent of spray from top to bottom, is the first thing you see. If you wander along the cliff opposite, a bow springs into being in the American Falls, accompanies you courteously on your walk, dwindles and dies as the mist ends, and awakens again as you reach the Canadian tumult. And the bold traveler who attempts the trip under the American Falls sees, when he dare open his eyes to anything, tiny baby rainbows, some four or five yards in span, leaping from rock to rock among the foam, and gamboling beside him, barely out of hand's reach, as he goes. One I saw in that place was a complete circle, such as I have never seen before, and so near that I could put my foot on it. It is a terrifying journey, beneath and behind the Falls. The senses are battered and bewildered by the thunder of the water and the assault of wind and spray; or rather, the sound is not of falling water, but merely of falling; a noise of unspecified ruin. So, if you are close behind the endless clamor, the sight cannot recognize liquid in the masses that hurl past. You are dimly and pitifully aware that sheets of light and darkness are falling in great curves in front of you. Dull omnipresent foam washes the face. Farther away, in the roar and hissing, clouds of spray seem literally to slide down some invisible plane of air.

 Beyond the foot of the Falls the river is like a slipping floor of marble, green with veins of dirty white, made by the scum that was foam. It slides very quietly and slowly down for a mile or two, sullenly exhausted. Then it turns to a dull sage green, and hurries more swiftly, smooth and ominous. As the walls of the ravine close in, trouble stirs, and the waters boil and eddy. These are the lower rapids, a sight more terrifying than the Falls, because less intelligible. Close in its bands of rock the river surges tumultuously forward, writhing and leaping as if inspired by a demon. It is pressed by the straits into a visibly convex form. Great planes of water slide past. Sometimes it is thrown up into a pinnacle of foam higher than a house, or leaps with incredible speed from the crest of one vast wave to another, along the shining curve between, like the spring of a wild beast. Its motion continually suggests muscular action. The power manifest in these rapids moves one with a different sense of awe and terror from that of the Falls. Here the inhuman life and strength are spontaneous, active, almost resolute; masculine vigor compared with the passive gigantic power, female, helpless and overwhelming, of the Falls. A place of fear.

One is drawn back, strangely, to a contemplation of the Falls, at every hour, and especially by night, when the cloud of spray becomes an immense visible ghost, straining and wavering high above the river, white and pathetic and translucent. The Victorian lies very close below the surface in every man. There one can sit and let great cloudy thoughts of destiny and the passage of empires drift through the mind; for such dreams are at home by Niagara. I could not get out of my mind the thought of a friend, who said that the rainbows over the Falls were like the arts and beauty and goodness, with regard to the stream of life—caused by it, thrown upon its spray, but unable to stay or direct or affect it, and ceasing when it ceased. In all comparisons that rise in the heart, the river, with its multitudinous waves and its single current, likens itself to a life, whether of an individual or of a community. A man's life is of many flashing moments, and yet one stream; a nation's flows through all its citizens, and yet is more than they. In such places, one is aware, with an almost insupportable and yet comforting certitude, that both men and nations are hurried onwards to their ruin or ending as inevitably as this dark flood. Some go down to it unreluctant, and meet it, like the river, not without nobility. And as incessant, as inevitable, and as unavailing as the spray that hangs over the Falls, is the white cloud of human crying... With some such thoughts does the platitudinous heart win from the confusion and thunder of a Niagara peace that the quietest plains or most stable hills can never give.

THE ALMOST PERFECT STATE

DON MARQUIS

I

No matter how nearly perfect an Almost Perfect State may be, it is not nearly enough perfect unless the individuals who compose it can, somewhere between death and birth, have a perfectly corking time for a few years. The most wonderful governmental system in the world does not attract us, as a system; we are after a system that scarcely knows it is a system; the great thing is to have the largest number of individuals as happy as may be, for a little while at least, some time before they die.

Infancy is not what it is cracked up to be. The child seems happy all the time to the adult, because the adult knows that the child is untouched by the real problems of life; if the adult were similarly untouched he is sure that he would be happy. But children, not knowing that they are having an easy time, have a good many hard times. Growing and learning and obeying the rules of their elders, or fighting against them, are not easy things to do. Adolescence is certainly far from a uniformly pleasant period. Early manhood might be the most glorious time of all were it not that the sheer excess of life and vigor gets a fellow into continual scrapes. Of middle age the best that can be said is that a middle aged person has likely learned how to have a little fun in spite of his troubles.

It is to old age that we look for reimbursement, the most of us. And most of us look in vain. For the most of us have been wrenched and racked, in one way or another, until old age is the most trying time of all.

In the Almost Perfect State every person shall have at least ten years before he dies of easy, carefree, happy living...things will be so arranged economically that this will be possible for each individual.

Personally we look forward to an old age of dissipation and indolence and unreverend disrepute. In fifty years we shall be ninety-two years old. We intend to work rather hard during those fifty years and accumulate enough to live on without working any more for the next ten years, for we have determined to die at the age of one hundred and two.

During the last ten years we shall indulge ourself in many things that we have been forced by circumstances to forego. We have always been compelled, and we shall be compelled for many years to come, to be prudent, cautious, staid, sober, conservative, industrious, respectful of established institutions, a model citizen. We have not liked it, but we have been unable to escape it. Our mind, our logical faculties, our observation, inform us that the conservatives have the right side of the argument in all human affairs. But the people whom we really prefer as associates, though we do not approve their ideas, are the rebels, the radicals, the wastrels, the vicious, the poets, the Bolshevists, the idealists, the nuts, the Lucifers, the agreeable good-for-nothings, the sentimentalists, the prophets, the freaks. We have never dared to know any of them, far less become intimate with them.

Between the years of ninety-two and a hundred and two, however, we shall be the ribald, useless, drunken outcast person we have always wished to be. We shall have a long white beard and long white hair; we shall not walk at all, but recline in a wheel chair and bellow for alcoholic beverages; in the winter we shall sit before the fire with our feet in a bucket of hot water, with a decanter of corn whiskey near at hand, and write ribald songs against organized society; strapped to one arm of our chair will be a forty-five caliber revolver, and we shall shoot out the lights when we want to go to sleep, instead of turning them off; when we want air we shall throw a silver candlestick through the front window and be damned to it; we shall address public meetings to which we have been invited because of our wisdom in a vein of jocund malice. We shall...but we don't wish to make any one envious of the good time that is coming to us...we look forward to a disreputable, vigorous, unhonored and disorderly old age.

(In the meantime, of course, you understand, you can't have us pinched and deported for our yearnings.)

We shall know that the Almost Perfect State is here when the kind of old age each person wants is possible to him. Of course, all of you may not want the kind we want...some of you may prefer prunes and morality to the bitter end. Some of you may be dissolute now and may look forward to becoming like one of the nice old fellows in a Wordsworth poem. But for our part we have always been a hypocrite and we shall have to continue being a hypocrite for a good many years yet, and we yearn to come out in our true colors at last. The point is, that no matter what you want to be, during those last ten years, that you may be, in the Almost Perfect State.

Any system of government under which the individual does all the sacrificing for the sake of the general good, for the sake of the community, the State, gets off on its wrong foot. We don't want things that cost us too much. We don't want too much strain all the time.

The best good that you can possibly achieve is not good enough if you have to strain yourself all the time to reach it. A thing is only worth doing, and doing again and again, if you can do it rather easily, and get some joy out of it.

Do the best you can, without straining yourself too much and too continuously, and leave the rest to God. If you strain yourself too much you'll have to ask God to patch you up. And for all you know, patching you up may take time that it was planned to use some other way.

BUT...overstrain yourself now and then. For this reason: The things you create easily and joyously will not continue to come easily and joyously unless you yourself are getting bigger all the time. And when you overstrain yourself you are assisting in the creation of a new self—if you get what we mean. And if you should ask us suddenly just what this has to do with the picture of the old guy in the wheel chair we should answer: Hanged if we know, but we seemed to sort o' run into it, somehow.

II

Interplanetary communication is one of the persistent dreams of the inhabitants of this oblate spheroid on which we move, breathe and suffer for lack of beer. There seems to be a feeling in many quarters that if we could get speech with the Martians, let us say, we might learn from them something to our advantage. There is a disposition to concede the superiority of the fellows Out There... just as some Americans capitulate without a struggle to poets from England, rugs from Constantinople, song and sausage from Germany, religious enthusiasts from Hindustan and cheese from Switzerland, although they have not tested the goods offered and really lack the discrimination to determine their quality. Almost the only foreign importations that were ever sneezed at in this country were Swedish matches and Spanish influenza.

But are the Martians...if Martians there be...any more capable than the persons dwelling between the Woolworth Building and the Golden Horn, between Shwe Dagon and the First Church, Scientist, in Boston, Mass.? Perhaps the Martians yearn toward earth, romantically, poetically, the Romeos swearing by its light to the Juliets; the idealists and philosophers fabling that already there exists upon it an *almost perfect state*—and now and then a wan prophet lifting his heart to its gleams, as a cup to be filled from Heaven with fresh waters of hope and courage. For this earth, it is also a star.

We know they are wrong about us, the lovers in the far stars, the philosophers, poets, the prophets...or are they wrong?

They are both right and wrong, as we are probably both right and wrong about them. If we tumbled into Mars or Arcturus or Sirius this evening we should find the people there discussing the shimmy, the jazz, the inconstancy of cooks and the iniquity of retail butchers, no doubt...and they would be equally disappointed by the way we flitter, frivol, flutter and flivver.

And yet, that other thing would be there too...that thing that made them look at our star as a symbol of grace and beauty.

Men could not think of the *almost perfect state* if they did not have it in them ultimately to create the *almost perfect state*.

We used sometimes to walk over the Brooklyn Bridge, that song in stone and steel of an engineer who was also a great artist, at dusk, when the tides of shadow flood in from the lower bay to break in a surf of glory and mystery and illusion against the tall towers of Manhattan. Seen from the middle arch of the bridge at twilight, New York with its girdle of shifting waters and its drift of purple cloud and its quick pulsations of unstable light is a miracle of splendor and beauty that lights up the heart like the laughter of a god.

But, descend. Go down into the city. Mingle with the details. The dirty old shed from which the 'L' trains and trolleys put out with their jammed and mangled thousands for flattest Flatbush and the unknown bourne of ulterior Brooklyn is still the same dirty old shed; on a hot, damp night the pasty streets stink like a paperhanger's overalls; you are trodden and over-ridden by greasy little profiteers and their hopping victims; you are encompassed round about by the ugly and the sordid, and the objectionable is exuded upon you from a myriad candid pores; your elation and your illusion vanish like ingenuous snowflakes that have kissed a hot dog sandwich on its fiery brow, and you say: 'Beauty? Aw, h—l! What's the use?'

And yet you have seen beauty. And beauty that was created by these people and people like these... You have seen the tall towers of Manhattan, wonderful under the stars. How did it come about that such growths came from such soil—that a breed lawless and sordid and prosaic has written such a mighty hieroglyphic against the sky? This glamor out of a pigsty...how come? How is it that this hideous, half-brute city is also beautiful and a fit habitation for demi-gods? How come?

It comes about because the wise and subtle deities permit

nothing worthy to be lost. It was with no thought of beauty that the builders labored; no conscious thought; they were masters or slaves in the bitter wars of commerce, and they never saw as a whole what they were making; no one of them did. But each one had had his dream. And the baffled dreams and the broken visions and the ruined hopes and the secret desires of each one labored with him as he labored; the things that were lost and beaten and trampled down went into the stone and steel and gave it soul; the aspiration denied and the hope abandoned and the vision defeated were the things that lived, and not the apparent purpose for which each one of all the millions sweat and toiled or cheated; the hidden things, the silent things, the winged things, so weak they are easily killed, the unacknowledged things, the rejected beauty, the strangled appreciation, the inchoate art, the submerged spirit—these groped and found each other and gathered themselves together and worked themselves into the tiles and mortar of the edifice and made a town that is a worthy fellow of the sunrise and the sea winds.

Humanity triumphs over its details.

The individual aspiration is always defeated of its perfect fruition and expression, but it is never lost; it passes into the conglomerate being of the race.

The way to encourage yourself about the human race is to look at it first from a distance; look at the lights on the high spots. Coming closer, you will be profoundly discouraged at the number of low spots, not to say two-spots. Coming still closer, you will become discouraged once more by the reflection that the same stuff that is in the high spots is also in the two-spots.

A FAMILIAR PREFACE

JOSEPH CONRAD

As a general rule we do not want much encouragement to talk about ourselves; yet this little book is the result of a friendly suggestion, and even of a little friendly pressure. I defended myself with some spirit; but, with characteristic tenacity, the friendly voice insisted, 'You know, you really must.'

It was not an argument, but I submitted at once. If one must!...

You perceive the force of a word. He who wants to persuade should put his trust not in the right argument, but in the right word. The power of sound has always been greater than the power of sense. I don't say this by way of disparagement. It is better for mankind to be impressionable than reflective. Nothing humanely great—great, I mean, as affecting a whole mass of lives—has come from reflection. On the other hand, you cannot fail to see the power of mere words; such words as Glory, for instance, or Pity. I won't mention any more. They are not far to seek. Shouted with perseverance, with ardor, with conviction, these two by their sound alone have set whole nations in motion and upheaved the dry, hard ground on which rests our whole social fabric. There's 'virtue' for you if you like!... Of course, the accent must be attended to. The right accent. That's very important. The capacious lung, the thundering or the tender vocal chords. Don't talk to me of your Archimedes' lever. He was an absent-minded person with a mathematical imagination. Mathematics commands all my respect, but I have no use for engines. Give me the right word and the right accent and I will move the world.

What a dream for a writer! Because written words have their accent, too. Yes! Let me only find the right word! Surely it must be lying somewhere among the wreckage of all the plaints and all the exultations poured out aloud since the first day when hope, the undying, came down on earth. It may be there, close by, disregarded, invisible, quite at hand. But it's no good. I believe there are men who can lay hold of a needle in a pottle of hay at the first try. For myself, I have never had such luck.

And then there is that accent. Another difficulty. For who is going to tell whether the accent is right or wrong till the word is shouted, and fails to be heard, perhaps, and goes down-wind, leaving the world unmoved? Once upon a time there lived an emperor who was a sage and something of a literary man. He jotted down on ivory tablets thoughts, maxims, reflections which chance has preserved for the edification of posterity. Among other sayings—I am quoting from memory—I remember this solemn admonition: 'Let all thy words have the accent of heroic truth.' The accent of heroic truth! This is very fine, but I am thinking that it is an easy matter for an austere emperor to jot down grandiose advice. Most of the working truths on this earth are humble, not heroic; and there have been times in the history of mankind when the accents of heroic truth have moved it to nothing but derision.

Nobody will expect to find between the covers of this little book words of extraordinary potency or accents of irresistible heroism. However humiliating for my self-esteem, I must confess that the counsels of Marcus Aurelius are not for me. They are more fit for a moralist than for an artist. Truth of a modest sort I can promise you, and also sincerity. That complete, praiseworthy sincerity which, while it delivers one into the hands of one's enemies, is as likely as not to embroil one with one's friends.

'Embroil' is perhaps too strong an expression. I can't imagine among either my enemies or my friends a being so hard up for something to do as to quarrel with me. 'To disappoint one's friends' would be nearer the mark. Most, almost all, friendships of the writing period of my life have come to me through my books; and I know that a novelist lives in his work. He stands there, the only reality in an invented world, among imaginary things, happenings, and people. Writing about them, he is only writing about himself. But the disclosure is not complete. He remains, to a certain extent, a figure behind the veil; a suspected rather than a seen presence—a movement and a voice behind the draperies of fiction. In these personal notes there is no such veil. And I cannot help thinking of a passage in the 'Imitation of Christ' where the ascetic author, who knew life so profoundly, says that 'there are persons esteemed on their reputation who by showing themselves destroy the opinion one had of them.' This is the danger incurred by an author of fiction who sets out to talk about himself without disguise.

While these reminiscent pages were appearing serially I was remonstrated with for bad economy; as if such writing were a form of self-indulgence wasting the substance of future volumes. It seems that I am not sufficiently literary. Indeed, a man who never wrote a line for print till he was thirty-six cannot bring himself to look upon his existence and his experience, upon the sum of his thoughts, sensations, and emotions, upon his memories and his regrets, and the whole possession of his past, as only so much material for his hands. Once before, some three years ago, when I published *The Mirror of the Sea*, a volume of impressions and memories, the same remarks were made to me. Practical remarks. But, truth to say, I have never understood the kind of thrift they recommend. I wanted to pay my tribute to the sea, its ships and its men, to whom I remain indebted for so much which has gone to make me what I am. That seemed to me the only shape in which I could offer it to their shades. There could not be a question in my mind of anything else. It is quite possible that I am a bad economist; but it is certain that I am incorrigible.

Having matured in the surroundings and under the special conditions of sea life, I have a special piety toward that form of my past; for its impressions were vivid, its appeal direct, its demands such as could be responded to with the natural elation of youth and strength equal to the call. There was nothing in them to perplex a young conscience. Having broken away from my origins under a storm of blame from every quarter which had the merest shadow of right to voice an opinion, removed by great distances from such natural affections as were still left to me, and even estranged, in a measure, from them by the totally unintelligible character of the life which had seduced me so mysteriously from my allegiance, I may safely say that through the blind force of circumstances the sea was to be all my world and the merchant service my only home for a long succession of years. No wonder, then, that in my two exclusively sea books—*The Nigger of the Narcissus*, and *The Mirror of the Sea* (and in the few short sea stories like 'Youth' and 'Typhoon')—I have tried with an almost filial regard to render the vibration of life in the great world of waters, in the hearts of the simple men who have for ages traversed its solitudes, and also that something sentient which seems to dwell in ships—the creatures of their hands and the objects of their care.

One's literary life must turn frequently for sustenance to memories and seek discourse with the shades, unless one has made up one's mind to write only in order to reprove mankind for what it is, or praise it for what it is not, or—generally—to teach it how to behave. Being neither quarrelsome, nor a flatterer, nor a sage, I have done none of these things, and I am prepared to put up serenely with the insignificance which attaches to persons who are not meddlesome in some way or other. But resignation is not indifference. I would not like to be left standing as a mere spectator on the bank of the great stream carrying onward so many lives. I would fain claim for myself the faculty of so much insight as can be expressed in a voice of sympathy and compassion.

It seems to me that in one, at least, authoritative quarter of criticism I am suspected of a certain unemotional, grim acceptance of facts—of what the French would call sécheresse du cœur. Fifteen years of unbroken silence before praise or blame testify sufficiently to my respect for criticism, that fine flower of personal expression in the garden of letters. But this is more of a personal matter, reaching the man behind the work, and therefore it may be alluded to in a volume which is a personal note in the margin of the public page. Not that I feel hurt in the least. The charge—if it amounted to a charge at all—was made in the most considerate terms; in a tone of regret.

My answer is that if it be true that every novel contains an element of autobiography—and this can hardly be denied, since the creator can only express himself in his creation—then there are some of us to whom an open display of sentiment is repugnant. I would not unduly praise the virtue of restraint. It is often merely temperamental. But it is not always a sign of coldness. It may be pride. There can be nothing more humiliating than to see the shaft of one's emotion miss the mark of either laughter or tears. Nothing more humiliating! And this for the reason that should the mark be missed, should the open display of emotion fail to move, then it must perish unavoidably in disgust or contempt. No artist can be reproached for shrinking from a risk which only fools run to meet and only genius dare confront with impunity. In a task which mainly consists in laying one's soul more or less bare to the world, a regard for decency, even at the cost of success, is but the regard for one's own dignity which is inseparably united with the dignity of one's work.

And then—it is very difficult to be wholly joyous or wholly sad on this earth. The comic, when it is human, soon takes upon itself a face of pain; and some of our griefs (some only, not all, for it is the capacity for suffering which makes man august in the eyes of men) have their source in weaknesses which must be recognized with smiling compassion as the common inheritance of us all. Joy and sorrow in this world pass into each other, mingling their forms and their murmurs in the twilight of life as mysterious as an overshadowed ocean, while the dazzling brightness of supreme hopes lies far off, fascinating and still, on the distant edge of the horizon.

Yes! I, too, would like to hold the magic wand giving that command over laughter and tears which is declared to be the highest achievement of imaginative literature. Only, to be a great magician one must surrender oneself to occult and irresponsible powers, either outside or within one's breast. We have all heard of simple men selling their souls for love or power to some grotesque devil. The most ordinary intelligence can perceive without much reflection that anything of the sort is bound to be a fool's bargain. I don't lay claim to particular wisdom because of my dislike and distrust of such transactions. It may be my sea training acting upon a natural disposition to keep good hold on the one thing really mine, but the fact is that I have a positive horror of losing even for one moving moment that full possession of myself which is the first condition of good service. And I have earned my notion of good service from my earlier into my later existence. I, who have never sought in the written word anything else but a form of the Beautiful—I have carried over that article of creed from the decks of ships to the more circumscribed space of my desk, and by that act, I suppose, I have become permanently imperfect in the eyes of the ineffable company of pure esthetes.

As in political so in literary action a man wins friends for himself mostly by the passion of his prejudices and by the consistent narrowness of his outlook. But I have never been able to love what was not lovable or hate what was not hateful out of deference for some general principle. Whether there be any courage in making this admission I know not. After the middle turn of life's way we consider dangers and joys with a tranquil mind. So I proceed in peace to declare that I have always suspected in the effort to bring into play the extremities of emotions the debasing touch of insincerity. In order to move others deeply we must deliberately allow ourselves to be carried away beyond the bounds of our normal sensibility—innocently enough, perhaps, and of necessity, like an actor who raises his voice on the stage above the pitch of natural conversation—but still we have to do that. And surely this is no great sin. But the danger lies in the writer becoming the victim of his own exaggeration, losing the exact notion of sincerity, and in the end coming to despise truth itself as something too cold, too blunt for his purpose—as, in fact, not good enough for his insistent emotion. From laughter and tears the descent is easy to snivelling and giggles.

These may seem selfish considerations; but you can't, in sound morals, condemn a man for taking care of his own integrity. It is his clear duty. And least of all can you condemn an artist pursuing, however humbly and imperfectly, a creative aim. In that interior world where his thought and his emotions go seeking for the experience of imagined adventures, there are no policemen, no law, no pressure of circumstance or dread of opinion to keep him within bounds. Who then is going to say Nay to his temptations if not his conscience?

And besides—this, remember, is the place and the moment of perfectly open talk—I think that all ambitions are lawful except those which climb upward on the miseries or credulities of mankind. All intellectual and artistic ambitions are permissible, up to and even beyond the limit of prudent sanity. They can hurt no one. If they are mad, then so much the worse for the artist. Indeed, as virtue is said to be, such ambitions are their own reward. Is it such a very mad presumption to believe in the sovereign power of one's art, to try for other means, for other ways of affirming this belief in the deeper appeal of one's work? To try to go deeper is not to be insensible. A historian of hearts is not a historian of emotions, yet he penetrates further, restrained as he may be, since his aim is to reach the wry fount of laughter and tears. The sight of human affairs deserves admiration and pity. They are worthy of respect, too. And he is not insensible who pays them the undemonstrative tribute of a sigh which is not a sob, and of a smile which is not a grin. Resignation, not mystic, not detached, but resignation open-eyed, conscious, and informed by love, is the only one of our feelings for which it is impossible to become a sham.

Not that I think resignation the last word of wisdom. I am too much the creature of my time for that. But I think that the proper wisdom is to will what the gods will without, perhaps, being certain what their will is—or even if they have a will of their own. And in this matter of life and art it is not the Why that matters so much to our happiness as the How. As the Frenchman said, '*Il y a toujours la manière*.' Very true. Yes. There is the manner.

The manner in laughter, in tears, in irony, in indignations and enthusiasms, in judgments—and even in love. The manner in which, as in the features and character of a human face, the inner truth is foreshadowed for those who know how to look at their kind.

Those who read me know my conviction that the world, the temporal world, rests on a few very simple ideas; so simple that they must be as old as the hills. It rests notably, among others, on the idea of Fidelity. At a time when nothing which is not revolutionary in some way or other can expect to attract much attention I have not been revolutionary in my writings. The revolutionary spirit is mighty convenient in this, that it frees one from all scruples as regards ideas. Its hard, absolute optimism is repulsive to my mind by the menace of fanaticism and intolerance it contains. No doubt one should smile at these things; but, imperfect Esthete, I am no better Philosopher. All claim to special righteousness awakens in me that scorn and anger from which a philosophical mind should be free.

O. W. FIRKINS

O. HENRY

There are two opinions concerning O. Henry. The middle class views him as the impersonation of vigor and brilliancy; part of the higher criticism sees in him little but sensation and persiflage. Between these views there is a natural relation; the gods of the heathens are ipso facto the demons of Christianity. Unmixed assertions, however, are commonly mixtures of truth and falsehood; there is room today for an estimate which shall respect both opinions and adopt neither.

There is one literary trait in which I am unable to name any writer of tales in any literature who surpasses O. Henry. It is not primary or even secondary among literary merits; it is less a value per se than the condition or foundation of values. But its utility is manifest, and it is rare among men: Chaucer and Shakespeare prove the possibility of its absence in masters of that very branch of art in which its presence would seem to be imperative. I refer to the designing of stories—not to the primary intuition or to skill in development, in both of which finer phases of invention O. Henry has been largely and frequently surpassed, but to the disposition of masses, to the blocking-out of plots. That a half-educated American provincial should have been original in a field in which original men have been copyists is enough of itself to make his personality observable.

Illustration, even of conceded truths, is rarely superfluous. I supply two instances. Two lads, parting in New York, agree to meet 'After Twenty Years' at a specified hour, date, and corner. Both are faithful; but the years in which their relation has slept in mutual silence and ignorance have turned the one into a dashing criminal, the other into a sober officer of the law. Behind the picturesque and captivating rendezvous lurks a powerful dramatic situation and a moral problem of arresting gravity. This is dealt with in six pages of 'The Four Million'. The 'Furnished Room', two stories further on, occupies twelve pages. Through the wilderness of apartments on the lower West Side a man trails a woman. Chance leads him to the very room in which the woman ended her life the week before. Between him and the truth the avarice of a sordid landlady interposes the curtain of a lie. In the bed in which the girl slept and died, the man sleeps and dies, and the entrance of the deadly fumes into his nostrils shuts the sinister and mournful coincidence forever from the knowledge of mankind. O. Henry gave these tales neither extension nor prominence; so far as I know, they were received without bravos or salvos. The distinction of a body of work in which such specimens are undistinguished hardly requires comment.

A few types among these stories may be specified. There are the Sydney Cartonisms, defined in the name; love-stories in which divided hearts, or simply divided persons, are brought together by the strategy of chance; hoax stories —deft pictures of smiling roguery; 'prince and pauper' stories, in which wealth and poverty face each other, sometimes enact each other; disguise stories, in which the wrong clothes often draw the wrong bullets; complemental stories, in which Jim sacrifices his beloved watch to buy combs for Della, who, meanwhile, has sacrificed her beloved hair to buy a chain for Jim.

This imperfect list is eloquent in its way; it smooths our path to the assertion that O. Henry's specialty is the enlistment of original method in the service of traditional appeals. The ends are the ends of fifty years ago; O. Henry transports us by aeroplane to the old homestead.

Criticism of O. Henry falls into those superlatives and antitheses in which his own faculty delighted. In mechanical invention he is almost the leader of his race. In a related quality—a defect—his leadership is even more conspicuous. I doubt if the sense of the probable, or, more precisely, of the available in the improbable, ever became equally weakened or deadened in a man who made his living by its exercise. The improbable, even the impossible, has its place in art, though that place is relatively low; and it is curious that works such as the *Arabian Nights* and *Grimm's Fairy Tales*, whose stock-in-trade is the incredible, are the works which give almost no trouble on the score of verisimilitude. The truth is that we reject not what it is impossible to prove, or even what it is possible to disprove, but what it is impossible to imagine. O. Henry asks us to imagine the unimaginable—that is his crime.

The right and wrong improbabilities may be illustrated from two burglar stories. 'Sixes and Sevens' contains an excellent tale of a burglar and a citizen who fraternize, in a comic midnight interview, on the score of their common sufferings from rheumatism. This feeling in practice would not triumph over fear and greed; but the feeling is natural, and everybody with a grain of nature in him can imagine its triumph. Nature tends towards that impossibility, and art, lifting, so to speak, the lid which fact drops upon nature, reveals nature in belying fact. In another story, in 'Whirligigs', a nocturnal interview takes place in which a burglar and a small boy discuss the etiquette of their mutual relation by formulas derived from short stories with which both are amazingly conversant. This is the wrong use of the improbable. Even an imagination inured to the virtues of burglars and the maturity of small boys will have naught to do with this insanity.

But O. Henry can go further yet. There are inventions in his tales the very utterance of which—not the mere substance but the utterance—on the part of a man not writing from Bedlam or for Bedlam impresses the reader as incredible. In a 'Comedy in Rubber', two persons become so used to spectatorship at transactions in the street that they drift into the part of spectators when the transaction is their own wedding. Can human daring or human folly go further? O. Henry is on the spot to prove that they can. In the 'Romance of a Busy Broker', a busy and forgetful man, in a freak of absent-mindedness, offers his hand to the stenographer whom he had married the night before.

The other day, in the journal of the Goncourts, I came upon

the following sentence: 'Never will the imagination approach the improbabilities and the antitheses of truth' (II, 9). This is dated February 21, 1862. Truth had still the advantage. O. Henry was not born till September of the same year.

Passing on to style, we are still in the land of antithesis. The style is gross—and fine. Of the plenitude of its stimulus, there can be no question. In 'Sixes and Sevens', a young man sinking under accidental morphia, is kept awake and alive by shouts, kicks, and blows. O. Henry's public seems imaged in that young man. But I draw a sharp distinction between the tone of the style and its pattern. The tone is brazen, or, better perhaps, brassy; its self-advertisement is incorrigible; it reeks with that air of performance which is opposed to real efficiency. But the pattern is another matter. The South rounds its periods like its vowels; O. Henry has read, not widely, but wisely, in his boyhood. His sentences are built—a rare thing in the best writers of today. In conciseness, that Spartan virtue, he was strong, though it must be confessed that the tale-teller was now and then hustled from the rostrum by his rival and enemy, the talker. He can introduce a felicity with a noiselessness that numbers him for a flying second among the sovereigns of English. 'In one of the second-floor front windows Mrs McCaskey awaited her husband. Supper was cooling on the table. Its heat went into Mrs McCaskey.'

I regret the tomfoolery; I wince at the slang. Yet even for these levities with which his pages are so liberally besprinkled or bedaubed, some half-apology may be circumspectly urged. In nonsense his ease is consummate. A horseman who should dismount to pick up a bauble would be childish; O. Henry picks it up without dismounting. Slang, again, is most pardonable in the man with whom its use is least exclusive and least necessary. There are men who, going for a walk, take their dogs with them; there are other men who give a walk to their dogs. Substitute slang for the dog, and the superiority of the first class to the second will exactly illustrate the superiority of O. Henry to the abject traffickers in slang.

In the 'Pendulum', Katy has a new patch in her crazy quilt which the ice man cut from the end of his four-in-hand. In the 'Day We Celebrate', threading the mazes of a banana grove is compared to 'paging the palm room of a New York hotel for a man named Smith'. O. Henry's is the type of mind to which images like this four-in-hand and this palm room are presented in exhaustless abundance and unflagging continuity. There was hardly an object in the merry-go-round of civilized life that had not offered at least an end or an edge to the avidity of his consuming eyes. Nothing escapes from the besom of his allusiveness, and the style is streaked and pied, almost to monotony, by the accumulation of lively details.

If O. Henry's style was crude, it was also rare; but it is part of the grimness of the bargain that destiny drives with us that the mixture of the crude and the rare should be a crude mixture, as the sons of whites and negroes are numbered with the blacks. In the kingdom of style O. Henry's estates were princely, but, to pay his debts, he must have sold them all.

Thus far in our inquiry extraordinary merits have been offset by extraordinary defects. To lift our author out of the class of brilliant and skilful entertainers, more is needed. Is more forthcoming? I should answer, yes. In O. Henry, above the knowledge of setting, which is clear and first-hand, but subsidiary, above the order of events, which is, generally speaking, fantastic, above the emotions, which are sound and warm, but almost purely derivative, there is a rather small, but impressive body of first-hand perspicacities and reactions. On these his endurance may hinge.

I name, first of all, O. Henry's feeling for New York. With the exception of his New Orleans, I care little for his South and West, which are a boyish South and West, and as little, or even less, for his Spanish-American communities. My objection to his opera-bouffe republics is, not that they are inadequate as republics (for that we were entirely prepared), but that they are inadequate as opera. He lets us see his show from the coulisses. The pretense lacks standing even among pretenses, and a faith must be induced before its removal can enliven us. But his New York has quality. It is of the family of Dickens's London and Hugo's Paris, though it is plainly a cadet in the family. Mr Howells, in his profound and valuable study of the metropolis in a 'Hazard of New Fortunes', is penetrating; O. Henry, on the other hand, is penetrated. His New York is intimate and clinging; it is caught in the mesh of the imagination.

O. Henry had rare but precious insights into human destiny and human nature. In these pictures he is not formally accurate; he could never or seldom set his truth before us in that moderation and proportion which truths acquire in the stringencies of actuality. He was apt to present his insight in a sort of parable or allegory, to upraise it before the eyes of mankind on the mast or flagpole of some vehement exaggeration. Epigram shows us truth in the embrace of a lie, and tales which are dramatized epigrams are subject to a like constraint. The force, however, is real. I could scarcely name anywhere a more powerful exposition of fatality than 'Roads of Destiny', the initial story in the volume which appropriates its title. It wanted only the skilled romantic touch of a Gautier or Stevenson to enroll this tale among the masterpieces of its kind in contemporary letters.

Now and then the ingredient of parable is hardly perceptible; we draw close to the bare fact. O. Henry, fortunate in plots, is peculiarly fortunate in his renunciation of plot. If contrivance is lucrative, it is also costly. There is an admirable little story called the 'Pendulum' (in *The Trimmed Lamp*), the simplicity of whose fable would have satisfied Coppée or Hawthorne. A man in a flat, by force of custom, has come to regard his wife as a piece of furniture. She departs for a few hours, and, by the break in usage, is restored, in his consciousness, to womanhood. She comes back, and relapses into furniture. That is all. O. Henry could not have given us less—or more. Farcical, clownish, if you will, the story resembles those clowns who carry daggers under their motley. When John Perkins takes up that inauspicious hat, the reader smiles, and quails. I will mention a few other examples of insights with the proviso that they are not specially commended to the man whose quest in the short story is the electrifying or the calorific. They include the 'Social Triangle', the 'Making of a New Yorker', and the 'Foreign Policy of Company 99', all in *The Trimmed Lamp,* the 'Brief Début of Tildy' in The Four Million, and the 'Complete Life of John Hopkins' in The Voice of the City. I cannot close this summary of good points without a passing reference to the not unsuggestive portrayal of humane and cheerful scoundrels in 'The Gentle Grafter'. The picture, if false to species, is faithful to genus.

O. Henry's egregiousness, on the superficial side, both in merits and defects, reminds us of those park benches so characteristic of his tales which are occupied by a millionaire at one end and a mendicant at the other. But, to complete the image, we must add as a casual visitor to that bench a seer or a student, who, sitting down between the previous comers and suspending the flamboyancies of their dialogue, should gaze with the pensive eye of Goldsmith or Addison upon the passing crowd.

In O. Henry American journalism and the Victorian tradition meet. His mind, quick to don the guise of modernity, was impervious to its spirit. The specifically modern movements, the scientific awakening, the religious upheaval and subsidence, the socialistic gospel, the enfranchisement of women—these never interfered with his artless and joyous pursuit of the old romantic motives of love, hate, wealth, poverty, gentility, disguise, and crime. On two points a moral record which, in his literature, is everywhere sound and stainless, rises almost to nobility. In an age when sexual excitement had become available and permissible, this worshiper of stimulus never touched with so much as a fingertip that insidious and meretricious fruit. The second point is his feeling for underpaid working-girls. His passionate concern for this wrong derives a peculiar emphasis from the general refusal of his books to bestow countenance or notice on philanthropy in its collective forms. When, in his dream of Heaven, he is asked: 'Are you one of the bunch?' (meaning one of the bunch of grasping and grinding employers), the response, through all its slang, is soul-stirring. 'Not on your immortality,' said I. 'I'm only the fellow that set fire to an orphan asylum and murdered a blind man for his pennies.' The author of that retort may have some difficulty with the sentries that watch the entrance of Parnassus; he will have none with the gatekeeper of the New Jerusalem.

THE STUDENT LIFE

WILLIAM OSLER

Except it be a lover, no one is more interesting as an object of study than a student. Shakespeare might have made him a fourth in his immortal group. The lunatic with his fixed idea, the poet with his fine frenzy, the lover with his frantic idolatry, and the student aflame with the desire for knowledge are of 'imagination all compact'. To an absorbing passion, a whole-souled devotion, must be joined an enduring energy, if the student is to become a devotee of the gray-eyed goddess to whose law his services are bound. Like the quest of the Holy Grail, the quest of Minerva is not for all. For the one, the pure life; for the other, what Milton calls 'a strong propensity of nature'. Here again the student often resembles the poet—he is born, not made. While the resultant of two molding forces, the accidental, external conditions, and the hidden germinal energies, which produce in each one of us national, family, and individual traits, the true student possesses in some measure a divine spark which sets at naught their laws. Like the Snark, he defies definition, but there are three unmistakable signs by which you may recognize the genuine article from a Boojum—an absorbing desire to know the truth, an unswerving steadfastness in its pursuit, and an open, honest heart, free from suspicion, guile, and jealousy.

At the outset do not be worried about this big question—Truth. It is a very simple matter if each one of you starts with the desire to get as much as possible. No human being is constituted to know the truth, the whole truth, and nothing but the truth; and even the best of men must be content with fragments, with partial glimpses, never the full fruition. In this unsatisfied quest the attitude of mind, the desire, the thirst—a thirst that from the soul must rise!—the fervent longing, are the be-all and the end-all. What is the student but a lover courting a fickle mistress who ever eludes his grasp? In this very elusiveness is brought out his second great characteristic—steadfastness of purpose. Unless from the start the limitations incident to our frail human faculties are frankly accepted, nothing but disappointment awaits you. The truth is the best you can get with your best endeavor, the best that the best men accept—with this you must learn to be satisfied, retaining at the same time with due humility an earnest desire for an ever larger portion. Only by keeping the mind plastic and receptive does the student escape perdition. It is not, as Charles Lamb remarks, that some people do not know what to do with truth when it is offered to them, but the tragic fate is to reach, after years of patient search, a condition of mind-blindness in which the truth is not recognized, though it stares you in the face. This can never happen to a man who has followed step by step the growth of a truth, and who knows the painful phases of its evolution. It is one of the great tragedies of life that every truth has to struggle to acceptance against honest but mind-blind students. Harvey knew his contemporaries well, and for twelve successive years demonstrated the circulation of the blood before daring to publish the facts on which the truth was based.

Only steadfastness of purpose and humility enable the student to shift his position to meet the new conditions in which new truths are born, or old ones modified beyond recognition. And, thirdly, the honest heart will keep him in touch with his fellow students, and furnish that sense of comradeship without which he travels an arid waste alone. I say advisedly an honest heart—the honest head is prone to be cold and stern, given to judgment, not mercy, and not always able to entertain that true charity which, while it thinketh no evil, is anxious to put the best possible interpretation upon the motives of a fellow worker. It will foster, too, an attitude of generous, friendly rivalry untinged by the green peril, jealousy, that is the best preventive of the growth of a bastard scientific spirit, loving seclusion and working in a lock-and-key laboratory, as timorous of light as is a thief.

You have all become brothers in a great society, not apprentices, since that implies a master, and nothing should be further from the attitude of the teacher than much that is meant in that word, used though it be in another sense, particularly by our French brethren in a most delightful way, signifying a bond of intellectual filiation. A fraternal attitude is not easy to cultivate—the chasm between the chair and the bench is difficult to bridge. Two things have helped to put up a cantilever across the gulf. The successful teacher is no longer on a height, pumping knowledge at high pressure into passive receptacles. The new methods have changed all this. He is no longer Sir Oracle, perhaps unconsciously by his very manner antagonizing minds to whose level he cannot possibly descend, but he is a senior student anxious to help his juniors. When a simple, earnest spirit animates a college, there is no appreciable interval between the teacher and the taught—both are in the same class, the one a little more advanced than the other. So animated, the student feels that he has joined a family whose honor is his honor, whose welfare is his own, and whose interests should be his first consideration.

The hardest conviction to get into the mind of a beginner is that the education upon which he is engaged is not a college course, not a medical course, but a life course, for which the work of a few years under teachers is but a preparation. Whether you will falter and fail in the race or whether you will be faithful to the end depends on the training before the start, and on your staying powers, points upon which I need not enlarge. You can all become good students, a few may become great students, and now and again one of you will be found who does easily and well what others cannot do at all, or very badly, which is John Ferriar's excellent definition of a genius.

In the hurry and bustle of a business world, which is the life of this continent, it is not easy to train first-class students. Under present conditions it is hard to get the needful seclusion, on which account it is that our educational market is so full of wayside fruit. I have always been much impressed by the advice of St

Chrysostom: 'Depart from the highway and transplant thyself in some enclosed ground, for it is hard for a tree which stands by the wayside to keep her fruit till it be ripe.' The dilettante is abroad in the land, the man who is always venturing on tasks for which he is imperfectly equipped, a habit of mind fostered by the multiplicity of subjects in the curriculum: and while many things are studied, few are studied thoroughly. Men will not take time to get to the heart of a matter. After all, concentration is the price the modern student pays for success. Thoroughness is the most difficult habit to acquire, but it is the pearl of great price, worth all the worry and trouble of the search. The dilettante lives an easy, butterfly life, knowing nothing of the toil and labor with which the treasures of knowledge are dug out of the past, or wrung by patient research in the laboratories. Take, for example, the early history of this country—how easy for the student of the one type to get a smattering, even a fairly full acquaintance with the events of the French and Spanish settlements. Put an original document before him, and it might as well be Arabic. What we need is the other type, the man who knows the records, who, with a broad outlook and drilled in what may be called the embryology of history, has yet a powerful vision for the minutiæ of life. It is these kitchen and backstair men who are to be encouraged, the men who know the subject in hand in all possible relationships. Concentration has its drawbacks. It is possible to become so absorbed in the problem of the 'enclitic de', or the structure of the flagella of the Trichomonas, or of the toes of the prehistoric horse, that the student loses the sense of proportion in his work, and even wastes a lifetime in researches which are valueless because not in touch with current knowledge. You remember poor Casaubon, in *Middlemarch*, whose painful scholarship was lost on this account. The best preventive to this is to get denationalized early. The true student is a citizen of the world, the allegiance of whose soul, at any rate, is too precious to be restricted to a single country. The great minds, the great works transcend all limitations of time, of language, and of race, and the scholar can never feel initiated into the company of the elect until he can approach all of life's problems from the cosmopolitan standpoint. I care not in what subject he may work, the full knowledge cannot be reached without drawing on supplies from lands other than his own—French, English, German, American, Japanese, Russian, Italian—there must be no discrimination by the loyal student who should willingly draw from any and every source with an open mind and a stern resolve to render unto all their dues. I care not on what stream of knowledge he may embark, follow up its course, and the rivulets that feed it flow from many lands. If the work is to be effective he must keep in touch with scholars in other countries. How often has it happened that years of precious time have been given to a problem already solved or shown to be insoluble, because of the ignorance of what had been done elsewhere. And it is not only book knowledge and journal knowledge, but a knowledge of men that is needed. The student will, if possible, see the men in other lands. Travel not only widens the vision and gives certainties in place of vague surmises, but the personal contact with foreign workers enables him to appreciate better the failings or successes in his own line of work, perhaps to look with more charitable eyes on the work of some brother whose limitations and opportunities have been more restricted than his own. Or, in contact with a mastermind, he may take fire, and the glow of the enthusiasm may be the inspiration of his life. Concentration must then be associated with large views on the relation of the problem, and a knowledge of its status elsewhere; otherwise it may land him in the slough of a specialism so narrow that it has depth and no breadth, or he may be led to make what he believes to be important discoveries, but which have long been current coin in other lands. It is sad to think that the day of the great polymathic student is at an end; that we may, perhaps, never again see a Scaliger, a Haller, or a Humboldt—men who took the whole field of knowledge for their domain and viewed it as from a pinnacle. And yet a great specializing generalist may arise, who can tell? Some twentieth-century Aristotle may be now tugging at his bottle, as little dreaming as are his parents or his friends of a conquest of the mind, beside which the wonderful victories of the Stagirite will look pale. The value of a really great student to the country is equal to half a dozen grain elevators or a new trans-continental railway. He is a commodity singularly fickle and variable, and not to be grown to order. So far as his advent is concerned there is no telling when or where he may arise. The conditions seem to be present even under the most unlikely externals. Some of the greatest students this country has produced have come from small villages and country places. It is impossible to predict from a study of the environment, which a 'strong propensity of nature', to quote Milton's phrase again, will easily bend or break.

The student must be allowed full freedom in his work, undisturbed by the utilitarian spirit of the Philistine, who cries, *Cui bono*? and distrusts pure science. The present remarkable position in applied science and in industrial trades of all sorts has been made possible by men who did pioneer work in chemistry, in physics, in biology, and in physiology, without a thought in their researches of any practical application. The members of this higher group of productive students are rarely understood by the common spirits, who appreciate as little their unselfish devotion as their unworldly neglect of the practical side of the problems.

Everywhere now the medical student is welcomed as an honored member of the guild. There was a time, I confess, and it is within the memory of some of us, when, like Falstaff, he was given to 'taverns and sack and wine and metheglins, and to drinkings and swearings and starings, pribbles and prabbles'; but all that has changed with the curriculum, and the 'Meds' now roar you as gently as the 'Theologs.' On account of the peculiar character of the subject-matter of your studies, what I have said upon the general life and mental attitude of the student applies with tenfold force to you. Man, with all his mental and bodily anomalies and diseases—the machine in order, the machine in disorder, and the business yours to put it to rights. Through all the phases of its career this most complicated mechanism of this wonderful world will be the subject of our study and of your care—the naked, new-born infant, the artless child, the lad and the lassie just aware of the tree of knowledge overhead, the strong man in the pride of life, the woman with the benediction of maternity on her brow, and the aged, peaceful in the contemplation of the past. Almost everything has been renewed in the science and in the art of medicine, but all through the long centuries there has been no variableness or shadow of change in the essential features of the life which is our contemplation and our care. The sick love-child of Israel's sweet singer, the plague-stricken hopes of the great Athenian statesman, Elpenor, bereft of his beloved Artemidora, and 'Tully's daughter mourned so tenderly', are not of any age or any race—they are here with us today, with the Hamlets, the Ophelias, and the Lears. Amid an eternal heritage of sorrow and suffering our work is laid, and this eternal note of sadness would be insupportable if the daily tragedies were not relieved by the spectacle of the heroism and devotion displayed by the actors. Nothing will sustain you more potently than the power to recognize in your humdrum routine, as perhaps it may be thought, the true poetry of life—the poetry of the commonplace, of the ordinary man, of the plain, toilworn woman, with their loves and their joys, their sorrows and their griefs. The comedy, too, of life will be spread before you, and nobody laughs more often than the doctor at the pranks Puck plays upon the Titanias and the Bottoms among his patients. The humorous side is really almost as frequently turned towards him as the tragic. Lift up one hand to heaven and thank your stars if they have given you the proper sense to enable you to appreciate the inconceivably droll situations in which we catch our fellow creatures. Unhappily, this is one of the free gifts of the gods, unevenly distributed, not bestowed on all, or on all in equal portions. In undue measure it is not without risk, and in any case in the doctor it is better appreciated by the eye than expressed on the tongue. Hilarity and good humor, a breezy cheerfulness, a nature 'sloping toward the southern side', as Lowell has it, help enormously both in the study and in the practice of medicine. To many of a somber and sour disposition it is hard to maintain good spirits amid the trials and tribulations of the day, and yet it is an unpardonable mistake to go about among patients with a long face.

Divide your attentions equally between books and men. The strength of the student of books is to sit still—two or three hours at a stretch—eating the heart out of a subject with pencil and notebook in hand, determined to master the details and intricacies, focussing all your energies on its difficulties. Get accustomed to test all sorts of book problems and statements for yourself, and take as little as possible on trust. The Hunterian 'Do not think, but try' attitude of mind is the important one to cultivate. The question came up one day, when discussing the grooves left on the nails after fever, how long it took for the nail to grow out, from root to edge. A majority of the class had no further interest; a few looked it up in books; two men marked their nails at the root with nitrate of silver, and a few months later had positive knowledge on the subject. They showed the proper spirit. The little points that come up in your reading try to test for yourselves. With one fundamental difficulty many of you will have to contend from the outset—a lack of proper preparation for really hard study. No one can have watched successive groups of young men pass through the special schools without profoundly regretting the haphazard, fragmentary character of their preliminary education. It does seem too bad that we cannot have a student in his eighteenth year sufficiently grounded in the humanities and in the sciences preliminary to medicine—but this is an educational problem upon which only a Milton or a Locke could discourse with profit. With pertinacity you can overcome the preliminary defects and once thoroughly interested, the work in books becomes a pastime. A serious drawback in the student life is the self-consciousness, bred of too close devotion to books. A man gets shy, 'dysopic', as old Timothy Bright calls it, and shuns the looks of men, and blushes like a girl.

The strength of a student of men is to travel—to study men, their habits, character, mode of life, their behavior under varied conditions, their vices, virtues, and peculiarities. Begin with a careful observation of your fellow students and of your teachers; then, every patient you see is a lesson in much more than the malady from which he suffers. Mix as much as you possibly can with the outside world, and learn its ways. Cultivated systematically, the student societies, the students' union, the gymnasium, and the outside social circle will enable you to conquer the diffidence so apt to go with bookishness and which may prove a very serious drawback in after-life. I cannot too strongly impress upon the earnest and attentive men among you the necessity of overcoming this unfortunate failing in your student days. It is not easy for everyone to reach a happy medium, and the distinction between a proper self-confidence and 'cheek', particularly in junior students, is not always to be made. The latter is met with chiefly among the student pilgrims who, in traveling down the Delectable Mountains, have gone astray and have passed to the left hand, where lieth the country of Conceit, the country in which you remember the brisk lad Ignorance met Christian.

I wish we could encourage on this continent among our best students the habit of wandering. I do not know that we are quite prepared for it, as there is still great diversity in the curricula, even among the leading schools, but it is undoubtedly a great advantage to study under different teachers, as the mental horizon is widened and the sympathies enlarged. The practice would do much to lessen that narrow 'I am of Paul and I am of Apollos' spirit which is hostile to the best interests of the profession.

There is much that I would like to say on the question of

work, but I can spare only a few moments for a word or two. Who will venture to settle upon so simple a matter as the best time for work? One will tell us there is no best time; all are equally good; and truly, all times are the same to a man whose soul is absorbed in some great problem. The other day I asked Edward Martin, the well-known story-writer, what time he found best for work. 'Not in the evening, and never between meals!' was his answer, which may appeal to some of my hearers. One works best at night; another, in the morning; a majority of the students of the past favor the latter. Erasmus, the great exemplar, says, 'Never work at night; it dulls the brain and hurts the health.' One day, going with George Ross through Bedlam, Dr Savage, at that time the physician in charge, remarked upon two great groups of patients—those who were depressed in the morning and those who were cheerful, and he suggested that the spirits rose and fell with the bodily temperature—those with very low morning temperatures were depressed, and vice versa. This, I believe, expresses a truth which may explain the extraordinary difference in the habits of students in this matter of the time at which the best work can be done. Outside of the asylum there are also the two great types, the student-lark who loves to see the sun rise, who comes to breakfast with a cheerful morning face, never so 'fit' as at 6 a.m. We all know the type. What a contrast to the student-owl with his saturnine morning face, thoroughly unhappy, cheated by the wretched breakfast bell of the two best hours of the day for sleep, no appetite, and permeated with an unspeakable hostility to his vis-à-vis, whose morning garrulity and good humor are equally offensive. Only gradually, as the day wears on and his temperature rises, does he become endurable to himself and to others. But see him really awake at 10 p.m., while our blithe lark is in hopeless coma over his books, from which it is hard to rouse him sufficiently to get his boots off for bed, our lean owl-friend, Saturn no longer in the ascendant, with bright eyes and cheery face, is ready for four hours of anything you wish—deep study, or Heart affluence in discursive talk ,and by 2 a.m. he will undertake to unsphere the spirit of Plato. In neither a virtue, in neither a fault we must recognize these two types of students, differently constituted, owing possibly—though I have but little evidence for the belief—to thermal peculiarities.

THE RUSSIAN QUARTER

THOMAS BURKE

I had known the quarter for many years before it interested me. It was not until I was prowling around on a Fleet Street assignment that I learned to hate it. A murder had been committed over a café in Lupin Street; a popular murder, fruity, cleverly done, and with a sex interest. Of course every newspaper and agency developed a virtuous anxiety to track the culprit, and all resources were directed to that end. Journalism is perhaps the only profession in which so fine a public spirit may be found. So it was that the North Country paper of which I was a hanger-on flung every available man into the fighting line, and the editor told me that I might, in place of the casual paragraphs for the London Letter, do something good on the Vassiloff murder.

It was a night of cold rain, and the pavements were dashed with smears of light from the shop windows. Through the streaming streets my hansom leaped; and as I looked from the window, and noted the despondent biliousness of Bethnal Green, I realized that the grass withereth, the flower fadeth.

I dismissed the cab at Brick Lane, and, continuing the tradition which had been instilled into me by my predecessor on the London Letter, I turned into one of the hostelries and had a vodka to keep the cold out. Little Russia was shutting up. The old shawled women, who sit at every corner with huge baskets of black bread and sweet cakes, were departing beneath umbrellas. The stalls of Osborn Street, usually dressed with foreign-looking confectionery, were also retiring. Indeed, everybody seemed to be slinking away, and as I sipped my vodka, and felt it burn me with raw fire, I cursed news editors and all publics which desired to read about murders. I was perfectly sure that I shouldn't do the least good; so I had another, and gazed through the kaleidoscopic window, rushing with rain, at the cheerful world that held me.

Oh, so sad it is, this quarter! By day the streets are a depression, with their frowzy doss-houses and their vapor-baths. Gray and sickly is the light. Gray and sickly, too, are the leering shops, and gray and sickly are the people and the children. Everything has followed the grass and the flowers. Childhood has no place; so above the roofs you may see the surly points of a Council School. Such games as happen are played but listlessly, and each little face is smirched. The gaunt warehouses hardly support their lopping heads, and the low, beetling, gabled houses of the alleys seem for ever to brood on nights of bitter adventure. Fit objects for contempt by day they may be, but when night creeps upon London, the hideous darkness that can almost be touched, then their faces become very powers of terror, and the cautious soul, wandered from the comfort of the main streets, walks and walks in a frenzy, seeking outlet and finding none. Sometimes a hoarse laugh will break sharp on his ear. Then he runs.

Well, I finished my second, and then sauntered out. As I was passing a cruel-looking passage, a girl stepped forward. She looked at me. I looked at her. She had the haunting melancholy of Russia in her face, but her voice was as the voice of Cockaigne. For she spoke and said:

'Funny-looking little guy, ain't you?'

I suppose I was. So I smiled and said: 'We are as God made us, old girl.'

She giggled…

I said I felt sure I should do no good on the Vassiloff murder. I didn't. For just then two of her friends came out of the court, each with a boy. It was apparent that she had no boy. I had no idea what the occasion might be, but the other four marched ahead, crying, 'Come on!' And, surprised, yet knowing of no good reason for being surprised, I felt the girl's arm slip into mine, and we joined the main column…

That is one of London's greatest charms: it is always ready to toss you little encounters of this sort, if you are out for them.

Across the road we went, through mire and puddle, and down a long, winding court. At about midway our friends disappeared, and, suddenly drawn to the right, I was pushed from behind up a steep, fusty stair. Then I knew where we were going. We were going to the tenements where most of the Russians meet of an evening. The atmosphere in these places is a little more cheerful than that of the cafés—if you can imagine a Russian ever rising to cheerfulness. Most of the girls lodge over the milliners' shops, and thither their friends resort. Every establishment here has a piano, for music, with them, is a somber passion rather than a diversion. You will not hear comic opera, but if you want to climb the lost heights of melody, stand in Bell Yard, and listen to a piano, lost in the high glooms, wailing the heart of Chopin, or Rubinstein or Glazounoff through the fingers of pale, moist girls, while the ghost of Peter the Painter parades the naphtha'd highways.

At the top of the stair I was pushed into a dark, fusty room, and guided to a low, fusty sofa or bed. Then someone struck a match, and a lamp was lit and set on the mantelshelf. It flung a soft, caressing radiance on its shabby home, and on its mistress, and on the other girls and boys. The boys were tough youngsters of the district, evidently very much at home, smoking Russian cigarettes and settling themselves on the bed in a manner that seemed curiously continental in Cockney toughs. I doubt if you would have loved the girls at that moment; and yet...you know... their black or brassy hair, their untidiness, and the cotton blouses half-dropped from their tumultuous breasts...The girl who had collared me disappeared for a moment, and then brought a tray of Russian tea. 'Help 'selves, boys!' We did so, and, watching the others, I discovered that it was the correct thing to lemon the ladies' tea for them and stir it well and light their cigarettes. I did so for Katarina—that was her name—while she watched me with little truant locks of hair running everywhere, and a slow, alluring smile that seemed to hold all the agony and mystery of the steppes.

The room, on which the wallpaper hung in dank strips,

contained a full-sized bed and a chair bedstead, a washstand, a samovar, a potpourri of a carpet, and certain mysteries of feminine toilet. A rickety three-legged table stood by the window, and Katarina's robes hung in a dainty riot of frill and color behind the door, which only shut when you thrust a peg of wood through a wired catch.

One of the boys sprawled himself, in clumsy luxury, on the bed, and his girl arranged herself at his side, and when she was settled her hair tumbled in a shower of hairpins, and everybody laughed like children. The other girl went to the piano, and her boy squatted on the floor at her feet.

She began to play... You would not understand, I suppose, the intellectual emotion of the situation. It is more than curious to sit in these rooms, in the filthiest spot in London, and listen to Moszkowsky, Tchaikowsky, and Sibelius, played by a factory girl. It is...something indefinable. I had visited similar places in Stepney before, but then I had not had a couple of vodkas, and I had not been taken in tow by an unknown girl. They play and play, while tea and cigarettes, and sometimes vodka or whisky, go round; and as the room gets warmer, so does one's sense of smell get sharper; so do the pale faces get moister; and so does one long more and more for a breath of cold air from the Ural Mountains. The best you can do is to ascend to the flat roof, and take a deep breath of Spitalfields ozone. Then back to the room for more tea and more music.

Sanya played... Despite the unventilated room, the greasy appointments, and other details that would have turned the stomach of Kensington, that girl at the piano, her dress cunningly disarranged, playing, as no one would have dreamed she could play, the finer intensities of Wieniawski and Moussorgsky, shook all sense of responsibility from me. The burdens of life vanished. News editors and their assignments be damned. Enjoy yourself, was what the cold, insidious music said. Take your moments when the fates send them; that was life's best lesson. Snatch the joy of the fleeting moment. Why ponder on time and tears?

Devilish little fingers they were, Sanya's. Her technique was not perhaps all that it might have been; she might not have won the Gold Medal of our white-shirted academies, but she had enough temperament to make half a dozen Bechstein Hall virtuosi. From valse to nocturne, from sonata to prelude, her fancy ran. With crashing chords she dropped from 'L'Automne Bacchanale' to the Nocturne in E flat; scarcely murmured of that, then tripped elvishly into Moszkowsky's Waltz, and from that she dropped to a song of Tchaikowsky, almost heartbreaking in its childish beauty, and then to the lecherous music of the second act of Tristan. Mazurka, polonaise, and nocturne wailed in the stuffy chamber; her little hands lit up the enchanted gloom of the place with bright thrills, until the bed and the dingy surroundings faded into phantoms and left only two stark souls in colloquy: Katarina's and mine.

Katarina had settled, I forget how, on the sofa, and was reclining very comfortably with her head on my shoulder and both arms about me. We did not talk. No questions passed as to why we had picked one another up. There we were, warmed with vodka and tea, at eleven o'clock at night, five stories above the clamorous world, while her friend shook the silly souls out of us. With the shy boldness of my native country, I stretched a hand and inclosed her fingers. She smiled; a curious smile that no other girl in London could have given; not a flushed smile, or a startled smile, or a satisfied smile, or a coy smile; but a smile of companionship, which seemed to have realized the tragedy of our living. So it was that she had, by slow stages, reached her comfortable position, for as my hand wandered from finger to wrist, from wrist to soft, rounded arm, and so inclosed her neck, she slipped and buried me in an avalanche of flaming, scented tresses.

Sanya at the piano shot a glance over her shoulder, a very sad-gay glance; she laughed, curiously, I almost said foreignly. I felt somehow as though I had been taken complete possession of by these people. I hardly belonged to myself. Fleet Street was but a street of dream. I seemed now to be awake and in an adorable captivity.

With a final volley of chords, the pianist slid from the chair, and sat by her boy on the carpet, smoothing his face with tobacco-stained fingers, and languishing, while her thick, over-ripe lips took his kisses as a baby bird takes food from its mother.

We talked—all of us—in jerks and snatches. Then the oil in the lamp began to give out, and the room grew dim. Someone said: 'Play something!' And some one said: 'Too tired!' The girl reclining on the bed grew snappy. She did not lean for caresses. She seemed morose, preoccupied, almost impatient. Twice she snapped up her boy on a casual remark. I believe I talked vodka'd nonsense...

But suddenly there came a whisper of soft feet on the landing, and a secret tap at the door. Someone opened it, and slipped out. One heard the lazy hum of voices in busy conversation. Then silence; and someone entered the room and shut the door. One of the boys asked, casually, 'What's up?' His question was not answered, but the girl who had gone to the door snapped something in a sharp tone which might have been either Russian or Yiddish. Katarina loosened herself from me, and sat up. The girl on the bed sat up. The three of them spat angry phrases about, I called over to one of the boys: 'What's the joke? Anything wrong?' and received a reply: 'Owshdiknow? I ain't a ruddy Russian, am I?'

Katarina suddenly drew back her flaming face. 'Here,' she said, 'you better go.'

'Go?'

'Yes—fathead! Go's what I said.'

'But—' I began, looking and feeling like a flabbergasted cat.

'Don't I speak plain? Go!'

I suppose a man never feels a finer idiot than when a woman tells him she doesn't want him. If he ever does, it is when a woman tells him that she loves him. Katarina had given me the bullet, and, of course, I felt a fool; but I derived some consolation from the fact that the other boys were being told off. Clearly, big things were in the air, about to happen. Something, evidently, had already happened. I wondered... Then I sat down on the sofa, and flatly told Katarina that I was not going unless I had a reason.

'Oh,' she said, blithely, 'ain't you? This is my room, ain't it? I brought you here, and you stay here just as long as I choose, and no longer. Who d'you think you are, saying you won't go? This is my room. I let you come here for a drink, and you just got to go when I say. See?'

I was about to make a second stand, when again there came a stealthy tap at the door, and the whispering of slippered feet. Sanya glided to the door, opened it, and disappeared. In a moment she came back, and called, 'Rina!' Katarina slipped from my embrace, went to the door, and disappeared too. One girl and three boys remained—in silence.

Next moment Katarina reappeared, and said something to Sanya. Sanya pulled her boy by the arm, and went out. The other girl pushed her boy at the neck and literally threw him out. Katarina came over to me, and said: 'Go, little fool!'

I said: 'Shan't unless I know what the game is.'

She stood over me; glared; searched for words to meet the occasion; found none. She gestured. I sat as rigid as an immobile comedian. Finally, she flung her arms, and swept away. At the door she turned; 'Blasted little fool! He'll do us both in if y'ain't careful. You don't know him. Both of us he'll have. Serveyeh right.'

She disappeared. I was alone. I heard the sup-sup of her slippered feet down the stair.

I got up, and moved to the door. I heard nothing. I stood by the window, my thoughts dancing a ragtime. I wondered what to do, and how, and whether. I wondered what was up exactly. I wondered...well, I just wondered. My thoughts got into a tangle, sank, and swam, and sank again. Then there was a sudden struggle and spurt from the lamp, and it went black out. From a room across the landing a clock ticked menacingly. I saw, by the thin light from the window, the smoke of a discarded cigarette curling up and up to the ceiling like a snake.

I went again to the door, peered down the steep stair and over the crazy balustrade. Nobody was about; no voices. I slipped swiftly down the five flights, met nobody. I stood in the slobbered vestibule. From afar I heard the sluck of the waters against the staples of the wharves, and the wicked hoot of the tugs.

It was then that a sudden nameless fear seized me; it was that simple terror that comes from nothing but ourselves. I am not usually afraid of any man or thing. I am normally nervous, and there are three or four things that have power to terrify me. But I am not, I think, afraid. At that moment, however, I was afraid of everything: of the room I had left, of the house, of the people, of the inviting lights of the warehouses and the threatening shoals of the alleys.

I stood a moment longer. Then I raced into Brick Lane, and out into the brilliance of Commercial Street.

A CLERGYMAN

MAX BEERBOHM

Fragmentary, pale, momentary; almost nothing; glimpsed and gone; as it were, a faint human hand thrust up, never to reappear, from beneath the rolling waters of Time, he forever haunts my memory and solicits my weak imagination. Nothing is told of him but that once, abruptly, he asked a question, and received an answer.

This was on the afternoon of April 7th, 1778, at Streatham, in the well-appointed house of Mr Thrale. Johnson, on the morning of that day, had entertained Boswell at breakfast in Bolt Court, and invited him to dine at Thrale Hall. The two took coach and arrived early. It seems that Sir John Pringle had asked Boswell to ask Johnson 'what were the best English sermons for style'. In the interval before dinner, accordingly, Boswell reeled off the names of several divines whose prose might or might not win commendation. 'Atterbury?' he suggested.

'JOHNSON: Yes, Sir, one of the best.
BOSWELL: Tillotson?
JOHNSON: Why, not now. I should not advise anyone to imitate Tillotson's style; though I don't know; I should be cautious of censuring anything that has been applauded by so many suffrages. South is one of the best, if you except his peculiarities, and his violence, and sometimes coarseness of language. Seed has a very fine style; but he is not very theological. Jortin's sermons are very elegant. Sherlock's style, too, is very elegant, though he has not made it his principal study. And you may add Smalridge.
BOSWELL: I like Ogden's Sermons on Prayer very much, both for neatness of style and subtility of reasoning.
JOHNSON: I should like to read all that Ogden has written.
BOSWELL: What I want to know is, what sermons afford the

best specimen of English pulpit eloquence.

JOHNSON: We have no sermons addressed to the passions, that are good for anything; if you mean that kind of eloquence.

A CLERGYMAN, whose name I do not recollect: Were not Dodd's sermons addressed to the passions?

JOHNSON: They were nothing, Sir, be they addressed to what they may.'

The suddenness of it! Bang!—and the rabbit that had popped from its burrow was no more.

I know not which is the more startling—the début of the unfortunate clergyman, or the instantaneousness of his end. Why hadn't Boswell told us there was a clergyman present? Well, we may be sure that so careful and acute an artist had some good reason. And I suppose the clergyman was left to take us unawares because just so did he take the company. Had we been told he was there, we might have expected that sooner or later he would join in the conversation. He would have had a place in our minds. We may assume that in the minds of the company around Johnson he had no place. He sat forgotten, overlooked; so that his self-assertion startled everyone just as on Boswell's page it startles us. In Johnson's massive and magnetic presence only some very remarkable man, such as Mr Burke, was sharply distinguishable from the rest. Others might, if they had something in them, stand out slightly. This unfortunate clergyman may have had something in him, but I judge that he lacked the gift of seeming as if he had. That deficiency, however, does not account for the horrid fate that befell him. One of Johnson's strongest and most inveterate feelings was his veneration for the Cloth. To any one in Holy Orders he habitually listened with a grace and charming deference. Today, moreover, he was in excellent good humor. He was at the Thrales', where he so loved to be; the day was fine; a fine dinner was in close prospect; and he had had what he always declared to be the sum of human felicity—a ride in a coach. Nor was there in the question put by the clergyman anything likely to enrage him. Dodd was one whom Johnson had befriended in adversity;

and it had always been agreed that Dodd in his pulpit was very emotional. What drew the blasting flash must have been not the question itself, but the manner in which it was asked. And I think we can guess what that manner was.

Say the words aloud: 'Were not Dodd's sermons addressed to the passions?' They are words which, if you have any dramatic and histrionic sense, cannot be said except in a high, thin voice.

You may, from sheer perversity, utter them in a rich and sonorous baritone or bass. But if you do so, they sound utterly unnatural. To make them carry the conviction of human utterance, you have no choice: you must pipe them.

Remember, now, Johnson was very deaf. Even the people whom he knew well, the people to whose voices he was accustomed, had to address him very loudly. It is probable that this unregarded, young, shy clergyman, when at length he suddenly mustered courage to 'cut in,' let his high, thin voice soar too high, insomuch that it was a kind of scream. On no other hypothesis can we account for the ferocity with which Johnson turned and rended him. Johnson didn't, we may be sure, mean to be cruel. The old lion, startled, just struck out blindly. But the force of paw and claws was not the less lethal. We have endless testimony to the strength of Johnson's voice; and the very cadence of those words, 'They were nothing, Sir, be they addressed to what they may,' convinces me that the old lion's jaws never gave forth a louder roar. Boswell does not record that there was any further conversation before the announcement of dinner. Perhaps the whole company had been temporarily deafened. But I am not bothering about them. My heart goes out to the poor dear clergyman exclusively.

I said a moment ago that he was young and shy; and I admit that I slipped those epithets in without having justified them to you by due process of induction. Your quick mind will have already supplied what I omitted. A man with a high, thin voice, and without power to impress anyone with a sense of his importance, a man so null in effect that even the retentive mind of Boswell did not retain his very name, would assuredly not be a self-confident man. Even if he were not naturally shy, social courage would soon have been sapped in him, and would in time have been destroyed, by experience. That he had not yet given himself up as a bad job, that he still had faint wild hopes, is proved by the fact that he did snatch the opportunity for asking that question. He must, accordingly, have been young. Was he the curate of the neighboring church? I think so. It would account for his having been invited. I see him as he sits there listening to the great Doctor's pronouncement on Atterbury and those others. He sits on the edge of a chair in the background. He has colorless eyes, fixed earnestly, and a face almost as pale as the clerical bands beneath his somewhat receding chin. His forehead is high and narrow, his hair mouse-colored. His hands are clasped tight before him, the knuckles standing out sharply. This constriction does not mean that he is steeling himself to speak. He has no positive intention of speaking. Very much, nevertheless, is he wishing in the back of his mind that he could say something—something whereat the great Doctor would turn on him and say, after a pause for thought, 'Why, yes, Sir. That is most justly observed' or 'Sir, this has never occurred to me. I thank you'—thereby fixing the observer forever high in the esteem of all. And now in a flash the chance presents itself. 'We have,' shouts Johnson, 'no sermons addressed to the passions, that are good for anything.' I see the curate's frame quiver with sudden impulse, and his mouth fly open, and—no, I can't bear it, I shut my eyes and ears. But audible, even so, is something shrill, followed by something thunderous.

Presently I reopen my eyes. The crimson has not yet faded from that young face yonder, and slowly down either cheek falls a glistening tear. Shades of Atterbury and Tillotson! Such weakness shames the Established Church. What would Jortin and Smalridge have said?—what Seed and South? And, by the way, who were they, these worthies? It is a solemn thought that so little is conveyed to us by names which to the palæo-Georgians conveyed so much. We discern a dim, composite picture of a big man in a big wig and a billowing black gown, with a big congregation beneath him. But we are not anxious to hear what he is saying. We know it is all very elegant. We know it will be printed and be bound in finely-tooled full calf, and no palæo-Georgian gentleman's library will be complete without it. Literate people in those days were comparatively few; but, bating that, one may say that sermons were as much in request as novels are today. I wonder, will mankind continue to be capricious? It is a very solemn thought indeed that no more than a hundred-and-fifty years hence the novelists of our time, with all their moral and political and sociological outlook and influence, will perhaps shine as indistinctly as do those old preachers, with all their elegance, now. 'Yes, Sir,' some great pundit may be telling a disciple at this moment, 'Wells is one of the best. Galsworthy is one of the best, if you except his concern for delicacy of style. Mrs Ward has a very firm grasp of problems, but is not very creational. Caine's books are very edifying. I should like to read all that Caine has written. Miss Corelli, too, is very edifying. And you may add Upton Sinclair.'

'What I want to know,' says the disciple, 'is, what English novels may be selected as specially enthralling.'

The pundit answers: 'We have no novels addressed to the passions that are good for anything, if you mean that kind of enthralment.'

And here some poor wretch (whose name the disciple will not remember) inquires: 'Are not Mrs Glyn's novels addressed to the passions?' and is in due form annihilated. Can it be that a time will come when readers of this passage in our pundit's Life will take more interest in the poor nameless wretch than in all the bearers of those great names put together, being no more able or anxious to discriminate between (say) Mrs Ward and Mr Sinclair than we are to set Ogden above Sherlock, or Sherlock above Ogden? It seems impossible. But we must remember that things are not always what they seem.

Every man illustrious in his day, however much he may be gratified by his fame, looks with an eager eye to posterity for a continuance of past favors, and would even live the remainder of his life in obscurity if by so doing he could insure that future generations would preserve a correct attitude towards him forever. This is very natural and human, but, like so many very natural and human things, very silly. Tillotson and the rest need not, after all, be pitied for our neglect of them. They either know nothing about it, or are above such terrene trifles. Let us keep our pity for the seething mass of divines who were not elegantly verbose, and had no fun or glory while they lasted. And let us keep a specially large portion for one whose lot was so much worse than merely undistinguished. If that nameless curate had not been at the Thrales' that day, or, being there, had kept the silence that so well became him, his life would have been drab enough, in all conscience. But at any rate an unpromising career would not have been nipped in the bud. And that is what in fact happened, I'm sure of it. A robust man might have rallied under the blow. Not so our friend. Those who knew him in infancy had not expected that he would be reared. Better for him had they been right. It is well to grow up and be ordained, but not if you are delicate and very sensitive, and shall happen to annoy the greatest, the most stentorian and roughest of contemporary personages. 'A Clergyman' never held up his head or smiled again after the brief encounter recorded for us by Boswell. He sank into a rapid decline. Before the next blossoming of Thrale Hall's almond trees he was no more. I like to think that he died forgiving Dr Johnson.

BED-BOOKS AND NIGHT-LIGHTS

H. M. TOMLINSON

The rain flashed across the midnight window with a myriad feet. There was a groan in outer darkness, the voice of all nameless dreads. The nervous candle-flame shuddered by my bedside. The groaning rose to a shriek, and the little flame jumped in a panic, and nearly left its white column. Out of the corners of the room swarmed the released shadows. Black specters danced in ecstasy over my bed. I love fresh air, but I cannot allow it to slay the shining and delicate body of my little friend the candle-flame, the comrade who ventures with me into the solitudes beyond midnight. I shut the window.

They talk of the candle-power of an electric bulb. What do they mean? It cannot have the faintest glimmer of the real power of my candle. It would be as right to express, in the same inverted and foolish comparison, the worth of 'those delicate sisters, the Pleiades'. That pinch of star dust, the Pleiades, exquisitely remote in deepest night, in the profound where light all but fails, has not the power of a sulphur match; yet, still apprehensive to the mind though tremulous on the limit of vision, and sometimes even vanishing, it brings into distinction those distant and difficult hints—hidden far behind all our verified thoughts—which we rarely properly view. I should like to know of any great arc-lamp which could do that. So the star-like candle for me. No other light follows so intimately an author's most ghostly suggestion. We sit, the candle and I, in the midst of the shades we are conquering, and sometimes look up from the lucent page to contemplate the dark hosts of the enemy with a smile before they overwhelm us; as they will, of course. Like me, the candle is mortal; it will burn out.

As the bed-book itself should be a sort of night-light, to assist its illumination, coarse lamps are useless. They would douse the book. The light for such a book must accord with it. It must be, like the book, a limited, personal, mellow, and companionable glow; the solitary taper beside the only worshiper in a sanctuary. That is why nothing can compare with the intimacy of candle-light for a bed-book. It is a living heart, bright and warm in central night, burning for us alone, holding the gaunt and towering shadows at bay. There the monstrous specters stand in our midnight room, the advance guard of the darkness of the world, held off by our valiant little glim, but ready to flood instantly and founder us in original gloom.

The wind moans without; ancient evils are at large and wandering in torment. The rain shrieks across the window. For a moment, for just a moment, the sentinel candle is shaken, and burns blue with terror. The shadows leap out instantly. The little flame recovers, and merely looks at its foe the darkness, and back to its own place goes the old enemy of light and man. The candle for me, tiny, mortal, warm, and brave, a golden lily on a silver stem!

'Almost any book does for a bed-book,' a woman once said to me. I nearly replied in a hurry that almost any woman would do for a wife; but that is not the way to bring people to conviction of sin. Her idea was that the bed-book is soporific, and for that reason she even advocated the reading of political speeches. That would be a dissolute act. Certainly you would go to sleep; but in what a frame of mind! You would enter into sleep with your eyes shut. It would be like dying, not only unshriven, but in the act of guilt.

What book shall it shine upon? Think of Plato, or Dante, or Tolstoy, or a Blue Book for such an occasion! I cannot. They will not do—they are no good to me. I am not writing about you. I know those men I have named are transcendent, the greater lights. But I am bound to confess at times they bore me. Though their feet are clay and on earth, just as ours, their stellar brows are sometimes dim in remote clouds. For my part, they are too big for bed-fellows. I cannot see myself, carrying my feeble and restricted glim, following (in pajamas) the statuesque figure of the Florentine where it stalks, aloof in its garb of austere pity, the sonorous deeps of Hades. Hades! Not for me; not after midnight! Let those go who like it.

As for the Russian, vast and disquieting, I refuse to leave all, including the blankets and the pillow, to follow him into the gelid tranquillity of the upper air, where even the colors are prismatic spicules of ice, to brood upon the erratic orbit of the poor mudball below called earth. I know it is my world also; but I cannot help that. It is too late, after a busy day, and at that hour, to begin overtime on fashioning a new and better planet out of cosmic dust. By breakfast-time, nothing useful would have been accomplished. We should all be where we were the night before. The job is far too long, once the pillow is nicely set.

For the truth is, there are times when we are too weary to remain attentive and thankful under the improving eye, kindly but severe, of the seers. There are times when we do not wish to be any better than we are. We do not wish to be elevated and improved. At midnight, away with such books! As for the literary pundits, the high priests of the Temple of Letters, it is interesting and helpful occasionally for an acolyte to swinge them a good hard one with an incense-burner, and cut and run, for a change, to something outside the rubrics. Midnight is the time when one can recall, with ribald delight, the names of all the Great Works which every gentleman ought to have read, but which some of us have not. For there is almost as much clotted nonsense written about literature as there is about theology.

There are few books which go with midnight, solitude, and a candle. It is much easier to say what does not please us then than what is exactly right. The book must be, anyhow, something benedictory by a sinning fellow-man. Cleverness would be repellent at such an hour. Cleverness, anyhow, is the level of mediocrity today; we are all too infernally clever. The first witty and perverse paradox blows out the candle. Only the sick in mind crave cleverness, as a morbid body turns to drink.

The late candle throws its beams a great distance; and its rays make transparent much that seemed massy and important. The mind at rest beside that light, when the house is asleep, and the consequential affairs of the urgent world have diminished to their right proportions because we see them distantly from another and a more tranquil place in the heavens where duty, honor, witty arguments, controversial logic on great questions, appear such as will leave hardly a trace of fossil in the indurated mud which presently will cover them—the mind then certainly smiles at cleverness.

For though at that hour the body may be dog-tired, the mind is white and lucid, like that of a man from whom a fever has abated. It is bare of illusions. It has a sharp focus, small and starlike, as a clear and lonely flame left burning by the altar of a shrine from which all have gone but one. A book which approaches that light in the privacy of that place must come, as it were, with honest and open pages.

I like Heine then, though. His mockery of the grave and great, in those sentences which are as brave as pennants in a breeze, is comfortable and sedative. One's own secret and awkward convictions, never expressed because not lawful and because it is hard to get words to bear them lightly, seem then to be heard aloud in the mild, easy, and confident diction of an immortal whose voice has the blitheness of one who has watched, amused and irreverent, the high gods in eager and secret debate on the best way to keep the gilt and trappings on the body of the evil they have created.

That first-rate explorer, Gulliver, is also fine in the light of the intimate candle. Have you read lately again his Voyage to the Houyhnhnms? Try it alone again in quiet. Swift knew all about our contemporary troubles. He has got it all down. Why was he called a misanthrope? Reading that last voyage of Gulliver in the select intimacy of midnight I am forced to wonder, not at Swift's hatred of mankind, not at his satire of his fellows, not at the strange and terrible nature of this genius who thought that much of us, but how it is that after such a wise and sorrowful revealing of the things we insist on doing, and our reasons for doing them, and what happens after we have done them, men do not change. It does seem impossible that society could remain unaltered, after the surprise its appearance should have caused it as it saw its face in that ruthless mirror. We point instead to the fact that Swift lost his mind in the end. Well, that is not a matter for surprise.

Such books, and France's *Isle of Penguins*, are not disturbing as bed-books. They resolve one's agitated and outraged soul, relieving it with some free expression for the accusing and questioning thoughts engendered by the day's affairs. But they do not rest immediately to hand in the book-shelf by the bed. They depend on the kind of day one has had. Sterne is closer. One would rather be transported as far as possible from all the disturbances of earth's envelope of clouds, and *Tristram Shandy* is sure to be found in the sun.

But best of all books for midnight are travel books. Once I was lost every night for months with Doughty in the *Arabia Deserta*. He is a craggy author. A long course of the ordinary facile stuff, such as one gets in the Press every day, thinking it is English, sends one thoughtless and headlong among the bitter herbs and stark boulders of Doughty's burning and spacious expanse; only to get bewildered, and the shins broken, and a great fatigue at first, in a strange land of fierce sun, hunger, glittering spar, ancient plutonic rock, and very Adam himself. But once you are acclimatized, and know the language—it takes time—there is no more London after dark, till, a wanderer returned from a forgotten land, you emerge from the interior of Arabia on the Red Sea coast again, feeling as though you had lost touch with the world you used to know. And if that doesn't mean good writing I know of no other test.

Because once there was a father whose habit it was to read with his boys nightly some chapters of the Bible—and cordially they hated that habit of his—I have that Book too; though I fear I have it for no reason that he, the rigid old faithful, would be pleased to hear about. He thought of the future when he read the Bible; I read it for the past. The familiar names, the familiar rhythm of its words, its wonderful well-remembered stories of things long past—like that of Esther, one of the best in English—the eloquent anger of the prophets for the people then who looked as though they were alive, but were really dead at heart, all is solace and home to me. And now I think of it, it is our home and solace that we want in a bed-book.

THE PRECEPT OF PEACE

LOUISE IMOGEN GUINEY

A certain sort of voluntary abstraction is the oldest and choicest of social attitudes. In France, where all esthetic discoveries are made, it was crowned long ago: la sainte indifférence is, or may be, a cult, and le saint indifférent an articled practitioner. For the Gallic mind, brought up at the knee of a consistent paradox, has found that not to appear concerned about a desired good is the only method to possess it; full happiness is given, in other words, to the very man who will never sue for it. This is a secret neat as that of the Sphinx: to 'go softly' among events, yet domineer them. Without fear: not because we are brave, but because we are exempt; we bear so charmed a life that not even Baldur's mistletoe can touch us to harm us. Without solicitude: for the essential thing is trained, falcon-like, to light from above upon our wrists, and it has become with us an automatic motion to open the hand, and drop what appertains to us no longer. Be it renown or a new hat, the shorter stick of celery, or:

The friends to whom we had no natural right,
The homes that were not destined to be ours,

...it is all one: let it fall away! since only so, by depletions, can we buy serenity and a blithe mien. It is diverting to study, at the feet of Antisthenes and of Socrates his master, how many indispensables man can live without; or how many he can gather together, make over into luxuries, and so abrogate them. Thoreau somewhere expresses himself as full of divine pity for the 'mover', who on May-Day clouds city streets with his melancholy household caravans: fatal impedimenta for an immortal. No: furniture is clearly a superstition. 'I have little, I want nothing; all my treasure is in Minerva's tower.' Not that the novice may not accumulate. Rather, let him collect beetles and Venetian interrogation-marks; if so be that he may distinguish what is truly extrinsic to him, and bestow these toys, eventually, on the children of Satan who clamor at the monastery gate. Of all his store, unconsciously increased, he can always part with sixteen-seventeenths, by way of concession to his individuality, and think the subtraction so much concealing marble chipped from the heroic figure of himself. He would be a donor from the beginning; before he can be seen to own, he will disencumber, and divide. Strange and fearful is his discovery, amid the bric-a-brac of the world, that this knowledge, or this material benefit, is for him alone. He would fain beg off from the acquisition, and shake the touch of the tangible from his imperious wings. It is not enough to cease to strive for personal favor; your true indifférent is Early Franciscan: caring not to have, he fears to hold. Things useful need never become to him things desirable. Towards all commonly-accounted sinecures, he bears the coldest front in Nature, like a magician walking a maze, and scornful of its flower-bordered detentions. 'I enjoy life,' says Seneca, 'because I am ready to leave it.' Meanwhile, they who act with too jealous respect for their morrow of civilized comfort, reap only indigestion, and crow's-foot traceries for their deluded eye-corners.

Now nothing is farther from le saint indifférent than cheap indifferentism, so-called: the sickness of sophomores. His business is to hide, not to display, his lack of interest in fripperies. It is not he who looks languid, and twiddles his thumbs for sick misplacedness, like Achilles among girls. On the contrary, he is a smiling industrious elf, monstrous attentive to the canons of polite society. In relation to others, he shows what passes for animation and enthusiasm; for at all times his character is founded on control of these qualities, not on the absence of them. It flatters his sense of superiority that he may thus pull wool about the ears of joint and several. He has so strong a will that it can be crossed and counter-crossed, as by himself, so by a dozen outsiders, without a break in his apparent phlegm. He has gone through volition, and come out at the other side of it; everything with him is a specific act: he has no habits. Le saint indifférent is a dramatic wight: he loves to refuse your proffered six per cent, when, by a little haggling, he may obtain three-and-a-half. For so he gets away with his own mental processes virgin: it is inconceivable to you that, being sane, he should so comport himself. Amiable, perhaps, only by painful propulsions and sore vigilance, let him appear the mere inheritor of easy good-nature. Unselfish out of sheer pride, and ever eager to claim the slippery side of the pavement, or the end cut of the roast (on the secret ground, be it understood, that he is not as Capuan men, who wince at trifles), let him have his ironic reward in passing for one whose physical connoisseurship is yet in the raw. That sympathy which his rule forbids his devoting to the usual objects, he expends, with some bravado, upon their opposites; for he would fain seem a decent partizan of some sort, not what he is, a bivalve intelligence, Tros Tyriusque. He is known here and there, for instance, as valorous in talk; yet he is by nature a solitary, and, for the most part, somewhat less communicative than

'The wind that sings to himself as he makes stride, Lonely and terrible, on the Andean height.'

Imagining nothing idler than words in the face of grave events, he condoles and congratulates with the genteelest air in the world. In short, while there is anything expected of him, while there are spectators to be fooled, the stratagems of the fellow prove inexhaustible. It is only when he is quite alone that he drops his jaw, and stretches his legs; then heigho! Arises like a smoke, and envelopes him becomingly, the beautiful native well-bred torpidity of the gods, of poetic boredom, of 'the Oxford manner.'

'How weary, stale, flat, and unprofitable!' sighed Hamlet of this mortal outlook. As it came from him in the beginning, that plaint, in its sincerity, can come only from the man of culture, who feels about him vast mental spaces and depths, and to whom the face of creation is but comparative and symbolic. Nor will he breathe it in the common ear, where it may woo misapprehensions, and breed ignorant rebellion. The unlettered must ever love or hate what is nearest him, and, for lack of perspective, think his own fist the size of the sun. The social prizes, which, with mellowed observers, rank as twelfth or thirteenth in order of desirability, such as wealth and a foothold in affairs, seem to him first and sole; and to them he clings like a barnacle. But to our indifférent, nothing is so vulgar as close suction. He will never tighten his fingers on loaned opportunity; he is a gentleman, the hero of the habitually relaxed grasp. A light unprejudiced hold on his profits strikes him as decent and comely, though his true artistic pleasure is still in 'fallings from us, vanishings.' It costs him little to lose and to forego, to unlace his tentacles, and from the many who push hard behind, to retire, as it were, on a never-guessed-at competency, 'richer than untempted kings.' He would not be a life-prisoner, in ever so charming a bower. While the tranquil Sabine Farm is his delight, well he knows that on the dark trail ahead of him, even Sabine Farms are not sequacious. Thus he learns betimes to play the guest under his own cedars, and, with disciplinary intent, goes often from them; and, hearing his heart-strings snap the third night he is away, rejoices that he is again a freedman. Where his foot is planted (though it root not anywhere), he calls that spot home. No Unitarian in locality, it follows that he is the best of travelers, tangential merely, and pleased with each new vista of the human Past. He sometimes wishes his understanding less, that he might itch deliciously with a prejudice. With cosmic congruities, great and general forces, he keeps, all along, a tacit understanding, such as one has with beloved relatives at a distance; and his finger, airily inserted in his outer pocket, is really upon the pulse of eternity. His vocation, however, is to bury himself in the minor and immediate task; and from his intent manner, he gets confounded, promptly and permanently, with the victims of commercial ambition.

The true use of the much-praised Lucius Cary, Viscount Falkland, has hardly been apprehended: he is simply the patron saint of indifférents. From first to last, almost alone in that discordant time, he seems to have heard far-off resolving harmonies, and to have been rapt away with foreknowledge. Battle, to which all knights were bred, was penitential to him. It was but a childish means: and to what end? He meanwhile—and no man carried his will in better abeyance to the scheme of the universe—wanted no diligence in camp or council. Cares sat handsomely on him who cared not at all, who won small comfort from the cause which his conscience finally espoused. He labored to be a doer, to stand well with observers; and none save his intimate friends read his agitation and profound weariness. 'I am so much taken notice of,' he writes, 'for an impatient desire for peace, that it is necessary I should likewise make it appear how it is not out of fear for the utmost hazard of war.' And so, driven from the ardor he had to the simulation of the ardor he lacked, loyally daring, a sacrifice to one of two transient opinions, and inly impartial as a star, Lord Falkland fell: the young never-to-be-forgotten martyr of Newburg field. The imminent deed he made a work of art; and the station of the moment the only post of honor. Life and death may be all one to such a man: but he will at least take the noblest pains to discriminate between Tweedledum and Tweedledee, if he has to write a book about the variations of their antennæ. And like the Carolian exemplar is the disciple. The indifférent is a good thinker, or a good fighter. He is no 'immartial minion,' as dear old Chapman suffers Hector to call Tydides. Nevertheless, his sign-manual is content with humble and stagnant conditions. Talk of scaling the Himalayas of life affects him, very palpably, as 'tall talk'. He deals not with things, but with the impressions and analogies of things. The material counts for nothing with him: he has moulted it away. Not so sure of the identity of the higher course of action as he is of his consecrating dispositions, he feels that he may make heaven again, out of sundries, as he goes. Shall not a beggarly duty, discharged with perfect temper, land him in 'the out-courts of Glory', quite as successfully as a grand Sunday-school excursion to front the cruel Paynim foe? He thinks so. Experts have thought so before him. Francis Drake, with the national alarum instant in his ears, desired first to win at bowls, on the Devon sward, 'and afterwards to settle with the Don.' No one will claim a buccaneering hero for an indifférent, however. The Jesuit novices were ball-playing almost at that very time, three hundred years ago, when some too speculative companion, figuring the end of the world in a few moments (with just leisure enough, between, to be shriven in chapel, according to his own thrifty mind), asked Louis of Gonzaga how he, on his part, should employ the precious interval. 'I should go on with the game,' said the most innocent and most ascetic youth among them. But to cite the behavior of any of the saints is to step over the playful line allotted. Indifference of the mundane brand is not to be confounded with their detachment, which is emancipation wrought in the soul, and the ineffable efflorescence of the Christian spirit. Like most supernatural virtues, it has a laic shadow; the counsel to abstain, and to be unsolicitous, is one not only of perfection, but also of polity. A very little nonadhesion to common affairs, a little reserve of unconcern, and the gay spirit of sacrifice, provide the moral immunity which is the only real estate. The indifférent believes in storms: since tales of shipwreck encompass him. But once among his own kind, he wonders that folk should be circumvented by merely extraneous powers! His favorite catch, woven in among escaped dangers, rises through the roughest weather, and daunts it:

'Now strike your sailes, ye jolly mariners, For we be come into a quiet rode.'

No slave to any vicissitude, his imagination is, on the contrary, the cheerful obstinate tyrant of all that is. He lives, as Keats once said of himself, 'in a thousand worlds', withdrawing at will from one to another, often curtailing his circumference to enlarge his liberty. His universe is a universe of balls, like those which the cunning Oriental carvers make out of ivory; each entire surface perforated with the same delicate pattern, each moving prettily and inextricably within the other, and all but the outer one impossible to handle. In some such innermost asylum the right sort of dare-devil sits smiling, while men rage or weep.

ON LYING AWAKE AT NIGHT

STEWART EDWARD WHITE

'Who hath lain alone to hear the wild goose cry?' About once in so often you are due to lie awake at night. Why this is so I have never been able to discover. It apparently comes from no predisposing uneasiness of indigestion, no rashness in the matter of too much tea or tobacco, no excitation of unusual incident or stimulating conversation. In fact, you turn in with the expectation of rather a good night's rest. Almost at once the little noises of the forest grow larger, blend in the hollow bigness of the first drowse; your thoughts drift idly back and forth between reality and dream; when—snap!—you are broad awake!

Perhaps the reservoir of your vital forces is full to the overflow of a little waste; or perhaps, more subtly, the great Mother insists thus that you enter the temple of her larger mysteries.

For, unlike mere insomnia, lying awake at night in the woods is pleasant. The eager, nervous straining for sleep gives way to a delicious indifference. You do not care. Your mind is cradled in an exquisite poppy-suspension of judgment and of thought. Impressions slip vaguely into your consciousness and as vaguely out again. Sometimes they stand stark and naked for your inspection; sometimes they lose themselves in the mist of half-sleep. Always they lay soft velvet fingers on the drowsy imagination, so that in their caressing you feel the vaster spaces from which they have come. Peaceful-brooding your faculties receive. Hearing, sight, smell—all are preternaturally keen to whatever of sound and sight and woods perfume is abroad through the night; and yet at the same time active appreciation dozes, so these things lie on it sweet and cloying like fallen rose-leaves.

In such circumstance you will hear what the voyageurs call the voices of the rapids. Many people never hear them at all.

They speak very soft and low and distinct beneath the steady roar and dashing, beneath even the lesser tinklings and gurglings whose quality superimposes them over the louder sounds. They are like the tear-forms swimming across the field of vision, which disappear so quickly when you concentrate your sight to look at them, and which reappear so magically when again your gaze turns vacant. In the stillness of your hazy half-consciousness they speak; when you bend your attention to listen, they are gone, and only the tumults and the tinklings remain.

But in the moments of their audibility they are very distinct. Just as often an odor will wake all a vanished memory, so these voices, by the force of a large impressionism, suggest whole scenes. Far off are the cling-clang-cling of chimes and the swell-and-fall murmur of a multitude en fête, so that subtly you feel the gray old town, with its walls, the crowded market-place, the decent peasant crowd, the booths, the mellow church building with its bells, the warm, dust-moted sun. Or, in the pauses between the swish-dash-dashings of the waters, sound faint and clear voices singing intermittently, calls, distant notes of laughter, as though many canoes were working against the current—only the flotilla never gets any nearer, nor the voices louder. The voyageurs call these mist people the Huntsmen; and look frightened. To each is his vision, according to his experience. The nations of the earth whisper to their exiled sons through the voices of the rapids. Curiously enough, by all reports, they suggest always peaceful scenes—a harvest-field, a street fair, a Sunday morning in a cathedral town, careless travelers—never the turmoils and struggles. Perhaps this is the great Mother's compensation in a harsh mode of life.

Nothing is more fantastically unreal to tell about, nothing more concretely real to experience, than this undernote of the quick water. And when you do lie awake at night, it is always making its unobtrusive appeal. Gradually its hypnotic spell works. The distant chimes ring louder and nearer as you cross the borderland of sleep. And then outside the tent some little woods noise snaps the thread. An owl hoots, a whippoorwill cries, a twig cracks beneath the cautious prowl of some night creature—at once the yellow sunlit French meadows puff away—you are staring at the blurred image of the moon spraying through the texture of your tent.

The voices of the rapids have dropped into the background, as have the dashing noises of the stream. Through the forest is a great silence, but no stillness at all. The whippoorwill swings down and up the short curve of his regular song; over and over an owl says his rapid whoo, whoo, whoo. These, with the ceaseless dash of the rapids, are the web on which the night traces her more delicate embroideries of the unexpected. Distant crashes, single and impressive; stealthy footsteps near at hand; the subdued scratching of claws; a faint sniff! sniff! sniff! of inquiry; the sudden clear tin-horn ko-ko-ko-óh of the little owl; the mournful, long-drawn-out cry of the loon, instinct with the spirit of loneliness; the ethereal call-note of the birds of passage high in the air; a patter, patter, patter, among the dead leaves, immediately stilled; and then at the last, from the thicket close at hand, the beautiful silver purity of the white-throated sparrow—the nightingale of the North—trembling with the ecstasy of beauty, as though a shimmering moonbeam had turned to sound; and all the while the blurred figure of the moon mounting to the ridge-line of your tent—these things combine subtly, until at last the great Silence of which they are a part overarches the night and draws you forth to contemplation.

No beverage is more grateful than the cup of spring water you drink at such a time; no moment more refreshing than that in which you look about you at the darkened forest. You have cast from you with the warm blanket the drowsiness of dreams. A coolness, physical and spiritual, bathes you from head to foot. All your senses are keyed to the last vibrations. You hear the littler night prowlers; you glimpse the greater. A faint, searching woods perfume of dampness greets your nostrils. And somehow, mysteriously, in a manner not to be understood, the forces of the world seem in suspense, as though a touch might crystallize infinite possibilities into infinite power and motion. But the touch lacks. The forces hover on the edge of action, unheeding the little noises. In all humbleness and awe, you are a dweller of the Silent Places.

At such a time you will meet with adventures. One night we put fourteen inquisitive porcupines out of camp. Near McGregor's Bay I discovered in the large grass park of my camp-site nine deer, cropping the herbage like so many beautiful ghosts. A friend tells me of a fawn that every night used to sleep outside his tent and within a foot of his head, probably by way of protection against wolves. Its mother had in all likelihood been killed. The instant my friend moved toward the tent opening the little creature would disappear, and it was always gone by earliest daylight. Nocturnal bears in search of pork are not uncommon. But even though your interest meets nothing but the bats and the woods shadows and the stars, that few moments of the sleeping world forces is a psychical experience to be gained in no other way. You cannot know the night by sitting up; she will sit up with you. Only by coming into her presence from the borders of sleep can you meet her face to face in her intimate mood.

The night wind from the river, or from the open spaces of the wilds, chills you after a time. You begin to think of your blankets. In a few moments you roll yourself in their soft wool. Instantly it is morning.

And, strange to say, you have not to pay by going through the day unrefreshed. You may feel like turning in at eight instead of nine, and you may fall asleep with unusual promptitude, but your journey will begin clear-headedly, proceed springily, and end with much in reserve. No languor, no dull headache, no exhaustion, follows your experience. For this once your two hours of sleep have been as effective as nine.

A WOODLAND VALENTINE

MARIAN STORM

Forces astir in the deepest roots grow restless beneath the lock of frost. Bulbs try the door. February's stillness is charged with a faint anxiety, as if the powers of light, pressing up from the earth's center and streaming down from the stronger sun, had troubled the buried seeds, who strive to answer their liberator, so that the guarding mother must whisper over and over, 'Not yet, not yet!' Better to stay behind the frozen gate than to come too early up into realms where the wolves of cold are still aprowl. Wisely the snow places a white hand over eager life unseen, but perceived in February's woods as a swimmer feels the changing moods of water in a lake fed by springs. Only the thick stars, closer and more companionable than in months of foliage, burn alert and serene. In February the Milky Way is revealed divinely lucent to lonely peoples—herdsmen, mountaineers, fishermen, trappers—who are abroad in the starlight hours of this grave and silent time of year. It is in the long, frozen nights that the sky has most red flowers.

February knows the beat of twilight wings. Drifting north again come birds who only pretended to forsake us—adventurers, not so fond of safety but that they dare risk finding how snow bunting and pine finch have plundered the cones of the evergreens, while chickadees, sparrows, and crows are supervising from established stations all the more domestic supplies available, a sparrow often making it possible to annoy even a duck out of her share of cracked corn. Ranged along a brown-draped oak branch in the waxing light, crows show a lordly glistening of feathers. (Sun on a sweeping wing in flight has the quality of sun on a ripple.) Where hemlocks gather, deep in somber woods, the great horned owl has thus soon, perhaps working amid snows at her task, built a nest wherein March will find sturdy balls of fluff. The thunderous love song of her mate sounds through the timber. By the time the wren has nested these winter babies will be solemn with the wisdom of their famous race.

There is no season like the end of February for cleaning out brooks. Hastening yellow waters toss a dreary wreckage of torn or ashen leaves, twigs, acorn cups, stranded rafts of bark, and buttonballs from the sycamore, never to come to seed. Standing on one bank or both, according to the sundering flood's ambition, the knight with staff and bold forefinger sets the water princess free. She goes then curtsying and dimpling over the shining gravel, sliding from beneath the ice that roofs her on the uplands down to the softer valleys, where her quickened step will be heard by the frogs in their mansions of mud, and the fish, recluses in rayless pools, will rise to the light she brings.

Down from the frozen mountains, in summer, birds and winds must bear the seed of alpine flowers—lilies that lean against unmelting snows, poppies, bright-colored herbs, and the palely gleaming, fringed beauties that change names with countries. How just and reasonable it would seem to be that flowers which edge the ice in July should consent to bloom in lowlands no colder in February! The pageant of blue, magenta, and scarlet on the austere upper slopes of the Rockies, where nights are bitter to the summer wanderer—why should it not flourish to leeward of a valley barn in months when icicles hang from the eaves in this tamer setting? But no. Mountain tempests are endurable to the silken-petaled. The treacherous lowland winter, with its coaxing suns followed by roaring desolation, is for blooms bred in a different tradition.

The light is clear but hesitant, a delicate wine, by no means the mighty vintage of April. February has no intoxication; the vague eagerness that gives the air a pulse where fields lie voiceless comes from the secret stirring of imprisoned life. Spring and sunrise are forever miracles, but the early hour of the wonder hardly hints the exuberance of its fulfilment. Even the forest dwellers move gravely, thankful for any promise of kindness from the lord of day as he hangs above a sea-gray landscape, but knowing well that their long duress is not yet to end. Deer pathetically haunt the outskirts of farms, gazing upon cattle feeding in winter pasture from the stack, and often, after dark, clearing the fences and robbing the same disheveled storehouse. Not a chipmunk winks from the top rail. The woodchuck, after his single expeditionary effort on Candlemas, which he is obliged to make for mankind's enlightenment, has retired without being seen, in sunshine or shadow, and has not the slightest intention of disturbing himself just yet. Though snowdrops may feel uneasy, he knows too much about the Ides of March! Quietest of all Northern woods creatures, the otter slides from one ice-hung waterfall to the next. The solitary scamperer left is the cottontail, appealing because he is the most pursued and politest of the furry; faithfully trying to give no offense, except when starvation points to winter cabbage, he is none the less fey. So is the mink, though he moves like a phantom.

Mosses, whereon March in coming treads first, show one hue brighter in the swamps. Pussy willows have made a gray dawn in viny caverns where the day's own dawn looks in but faintly, and the flushing of the red willow betrays reveries of a not impossible cowslip upon the bank beneath. The blue jay has mentioned it in the course of his voluble recollections. He is unwilling to prophesy arbutus, but he will just hint that when the leaves in the wood lot show through snow as early as this... Once he found a hepatica bud the last day of February... Speaking with his old friend, the muskrat, last week... And when you can see red pebbles in the creek at five o'clock in the afternoon... But it is no use to expect yellow orchids on the west knoll this spring, for some people found them there last year, and after that you might as well... Of course cowslips beside red willows are remarkably pretty, just as blue jays in a cedar with blue berries... He is interminable, but then he has seen a great deal of life. And February needs her blue jays' unwearied and conquering faith.

THE ELEMENTS OF POETRY

GEORGE SANTAYANA

If poetry in its higher reaches is more philosophical than history, because it presents the memorable types of men and things apart from unmeaning circumstances, so in its primary substance and texture poetry is more philosophical than prose because it is nearer to our immediate experience. Poetry breaks up the trite conceptions designated by current words into the sensuous qualities out of which those conceptions were originally put together. We name what we conceive and believe in, not what we see; things, not images; souls, not voices and silhouettes. This naming, with the whole education of the senses which it accompanies, subserves the uses of life; in order to thread our way through the labyrinth of objects which assault us, we must make a great selection in our sensuous experience; half of what we see and hear we must pass over as insignificant, while we piece out the other half with such an ideal complement as is necessary to turn it into a fixed and well-ordered conception of the world. This labor of perception and understanding, this spelling of the material meaning of experience, is enshrined in our workaday language and ideas; ideas which are literally poetic in the sense that they are 'made' (for every conception in an adult mind is a fiction), but which are at the same time prosaic because they are made economically, by abstraction, and for use.

When the child of poetic genius, who has learned this intellectual and utilitarian language in the cradle, goes afield and gathers for himself the aspects of nature, he begins to encumber his mind with the many living impressions which the intellect rejected, and which the language of the intellect can hardly convey; he labors with his nameless burden of perception, and wastes himself in aimless impulses of emotion and reverie, until finally the method of some art offers a vent to his inspiration, or to such part of it as can survive the test of time and the discipline of expression.

The poet retains by nature the innocence of the eye, or recovers it easily; he disintegrates the fictions of common perception into their sensuous elements, gathers these together again into chance groups as the accidents of his environment or the affinities of his temperament may conjoin them; and this wealth of sensation and this freedom of fancy, which make an extraordinary ferment in his ignorant heart, presently bubble over into some kind of utterance.

The fullness and sensuousness of such effusions bring them nearer to our actual perceptions than common discourse could come; yet they may easily seem remote, overloaded, and obscure to those accustomed to think entirely in symbols, and never to be interrupted in the algebraic rapidity of their thinking by a moment's pause and examination of heart, nor ever to plunge for a moment into that torrent of sensation and imagery over which the bridge of prosaic associations habitually carries us safe and dry to some conventional act. How slight that bridge commonly is, how much an affair of trestles and wire, we can hardly conceive until we have trained ourselves to an extreme sharpness of introspection. But psychologists have discovered, what laymen generally will confess, that we hurry by the procession of our mental images as we do by the traffic of the street, intent on business, gladly forgetting the noise and movement of the scene, and looking only for the corner we would turn or the door we would enter. Yet in our alertest moment the depths of the soul are still dreaming; the real world stands drawn in bare outline against a background of chaos and unrest. Our logical thoughts dominate experience only as the parallels and meridians make a checkerboard of the sea. They guide our voyage without controlling the waves, which toss forever in spite of our ability to ride over them to our chosen ends. Sanity is a madness put to good uses; waking life is a dream controlled.

Out of the neglected riches of this dream the poet fetches his wares. He dips into the chaos that underlies the rational shell of the world and brings up some superfluous image, some emotion dropped by the way, and reattaches it to the present object; he reinstates things unnecessary, he emphasizes things ignored, he paints in again into the landscape the tints which the intellect has allowed to fade from it. If he seems sometimes to obscure a fact, it is only because he is restoring an experience. The first element which the intellect rejects in forming its ideas of things is the emotion which accompanies the perception; and this emotion is the first thing the poet restores. He stops at the image, because he stops to enjoy. He wanders into the bypaths of association because the bypaths are delightful. The love of beauty which made him give measure and cadence to his words, the love of harmony which made him rhyme them, reappear in his imagination and make him select there also the material that is itself beautiful, or capable of assuming beautiful forms. The link that binds together the ideas, sometimes so wide apart, which his wit assimilates, is most often the link of emotion; they have in common some element of beauty or of horror.

NOCTURNE

SIMEON STRUNSKY

Once every three months, with fair regularity, she was brought into the Night Court, found guilty and fined. She came in between eleven o'clock and midnight, when the traffic of the court is at its heaviest, and it would be an hour, perhaps, before she was called to the bar. When her turn came she would rise from her seat at one end of the prisoners' bench and confront the magistrate.

Her eyes did not reach to the level of the magistrate's desk. A policeman in citizen's clothes would mount the witness stand, take oath with a seriousness of mien which was surprising, in view of the frequency with which he was called upon to repeat the formula, and testify in an illiterate drone to a definite infraction of the law of the State, committed in his presence and with his encouragement. While he spoke the magistrate would look at the ceiling. When she was called upon to answer she defended herself with an obvious lie or two, while the magistrate looked over her head. He would then condemn her to pay the sum of ten dollars to the State and let her go.

She came to look forward to her visits at the Night Court.

◆

The Night Court is no longer a center of general interest. During the first few months after it was established, two or three years ago, it was one of the great sights of a great city. For the newspapers it was a rich source of human-interest stories. It replaced Chinatown in its appeal to visitors from out-of-town. It stirred even the languid pulses of the native inhabitant with its offerings of something new in the way of 'life'. The sociologists, sincere and amateur, crowded the benches and took notes.

Today the novelty is worn off. The newspapers long ago abandoned the Night Court, clergymen go to it rarely for their texts, and the tango has taken its place. But the sociologists and the casual visitor have not disappeared. Serious people, anxious for an immediate vision of the pity of life, continue to fill the benches comfortably. No session of the court is without its little group of social investigators, among whom the women are in the majority. Many of them are young women, exceedingly sympathetic, handsomely gowned, and very well taken care of.

As she sat at one end of the prisoners' bench waiting her turn before the magistrate's desk, she would cast a sidelong glance over the railing that separated her from the handsomely gowned, gently bred, sympathetic young women in the audience. She observed with extraordinary admiration and delight those charming faces softened in pity, the graceful bearing, the admirably constructed yet simple coiffures, the elegance of dress, which she compared with the best that the windows in Sixth Avenue could show. She was amazed to find such gowns actually being worn instead of remaining as an unattainable ideal on smiling lay figures in the shop windows.

Occupants of the prisoners' bench are not supposed to stare at the spectators. She had to steal a glance now and then. Her visits to the Night Court had become so much a matter of routine that she would venture a peep over the railing while the case immediately preceding her own was being tried. Once or twice she was surprised by the clerk who called her name. She stood up mechanically and faced the magistrate as Officer Smith, in civilian clothes, mounted the witness stand.

She had no grudge against Officer Smith. She did not visualize him either as a person or as a part of a system. He was merely an incident of her trade. She had neither the training nor the imagination to look behind Officer Smith and see a communal policy which has not the power to suppress, nor the courage to acknowledge, nor the skill to regulate, and so contents itself with sending out full-fed policemen in civilian clothes to work up the evidence that defends society against her kind through the imposition of a ten-dollar fine.

To some of the women on the visitors' benches the cruelty of the process came home: this business of setting a two-hundred-pound policeman in citizen's clothes, backed up by magistrates, clerks, court criers, interpreters, and court attendants, to worrying a ten-dollar fine out of a half-grown woman under an enormous imitation ostrich plume. The professional sociologists were chiefly interested in the money cost of this process to the tax-payer, and they took notes on the proportion of first offenders. Yet the Night Court is a remarkable advance in civilization. Formerly, in addition to her fine, the prisoner would pay a commission to the professional purveyor of bail.

Sometimes, if the magistrate was young or new to the business, she would be given a chance against Officer Smith. She would be called to the witness chair and under oath be allowed to elaborate on the obvious lies which constituted her usual defense. This would give her the opportunity, between the magistrate's questions, of sweeping the courtroom with a full, hungry look for as much as half a minute at a time. She saw the women in the audience only, and their clothes. The pity in their eyes did not move her, because she was not in the least interested in what they thought, but in how they looked and what they wore. They were part of a world which she would read about—she read very little—in the society columns of the Sunday newspaper. They were the women around whom headlines were written and whose pictures were printed frequently on the first page.

She could study them with comparative leisure in the Night Court. Outside in the course of her daily routine she might catch an occasional glimpse of these same women, through the windows of a passing taxi, or in the matinée crowds, or going in and out of the fashionable shops. But her work took her seldom into the region of taxicabs and fashionable shops. The nature of her occupation kept her to furtive corners and the dark side of streets. Nor was she at such times in the mood for just appreciation of the beautiful things in life. More than any other walk of life, hers was of an exacting nature, calling for intense powers of concentration both as regards the public and the police. It was different in the Night Court. Here, having nothing to fear and nothing out of the usual to hope for, she might give herself up to the esthetic contemplation of a beautiful world of which, at any other time, she could catch mere fugitive aspects.

Sometimes I wonder why people think that life is only what they see and hear, and not what they read of. Take the Night Court. The visitor really sees nothing and hears nothing that he has not read a thousand times in his newspaper and had it described in greater detail and with better-trained powers of observation than he can bring to bear in person. What new phase of life is revealed by seeing in the body, say, a dozen practitioners of a trade of whom we know there are several tens of thousands in New York? They have been described by the human-interest reporters, analyzed by the statisticians, defended by the social revolutionaries, and explained away by the optimists. For that matter, to the faithful reader of the newspapers, daily and Sunday, what can there be new in this world from the Pyramids by moonlight to the habits of the night prowler? Can the upper classes really acquire for themselves, through slumming parties and visits to the Night Court, anything like the knowledge that books and newspapers can furnish them? Can the lower classes ever hope to obtain that complete view of the Fifth Avenue set which the Sunday columns offer them? And yet there the case stands: only by seeing and hearing for ourselves, however imperfectly, do we get the sense of reality.

That is why our criminal courts are probably our most influential schools of democracy. More than our settlement houses, more than our subsidized dancing-schools for shopgirls, they encourage the get-together process through which one-half the world learns how the other half lives. On either side of the railing of the prisoners' cage is an audience and a stage.

That is why she would look forward to her regular visits at the Night Court. She saw life there.

BEER AND CIDER

GEORGE SAINTSBURY

There is no beverage which I have liked 'to live with' more than Beer; but I have never had a cellar large enough to accommodate much of it, or an establishment numerous enough to justify the accommodation. In the good days when servants expected beer, but did not expect to be treated otherwise than as servants, a cask or two was necessary; and persons who were 'quite' generally took care that the small beer they drank should be the same as that which they gave to their domestics, though they might have other sorts as well. For these better sorts at least the good old rule was, when you began on one cask always to have in another. Even Cobbett, whose belief in beer was the noblest feature in his character, allowed that it required some keeping. The curious 'white ale', or lober agol—which, within the memory of man, used to exist in Devonshire and Cornwall, but which, even half a century ago, I have vainly sought there—was, I believe, drunk quite new; but then it was not pure malt and not hopped at all, but had eggs ('pullet-sperm in the brewage') and other foreign bodies in it.

I did once drink, at St David's, ale so new that it frothed from the cask as creamily as if it had been bottled: and I wondered whether the famous beer of Bala, which Borrow found so good at his first visit and so bad at his second, had been like it.

On the other hand, the very best Bass I ever drank had had an exactly contrary experience. In the year 1875, when I was resident at Elgin, I and a friend now dead, the Procurator-Fiscal of the district, devoted the May 'Sacrament holidays', which were then still kept in those remote parts, to a walking tour up the Findhorn and across to Loch Ness and Glen Urquhart. At the Freeburn Inn on the first-named river we found some beer of singular excellence: and, asking the damsel who waited on us about it, were informed that a cask of Bass had been put in during the previous October, but, owing to a sudden break in the weather and the departure of all visitors, had never been tapped till our arrival.

Beer of ordinary strength left too long in the cask gets 'hard' of course; but no one who deserves to drink it would drink it from anything but the cask if he could help it. Jars are makeshifts, though useful makeshifts: and small beer will not keep in them for much more than a week. Nor are the very small barrels, known by various affectionate diminutives ('pin', etc.) in the country districts, much to be recommended. 'We'll drink it in the firkin, my boy!' is the lowest admission in point of volume that should be allowed. Of one such firkin I have a pleasant memory and memorial, though it never reposed in my home cellar. It was just before the present century opened, and some years before we Professors in Scotland had, of our own motion and against considerable opposition, given up half of the old six months' holiday without asking for or receiving a penny more salary. (I have since chuckled at the horror and wrath with which Mr Smillie and Mr Thomas would hear of such profligate conduct.) One could therefore move about with fairly long halts: and I had taken from a friend a house at Abingdon for some time. So, though I could not even then drink quite as much beer as I could thirty years earlier a little higher up the Thames, it became necessary to procure a cask. It came—one of Bass's minor mildnesses—affectionately labeled 'Mr George Saintsbury. Full to the bung.' I detached the card, and I believe I have it to this day as my choicest (because quite unsolicited) testimonial.

Very strong beer permits itself, of course, to be bottled and kept in bottles: but I rather doubt whether it also is not best from the wood; though it is equally of course, much easier to cellar it and keep it bottled. Its kinds are various and curious. 'Scotch ale' is famous, and at its best (I never drank better than Younger's) excellent: but its tendency, I think, is to be too sweet.

I once invested in some—not Younger's—which I kept for nearly sixteen years, and which was still treacle at the end. Bass's No 1 requires no praises. Once when living in the Cambridgeshire village mentioned earlier I had some, bottled in Cambridge itself, of great age and excellence. Indeed, two guests, though both of them were Cambridge men, and should have had what Mr Lang once called the 'robust' habits of that University, fell into one ditch after partaking of it. (I own that the lanes thereabouts are very dark.) In former days, though probably not at present, you could often find rather choice specimens of strong beer produced at small breweries in the country. I remember such even in the Channel Islands. And I suspect the Universities themselves have been subject to 'declensions and fallings off'. I know that in my undergraduate days at Merton we always had proper beer-glasses, like the old 'flute' champagnes, served regularly at cheese-time with a most noble beer called 'Archdeacon', which was then actually brewed in the sacristy of the College chapel. I have since—a slight sorrow to season the joy of reinstatement there—been told that it is now obtained from outside. And All Souls is the only other college in which, from actual recent experience, I can imagine the possibility of the exorcism,

Strongbeerum! Discede a lay-fratre Petro,

if lay-brother Peter were so silly as to abuse, or play tricks with, the good gift.

I have never had many experiences of real 'home-brewed', but two which I had were pleasing. There was much home-brewing in East Anglia at the time I lived there, and I once got the village carpenter to give me some of his own manufacture. It was as good light ale as I ever wish to drink (many times better than the wretched stuff that Dora has foisted on us), and he told me that, counting in every expense for material, cost and wear of plant, etc., it came to about a penny a quart. The other was very different. The late Lord de Tabley—better or at least longer known as Mr Leicester Warren—once gave a dinner at the Athenæum at which I was present, and had up from his Cheshire cellars some of the old ale for which that county is said to be famous, to make flip after dinner. It was shunned by most of the pusillanimous guests, but not by me, and it was excellent. But I should like to have tried it unflipped.

I never drank mum, which all know from *The Antiquary*, some from 'The Rhyme of Sir Lancelot Bogle', and some again from the notice which Mr Gladstone's love of Scott (may it plead for him!) gave it once in some Budget debate, I think. It is said to be brewed of wheat, which is not in its favor (wheat was meant to be eaten, not drunk) and very bitter, which is. Nearly all bitter drinks are good. The only time I ever drank 'spruce' beer I did not like it. The comeliest of black malts is, of course, that noble liquor called of Guinness. Here at least I think England cannot match Ireland, for our stouts are, as a rule, too sweet and 'clammy'. But there used to be in the country districts a sort of light porter which was one of the most refreshing liquids conceivable for hot weather. I have drunk it in Yorkshire at the foot of Roseberry Topping, out of big stone bottles like champagne magnums. But that was nearly sixty years ago. Genuine lager beer is no more to be boycotted than genuine hock, though, by the way, the best that I ever drank (it was at the good town of King's Lynn) was Low not High Dutch in origin. It was so good that I wrote to the shippers at Rotterdam to see if I could get some sent to Leith, but the usual difficulties in establishing connection between wholesale dealers and individual buyers prevented this. It was, however, something of a consolation to read the delightful name, 'our top-and-bottom-fermentation beer', in which the manufacturer's letter, in very sound English for the most part, spoke of it. English lager I must say I have never liked; perhaps I have been unlucky in my specimens. And good as Scotch strong beer is, I cannot say that the lighter and medium kinds are very good in Scotland. In fact, in Edinburgh I used to import beer of this kind from Lincolnshire, where there is no mistake about it. My own private opinion is that John Barleycorn, north of Tweed, says: 'I am for whisky, and not for ale.'

'Cider and perry,' says Burton, 'are windy drinks'; yet he observes that the inhabitants of certain shires in England (he does not, I am sorry to say, mention Devon) of Normandy in France, and of Guipuzcoa in Spain, 'are no whit offended by them'. I have never liked perry on the few occasions on which I have tasted it; perhaps because its taste has always reminded me of the smell of some stuff that my nurse used to put on my hair when I was small. But I certainly have been no whit offended by cider, either in divers English shires, including very specially those which Burton does not include, Devon, Dorset, and Somerset, or in Normandy. The Guipuzcoan variety I have, unfortunately, had no opportunity of tasting. Besides, perry seems to me to be an abuse of that excellent creature the pear, whereas cider-apples furnish one of the most cogent arguments to prove that Providence had the production of alcoholic liquors directly in its eye. They are good for nothing else whatever, and they are excellent good for that. I think I like the weak ciders, such as those of the west and the Normandy, better than the stronger ones, and draught cider much better than bottled. That of Norfolk, which has been much commended of late, I have never tasted; but I have had both Western and West-Midland cider in my cellar, often in bottle and once or twice in cask. It is a pity that the liquor—extremely agreeable to the taste, one of the most thirst-quenching to be anywhere found, of no overpowering alcoholic strength as a rule, and almost sovereign for gout—is not to be drunk without caution, and sometimes has to be given up altogether from other medical aspects. Qualified with brandy—a mixture which was first imparted to me at a roadside inn by a very amiable Dorsetshire farmer whom I met while walking from Sherborne to Blandford in my first Oxford 'long'—it is capital: and cider-cup who knoweth not? If there be any such, let him not wait longer than tomorrow before establishing knowledge. As for the pure juice of the apple, four gallons a day per man used to be the harvest allowance in Somerset when I was a boy. It is refreshing only to think of it now.

Of mead or metheglin, the third indigenous liquor of Southern Britain, I know little. Indeed, I should have known nothing at all of it had it not been that the parish-clerk and sexton of the Cambridgeshire village where I lived, and the caretaker of a vinery which I rented, was a bee-keeper and mead-maker. He gave me some once. I did not care much for it. It was like a sweet weak beer, with, of course, the special honey flavor. But I should imagine that it was susceptible of a great many different modes of preparation, and it is obvious, considering what it is made of, that it could be brewed of almost any strength. Old literary notices generally speak of it as strong.

BEYOND LIFE

JAMES BRANCH CABELL

I ask of literature precisely those things of which I feel the lack in my own life. I appeal for charity, and implore that literature afford me what I cannot come by in myself...

For I want distinction for that existence which ought to be peculiarly mine, among my innumerable fellows who swarm about earth like ants. Yet which one of us is noticeably, or can be appreciably different, in this throng of human ephemeræ and all their millions and inestimable millions of millions of predecessors and oncoming progeny? And even though one mote may transiently appear exceptional, the distinction of those who in their heydays are 'great' personages—much as the Emperor of Lilliput overtopped his subjects by the breadth of Captain Gulliver's nail—must suffer loss with time, and must dwindle continuously, until at most the man's recorded name remains here and there in sundry pedants' libraries. There were how many dynasties of Pharaohs, each one of whom was absolute lord of the known world, and is today forgotten? Among the countless popes who one by one were adored as the regent of Heaven upon earth, how many persons can today distinguish? And does not time breed emperors and czars and presidents as plentiful as blackberries, and as little thought of when their season is out? For there is no perpetuity in human endeavor: we strut upon a quicksand: and all that any man may do for good or ill is presently forgotten, because it does not matter. I wail to a familiar tune, of course, in this lament for the evanescence of human grandeur and the perishable renown of kings. And indeed to the statement that imperial Cæsar is turned to clay and Mizraim now cures wounds, and that in short Queen Anne is dead, we may agree lightly enough; for it is, after all, a matter of no personal concern:

but how hard it is to concede that the banker and the rector and the traffic-officer, to whom we more immediately defer, and we ourselves, and the little gold heads of our children, may be of no importance, either!... In art it may so happen that the thing which a man makes endures to be misunderstood and gabbled over: yet it is not the man himself. We retain the Iliad, but oblivion has swallowed Homer so deep that many question if he ever existed at all... So we pass as a cloud of gnats, where I want to live and be thought of, if only by myself, as a distinguishable entity. And such distinction is impossible in the long progress of suns, whereby in thought to separate the personality of any one man from all others that have lived, becomes a task to stagger Omniscience...

I want my life, the only life of which I am assured, to have symmetry or, in default of that, at least to acquire some clarity. Surely it is not asking very much to wish that my personal conduct be intelligible to me! Yet it is forbidden to know for what purpose this universe was intended, to what end it was set a-going, or why I am here, or even what I had preferably do while here. It vaguely seems to me that I am expected to perform an allotted task, but as to what it is I have no notion... And indeed, what have I done hitherto, in the years behind me? There are some books to show as increment, as something which was not anywhere before I made it, and which even in bulk will replace my buried body, so that my life will be to mankind no loss materially. But the course of my life, when I look back, is as orderless as a trickle of water that is diverted and guided by every pebble and crevice and grass-root it encounters. I seem to have done nothing with pre-meditation, but rather, to have had things done to me. And for all the rest of my life, as I know now, I shall have to shave every morning in order to be ready for no more than this!... I have attempted to make the best of my material circumstances always; nor do I see today how any widely varying course could have been wiser or even feasible: but material things have nothing to do with that life which moves in me. Why, then, should they direct and heighten and provoke and curb every action of life?

It is against the tyranny of matter I would rebel—against life's absolute need of food, and books, and fire, and clothing, and flesh, to touch and to inhabit, lest life perish... No, all that which I do here or refrain from doing lacks clarity, nor can I detect any symmetry anywhere, such as living would assuredly display, I think, if my progress were directed by any particular motive... It is all a muddling through, somehow, without any recognizable goal in view, and there is no explanation of the scuffle tendered or anywhere procurable. It merely seems that to go on living has become with me a habit...

And I want beauty in my life. I have seen beauty in a sunset and in the spring woods and in the eyes of divers women, but now these happy accidents of light and color no longer thrill me. And I want beauty in my life itself, rather than in such chances as befall it. It seems to me that many actions of my life were beautiful, very long ago, when I was young in an evanished world of friendly girls, who were all more lovely than any girl is nowadays. For women now are merely more or less good-looking, and as I know, their looks when at their best have been painstakingly enhanced and edited... But I would like this life which moves and yearns in me, to be able itself to attain to comeliness, though but in transitory performance. The life of a butterfly, for example, is just a graceful gesture: and yet, in that its loveliness is complete and perfectly rounded in itself, I envy this bright flicker through existence. And the nearest I can come to my ideal is punctiliously to pay my bills, be polite to my wife, and contribute to deserving charities: and the program does not seem, somehow, quite adequate. There are my books, I know; and there is beauty 'embalmed and treasured up' in many pages of my books, and in the books of other persons, too, which I may read at will: but this desire inborn in me is not to be satiated by making marks upon paper, nor by deciphering them... In short, I am enamored of that flawless beauty of which all poets have perturbedly divined the existence somewhere, and which life as men know it simply does not afford nor anywhere foresee...

And tenderness, too—but does that appear a mawkish thing to desiderate in life? Well, to my finding human beings do not like one another. Indeed, why should they, being rational creatures? All babies have a temporary lien on tenderness, of course: and therefrom children too receive a dwindling income, although on looking back, you will recollect that your childhood was upon the whole a lonesome and much put-upon period. But all grown persons ineffably distrust one another... In courtship, I grant you, there is a passing aberration which often mimics tenderness, sometimes as the result of honest delusion, but more frequently as an ambuscade in the endless struggle between man and woman. Married people are not ever tender with each other, you will notice: if they are mutually civil it is much: and physical contacts apart, their relation is that of a very moderate intimacy. My own wife, at all events, I find an unfailing mystery, a Sphinx whose secrets I assume to be not worth knowing: and, as I am mildly thankful to narrate, she knows very little about me, and evinces as to my affairs no morbid interest. That is not to assert that if I were ill she would not nurse me through any imaginable contagion, nor that if she were drowning I would not plunge in after her, whatever my delinquencies at swimming: what I mean is that, pending such high crises, we tolerate each other amicably, and never think of doing more... And from our blood-kin we grow apart inevitably. Their lives and their interests are no longer the same as ours, and when we meet it is with conscious reservations and much manufactured talk. Besides, they know things about us which we resent... And with the rest of my fellows, I find that convention orders all our dealings, even with children, and we do and say what seems more or less expected. And I know that we distrust one another all the while, and instinctively conceal or misrepresent our actual thoughts and emotions when there is no very apparent need... Personally, I do not like human beings because I am not aware, upon the whole, of any generally distributed qualities which entitle them as a race to admiration and affection. But toward people in books—such as Mrs Millamant, and Helen of

Troy, and Bella Wilfer, and Mélusine, and Beatrix Esmond—I may intelligently overflow with tenderness and caressing words, in part because they deserve it, and in part because I know they will not suspect me of being 'queer' or of having ulterior motives...

And I very often wish that I could know the truth about just any one circumstance connected with my life... Is the phantasmagoria of sound and noise and color really passing or is it all an illusion here in my brain? How do you know that you are not dreaming me, for instance? In your conceded dreams, I am sure, you must invent and see and listen to persons who for the while seem quite as real to you as I do now. As I do, you observe, I say! And what thing is it to which I so glibly refer as I? If you will try to form a notion of yourself, of the sort of a something that you suspect to inhabit and partially to control your flesh and blood body, you will encounter a walking bundle of superfluities: and when you mentally have put aside the extraneous things—your garments and your members and your body, and your acquired habits and your appetites and your inherited traits and your prejudices, and all other appurtenances which considered separately you recognize to be no integral part of you—there seems to remain in those pearl-colored brain-cells, wherein is your ultimate lair, very little save a faculty for receiving sensations, of which you know the larger portion to be illusory. And surely, to be just a very gullible consciousness provisionally existing among inexplicable mysteries, is not an enviable plight. And yet this life—to which I cling tenaciously—comes to no more. Meanwhile I hear men talk about 'the truth'; and they even wager handsome sums upon their knowledge of it: but I align myself with 'jesting Pilate', and echo the forlorn query that recorded time has left unanswered...

Then, last of all, I desiderate urbanity. I believe this is the rarest quality in the world. Indeed, it probably does not exist anywhere. A really urbane person—a mortal open-minded and affable to conviction of his own shortcomings and errors, and unguided in anything by irrational blind prejudices—could not but in a world of men and women be regarded as a monster. We are all of us, as if by instinct, intolerant of that which is unfamiliar: we resent its impudence: and very much the same principle which prompts small boys to jeer at a straw-hat out of season induces their elders to send missionaries to the heathen. The history of the progress of the human race is but the picaresque romance of intolerance, a narrative of how—what is it Milton says?—'truth never came into the world but, like a bastard, to the ignominy of him that brought her forth, till time hath washed and salted the infant, declared her legitimate, and churched the father of his young Minerva'. And I, who prattle to you, very candidly confess that I have no patience with other people's ideas unless they coincide with mine: for if the fellow be demonstrably wrong I am fretted by his stupidity, and if his notion seem more nearly right than mine I am infuriated... Yet I wish I could acquire urbanity, very much as I would like to have wings. For in default of it, I cannot even manage to be civil to that piteous thing called human nature, or to view its parasites, whether they be politicians or clergymen of popular authors, with one-half the commiseration which the shifts they are put to, quite certainly, would rouse in the urbane...

So I in point of fact desire of literature, just as you guessed, precisely those things of which I most poignantly and most constantly feel the lack in my own life. And it is that which romance affords her postulants. The philtres of romance are brewed to free us from this unsatisfying life that is calendared by fiscal years, and to contrive a less disastrous elusion of our own personalities than many seek dispersedly in drink and drugs and lust and fanaticism, and sometimes in death. For, beset by his own rationality, the normal man is goaded to evade the strictures of his normal life, upon the incontestable ground that it is a stupid and unlovely routine; and to escape likewise from his own personality, which bores him quite as much as it does his associates. So he hurtles into these very various roads from reality, precisely as a goaded sheep flees without notice of what lies ahead...

And romance tricks him, but not to his harm. For, be it remembered that man alone of animals plays the ape to his dreams.

Romance it is undoubtedly who whispers to every man that life is not a blind and aimless business, not all a hopeless waste and confusion; and that his existence is a pageant (appreciatively observed by divine spectators), and that he is strong and excellent and wise: and to romance he listens, willing and thrice willing to be cheated by the honeyed fiction. The things of which romance assures him are very far from true: yet it is solely by believing himself a creature but little lower than the cherubim that man has by interminable small degrees become, upon the whole, distinctly superior to the chimpanzee: so that, however extravagant may seem these flattering whispers today, they were immeasurably more remote from veracity when men first began to listen to their sugared susurrus, and steadily the discrepancy lessens. Today these things seem quite as preposterous to calm consideration as did flying yesterday: and so, to the Gradgrindians, romance appears to discourse foolishly, and incurs the common fate of prophets: for it is about tomorrow and about the day after tomorrow, that romance is talking, by means of parables. And all the while man plays the ape to fairer and yet fairer dreams, and practice strengthens him at mimickry...

To what does the whole business tend?—why, how in heaven's name should I know? We can but be content to note that all goes forward, toward something... It may be that we are nocturnal creatures perturbed by rumors of a dawn which comes inevitably, as prologue to a day wherein we and our children have no part whatever. It may be that when our arboreal propositus descended from his palm-tree and began to walk upright about the earth, his progeny were forthwith committed to a journey in which today is only a way-station. Yet I prefer to take it that we are components of an unfinished world, and that we are but as seething atoms which ferment toward its making, if merely because man as he now exists can hardly be the finished product of any Creator whom one could very heartily revere. We are being made into something quite unpredictable, I imagine: and through the purging and the smelting, we are sustained by an instinctive knowledge that we are being made into something better. For this we know, quite incommunicably, and yet as surely as we know that we will to have it thus.

And it is this will that stirs in us to have the creatures of earth and the affairs of earth, not as they are, but 'as they ought to be', which we call romance. But when we note how visibly it sways all life we perceive that we are talking about God.

THE FISH REPORTER

ROBERT CORTES HOLLIDAY

Men of genius, blown by the winds of chance, have been, now and then, mariners, bar-keeps, schoolmasters, soldiers, politicians, clergymen, and what not. And from these pursuits have they sucked the essence of yarns and in the setting of these activities found a flavor to stir and to charm hearts untold. Now, it is a thousand pities that no man of genius has ever been a fish reporter. Thus has the world lost great literary treasure, as it is highly probable that there is not under the sun any prospect so filled with the scents and colors of story as that presented by the commerce in fish.

Take whale oil. Take the funny old buildings on Front Street, out of paintings, I declare, by Howard Pyle, where the large merchants in whale oil are. Take salt fish. Do you know the oldest salt-fish house in America, down by Coenties Slip? Ah! You should. The ghost of old Long John Silver, I suspect, smokes an occasional pipe in that old place. And many are the times I've seen the slim shade of young Jim Hawkins come running out. Take Labrador cod for export to the Mediterranean lands or to Porto Rico via New York. Take herrings brought to this port from Iceland, from Holland, and from Scotland; mackerel from Ireland, from the Magdalen Islands, and from Cape Breton; crabmeat from Japan; fishballs from Scandinavia; sardines from Norway and from France; caviar from Russia; shrimp which comes from Florida, Mississippi, and Georgia, or salmon from Alaska, and Puget Sound, and the Columbia River.

Take the obituaries of fishermen. 'In his prime, it is said, there was not a better skipper in the Gloucester fishing fleet.' Take disasters to schooners, smacks and trawlers. 'The crew were landed, but lost all their belongings.' New vessels, sales, etc. 'The sealing schooner, *Tillie B.*, whose career in the South Seas is well known, is reported to have been sold to a moving-picture firm.' Sponges from the Caribbean Sea and the Gulf of Mexico. 'To most people, familiar only with the sponges of the shops, the animal as it comes from the sea would be rather unrecognizable.' Why, take anything you please! It is such stuff as stories are. And as you eat your fish from the store how little do you reck of the glamor of what you are doing!

However, as it seems to me unlikely that a man of genius will be a fish reporter shortly I will myself do the best I can to paint the tapestry of the scenes of his calling. The advertisement in the newspaper read: 'Wanted—Reporter for weekly trade paper.' Many called, but I was chosen. Though, doubtless, no man living knew less about fish than I.

The newsstands are each like a fair, so laden are they with magazines in bright colors. It would seem almost as if there were a different magazine for every few hundred and seven-tenth person, as the statistics put these matters. And yet, it seems, there is a vast, a very vast, periodical literature of which we, that is, magazine readers in general, know nothing whatever. There is, for one, that fine, old, standard publication, *Barrel and Box*, devoted to the subjects and the interests of the coopering industry; there is too, *The Dried Fruit Packer* and *Western Canner*, as alert a magazine as one could wish—in its kind; and from the home of classic American literature comes *The New England Tradesman and Grocer*. And so on. At the place alone where we went to press twenty-seven trade journals were printed every week, from one for butchers to one for bankers.

The Fish Industries Gazette—Ah, yes! For some reason not clear (though it is an engaging thing, I think) the word 'gazette' is the great word among the titles of trade journals. There are *The Jewellers' Gazette* and *The Women's Wear Gazette* and *The Poulterers' Gazette* (of London), and *The Maritime Gazette* (of Halifax), and other gazettes quite without number. This word 'gazette' makes its appeal, too, curiously enough, to those who christen country papers; and trade journals have much of the intimate charm of country papers. The 'trade' in each case is a kind of neighborly community, separated in its parts by space, but joined in unity of sympathy. 'Personals' are a vital feature of trade papers. 'Walter Conner, who for some time has conducted a bakery and fish market at Hudson, N. Y., has removed to Fort Edward, leaving his brother Ed in charge at the Hudson place of business.'

The Fish Industries Gazette, as I say, was one of several in its field, in friendly rivalry with *The Oyster Trade* and *Fisherman* and *The Pacific Fisheries*. It comprised two departments: the fresh fish and oyster department, and myself. I was, as an editorial announcement said at the beginning of my tenure of office, a 'reorganization of our salt, smoked, and pickled fish department.' The delectable, mellow spirit of the country paper, so removed from the crash and whirr of metropolitan journalism, rested in this, too, that upon *The Gazette* I did practically everything on the paper except the linotyping. Reporter, editorial writer, exchange editor, make-up man, proof-reader, correspondent, advertisement solicitor, was I.

As exchange editor, did I read all the papers in the English language in eager search of fish news. And while you are about the matter, just find me a finer bit of literary style evoking the romance of the vast wastes of the moving sea, in Stevenson, Defoe, anywhere you please, than such a news item as this: 'Capt Ezra Pound, of the bark Elnora, of Salem, Mass., spoke a lonely vessel in latitude this and longitude that, September 8. She proved to be the whaler *Wanderer*, and her captain said that she had been nine months at sea, that all on board were well, and that he had stocked so many barrels of whale oil.'

As exchange editor was it my business to peruse reports from Eastport, Maine, to the effect that one of the worst storms in recent years had destroyed large numbers of the sardine weirs there. To seek fish recipes, of such savory sound as those for 'broiled redsnapper', 'shrimps bordelaise', and 'baked fish croquettes'. To follow fishing conditions in the North Sea occasioned by the Great War. To hunt down jokes of piscatory humor. 'The man who drinks like a fish does not take kindly to water.—Exchange.' To find other 'fillers' in the consular reports and elsewhere: 'Fish culture in India', '1800 Miles in a Dory', 'Chinese Carp for the Philippines', 'Americans as Fish Eaters'. And, to use a favorite term of trade papers, 'etc., etc.' Then to 'paste up' the winnowed fruits of this beguiling research.

As editorial writer, to discuss the report of the commission recently sent by congress to the Pribilof Islands, Alaska, to report on the condition of our national herd of fur seals; to discuss the official interpretation here of the Government ruling on what constitutes 'boneless' codfish; to consider the campaign in Canada to promote there a more popular consumption of fish, and to brightly remark à propos of this that 'a fish a day keeps the doctor away'; to review the current issue of *The Journal of the Fisheries Society of Japan*, containing leading articles on 'Are Fishing Motor Boats Able to Encourage in Our Country' and 'Fisherman the Late Mr H. Yamaguchi Well Known'; to combat the prejudice against dogfish as food, a prejudice like that against eels, in some quarters eyed askance as 'calling cousins with the great sea-serpent', as Juvenal says; to call attention to the doom of one of the most picturesque monuments in the story of fish, the passing of the pleasant and celebrated old Trafalgar Hotel at Greenwich, near London, scene of the famous Ministerial white-bait dinners of the days of Pitt; to make a jest on an exciting idea suggested by some medical man that some of the features of a Ritz-Carlton Hotel, that is, baths, be introduced into the fo'c's'les of Grand Banks fishing vessels; to keep an eye on the activities of our Bureau of Fisheries; to hymn a praise to the monumental new Fish Pier at Boston; to glance at conditions at the premier fish market of the world, Billingsgate; to herald the fish display at the Canadian National Exhibition at Toronto, and, indeed, etc., and again etc.

As general editorial roustabout, to find each week a 'leader', a translation, say, from *In Allgemeine Fishcherei-Zeitung*, or

Economic Circular No 10, 'Mussels in the Tributaries of the Missouri', or the last biennial report of the Superintendent of Fisheries of Wisconsin, or a scientific paper on 'The Porpoise in Captivity' reprinted by permission of *Zoologica*, of the New York Zoölogical Society. To find each week for reprint a poem appropriate in sentiment to the feeling of the paper. One of the 'Salt Water Ballads' would do, or John Masefield singing of 'the whale's way', or 'Down to the white dipping sails'; or Rupert Brooke: 'And in that heaven of all their wish, There shall be no more land, say fish'; or a 'weather rhyme' about 'mackerel skies', when 'you're sure to get a fishing day'; or something from the New York Sun about 'the lobster pots of Maine'; or Oliver Herford, in the Century, 'To a Goldfish'; or, best of all, an old song of fishing ways of other days.

And to compile from the *New York Journal* of Commerce better poetry than any of this, tables, beautiful tables of 'imports into New York': 'Oct 15.—From Bordeaux, 225 cs. cuttlefish bone; Copenhagen, 173 pkgs. fish; Liverpool, 969 bbls. herrings, 10 walrus hides, 2,000 bags salt; La Guayra, 6 cs. fish sounds; Belize, 9 bbls. sponges; Rotterdam, 7 pkgs. seaweed, 9,000 kegs herrings; Barcelona, 235 cs. sardines; Bocas Del Toro, 5 cs. turtle shells; Genoa, 3 boxes corals; Tampico, 2 pkgs. sponges; Halifax, 1 cs. seal skins, 35 bbls. cod liver oil, 215 cs. lobsters, 490 bbls. codfish; Akureyri, 4,150 bbls. salted herrings,' and much more. Beautiful tables of 'exports from New York'. 'To Australia' (cleared Sep 1); 'to Argentina';—Haiti, Jamaica, Guatemala, Scotland, Salvador, Santo Domingo, England, and to places many more. And many other gorgeous tables, too. 'Fishing vessels at New York,' for one, listing the 'trips' brought into this port by the *Stranger*, the *Sarah O'Neal*, the *Nourmahal*, a farrago of charming sounds, and a valuable tale of facts.

As make-up man, of course, so to 'dress' the paper that the 'markets', Oporto, Trinidad, Porto Rico, Demerara, Havana, would be together; that 'Nova Scotia Notes'—'Weather conditions for curing have been more favorable since October set in'—would follow 'Halifax Fish Market'—'Last week's arrivals were: Oct. 13, schr. Hattie Loring, 960 quintals,' etc.—that 'Pacific Coast Notes'—'The tug Tatoosh will perform the service for the Seattle salmon packers of towing a vessel from Seattle to this port via the Panama Canal'—would follow 'Canned Salmon'; that shellfish matter would be in one place; reports of saltfish where such should be; that the weekly tale of the canned fish trade politically embraced the canned fish advertising; and so on and so on.

Finest of all, as reporter, to go where the fish reporter goes. There the sight-seeing cars never find their way; the hurried commuter has not his path, nor knows of these things at all; and there that racy character who, voicing a multitude, declares that he would rather be a lamp post on Broadway than Mayor of St Louis, goes not for to see. Up lower Greenwich Street the fish reporter goes, along an eerie, dark, and narrow way, beneath a strange, thundering roof, the 'L' overhead. He threads his way amid seemingly chaotic, architectural piles of boxes, of barrels, crates, casks, kegs, and bulging bags; roundabout many great fetlocked draught horses, frequently standing or plunging upon the sidewalk, and attached to many huge trucks and wagons; and much of the time in the street he is compelled to go, finding the sidewalks too congested with the traffic of commerce to admit of his passing there.

You probably eat butter, and eggs, and cheese. Then you would delight in Greenwich Street. You could feast your highly creditable appetite for these excellent things for very nearly a solid mile upon the signs of 'wholesale dealers and commission merchants' in them. The letter press, as you might say, of the fish reporter's walk is a noble pæan to the earth's glorious yield for the joyous sustenance of man. For these princely merchants' signs sing of opulent stores of olive oil, of sausages, beans, soups, extracts, and spices, sugar, Spanish, Bermuda, and Havana onions, 'fine' apples, teas, coffee, rice, chocolates, dried fruits and raisins, and of loaves and of fishes, and of 'fish products'. Lo! Dark and dirty and thundering Greenwich Street is today's translation of the Garden of Eden.

Here is a great house whose sole vocation is the importation of caviar for barter here. Caviar from over-seas now comes, when it comes at all, mainly by the way of Archangel, recently put on the map, for most of us, by the war. The fish reporter is told, however, if it be summer, that there cannot be much doing in the way of caviar until fall, 'when the spoonbill start coming in'. And on he goes to a great saltfish house, where many men in salt-stained garments are running about, their arms laden with large flat objects, of sharp and jagged edge, which resemble dried and crackling hides of some animal curiously like a huge fish; and numerous others of 'the same' are trundling round wheelbarrow-like trucks likewise so laden. Where stacks of these hides stand on their tails against the walls, and goodness knows how many big boxes are, containing, as those open show, beautifully soft, thick, cream-colored slabs, which is fish. And where still other men, in overalls stained like a painter's palette, are knocking off the heads of casks and dipping out of brine still other kinds of fish for inspection.

Here it is said by the head of the house, by the stove (it is chill weather) in his office like a shipmaster's cabin: 'Strong market on foreign mackerel. Mines hinder Norway catch. Advices from abroad report that German resources continue to purchase all available supplies from the Norwegian fishermen. No Irish of any account. Recent shipment sold on the deck at high prices. Fair demand from the Middle West.'

So, by stages, on up to turn into North Moore Street, looking down a narrow lane between two long bristling rows of wagons pointed out from the curbs, to the façades of the North River docks at the bottom, with the tops of the buff funnels of ocean liners, and Whistleranean silhouettes of derricks, rising beyond. Hereabout are more importers, exporters, and 'producers' of fish, famous in their calling beyond the celebrities of popular publicity. And he that has official entrée may learn, by mounting dusky stairs, half-ladder and half-stair, and by passing through low-ceilinged chambers freighted with many barrels, to the sanctums of the fish lords, what's doing in the foreign herring way, and get the current market quotations, at present sky-high, and hear that the American shore mackerel catch is very fine stock.

Then roundabout, with a step into the broad vista of homely Washington Street, and a turn through Franklin Street, where is the man decorated by the Imperial Japanese Government with a gold medal, if he should care to wear it, for having distinguished himself in the development of commerce in the marine products of Japan, back to Hudson Street. An authentic railroad is one of the spectacular features of Hudson Street.

Here down the middle of the way are endless trains, stopping, starting, crashing, laden to their ears with freight, doubtless all to eat. Tourists should come from very far to view Hudson Street. Here is a spectacle as fascinating, as awe-inspiring, as extraordinary as any in the world. From dawn until darkness falls, hour after hour, along Hudson Street slowly, steadily moves a mighty procession of great trucks. One would not suppose there were so many trucks on the face of the earth. It is a glorious sight, and any man whose soul is not dead should jump with joy to see it. And the thunder of them altogether as they bang over the stones is like the music of the spheres.

There is on Hudson Street a tall handsome building where the fish reporter goes, which should be enjoyed in this way: Up in the lift you go to the top, and then you walk down, smacking your lips. For all the doors in that building are brimming with poetry. And the tune of it goes like this: 'Toasted Corn-Flake Co.', 'Seaboard Rice', 'Chili Products', 'Red Bloom Grape Juice Sales Office', 'Porto Rico and Singapore Pineapple Co.', 'Sunnyland Foodstuffs', 'Importers of Fruit Pulps, Pimentos', 'Sole Agents U. S. A. Italian Salad Oil', 'Raisin Growers', 'Log Cabin Syrups', 'Jobbers in Beans, Peas', 'Chocolate and Cocoa Preparations', 'Ohio Evaporated Milk Co.', 'Bernese Alps and Holland Condensed Milk Co.', 'Brazilian Nuts Co.', 'Brokers Pacific Coast Salmon', 'California Tuna Co.', and thus on and on.

The fish reporter crosses the street to see the head of the

Sardine Trust, who has just thrown the market into excitement by a heavy cut in prices of last year's pack. Thence, pausing to refresh himself by the way at a sign 'Agency for Reims Champagne and Moselle Wines—Bordeaux Clarets and Sauternes', over to Broadway to interview the most august persons of all, dealers in fertilizer, 'fish scrap'. These mighty gentlemen live, when at business, in palatial suites of offices constructed of marble and fine woods and laid with rich rugs. The reporter is relayed into the innermost sanctum by a succession of richly clothed attendants. And he learns, it may be, that fishing in Chesapeake Bay is so poor that some of the 'fish factories' may decide to shut down. Acid phosphate, it is said, is ruling at $13 f.o.b. Baltimore.

And so the fish reporter enters upon the last lap of his rounds. Through, perhaps, the narrow, crooked lane of Pine Street he passes, to come out at length upon a scene set for a sea tale. Here would a lad, heir to vast estates in Virginia, be kidnapped and smuggled aboard to be sold a slave in Africa. This is Front Street. A white ship lies at the foot of it. Cranes rise at her side. Tugs, belching smoke, bob beyond. All about are ancient warehouses, redolent of the Thames, with steep roofs and sometimes stairs outside, and with tall shutters, a crescent-shaped hole in each. There is a dealer in weather-vanes. Other things dealt in hereabout are these: chronometers, 'nautical instruments,' wax gums, cordage and twine, marine paints, cotton wool and waste, turpentine, oils, greases, and rosin. Queer old taverns, public houses, are here, too. Why do not their windows rattle with a 'Yo, ho, ho'?

There is an old, old house whose business has been fish oil within the memory of men. And here is another. Next, through Water Street, one comes in search of the last word on salt fish. Now the air is filled with gorgeous smell of roasting coffee. Tea, coffee, sugar, rice, spices, bags and bagging here have their home. And there are haughty bonded warehouses filled with fine liquors. From his white cabin at the top of a venerable structure comes the dean of the saltfish business. 'Export trade fair,' he says; 'good demand from South America.'

THE FIFTY-FIRST DRAGON

HEYWOOD BROUN

Of all the pupils at the knight school Gawaine le Cœur-Hardy was among the least promising. He was tall and sturdy, but his instructors soon discovered that he lacked spirit. He would hide in the woods when the jousting class was called, although his companions and members of the faculty sought to appeal to his better nature by shouting to him to come out and break his neck like a man. Even when they told him that the lances were padded, the horses no more than ponies and the field unusually soft for late autumn, Gawaine refused to grow enthusiastic. The Headmaster and the Assistant Professor of Pleasaunce were discussing the case one spring afternoon and the Assistant Professor could see no remedy but expulsion.

'No,' said the Headmaster, as he looked out at the purple hills which ringed the school, 'I think I'll train him to slay dragons.'

'He might be killed,' objected the Assistant Professor.

'So he might,' replied the Headmaster brightly, but he added, more soberly, 'we must consider the greater good. We are responsible for the formation of this lad's character.'

'Are the dragons particularly bad this year?' interrupted the Assistant Professor. This was characteristic. He always seemed restive when the head of the school began to talk ethics and the ideals of the institution.

'I've never known them worse,' replied the Headmaster. 'Up in the hills to the south last week they killed a number of peasants, two cows and a prize pig. And if this dry spell holds there's no telling when they may start a forest fire simply by breathing around indiscriminately.'

'Would any refund on the tuition fee be necessary in case of an accident to young Cœur-Hardy?'

'No,' the principal answered, judicially, 'that's all covered in the contract. But as a matter of fact he won't be killed. Before I send him up in the hills I'm going to give him a magic word.'

'That's a good idea,' said the Professor. 'Sometimes they work wonders.'

From that day on Gawaine specialized in dragons. His course included both theory and practice. In the morning there were long lectures on the history, anatomy, manners and customs of dragons. Gawaine did not distinguish himself in these studies. He had a marvelously versatile gift for forgetting things. In the afternoon he showed to better advantage, for then he would go down to the South Meadow and practise with a battle-ax. In this exercise he was truly impressive, for he had enormous strength as well as speed and grace. He even developed a deceptive display of ferocity. Old alumni say that it was a thrilling sight to see Gawaine charging across the field toward the dummy paper dragon which had been set up for his practice. As he ran he would brandish his ax and shout 'A murrain on thee!' or some other vivid bit of campus slang. It never took him more than one stroke to behead the dummy dragon.

Gradually his task was made more difficult. Paper gave way to papier-mâché and finally to wood, but even the toughest of these dummy dragons had no terrors for Gawaine. One sweep of the ax always did the business. There were those who said that when the practice was protracted until dusk and the dragons threw long, fantastic shadows across the meadow Gawaine did not charge so impetuously nor shout so loudly. It is possible there was malice in this charge. At any rate, the Headmaster decided by the end of June that it was time for the test. Only the night before a dragon had come close to the school grounds and had eaten some of the lettuce from the garden. The faculty decided that Gawaine was ready. They gave him a diploma and a new battle-ax and the Headmaster summoned him to a private conference.

'Sit down,' said the Headmaster. 'Have a cigarette.'

Gawaine hesitated.

'Oh, I know it's against the rules,' said the Headmaster. 'But after all, you have received your preliminary degree. You are no longer a boy. You are a man. Tomorrow you will go out into the world, the great world of achievement.'

Gawaine took a cigarette. The Headmaster offered him a match, but he produced one of his own and began to puff away with a dexterity which quite amazed the principal.

'Here you have learned the theories of life,' continued the Headmaster, resuming the thread of his discourse, 'but after all, life is not a matter of theories. Life is a matter of facts. It calls on the young and the old alike to face these facts, even though they are hard and sometimes unpleasant. Your problem, for example, is to slay dragons.'

'They say that those dragons down in the south wood are five hundred feet long,' ventured Gawaine, timorously.

'Stuff and nonsense!' said the Headmaster. 'The curate saw one last week from the top of Arthur's Hill. The dragon was sunning himself down in the valley. The curate didn't have an opportunity to look at him very long because he felt it was his duty to hurry back to make a report to me. He said the monster, or shall I say, the big lizard?—wasn't an inch over two hundred feet. But the size has nothing at all to do with it. You'll find the big ones even easier than the little ones. They're far slower on their feet and less aggressive, I'm told. Besides, before you go I'm going to equip you in such fashion that you need have no fear of all the dragons in the world.'

'I'd like an enchanted cap,' said Gawaine.

'What's that?' answered the Headmaster, testily.

'A cap to make me disappear,' explained Gawaine.

The Headmaster laughed indulgently. 'You mustn't believe all those old wives' stories,' he said. 'There isn't any such thing. A cap to make you disappear, indeed! What would you do with it? You haven't even appeared yet. Why, my boy, you could walk from here to London, and nobody would so much as look at you. You're nobody. You couldn't be more invisible than that.'

Gawaine seemed dangerously close to a relapse into his old habit of whimpering. The Headmaster reassured him: 'Don't worry; I'll give you something much better than an enchanted cap. I'm going to give you a magic word. All you have to do is to repeat this magic charm once and no dragon can possibly harm a hair of your head. You can cut off his head at your leisure.'

He took a heavy book from the shelf behind his desk and began to run through it. 'Sometimes,' he said, 'the charm is a whole phrase or even a sentence. I might, for instance, give you 'To make the'—No, that might not do. I think a single word would be best for dragons.'

'A short word,' suggested Gawaine.

'It can't be too short or it wouldn't be potent. There isn't so much hurry as all that. Here's a splendid magic word: "Rumplesnitz". Do you think you can learn that?'

Gawaine tried and in an hour or so he seemed to have the word well in hand. Again and again he interrupted the lesson to inquire, 'And if I say "Rumplesnitz" the dragon can't possibly hurt me?' And always the Headmaster replied, 'If you only say "Rumplesnitz", you are perfectly safe.'

Toward morning Gawaine seemed resigned to his career. At daybreak the Headmaster saw him to the edge of the forest and pointed him to the direction in which he should proceed. About a mile away to the southwest a cloud of steam hovered over an open meadow in the woods and the Headmaster assured Gawaine that under the steam he would find a dragon. Gawaine went forward slowly. He wondered whether it would be best to approach the dragon on the run as he did in his practice in the South Meadow or to walk slowly toward him, shouting 'Rumplesnitz' all the way.

The problem was decided for him. No sooner had he come to the fringe of the meadow than the dragon spied him and began to charge. It was a large dragon and yet it seemed decidedly aggressive in spite of the Headmaster's statement to the contrary. As the dragon charged it released huge clouds of hissing steam through its nostrils. It was almost as if a gigantic teapot had gone mad. The dragon came forward so fast and Gawaine was so frightened that he had time to say 'Rumplesnitz' only once. As he said it, he swung his battle-ax and off popped the head of the dragon. Gawaine had to admit that it was even easier to kill a real dragon than a wooden one if only you said 'Rumplesnitz'.

Gawaine brought the ears home and a small section of the tail. His school mates and the faculty made much of him, but the Headmaster wisely kept him from being spoiled by insisting that he go on with his work. Every clear day Gawaine rose at dawn and went out to kill dragons. The Headmaster kept him at home when it rained, because he said the woods were damp and unhealthy at such times and that he didn't want the boy to run needless risks. Few good days passed in which Gawaine failed to get a dragon. On one particularly fortunate day he killed three, a husband and wife and a visiting relative. Gradually he developed a technique. Pupils who sometimes watched him from the hilltops a long way off said that he often allowed the dragon to come within a few feet before he said 'Rumplesnitz'. He came to say it with a mocking sneer. Occasionally he did stunts. Once when an excursion party from London was watching him he went into action with his right hand tied behind his back. The dragon's head came off just as easily.

As Gawaine's record of killings mounted higher the Headmaster found it impossible to keep him completely in hand. He fell into the habit of stealing out at night and engaging in long drinking bouts at the village tavern. It was after such a debauch that he rose a little before dawn one fine August morning and started out after his fiftieth dragon. His head was heavy and his mind sluggish. He was heavy in other respects as well, for he had adopted the somewhat vulgar practice of wearing his medals, ribbons and all, when he went out dragon hunting. The decorations began on his chest and ran all the way down to his abdomen. They must have weighed at least eight pounds.

Gawaine found a dragon in the same meadow where he had killed the first one. It was a fair-sized dragon, but evidently an old one. Its face was wrinkled and Gawaine thought he had never seen so hideous a countenance. Much to the lad's disgust, the monster refused to charge and Gawaine was obliged to walk toward him. He whistled as he went. The dragon regarded him hopelessly, but craftily. Of course it had heard of Gawaine. Even when the lad raised his battle-ax the dragon made no move. It knew that there was no salvation in the quickest thrust of the head, for it had been informed that this hunter was protected by an enchantment. It merely waited, hoping something would turn up. Gawaine raised the battle-ax and suddenly lowered it again. He had grown very pale and he trembled violently. The dragon suspected a trick. 'What's the matter?' it asked, with false solicitude.

'I've forgotten the magic word,' stammered Gawaine.

'What a pity,' said the dragon. 'So that was the secret. It doesn't seem quite sporting to me, all this magic stuff, you know. Not cricket, as we used to say when I was a little dragon; but after all, that's a matter of opinion.'

Gawaine was so helpless with terror that the dragon's confidence rose immeasurably and it could not resist the temptation to show off a bit.

'Could I possibly be of any assistance?' it asked. 'What's the first letter of the magic word?'

'It begins with an "r",' said Gawaine weakly.

'Let's see,' mused the dragon, 'that doesn't tell us much, does it? What sort of a word is this? Is it an epithet, do you think?'

Gawaine could do no more than nod.

'Why, of course,' exclaimed the dragon, 'reactionary Republican.'

Gawaine shook his head.

'Well, then,' said the dragon, 'we'd better get down to business. Will you surrender?'

With the suggestion of a compromise Gawaine mustered up enough courage to speak.

'What will you do if I surrender?' he asked.

'Why, I'll eat you,' said the dragon.

'And if I don't surrender?'

'I'll eat you just the same.'

'Then it doesn't mean any difference, does it?' moaned Gawaine.

'It does to me,' said the dragon with a smile. 'I'd rather you didn't surrender. You'd taste much better if you didn't.'

The dragon waited for a long time for Gawaine to ask 'Why?' but the boy was too frightened to speak. At last the dragon had to give the explanation without his cue line. 'You see,' he said, 'if you don't surrender you'll taste better because you'll die game.'

This was an old and ancient trick of the dragon's. By means of some such quip he was accustomed to paralyze his victims with laughter and then to destroy them. Gawaine was sufficiently paralyzed as it was, but laughter had no part in his helplessness. With the last word of the joke the dragon drew back his head and struck. In that second there flashed into the mind of Gawaine the magic word 'Rumplesnitz', but there was no time to say it. There was time only to strike and, without a word, Gawaine met the onrush of the dragon with a full swing. He put all his back and shoulders into it. The impact was terrific and the head of the dragon flew away almost a hundred yards and landed in a thicket.

Gawaine did not remain frightened very long after the death of the dragon. His mood was one of wonder. He was enormously puzzled. He cut off the ears of the monster almost in a trance. Again and again he thought to himself, 'I didn't say "Rumplesnitz"!' He was sure of that and yet there was no question that he had killed the dragon. In fact, he had never killed one so utterly. Never before had he driven a head for anything like the same distance. Twenty-five yards was perhaps his best previous record. All the way back to the knight school he kept rumbling about in his mind seeking an explanation for what had occurred. He went to the Headmaster immediately and after closing the door told him what had happened. 'I didn't say "Rumplesnitz",' he explained with great earnestness.

The Headmaster laughed. 'I'm glad you've found out,' he said.

'It makes you ever so much more of a hero. Don't you see that? Now you know that it was you who killed all these dragons and not that foolish little word "Rumplesnitz".'

Gawaine frowned. 'Then it wasn't a magic word after all?' he asked.

'Of course not,' said the Headmaster, 'you ought to be too old for such foolishness. There isn't any such thing as a magic word.'

'But you told me it was magic,' protested Gawaine. 'You said it was magic and now you say it isn't.'

'It wasn't magic in a literal sense,' answered the Headmaster, 'but it was much more wonderful than that. The word gave you confidence. It took away your fears. If I hadn't told you that you might have been killed the very first time. It was your battle-ax did the trick.'

Gawaine surprised the Headmaster by his attitude. He was obviously distressed by the explanation. He interrupted a long philosophic and ethical discourse by the Headmaster with, 'If I hadn't of hit 'em all mighty hard and fast any one of 'em might have crushed me like a, like a—' He fumbled for a word.

'Egg shell,' suggested the Headmaster.

'Like a egg shell,' assented Gawaine, and he said it many times. All through the evening meal people who sat near him heard him muttering, 'Like a egg shell, like a egg shell.'

The next day was clear, but Gawaine did not get up at dawn. Indeed, it was almost noon when the Headmaster found him cowering in bed, with the clothes pulled over his head. The principal called the Assistant Professor of Pleasaunce, and together they dragged the boy toward the forest.

'He'll be all right as soon as he gets a couple more dragons under his belt,' explained the Headmaster.

The Assistant Professor of Pleasaunce agreed. 'It would be a shame to stop such a fine run,' he said. 'Why, counting that one yesterday, he's killed fifty dragons.'

They pushed the boy into a thicket above which hung a meager cloud of steam. It was obviously quite a small dragon.

But Gawaine did not come back that night or the next. In fact, he never came back. Some weeks afterward brave spirits from the school explored the thicket, but they could find nothing to remind them of Gawaine except the metal parts of his medals. Even the ribbons had been devoured.

The Headmaster and the Assistant Professor of Pleasaunce agreed that it would be just as well not to tell the school how Gawaine had achieved his record and still less how he came to die. They held that it might have a bad effect on school spirit. Accordingly, Gawaine has lived in the memory of the school as its greatest hero. No visitor succeeds in leaving the building today without seeing a great shield which hangs on the wall of the dining hall. Fifty pairs of dragons' ears are mounted upon the shield and underneath in gilt letters is 'Gawaine le Cœur-Hardy', followed by the simple inscription, 'He killed fifty dragons.' The record has never been equaled.

DOGS AND MEN

HENRY C. MERWIN

There are men and women in the world who, of their own free will, live a dogless life, not knowing what they miss; and for them this essay, securely placed in the dignified Atlantic, there to remain so long as libraries and books shall endure, is chiefly written. Let them not pass it by in scorn, but rather stop to consider what can be said of the animal as a fellow being entitled to their sympathy, and having, perhaps, a like destiny with themselves.

As to those few persons who are not only dogless but dog-haters, they should excite pity rather than resentment. The man who hates a good dog is abnormal, and cannot help it. I once knew such a man, a money-lender long since passed away, whose life was largely a crusade against dogs, carried on through newspapers, pamphlets, and in conversation.

He used to declare that he had often been bitten by these animals, and that, on one occasion, a terrier actually jumped on the street-car in which he was riding, took a small piece out of his leg (a mere soupçon, no doubt), and then jumped off—all without apparent provocation, and in a moment of time. Probably this story, strange as it may sound, was substantially true. The perceptions of the dog are wonderfully acute. A recent occurrence may serve as the converse of the money-lender's story. A lost collie, lame and nearly starved, was taken in, fed, and cared for by a household of charitable persons, who, however, did not like or understand dogs, and were anxious to get rid of this one, provided that a good home could be found for him. In the course of a week there came to call upon them in her buggy an old lady who is extremely fond of dogs, and who possesses that combination of a masterful spirit with deep affection which acts like witchcraft upon the lower animals. The collie was brought out, and the story of his arrival was related at length. Meanwhile the old lady and the dog looked each other steadfastly in the eye. 'Do you want to come with me, doggie?' she said at last, not really meaning to take him. Up jumped the dog, and sat down beside her, and could not be dislodged by any entreaties or commands—and all parties were loath to use force. She took him home, but brought him back the next day, intending to leave him behind her. Again, however, the dog refused to be parted from his new and real friend. He bestowed a perfunctory wag of the tail upon his benefactors—he was not ungrateful; but, like all dogs, he sought not chiefly meat and bones and a comfortable place by the fire, but affection and caresses. The dog does not live that would refuse to forsake his dinner for the companionship of his master.

The mission of the dog—I say it with all reverence—is the same as the mission of Christianity, namely, to teach mankind that the universe is ruled by love. Ownership of a dog tends to soften the hard hearts of men. There are two great mysteries about the lower animals: one, the suffering which they have to endure at the hands of man; the other, the wealth of affection which they possess, and which for the most part is unexpended. All animals have this capacity for loving other creatures, man included. Crows, for example, show it to a remarkable degree. 'As much latent affection goes to waste in every flock of crows that flies overhead as would fit a human household for heaven.' A crow and a dog, if kept together, will become almost as fond of each other as of their master.

Surely this fact, this capacity of the lower animals to love, not only man, but one another, is the most significant, the most deserving to be pondered, the most important in respect to their place in the universe, of all the facts that can be learned about them. Compared with it, how trivial is anything that the zoologist or biologist or the physiologist can tell us about the nature of the lower animals!

The most beautiful sight in the world, I once heard it said

(by myself, to be honest), is the expression in the eyes of an intelligent, sweet-tempered pup—a pup old enough to take an interest in things about him, and yet so young as to imagine that everybody will be good to him; so young as not to fear that any man or boy will kick him, or that any dog will take away his bone. In the eyes of such a pup there is a look of confiding innocence, a consciousness of his own weakness and inexperience, a desire to love and to be loved, which are irresistible. In older dogs one is more apt to notice an eager, anxious, inquiring look, as if they were striving to understand things which the Almighty had placed beyond their mental grasp; and the nearest approach to a really human expression is seen in dogs suffering from illness. Heine, who, as the reader well knows, served a long apprenticeship to pain, somewhere says that pain refines even the lower animals; and all who are familiar with dogs in health and in disease will see the truth of this statement. I have seen in the face of an intelligent dog, suffering acutely from distemper, a look so human as to be almost terrifying; as if I had accidentally caught a glimpse of some deep-lying trait in the animal which nature had intended to conceal from mortal gaze.

The dog, in fact, makes a continual appeal to the sympathies of his human friends, and thus tends to prevent them from becoming hard or narrow. There are certain families, especially perhaps in New England, and most of all, no doubt, in Boston, who need to be regenerated, and might be regenerated by keeping a dog, provided that they went about it in the proper spirit. A distinguished preacher and author, himself a Unitarian, remarked recently in an address to Unitarians that they were usually the most self-satisfied people that he ever met. It was a casual remark, and perhaps neither he nor those who heard it appreciated its full significance. However, the preacher was probably thinking, not so much of Unitarians as of a certain kind of person often found in this neighborhood, and not necessarily professing any particular form of religion. We all know the type. When a man invariably has money in the bank, and is respectable and respected, was graduated at Harvard, has a decorous wife and children, has never been carried away by any passion or enthusiasm, knows the right people, and conforms strictly to the customs of good society; and when this sort of thing has been going on for, perhaps, two or three generations, then there is apt to creep into the blood a coldness that would chill the heart of a bronze statue. Such persons are really degenerates of their peculiar kind, and need to be saved, perhaps by desperate measures. Let them elope with the cook; let them get religion of a violent Methodistic, or of an intense Ritualistic, kind (the two forms have much in common); or if they cannot get religion, let them get a dog, give him the run of the house, love him and spoil him, and so, by the blessing of Providence, their salvation may be effected.

Reformers and philanthropists should always keep dogs, in order that the spontaneous element may not wholly die out of them. Their tendency is to regard the human race as a problem, and particular persons as 'cases' to be dealt with, not according to one's impulses, but according to certain rules approved by good authority, and supposed to be consistent with sound economic principles. To my old friend—, who once liked me for myself, without asking why, I have long ceased to be an individual, and am now simply an item of humanity to whom he owes such duty as my particular wants or vices would seem to indicate. But if he had a dog he could not regard him in that impersonal way, or worry about the dog's morals: he would simply take pleasure in his society, and love him for what he was, without considering what he might have been.

I know and honor one philanthropist who, in middle life or thereabout, became for the first time the possessor of a dog; and thenceforth there was disclosed in him a genuine vein of sentiment and affection which many years of doing good and virtuous living had failed to eradicate. Often had I heard of his civic deeds and of his well-directed charities, but my heart never quite warmed toward him until I learned that, with spectacles on nose and comb in hand, he had spent three laborious hours in painfully going over his spaniel, and eliminating those parasitic guests which sometimes infest the coat of the cleanest and most aristocratic dog. I am not ashamed to say that I have a confidence in his wisdom now which I did not have before, knowing that his head will never be allowed to tyrannize over his heart. His name should be recorded here, were it not that his modesty might be offended by the act. (Three letters would suffice to print it.)

In speaking of the dog as a kind of missionary in the household, I mean, it need hardly be said, something more than mere ownership of the animal. It will not suffice to pay a large sum for a dog of fashionable breed, equip him with a costly collar, and then relegate him to the stable or the kitchen. He should be one of the family, living on equal terms with the others, and their constant companion. The dog's life is short at the best, and every moment of it will be needed for his development. It is wonderful how, year by year, the household pet grows in intelligence, how many words he learns the meaning of, how quick he becomes in interpreting the look, the tone of voice, the mood of the person whom he loves. He is old at ten or eleven, and seldom lives beyond thirteen or fourteen. If he lived to be fifty, he would know so much that we should be uneasy, perhaps terrified, in his presence.

A certain amount of discipline is necessary for a dog. If left to his own devices, he is apt to become somewhat dissipated, to spend his evenings out, to scatter among many the affection which should be reserved for a few. But, on the other hand, a dog may easily receive too much discipline; he becomes like the child of a despotic father. A dog perfectly trained, from the martinet point of view—one who never 'jumps up' on you, never lays an entreating paw on your arm, never gets into a chair, or enters the drawing-room—such a dog is a sad sight to one who really knows and loves the animal. It is against his nature to be so repressed. Over-careful housewives, and persons who are burdened with costly surroundings, talk of injury to carpets and other furniture if the dog has a right of entry everywhere in the house. But what is furniture for? Is it for display, is it a guaranty of the wealth of the owners, or is it for use? Blessed are they whose furniture is so inexpensive or so shabby that children and dogs are not excluded from its sacred precincts. Perhaps the happiest household to which I ever had the honor of being admitted was one where it was sometimes a little difficult to find a comfortable vacant chair: the dogs always took the arm-chairs. Alas, where are those hospitable chairs now? Where the dogs that used to sit up in them, and wink and yawn, and give their paws in humorous embarrassment?

'The drawing-room was made for dogs, and not dogs for the drawing-room,' would be Lady Barnes's thesis, did she formulate it. It was this same Lady Barnes—Rhoda Broughton's—who once said, 'I have no belief in Eliza, the housemaid I leave in charge here. When last I came down from London the dogs were so unnaturally good that I felt sure she bullied them. I spoke very seriously to her, and this time, I am glad to say, they are as disobedient as ever, and have done even more mischief than when I am at home.' And she laughed with a delicate relish of her own folly.

Of all writers of fiction, by the way, is there any whose dogs quite equal those of Rhoda Broughton? Even the beloved author of Rab and His Friends, even Sir Walter himself, with his immortal Dandie Dinmonts, has not, it seems to me, given us such life-like and home-like pictures of dogs as those which occur in her novels. They seem to be there, not of set purpose, but as if dogs were such an essential part of her own existence that they crept into her books almost without her knowing it. No room in her novels is complete without a dog or two; and every remark that she makes about them has the quality of a caress. Even in a tragic moment, the heroine cannot help observing, that 'Mink is lying on his small hairy side in a sunpatch, with his little paws crossed like the hands of a dying saint.'

'Mr Brown,' that dear, faithful mongrel, is forever associated with the unfortunate Joan; and Brenda's 'wouff' will go resounding down the halls of time so long as novels are read.

Perhaps the final test of anybody's love of dogs is willingness to permit them to make a camping-ground of the bed. There is no other place in the world that suits the dog quite so well. On the bed he is safe from being stepped upon; he is out of the way of draughts; he has a commanding position from which to survey what goes on in the world; and, above all, the surface is soft and yielding to his outstretched limbs. No mere man can ever be so comfortable as a dog looks.

Some persons object to having a dog on the bed at night; and it must be admitted that he lies a little heavily upon one's limbs; but why be so base as to prefer comfort to companionship! To wake up in the dark night, and put your hand on that warm soft body, to feel the beating of that faithful heart—is not this better than undisturbed sloth? The best night's rest I ever had was once when a cocker spaniel puppy, who had just recovered from stomach-ache (dose one to two soda-mints), and was a little frightened by the strange experience, curled up on my shoulder like a fur tippet, gently pushed his cold, soft nose into my neck, and there slept sweetly and soundly until morning.

Companionship with his master is the dog's remedy for every ill, and only an extreme case will justify sending him away or boarding him out. To put a dog in a hospital, unless there is some surgical or other like necessity for doing so, is an act of doubtful kindness. Many and many a dog has died from homesickness. If he is ill, keep him warm and quiet, give him such simple remedies as you would give to a child: pour beef tea or malted milk down his throat, or even a little whiskey, if he is weak from want of food; and let him live or die, as did our fathers and our fathers' dogs—at home.

Many dogs are sensitive to an excessive degree, so sensitive indeed that any correction of them, beyond such as can be conveyed by a word, amounts to positive cruelty. A dog of that kind may easily be thrown by harsh treatment into a state of nervous disorder, and will be really unable to do what is required of him. In that state he often presents an appearance of obstinacy, whereas in fact he is suffering from a sort of nervous atrophy or paralysis, closely resembling that of a 'balky' horse.

This nervous temperament makes the dog susceptible to misery in many forms, but the worst evil that can befall is to be lost. The very words 'lost dog' call up such pictures of canine misery as can never be forgotten by those who have witnessed them. I have seen a lost dog, lame, emaciated, wounded, footsore, hungry, and thirsty, yet suffering so intensely from fear, and loneliness, and despair—from the mere sense of being lost—as to be absolutely unconscious of his bodily condition. The mental agony was so much greater that it swallowed up the physical pain.

A little Boston terrier, who was lost in a large city for two or three days, became so wrecked in his nervous system that no amount of care or petting could restore him to equanimity, and it was found necessary to kill him. Oh, reader, pass not by the lost dog! Succor him if you can; preserve him from what is worse than death. It is easy to recognize him by the look of nervous terror in his eye, by his drooping tail, by his uncertain movements.

There is a remorseful experience of my own, of which I should be glad to unburden myself to the reader. It once became my duty to kill a dog afflicted with some incurable disease. Instead of doing it myself, as I should have done, I took him to a place where lost dogs are received, and where those for whom no home can be found are mercifully destroyed. There, instead of myself leading him to the death-chamber, as, again, I should have done, I handed him over to the executioner. The dog was an abnormally nervous and timid one; and as he was dragged most unwillingly away, he turned around, as nearly as he could, and cast back at me a look of horror, of fear, of agonized appeal—a look that has haunted me for years.

Whether he had any inkling of what was in store for him, I do not know, but it is highly probable that he had. Dogs and other animals are wonderful mind-readers. I have known three cases in which some discussion about the necessity of killing an old dog, held in his presence, was quickly followed by the sudden, unaccountable disappearance of the animal; and no tidings of him could ever be obtained, although the greatest pains were taken to obtain them. Horses are inferior only to dogs in this capacity. Often, especially in the case of vicious or half-broken horses, an intention will flash from the mind of the horse to the mind of the rider or driver, and vice versa, without the slightest indication being given by horse or man. Men who ride race-horses have told me that a sudden conviction in their own minds, in the course of a race, that they could not win has passed immediately to the horse, and caused him to slacken his speed, although they had not ceased to urge him. It is notorious in the trotting world that faint-hearted and pessimistic drivers often lose races which they ought to win.

As to remarkable stories about this or that animal, perhaps it might be said that they are probably true when they illustrate the animal's perceptive abilities, and are probably false when they depend upon his power to originate. There appeared lately an account of a race between loons in the wild state: how the loons got together and arranged the preliminaries (whether they made books on the event or adopted the pool system of betting was not stated), how the race was run, or rather flown, amid intense loon excitement, and how the victor was greeted with screams of applause!

Some power of origination animals, and dogs especially, certainly have. There is the familiar trick which dogs play when one, to get a bone away from another, rushes off a little space, gives the bark which signifies the presence of an intruder, then comes back and quietly runs away with the bone which the other dog, in his curiosity to see who is coming, has impulsively dropped. This is an example, not of reasoning only, but of origination.

In general, however, when dogs surprise us, as they frequently do, it is by the delicacy and acuteness of their perceptive powers. How unerringly do they distinguish between different classes of persons, as, for example, between the members of the family and the servants; and again, between the servants and the friends of the household! Unquestionably the dog has three sets of manners for these three classes of persons. He will take liberties in the kitchen that he would never dream of taking in the dining-room. We have known our cook to fly in terror from the kitchen because Figaro, a masterful cocker spaniel, threatened to bite her if she did not give him a piece of meat forthwith. Figaro reasoned that the cook was partly his cook, and that he had a right to bully her if he could.

As for the different members of the family, the dog will 'size them up' with an unerring instinct. It is impossible to conceal any weakness of character from him; and if you are strong, he will know that, too. As I write these lines, the vision of 'Mr Guppy' rises before me. Mr Guppy was a very small Boston terrier with a white head, but otherwise of a brindle color. He had a beautiful 'mug', much like that of a bull dog, with a short nose, wide jaws, and plenty of loose skin hanging about his stout little neck. It must be admitted that he was somewhat self-indulgent, being continually on the watch for a chance to lie close by the fire—a situation considered by his friends to be unwholesome for him. Mr Guppy understood me very well. He knew that I was a poor, weak, easy-going, absent-minded creature, with whom he could take liberties; accordingly, when we were alone together, the rogue would lie sleeping with his head on the hearth, while I was absorbed in my book. But hark! There is a step on the stairs, of one whom Mr Guppy both loved and feared more than any dog ever loved or feared me; and forthwith the little impostor would rise and crawl softly back to his place on a rug in the corner; and there he would be found lying and winking, with an expression of perfect innocence, when the disciplinarian entered the room.

Dogs have the same sensitiveness that we associate with well-bred men and women. Their politeness is remarkable. Offer a dog water when he is not thirsty, and he will almost always take a lap or two, just out of civility, and to show his gratitude. I know a group of dogs that never forget to come and tell their mistress when they have had their dinner, feeling sure that she will sympathize with them; and if they have failed to get it, they will notify her immediately of the omission. If you happen to step on a dog's tail or paw, how eagerly—after one irrepressible yelp of pain—will he tell you by his caresses that he knows you did not mean to hurt him and forgives you!

In their relations with one another, also, dogs have a keen sense of etiquette. A well-known traveler makes this unexpected remark about a tribe of naked black men, living on one of the South Sea Islands: 'In their everyday intercourse there is much that is stiff, formal, and precise.' Almost the same remark might be made about dogs. Unless they are on very intimate terms, they take great pains never to brush against or even to touch one another. For one dog to step over another is a dangerous breach of etiquette unless they are special friends. It is no uncommon thing for two dogs to belong to the same person, and live in the same house, and yet never take the slightest notice of each other. We have a spaniel so dignified that he will never permit another member of the dog family to pillow his head on him; but, with the egotism of a true aristocrat, he does not hesitate to make use of the other dogs for that purpose.

Often canine etiquette is so subtle that one has much difficulty in following it out. In our household are two uncongenial dogs, who, in ordinary circumstances, completely ignore each other, and between whom any familiarity would be resented fiercely. And yet, when we are all out walking, if I am obliged to scold or punish one of these two, the other will run up to the offender, bark at him, and even jostle him, as if he were saying, 'Well, old man, you got it that time; aren't you ashamed of yourself?' And the other dog, feeling that he is in the wrong, I suppose, submits meekly to the insult.

A family of six dogs used to pair off in couples, each couple being on terms of special intimacy and affection; and besides these relationships, there were many others among them. For example, they all deferred to the oldest dog, although he was smaller and weaker than the rest. If a fight began, he would jump in between the contestants and stop it; if a dog misbehaved, he would rush at the offender with a warning growl; and this exercise of authority was never resented. The other dogs seemed to respect his weight of years, his character, which was of the highest, and his moral courage, which was undoubted. This same dog—his name was Pedro—had many human traits. He and his companions slept together on a sofa upstairs, where, of a cold night, they would curl up together in an indistinguishable heap. Sometimes the old dog would put himself to bed before the others, and then, finding that he needed the warmth and companionship of their presence, he would go into the hall, put his head between the balusters, and whine softly until they came upstairs to join him.

That animals reason is a fact of everyday experience. That they can communicate their wants and feelings to one another and to man is equally plain. 'When a cat or a dog,' wrote the late Mr Romanes, 'pulls one's dress to lead one to the kittens or puppies in need of assistance, the animal is behaving in the same manner as a deaf mute might behave when invoking assistance from a friend. That is to say, the animal is translating the logic of feelings into the logic of signs; and so far as this particular action is concerned, it is psychologically indistinguishable from that which is performed by the deaf mute.'

Mentally, we are not so many epochs removed from the other animals, and emotionally the connection is closer yet. I will not discuss the question whether dumb animals have any sense of right and wrong. I believe that they have this sense in a rudimentary degree; or at least that it is latent in them, and may be developed. The popular instinctive notions about animals, the result of the experience of the race, seem to justify this view. 'If we say a vicious horse,' remarked Dr Arnold, 'why not a virtuous horse?' And we do speak of a 'kind' horse.

Moreover, it is obvious that dogs have a sense of humor; and they have also a sense of shame, perfectly distinct from the fear of punishment. Of this sense of shame let me give one example. The dog's eyesight, so far at least as stationary objects are concerned, is very poor, his real reliance being on his sense of smell; and I have often seen a dog mistake one of his own family for a strange animal, run toward him, with every sign of hostility, and then, when he came within a few feet of the other dog, suddenly drop his tail between his legs and slink away, as if he feared that somebody had noticed his absurd mistake.

Can it be that an animal should possess a sense of humor and a sense of shame, without having also some elementary sense of right and wrong? But even if it be thought that he is devoid of that sense, it is certain that he has those kindly impulses from which it has been developed. All that is best in man springs from something which is practically the same in the dog that it is in him, namely, the instinct of pity or benevolence. To that instinct, as it exists in the lower animals, Darwin attributed the origin of conscience in man; and there are now few, if any, philosophers who would give a different account of it.

I have seen a pup not six months old run to comfort another pup that cried out from pain; and the impulse that prompted this act was essentially the same as that which impels the noblest of mankind when they befriend the poor or the afflicted. We are akin to the lower animals morally, as well as physically and mentally.

But this is a modern discovery. It is astonishing and confusing to realize how little organized Christianity has done for the lower animals. The ecclesiastical conception of them was simply that they were creatures without souls, and therefore had no rights as against, or at the hands of, mankind. To this day that conception remains, although it is qualified, of course, by other and more humane considerations. Even Cardinal Newman said,—

'We have no duties toward the brute creation; there is no relation of justice between them and us. Of course, we are bound not to treat them ill, for cruelty is an offense against the holy law which our Maker has written on our hearts, and it is displeasing to Him. But they can claim nothing at our hand; into our hand they are absolutely delivered. We may use them, we may destroy them at our pleasure: not our wanton pleasure, but still for our own ends, for our own benefit and satisfaction, provided that we can give a rational account of what we do.'

This position, although not perhaps cruel in itself, inevitably results in immeasurable cruelties. When an English traveler remonstrated with a Spanish lady for throwing a sick kitten out of the second-story window, she justified herself by saying that the kitten had no soul; and that is the national point of view.

Protestantism has been almost as indifferent as Catholicism to the lower animals. In fact, the conscience which exists outside of the church, Catholic or Protestant, has in this matter, outstripped the conscience of the church. 'Cruelty,' said Du Maurier, 'is the only unpardonable sin'; and the world is slowly but surely coming to that opinion. The long-deferred awakening of mankind to the sufferings of dumb animals was not due to a decline of the ecclesiastical conception of them, although it has declined; nor even to the new knowledge concerning the common origin of man and beast—indeed, it slightly preceded that knowledge; but it was due to the gradual enlightenment and moral improvement of the race, especially of the English-speaking race.

The nineteenth century, as we are often told, saw more discoveries and inventions than had been made in the preceding six thousand years; but I believe that in future ages not one of those discoveries and inventions, nor all together, will bulk so large as factors in the development and uplifting of man, as will those humane laws and societies which first came into existence in that century.

We overvalue intellectual as compared with moral and emotional gifts. The material civilization upon which we pride ourselves is almost wholly the achievement of the intellect. Fame and wealth, luxury, cultivation, and leisure—all the big prizes of the world, in fact—are obtained by the successful exercise of the intellect. The moral qualities, of themselves, can procure us nothing but a clear conscience, and the approval, perhaps mixed with contempt, of our neighbors.

And yet, when the intellectual qualities are brought to the test of reality; when one's view of them is not clouded by pride, avarice, or passion, then how amazingly does their value shrink and shrivel! When a man lies on his deathbed, for example, his intellectual achievements, though of the highest order, will seem as nothing to him—he will ask himself simply whether he has lived a good or a bad life; and after his death his family and his friends will look at the matter in precisely the same way.

Even the progress of mankind is far more moral than intellectual. Competent authorities tell us that the Anglo-Saxon of today is mentally inferior to the Greek who lived two thousand years ago: and if the human race has improved during that time, it is not so much because man has advanced in knowledge as because he has acquired more sympathy with his inferiors, be they brute or human, more generosity, more mercy toward them. Not Stevenson, nor Faraday, nor Morse, nor Fulton, nor Bell, did so much for the human race, to say nothing of the other animals, as did that dueling Irishman who, in the year 1822, proposed in the English Parliament, amid shrieks and howls of derision, what afterward became the first law for the protection of dumb animals ever placed on the statute-book of any country. Every movement for the relief of the brute creation has originated in England; and when we damn, as we righteously may, John Bull for one thing and another, let us remember this fact to his eternal honor!

It is hard to part from an old dog-friend with no hope of ever meeting him again, hard to believe that the spirit of love which burned so steadfastly in him is quenched forever. But for those who hold what I have called the ecclesiastical conception of the lower animals, no other view is possible. That devout Catholic and exquisite poet, Dr Parsons, has beautifully expressed this fact:

> When parents die there's many a word to say—
> Kind words, consoling—one can always pray;
> When children die 't is natural to tell
> Their mother, 'Certainly with them 't is well!'
> But for a dog, 't was all the life he had,
> Since death is end of dogs, or good or bad.
> This was his world, he was contented here;

> Imagined nothing better, naught more dear,
> Than his young mistress; sought no higher sphere;
> Having no sin, asked not to be forgiven;
> Ne'er guessed at God nor ever dreamed of heaven.
> Now he has passed away, so much of love
> Goes from our life, without one hope above!

But is there no hope? Is there not as much—or, if the reader prefers, as little—hope for the dog as there is for man? I remember reading years ago in a prominent magazine the statement that doubtless a few men, the very wickedest, will become extinct at death, whereas the rest of mankind will be immortal. This view had some adherents then, but would now be regarded by almost everybody as irrational. Who can believe that between the best and the worst man there is any such gulf as would justify so diverse a fate!

Moreover we have learned that there are no chasms or jumps in nature. One thing slides into another; every creature is a link between two other creatures; and man himself can be traced back physically, mentally, and morally, to the lower animals. Is it not then reasonable to suppose that immortality belongs to all forms of life or to none? That if man is immortal, the dog is immortal, too? Even to speculate upon this subject seems almost ridiculous, our knowledge is so limited; and yet it is hard to refrain from speculation. The transmigration of souls may be a fact, or men and dogs and all other forms of life may be simply forms, temporary phases, proceeding from one source, and returning thereto. But alas, every supposition that we can make is rendered almost, if not quite, untenable by the mere fact that the human intellect has conceived it—it is so unlikely that we should hit upon the right solution!

In this situation, what we seem bound to do is to refrain from hasty, and especially from egotistic conclusions, to keep our minds open, to regard the lower animals, not only with pity, but with a certain reverence. We do not know what or whence they are;

but we do know that their nature resembles ours; that they have Individuality, as we have it; that they feel pain, both physical and mental; that they are capable of affection; that, although innocent, as we believe, their sufferings have been, and are, unspeakable. Is there no mystery here?

To many men, to most men, perhaps, a dog is simply an animated machine, developed or created for the convenience of the human race. It may be so; and yet again it may be that the dog has his own rightful place in the universe, irrespective and independent of man, and that an injury done to him is an insult to the Creator.

THE DEVIL BABY AT HULL-HOUSE

JANE ADDAMS

I

The knowledge of the existence of the Devil Baby burst upon the residents of Hull-House one day when three Italian women, with an excited rush through the door, demanded that he be shown them. No amount of denial convinced them that he was not there, for they knew exactly what he was like, with his cloven hoofs, his pointed ears and diminutive tail; moreover, the Devil Baby had been able to speak as soon as he was born and was most shockingly profane.

The three women were but the forerunners of a veritable multitude; for six weeks the streams of visitors from every part of the city and suburbs to this mythical baby poured in all day long, and so far into the night that the regular activities of the settlement were almost swamped.

The Italian version, with a hundred variations, dealt with a pious Italian girl married to an atheist. Her husband vehemently tore a holy picture from the bedroom wall, saying that he would quite as soon have a devil in the house as that; whereupon the devil incarnated himself in her coming child. As soon as the Devil Baby was born, he ran about the table shaking his finger in deep reproach at his father, who finally caught him and in fear and trembling brought him to Hull-House. When the residents there, in spite of the baby's shocking appearance, wishing to save his soul, took him to church for baptism, they found that the shawl was empty, and the Devil Baby, fleeing from the holy water, ran lightly over the backs of the pews.

The Jewish version, again with variations, was to the effect that the father of six daughters had said before the birth of a seventh child that he would rather have a devil in the house than another girl, whereupon the Devil Baby promptly appeared.

Save for a red automobile which occasionally figured in the story, and a stray cigar which, in some versions, the newborn child snatched from his father's lips, the tale might have been fashioned a thousand years ago.

Although the visitors to the Devil Baby included people of every degree of prosperity and education—even physicians and trained nurses who assured us of their scientific interest—the story constantly demonstrated the power of an old wives' tale among thousands of people in modern society who are living in a corner of their own, their vision fixed, their intelligence held by some iron chain of silent habit. To such primitive people the metaphor apparently is still the very 'stuff of life'; or, rather, no other form of statement reaches them, and the tremendous tonnage of current writing for them has no existence. It was in keeping with their simple habits that the reputed presence of the Devil Baby at Hull-House did not reach the newspapers until the fifth week of his sojourn—after thousands of people had already been informed of his whereabouts by the old method of passing news from mouth to mouth.

During the weeks of excitement it was the old women who really seemed to have come into their own, and perhaps the most significant result of the incident was the reaction of the story upon them. It stirred their minds and memories as with a magic touch; it loosened their tongues and revealed the inner life and thoughts of those who are so often inarticulate. These old women enjoyed a moment of triumph, as if they had made good at last and had come into a region of sanctions and punishments which they understood.

Throughout six weeks, as I went about Hull-House, I would hear a voice at the telephone repeating for the hundredth time that day, 'No, there is no such baby'; 'No, we never had it here'; 'No, he couldn't have seen it for fifty cents'; 'We didn't send it anywhere because we never had it'; 'I don't mean to say that your sister-in-law lied, but there must be some mistake'; 'There is no use getting up an excursion from Milwaukee, for there isn't any Devil Baby at Hull-House'; 'We can't give reduced rates because we are not exhibiting anything'; and so on and on. As I came near the front door, I would catch snatches of arguments that were often acrimonious: 'Why do you let so many people believe it, if it isn't here?'; 'We have taken three lines of cars to come, and we have as much right to see it as anybody else'; 'This is a pretty big place, of course you could hide it easy enough'; 'What you saying that for—are you going to raise the price of admission?' We had doubtless struck a case of what the psychologists call the 'contagion of emotion,' added to that 'æsthetic sociability' which impels any one of us to drag the entire household to the window when a procession comes into the street or a rainbow appears in the sky.

But the Devil Baby of course was worth many processions and rainbows, and I will confess that, as the empty show went on day after day, I quite revolted against such a vapid manifestation of an admirable human trait. There was always one exception, however: whenever I heard the high eager voices of old women, I was irresistibly interested, and left anything I might be doing in order to listen to them.

II

Perhaps my many talks with these aged visitors crystallized thoughts and impressions that I had been receiving through years; or the tale itself may have ignited a fire, as it were, whose light illumined some of my darkest memories of neglected and uncomfortable old age, of old peasant women who had ruthlessly probed into the ugly depths of human nature in themselves and others. Many of them who came to see the Devil Baby had been forced to face tragic human experiences; the powers of brutality and horror had had full scope in their lives, and for years they had had acquaintance with disaster and death. Such old women do not shirk life's misery by feeble idealism, for they are long past the stage of make-believe. They relate without flinching the most hideous experiences. 'My face has had this queer twist for now nearly sixty years; I was ten when it got that way, the night after I saw my father do my mother to death with his knife.'

'Yes, I had fourteen children; only two grew to be men and both of them were killed in the same explosion. I was never sure they brought home the right bodies.' But even the most hideous sorrows which the old women related had apparently subsided into the paler emotion of ineffectual regret, after Memory had long done her work upon them; the old people seemed, in some unaccountable way, to lose all bitterness and resentment against life, or rather they were so completely without it that they must have lost it long since.

Perhaps those women, because they had come to expect nothing more from life and had perforce ceased from grasping and striving, had obtained, if not renunciation, at least that quiet endurance which allows the wounds of the spirit to heal. Through their stored-up habit of acquiescence, they vouchsafed a fleeting glimpse of that translucent wisdom so often embodied in old women, but so difficult to portray. I recall a conversation with one of them, a woman whose fine mind and indomitable spirit I had long admired; I had known her for years, and yet the recital of her sufferings, added to those which the Devil Baby had already induced other women to tell me, pierced me afresh.

'I had eleven children, some born in Bohemia and some born here; nine of them boys; all of the children died when they were little, but my dear Liboucha, you know all about her. She died last winter in the insane asylum. She was only twelve years old when her father, in a fit of delirium tremens, killed himself after he had chased us around the room trying to kill us first. She saw it all; the blood splashed on the wall stayed in her mind the worst; she shivered and shook all that night through, and the next morning she had lost her voice, couldn't speak out loud for terror. After a while her voice came back, although it was never very natural, and she went to school again. She seemed to do as well as ever and was awful pleased when she got into High School. All the money we had, I earned scrubbing in a public dispensary, although sometimes I got a little more by interpreting for the patients, for I know three languages, one as well as the other. But I was determined that, whatever happened to me, Liboucha was to be educated. My husband's father was a doctor in the old country, and Liboucha was always a clever child. I wouldn't have her live the kind of life I had, with no use for my mind except to make me restless and bitter. I was pretty old and worn out for such hard work, but when I used to see Liboucha on a Sunday morning, ready for church, in her white dress with her long yellow hair braided round her beautiful pale face, lying there in bed as I was—being brought up a freethinker and needing to rest my aching bones for the next week's work—I'd feel almost happy, in spite of everything.

'But of course no such peace could last in my life; the second year at High School, Liboucha began to seem different and do strange things. You know the time she wandered away for three days and we were all wild with fright, although a kind woman had taken her in and no harm came to her. I could never be easy after that; she was always gentle, but she was awful sly about running away, and at last I had to send her to the asylum. She stayed there off and on for five years, but I saw her every week of my life and she was always company for me, what with sewing for her, washing and ironing her clothes, cooking little things to take out to her and saving a bit of money to buy fruit for her. At any rate, I had stopped feeling so bitter, and got some comfort out of seeing the one thing that belonged to me on this side of the water, when all of a sudden she died of heart-failure, and they never took the trouble to send for me until the next day.'

She stopped, as if wondering afresh that the Fates could have been so casual, but with a sudden illumination, as if she had been awakened out of the burden and intensity of her restricted personal interests into a consciousness of those larger relations which are, for the most part, so strangely invisible. It was as if the young mother of the grotesque Devil Baby, that victim of wrongdoing on the part of others, had revealed to this tragic woman, much more clearly than soft words had ever done, that the return of a deed of violence upon the head of the innocent is inevitable; as if she had realized that, although she was destined to walk all the days of her life with that piteous multitude who bear the undeserved wrongs of the world, she would walk henceforth with a sense of companionship.

Among the visitors were pitiful old women who, although they had already reconciled themselves to much misery, were still enduring more. 'You might say it's a disgrace to have your son beat you up for the sake of a bit of money you've earned by scrubbing—your own man is different—but I haven't the heart to blame the boy for doing what he's seen all his life; his father forever went wild when the drink was in him and struck me to the very day of his death. The ugliness was born in the boy as the marks of the devil was born in the poor child upstairs.'

This more primitive type embodies the eternal patience of those humble toiling women who through the generations have been held of little value, save as their drudgery ministered to their men. One of them related her habit of going through the pockets of her drunken son every pay-day, and complained that she had never got so little as the night before, only twenty-five cents out of fifteen dollars he had promised for the rent long overdue. 'I had to get that as he lay in the alley before the door; I couldn't pull him in, and the copper who helped him home left as soon as he heard me coming and pretended he didn't see me. I have no food in the house nor coffee to sober him up with. I know perfectly well that you will ask me to eat something here, but if I can't carry it home, I won't take a bite nor a sup. I have never told you so much before. Since one of the nurses said he could be arrested for my nonsupport, I've been awfully close-mouthed. It's the foolish way all the women in our street are talking about the Devil Baby that's loosened my tongue—more shame to me.'

There are those, if possible more piteous still, who have

become absolutely helpless and can therefore no longer perform the household services exacted from them. One last wish has been denied them. 'I hoped to go before I became a burden, but it was not to be'; and the long days of unwonted idleness are darkened by the haunting fear that 'they' will come to think the burden too heavy and decide that the poorhouse is 'the best.' Even then there is no word of blame for undutiful children or heedless grandchildren, for apparently all that is petty and transitory falls away from austere old age; the fires are burned out, resentments, hatreds, and even cherished sorrows have become actually unintelligible. It is as if the horrors through which these old people had passed had never existed for them; and, facing death as they are, they seem anxious to speak only such words of groping wisdom as they can command.

This aspect of memory has never been more clearly stated than by Gilbert Murray in his *Life of Euripides*. He tells us that the aged poet, when he was officially declared to be one of 'the old men of Athens', said, 'Even yet the age-worn minstrel can turn Memory into song'; and the memory of which he spoke was that of history and tradition, rather than his own. The aged poet turned into song even the hideous story of Medea, transmuting it into 'a beautiful remote song about far-off children who have been slain in legend, children who are now at peace and whose ancient pain has become part mystery and part music. Memory—that Memory who is the mother of the Muses—having done her work upon them.'

The vivid interest of so many old women in the story of the Devil Baby may have been an unconscious, although powerful, testimony that tragic experiences gradually become dressed in such trappings in order that their spent agony may prove of some use to a world which learns at the hardest; and that the strivings and sufferings of men and women long since dead, their emotions no longer connected with flesh and blood, are thus transmuted into legendary wisdom. The young are forced to heed the warning in such a tale, although for the most part it is so easy for them to disregard the words of the aged. That the old women who came to visit the Devil Baby believed that the story would secure them a hearing at home, was evident, and as they prepared themselves with every detail of it, their old faces shone with a timid satisfaction. Their features, worn and scarred by harsh living, even as effigies built into the floor of an old church become dim and defaced by rough-shod feet, grew poignant and solemn. In the midst of their double bewilderment, both that the younger generation were walking in such strange paths and that no one would listen to them, for one moment there flickered up that last hope of a disappointed life, that it may at least serve as a warning while affording material for exciting narrations.

Sometimes in talking to one of them, who was 'but a hair's breadth this side of the darkness', one realized that old age has its own expression for the mystic renunciation of the world. The impatience with all non-essentials, the craving to be free from hampering bonds and soft conditions, was perhaps typified in our own generation by Tolstoi's last impetuous journey, the light of his genius for a moment making comprehensible to us that unintelligible impulse of the aged.

Often, in the midst of a conversation, one of these touching old women would quietly express a longing for death, as if it were a natural fulfillment of an inmost desire. Her sincerity and anticipation were so genuine that I would feel abashed in her presence, ashamed to 'cling to this strange thing that shines in the sunlight, and to be sick with love for it.' Such impressions were in their essence transitory, but one result from the hypothetical visit of the Devil Baby to Hull-House will, I think, remain: a realization of the sifting and reconciling power inherent in Memory, itself. The old women, with much to aggravate and little to soften the habitual bodily discomforts of old age, exhibited an emotional serenity so vast and reassuring that I found myself perpetually speculating as to how soon the fleeting and petty emotions which seem so unduly important to us now might be thus transmuted; at what moment we might expect the inconsistencies and perplexities of life to be brought under this appeasing Memory, with its ultimate power to increase the elements of Beauty and Significance and to reduce, if not to eliminate, stupidity and resentment.

III

As our visitors to the Devil Baby came day by day, it was gradually evident that the simpler women were not moved wholly by curiosity, but that many of them prized the story as a valuable instrument in the business of living.

The legend exhibited all the persistence of one of those tales which have doubtless been preserved through the centuries because of their taming effects upon recalcitrant husbands and fathers. Shamefaced men brought by their women-folk to see the baby but ill-concealed their triumph when there proved to be no such visible sign of retribution for domestic derelictions. On the other hand, numbers of men came by themselves. One group from a neighboring factory, on their 'own time', offered to pay twenty-five cents, a half-dollar, two dollars apiece to see the child, insisting that it must be at Hull-House because 'the women-folks had seen it'. To my query as to whether they supposed we would exhibit for money a poor little deformed baby, if one had been born in the neighborhood, they replied, 'Sure, why not?' and, 'It teaches a good lesson, too,' they added as an afterthought, or perhaps as a concession to the strange moral standards of a place like Hull-House. All the members of this group of hardworking men, in spite of a certain swagger toward one another and a tendency to bully the derelict showman, wore that hang-dog look betraying the sense of unfair treatment which a man is so apt to feel when his womankind makes an appeal to the supernatural. In their determination to see the child, the men recklessly divulged much more concerning their motives than they had meant to do, and their talk confirmed my impression that such a story may still act as a restraining influence in that sphere of marital conduct, which, next to primitive religion itself, we are told, has always afforded the most fertile field for irrational tabus and savage punishments.

What story more than this could be calculated to secure sympathy for the mother of too many daughters, and contumely for the irritated father? The touch of mysticism, the supernatural sphere in which it was placed, would render a man perfectly helpless.

The story of the Devil Baby, evolved today as it might have been centuries before in response to the imperative needs of anxious wives and mothers, recalled the theory that woman first fashioned the fairy-story, that combination of wisdom and romance, in an effort to tame her mate and to make him a better father to her children, until such stories finally became a rude creed for domestic conduct, softening the treatment that men accorded to women.

These first pitiful efforts of women, so wide-spread and powerful that we have not yet escaped their influence, still cast vague shadows upon the vast spaces of life, shadows that are dim and distorted because of their distant origin. They remind us that for thousands of years women had nothing to oppose against unthinkable brutality save 'the charm of words', no other implement with which to subdue the fiercenesses of the world about them.

During the weeks that the Devil Baby drew multitudes of visitors to Hull-House, my mind was opened to the fact that new knowledge derived from concrete experience is continually being made available for the guidance of human life; that humble women are still establishing rules of conduct as best they may, to counteract the base temptations of a man's world. Thousands of women, for instance, make it a standard of domestic virtue that a man must not touch his pay envelope, but bring it home unopened to his wife. High praise is contained in the phrase, 'We have been married twenty years and he never once opened his own envelope'; or covert blame in the statement, 'Of course he got to gambling; what can you expect from a man who always opens his own pay?'

The women are so fatalistically certain of this relation of punishment to domestic sin, of reward to domestic virtue, that when they talk about it, as they so constantly did in connection with the Devil Baby, it often sounds as if they were using the words of a widely known ritual. Even the young girls seized upon it as a palpable punishment, to be held over the heads of reckless friends. That the tale was useful was evidenced by many letters similar to the anonymous epistle here given.

'me and my friends we work in talor shop and when we are going home on the roby street car where we get off that car at blue island ave. we will meet some fellows sitting at that street where they drink some beer from pail, they keep look in cars all time and they will wait and see if we will come sometimes we will have to work, but they will wait so long they are tired and they don't care they get rest so long but a girl what works in twine mill saw them talk with us we know her good and she say what youse talk with old drunk man for we shall come to thier dance when it will be they will tell us and we should know all about where to see them that girl she say oh if you will go with them you will get devils baby like some other girls did who we knows, she say Jane Addams she will show one like that in Hull House if you will go down there we shall come sometime and we will see if that is trouth we do not believe her for she is friendly with them old men herself when she go out from her work they will wink to her and say something else to. We will go down and see you and make a lie from what she say.'

IV

The story evidently held some special comfort for hundreds of forlorn women, representatives of that vast horde of the denied and proscribed, who had long found themselves confronted by those mysterious and impersonal wrongs which are apparently nobody's fault but seem to be inherent in the very nature of things.

Because the Devil Baby embodied an undeserved wrong to a poor mother, whose tender child had been claimed by the forces of evil, his merely reputed presence had power to attract to Hull-House hundreds of women who had been humbled and disgraced by their children; mothers of the feeble-minded, of the vicious, of the criminal, of the prostitute. In their talk it was as if their long rôle of maternal apology and protective reticence had at last broken down; as if they could speak out freely because for once a man responsible for an ill-begotten child had been 'met up with' and had received his deserts. Their sinister version of the story was that the father of the Devil Baby had married without confessing a hideous crime committed years before, thus basely deceiving both his innocent young bride and the good priest who performed the solemn ceremony; that the sin had become incarnate in his child, which, to the horror of the young and trusting mother, had been born with all the outward aspects of the devil himself.

As if drawn by a magnet, week after week, a procession of forlorn women in search of the Devil Baby came to Hull-House from every part of the city, issuing forth from the many homes in which dwelt 'the two unprofitable goddesses, Poverty and Impossibility'. With an understanding that was quickened perhaps by my own acquaintance with the mysterious child, I listened to many tragic tales from the visiting women: of premature births, 'because he kicked me in the side'; of children maimed and burned, because 'I had no one to leave them with when I went to work.' These women had seen the tender flesh of growing little bodies given over to death because 'he wouldn't let me send for the doctor', or because 'there was no money to pay for the medicine'. But even these mothers, rendered childless through insensate brutality, were less pitiful than some of the others, who might well have cried aloud of their children as did a distracted mother of her child centuries ago—

> That God should send this one thing more
> Of hunger and of dread, a door
> Set wide to every wind of pain!

Such was the mother of a feeble-minded boy who said, 'I didn't have a devil baby myself, but I bore a poor "innocent", who made me fight devils for twenty-three years.' She told of her son's experiences, from the time the other little boys had put him up to stealing that they might hide in safety and leave him to be found with 'the goods' on him, until, grown into a huge man, he fell into the hands of professional burglars; he was evidently the dupe and stool-pigeon of the vicious and criminal until the very day he was locked into the State Penitentiary. 'If people played with him a little, he went right off and did anything they told him to, and now he's been sent up for life. We call such innocents "God's Fools" in the old country, but over here the Devil himself gets them. I've fought off bad men and boys from the poor lamb with my very fists; nobody ever came near the house except such like and the police officers who were always arresting him.'

There were a goodly number of visitors, of the type of those to be found in every large city, who are on the verge of nervous collapse or who exhibit many symptoms of mental aberration and yet are sufficiently normal to be at large most of the time and to support themselves by drudgery which requires little mental effort, although the exhaustion resulting from the work they are able to do is the one thing from which they should be most carefully protected. One such woman, evidently obtaining inscrutable comfort from the story of the Devil Baby even after she had become convinced that we harbored no such creature, came many times to tell of her longing for her son who had joined the army some eighteen months before and was stationed in Alaska. She always began with the same words. 'When spring comes and the snow melts so that I know he could get out, I can hardly stand it. You know I was once in the Insane Asylum for three years at a stretch, and since then I haven't had much use of my mind except to worry with. Of course I know that it is dangerous for me, but what can I do? I think something like this: 'The snow is melting, now he could get out, but his officers won't let him off, and if he runs away he'll be shot for a deserter—either way I'll never see him again; I'll die without seeing him—and then I begin all over again with the snow.' After a pause, she said, 'The recruiting officer ought not to have taken him; he's my only son and I'm a widow; it's against the rules, but he was so crazy to go that I guess he lied a little. At any rate, the government has him now and I can't get him back. Without this worry about him, my mind would be all right; if he was here he would be earning money and keeping me and we would be happy all day long.'

Recalling the vagabondish lad who had never earned much money and had certainly never 'kept' his hard-working mother, I ventured to suggest that, even if he were at home, he might not have worked these hard times, that he might get into trouble and be arrested—I did not need to remind her that he had already been arrested twice—that he was now fed and sheltered and under discipline, and I added hopefully something about seeing the world. She looked at me out of her withdrawn harried eyes, as if I were speaking a foreign tongue. 'That wouldn't make any real difference to me—the work, the money, his behaving well and all that, if I could cook and wash for him; I don't need all the money I earn scrubbing that factory; I only take bread and tea for supper, and I choke over that, thinking of him.'

V

A sorrowful woman clad in heavy black, who came one day, exhibited such a capacity for prolonged weeping that it was evidence in itself of the truth of at least half her statement, that she had cried herself to sleep every night of her life for fourteen years in fulfillment of a 'curse' laid upon her by an angry man that 'her pillow would be wet with tears as long as she lived'. Her respectable husband had kept a shop in the Red Light district, because he found it profitable to sell to the men and women who lived there. She had kept house in the rooms 'over the store', from the time she was a bride newly come from Russia, and her five daughters had been born there, but never a son to gladden her husband's heart.

She took such a feverish interest in the Devil Baby that when

I was obliged to disillusion her, I found it hard to take away her comfort in the belief that the Powers that Be are on the side of the woman, when her husband resents too many daughters. But, after all, the birth of daughters was but an incident in her tale of unmitigated woe, for the scoldings of a disappointed husband were as nothing to the curse of a strange enemy, although she doubtless had a confused impression that if there was retribution for one in the general scheme of things, there might be for the other.

When the weeping woman finally put the events of her disordered life in some sort of sequence, it was clear that about fifteen years ago she had reported to the police a vicious house whose back door opened into her own yard. Her husband had forbidden her to do anything about it and had said that it would only get them into trouble; but she had been made desperate one day when she saw her little girl, then twelve years old, come out of the door, gleefully showing her younger sister a present of money. Because the poor woman had tried for ten years, without success, to induce her husband to move from the vicinity of such houses, she was certain that she could save her child only by forcing out 'the bad people' from her own door-yard. She therefore made her one frantic effort, found her way to the city hall, and there reported the house to the chief himself. Of course, 'the bad people' stood in with the police, and nothing happened to them except, perhaps, a fresh levy of blackmail; but the keeper of the house, beside himself with rage, made the dire threat and laid the curse upon her. In less than a year from that time he had enticed her daughter into a disreputable house in another part of the district. The poor woman, ringing one doorbell after another, had never been able to find her; but the girl's sisters, who in time came to know where she was, had been dazzled by her mode of life. The weeping mother was quite sure that two of her daughters, while still outwardly respectable and 'working downtown', earned money in the devious ways which they had learned all about when they were little children, although for the past five years the now prosperous husband had allowed the family to live in a suburb where the two younger daughters were 'growing up respectable'.

At moments it seemed possible that these simple women, representing an earlier development, eagerly seized upon the story simply because it was primitive in form and substance. Certainly one evening a long-forgotten ballad made an unceasing effort to come to the surface of my mind, as I talked to a feeble woman who, in the last stages of an incurable disease from which she soon afterwards died, had been helped off the street-car in front of Hull-House.

The ballad tells that the lover of a proud and jealous mistress, who demanded as a final test of devotion that he bring her the heart of his mother, had quickly cut the heart from his mother's breast and impetuously returned to his lady bearing it upon a salver; but that, when stumbling in his gallant haste, he stooped to replace upon the silver plate his mother's heart which had rolled upon the ground, the heart, still beating with tender solicitude, whispered the hope that her child was not hurt.

The ballad itself was scarcely more exaggerated than the story of our visitor that evening, who had made the desperate effort of a journey from home in order to see the Devil Baby. I was familiar with her vicissitudes: the shiftless drinking husband and the large family of children, all of whom had brought her sorrow and disgrace; and I knew that her heart's desire was to see again before she died her youngest son, who was a life prisoner in the penitentiary. She was confident that the last piteous stage of her disease would secure him a week's parole, founding this forlorn hope upon the fact that 'they sometimes let them out to attend a mother's funeral, and perhaps they'd let Joe come a few days ahead; he could pay his fare afterwards from the insurance money. It wouldn't take much to bury me'.

Again we went over the hideous story. Joe had violently quarreled with a woman, the proprietor of the house in which his disreputable wife lived, because she withheld from him a part of his wife's 'earnings', and in the altercation had killed her—a situation, one would say, which it would be difficult for even a mother to condone. But not at all: her thin gray face worked with emotion, her trembling hands restlessly pulled at her shabby skirt as the hands of the dying pluck at the sheets, but she put all the vitality she could muster into his defense. She told us he had legally married the girl who supported him, 'although Lily had been so long in that life that few men would have done it. Of course such a girl must have a protector or everybody would fleece her; poor Lily said to the day of her death that he was the kindest man she ever knew, and treated her the whitest; that she herself was to blame for the murder because she told on the old miser, and Joe was so hot-headed she might have known that he would draw a gun for her'. The gasping mother concluded, 'He was always that handsome and had such a way. One winter when I was scrubbing in an office-building, I'd never get home much before twelve o'clock; but Joe would open the door for me just as pleasant as if he hadn't been waked out of a sound sleep.'

She was so triumphantly unconscious of the incongruity of a sturdy son in bed while his mother earned his food, that her auditors said never a word, and in silence we saw a hero evolved before our eyes: a defender of the oppressed, the best beloved of his mother, who was losing his high spirits and eating his heart out behind prison bars. He could well defy the world even there, surrounded as he was by that invincible affection which assures both the fortunate and unfortunate alike that we are loved, not according to our deserts, but in response to some profounder law.

This imposing revelation of maternal solicitude was an instance of what continually happened in connection with the Devil Baby. In the midst of the most tragic recitals there remained that something in the souls of these mothers which has been called the great revelation of tragedy, or sometimes the great illusion of tragedy—that which has power in its own right to make life acceptable and at rare moments even beautiful.

At least, during the weeks when the Devil Baby seemed to occupy every room in Hull-House, one was conscious that all human vicissitudes are in the end melted down into reminiscence, and that a metaphorical statement of those profound experiences which are implicit in human nature itself, however crude in form the story may be, has a singular power of healing the distracted spirit.

If it has always been the mission of literature to translate the particular act into something of the universal, to reduce the element of crude pain in the isolated experience by bringing to the sufferer a realization that his is but the common lot, this mission may have been performed by such stories as this for simple hard-working women, who, after all, at any given moment compose the bulk of the women in the world.

EVERY MAN'S NATURAL DESIRE TO BE SOMEBODY ELSE

SAMUEL MCCHORD CROTHERS

I

Several years ago a young man came to my study with a manuscript which he wished me to criticize.

'It is only a little bit of my work,' he said modestly, 'and it will not take you long to look it over. In fact it is only the first chapter, in which I explain the Universe.'

I suppose that we have all had moments of sudden illumination when it occurred to us that we had explained the Universe, and it was so easy for us that we wondered why we had not done it before. Some thought drifted into our mind and filled us with vague forebodings of omniscience. It was not an ordinary thought, that explained only a fragment of existence. It explained everything. It proved one thing and it proved the opposite just as well. It explained why things are as they are, and if it should turn out that they are not that way at all, it would prove that fact also. In the light of our great thought chaos seemed rational.

Such thoughts usually occur about four o'clock in the morning. Having explained the Universe, we relapse into satisfied slumber. When, a few hours later, we rise, we wonder what the explanation was.

Now and then, however, one of these highly explanatory ideas remains to comfort us in our waking hours. Such a thought is that which I here throw out, and which has doubtless at some early hour occurred to most of my readers. It is that every man has a natural desire to be somebody else.

This does not explain the Universe, but it explains that perplexing part of it which we call Human Nature. It explains why so many intelligent people, who deal skillfully with matters of fact, make such a mess of it when they deal with their fellow creatures. It explains why we get on as well as we do with strangers, and why we do not get on better with our friends. It explains why people are so often offended when we say nice things about them, and why it is that, when we say harsh things about them, they take it as a compliment. It explains why people marry their opposites and why they live happily ever afterwards. It also explains why some people don't. It explains the meaning of tact and its opposite.

The tactless person treats a person according to a scientific method as if he were a thing. Now, in dealing with a thing, you must first find out what it is, and then act accordingly. But with a person, you must first find out what he is and then carefully conceal from him the fact that you have made the discovery.

The tactless person can never be made to understand this. He prides himself on taking people as they are without being aware that that is not the way they want to be taken.

He has a keen eye for the obvious, and calls attention to it. Age, sex, color, nationality, previous condition of servitude, and all the facts that are interesting to the census-taker, are apparent to him and are made the basis of his conversation. When he meets one who is older than he, he is conscious of the fact, and emphasizes by every polite attention the disparity in years. He has an idea that at a certain period in life the highest tribute of respect is to be urged to rise out of one chair and take another that is presumably more comfortable. It does not occur to him that there may remain any tastes that are not sedentary. On the other hand, he sees a callow youth and addresses himself to the obvious callowness, and thereby makes himself thoroughly disliked. For, strange to say, the youth prefers to be addressed as a person of precocious maturity.

The literalist, observing that most people talk shop, takes it for granted that they like to talk shop. This is a mistake. They do it because it is the easiest thing to do, but they resent having attention called to their limitations. A man's profession does not necessarily coincide with his natural aptitude or with his predominant desire. When you meet a member of the Supreme Court you may assume that he is gifted with a judicial mind. But it does not follow that that is the only quality of mind he has; nor that when, out of court, he gives you a piece of his mind, it will be a piece of his judicial mind that he gives.

My acquaintance with royalty is limited to photographs of royal groups, which exhibit a high degree of domesticity. It would seem that the business of royalty when pursued as a steady job becomes tiresome, and that when they have their pictures taken they endeavor to look as much like ordinary folks as possible—and they usually succeed.

The member of one profession is always flattered by being taken for a skilled practitioner of another. Try it on your minister. Instead of saying, 'That was an excellent sermon of yours this morning,' say, 'As I listened to your cogent argument, I thought what a successful lawyer you would have made.' Then he will say, 'I did think of taking to the law.'

If you had belonged to the court of Frederick the Great, you would have proved a poor courtier indeed if you had praised His Majesty's campaigns. Frederick knew that he was a Prussian general, but he wanted to be a French literary man. If you wished to gain his favor, you should have told him that in your opinion he excelled Voltaire.

We do not like to have too much attention drawn to our present circumstances. They may be well enough in their way, but we can think of something which would be more fitting for us. We have either seen better days or we expect them.

Suppose you had visited Napoleon in Elba and had sought to ingratiate yourself with him.

'Sire,' you would have said, 'this is a beautiful little empire of yours, so snug and cosy and quiet. It is just such a domain as is suited to a man in your condition. The climate is excellent. Everything is peaceful. It must be delightful to rule where everything is arranged for you and the details are taken care of by others. As I came to your dominion I saw a line of British frigates guarding your shores. The evidences of such thoughtfulness are everywhere.'

Your praise of his present condition would not have endeared you to Napoleon. You were addressing him as the Emperor of Elba. In his own eyes he was Emperor, though in Elba.

It is such a misapprehension which irritates any mature human being when his environment is taken as the measure of his personality.

The man with a literal mind moves in a perpetual comedy of errors. It is not a question of two Dromios. There are half a dozen Dromios under one hat.

How casually introductions are made, as if it were the easiest thing in the world to make two human beings acquainted! Your friend says, 'I want you to know Mr Stifflekin,' and you say that you are happy to know him. But does either of you know the enigma that goes under the name of Stifflekin? You may know what he looks like and where he resides and what he does for a living. But that is all in the present tense. To really know him you must not only know what he is but what he used to be; what he used to think he was; what he used to think he ought to be and might be if he worked hard enough. You must know what he might have been if certain things had happened otherwise, and you must know what might have happened otherwise if he had been otherwise. All these complexities are a part of his own dim apprehension of himself. They are what make him so much more interesting to himself than he is to anyone else.

It is this consciousness of the inadequacy of our knowledge which makes us so embarrassed when we offer any service to another. Will he take it in the spirit in which it is given?

That was an awkward moment when Stanley, after all his hardships in his search for Dr Livingstone, at last found the Doctor by a lake in Central Africa. Stanley held out his hand and said stiffly, 'Dr Livingstone, I presume?' Stanley had heroically plunged through the equatorial forests to find Livingstone and to bring him back to civilization. But Livingstone was not particularly anxious to be found, and had a decided objection to being brought back to civilization. What he wanted was a new adventure. Stanley did not find the real Livingstone till he discovered that the old man was as young at heart as himself. The two men became acquainted only when they began to plan a new expedition to find the source of the Nile.

II

The natural desire of every man to be somebody else explains many of the minor irritations of life. It prevents that perfect organization of society in which everyone should know his place and keep it. The desire to be somebody else leads us to practice on work that does not strictly belong to us. We all have aptitudes and talents that overflow the narrow bounds of our trade or profession. Every man feels that he is bigger than his job, and he is all the time doing what theologians call 'works of supererogation'.

The serious-minded housemaid is not content to do what she is told to do. She has an unexpended balance of energy. She wants to be a general household reformer. So she goes to the desk of the titular master of the house and gives it a thorough reformation. She arranges the papers according to her idea of neatness. When the poor gentleman returns and finds his familiar chaos transformed into a hateful order, he becomes a reactionary.

The serious manager of a street railway company is not content with the simple duty of transporting passengers cheaply and comfortably. He wants to exercise the functions of a lecturer in an ethical culture society. While the transported victim is swaying precariously from the end of a strap he reads a notice urging him to practice Christian courtesy and not to push. While the poor wretch pores over this counsel of perfection, he feels like answering as did Junius to the Duke of Grafton, 'My Lord, injuries may be atoned for and forgiven, but insults admit of no compensation.'

A man enters a barber's shop with the simple desire of

being shaved. But he meets with the more ambitious desires of the barber. The serious barber is not content with any slight contribution to human welfare. He insists that his client shall be shampooed, manicured, massaged, steamed beneath boiling towels, cooled off by electric fans and, while all this is going on, that he shall have his boots blacked.

Have you never marveled at the patience of people in having so many things done to them that they don't want, just to avoid hurting the feelings of professional people who want to do more than is expected of them? You watch the stoical countenance of the passenger in a Pullman car as he stands up to be brushed. The chances are that he doesn't want to be brushed. He would prefer to leave the dust on his coat rather than to be compelled to swallow it. But he knows what is expected of him. It is a part of the solemn ritual of traveling. It precedes the offering.

The fact that every man desires to be somebody else explains many of the aberrations of artists and literary men. The painters, dramatists, musicians, poets, and novelists are just as human as housemaids and railway managers and porters. They want to do 'all the good they can to all the people they can in all the ways they can'. They get tired of the ways they are used to and like to try new combinations. So they are continually mixing things. The practitioner of one art tries to produce effects that are proper to another art.

A musician wants to be a painter and use his violin as if it were a brush. He would have us see the sunset glories that he is painting for us. A painter wants to be a musician and paint symphonies, and he is grieved because the uninstructed cannot hear his pictures, although the colors do swear at each other. Another painter wants to be an architect and build up his picture as if it were made of cubes of brick. It looks like brick-work, but to the natural eye it doesn't look like a picture. A prose-writer gets tired of writing prose, and wants to be a poet. So he begins every line with a capital letter, and keeps on writing prose.

You go to the theatre with the simple-minded Shakespearean

idea that the play's the thing. But the playwright wants to be a pathologist. So you discover that you have dropped into a grewsome clinic. You sought innocent relaxation, but you are one of the non-elect and have gone to the place prepared for you. You must see the thing through. The fact that you have troubles of your own is not a sufficient claim for exemption.

Or you take up a novel expecting it to be a work of fiction. But the novelist has other views. He wants to be your spiritual adviser. He must do something to your mind, he must rearrange your fundamental ideas, he must massage your soul, and generally brush you off. All this in spite of the fact that you don't want to be brushed off and set to rights. You don't want him to do anything to your mind. It's the only mind you have and you need it in your own business.

III

But if the desire of every man to be somebody else accounts for many whimsicalities of human conduct and for many aberrations in the arts, it cannot be lightly dismissed as belonging only to the realm of comedy. It has its origin in the nature of things. The reason why every man wants to be somebody else is that he can remember the time when he was somebody else. What we call personal identity is a very changeable thing, as all of us realize when we look over old photographs and read old letters.

The oldest man now living is but a few years removed from the undifferentiated germ-plasm, which might have developed into almost anything. In the beginning he was a bundle of possibilities. Every actuality that is developed means a decrease in the rich variety of possibilities. In becoming one thing it becomes impossible to be something else.

The delight in being a boy lies in the fact that the possibilities are still manifold. The boy feels that he can be anything that he desires. He is conscious that he has capacities that would make him a successful banker. On the other hand, there are attractions in a life of adventure in the South Seas. It would be pleasant to lie under a bread-fruit tree and let the fruit drop into his mouth, to the admiration of the gentle savages who would gather about him. Or he might be a saint—not a commonplace modern saint who does chores and attends tiresome committee meetings, but a saint such as one reads about, who gives away his rich robes and his purse of gold to the first beggar he meets, and then goes on his carefree way through the forest to convert interesting robbers. He feels that he might practice that kind of unscientific charity, if his father would furnish him with the money to give away.

But by and by he learns that making a success in the banking business is not consistent with excursions to the South Seas or with the more picturesque and unusual forms of saintliness. If he is to be in a bank he must do as the bankers do.

Parents and teachers conspire together to make a man of him, which means making a particular kind of man of him. All mental processes which are not useful must be suppressed. The sum of their admonitions is that he must pay attention. That is precisely what he is doing. He is paying attention to a variety of things that escape the adult mind. As he wriggles on the bench in the school-room, he pays attention to all that is going on. He attends to what is going on out-of-doors; he sees the weak points of his fellow pupils, against whom he is planning punitive expeditions; and he is delightfully conscious of the idiosyncrasies of the teacher. Moreover, he is a youthful artist and his sketches from life give acute joy to his contemporaries when they are furtively passed around.

But the schoolmaster says sternly, 'My boy, you must learn to pay attention; that is to say, you must not pay attention to so many things, but you must pay attention to one thing, namely, the second declension.'

Now, the second declension is the least interesting thing in the room, but unless he confines his attention to it he will never learn it. Education demands narrowing of attention in the interest of efficiency.

A man may, by dint of application to a particular subject,

become a successful merchant or real-estate man or chemist or overseer of the poor. But he cannot be all these things at the same time. He must make his choice. Having in the presence of witnesses taken himself for better or worse, he must, forsaking all others, cleave to that alone. The consequence is that, by the time he is forty, he has become one kind of a man, and is able to do one kind of work. He has acquired a stock of ideas true enough for his purposes, but not so transcendentally true as to interfere with his business. His neighbors know where to find him, and they do not need to take a spiritual elevator. He does business on the ground floor. He has gained in practicality, but has lost in the quality of interestingness.

The old prophet declared that the young men dream dreams and the old men see visions, but he did not say anything about the middle-aged men. They have to look after the business end.

But has the man whose working hours are so full of responsibilities changed so much as he seems to have done? When he is talking shop is he 'all there'? I think not. There are elusive personalities that are in hiding. As the rambling mansions of the old Catholic families had secret panels opening into the 'priest's hole', to which the family resorted for spiritual comfort, so in the mind of the most successful man there are secret chambers where are hidden his unsuccessful ventures, his romantic ambitions, his unfulfilled promises. All that he dreamed of as possible is somewhere concealed in the man's heart. He would not for the world have the public know how much he cares for the selves that have not had a fair chance to come into the light of day. You do not know a man until you know his lost Atlantis, and his Utopia for which he still hopes to set sail.

When Dogberry asserted that he was 'as pretty a piece of flesh as any is in Messina', and 'one that hath two gowns and everything handsome about him', he was pointing out what he deemed to be quite obvious. It was in a more intimate tone that he boasted, 'and a fellow that hath had losses'.

When Julius Cæsar rode through the streets of Rome in his

chariot, his laurel crown seemed to the populace a symbol of his present greatness. But gossip has it that Cæsar at that time desired to be younger than he was, and that before appearing in public he carefully arranged his laurel wreath so as to conceal the fact that he had had losses.

Much that passes for pride in the behavior of the great comes from the fear of the betrayal of emotions that belong to a simpler manner of life. When the sons of Jacob saw the great Egyptian officer to whom they appealed turn away from them, they little knew what was going on. 'And Joseph made haste, for his bowels did yearn upon his brother: and he sought where to weep, and he entered into his chamber, and wept there. And he washed his face, and went out, and refrained himself.' Joseph didn't want to be a great man. He wanted to be human. It was hard to refrain himself.

IV

What of the lost arts of childhood, the lost audacities and ambitions and romantic admirations of adolescence? What becomes of the sympathies which make us feel our kinship to all sorts of people? What becomes of the early curiosity in regard to things which were none of our business? We ask as Saint Paul asked of the Galatians, 'Ye began well; who did hinder you?'

The answer is not wholly to our discredit. We do not develop all parts of our nature because we are not allowed to do so. Walt Whitman might exult over the Spontaneous Me. But nobody is paid for being spontaneous. A spontaneous switchman on the railway would be a menace to the traveling public. We prefer some one less temperamental.

As civilization advances and work becomes more specialized, it becomes impossible for anyone to find free and full development for all his natural powers in any recognized occupation. What then becomes of the other selves? The answer must be that playgrounds must be provided for them outside the confines of daily business. As work becomes more engrossing and narrowing, the need is more urgent for recognized and carefully guarded periods of leisure.

The old Hebrew sage declared, 'Wisdom cometh from the opportunity of leisure.' It does not mean that a wise man must belong to what we call the leisure classes. It means that, if one has only a little free time at his disposal, he must use that time for the refreshment of his hidden selves. If he cannot have a sabbath rest of twenty-four hours, he must learn to sanctify little sabbaths, it may be of ten minutes' length. In them he shall do no manner of work. It is not enough that the self that works and receives wages shall be recognized and protected; the world must be made safe for our other selves. Does not the Declaration of Independence say that every man has an inalienable right to the pursuit of happiness?

The old-time minister, after he had exhorted the believers at considerable length, used to turn to a personage who for homiletical purposes was known as the Objector. To him he addressed his most labored arguments. At this point I am conscious of the presence of the Objector.

'All you say,' he remarks, 'in praise of your favorite platitude is true to a fault. But what has all this to do with the War? There is only one thing in these days worth thinking about—at least, it is the only thing we can think about.'

'I agree with you, courteous Objector. No matter where we start, we all come back to this point: Who was to blame for the War, and how is it coming out? Our explanatory idea has a direct bearing on the question before us. The Prussian militarists had a painstaking knowledge of facts, but they had a contempt for human nature. Their tactlessness was almost beyond belief. They treated persons as if they were things. They treated facts with deadly seriousness, but had no regard for feelings. They had spies all over the world to report all that could be seen, but they took no account of what could not be seen. So, while they were dealing scientifically with the obvious facts and forces, all the hidden powers of the human soul were being turned against them. Prussianism insists on highly specialized men who have no sympathies to interfere with their efficiency. Having adopted a standard, all variation must be suppressed. It is against this effort to suppress the human variations that we are fighting. We don't want all men to be reduced to one pattern.'

'But what about the Kaiser? Does your formula explain him? Does he want to be somebody else?'

'I confess, dear Objector, that it is probably a new idea to him; but he may come to it.'

THE TEMPLE'S DIFFICULT DOOR

ROBERT M. GAY

Do you remember the little old white church which, when we were boys, we attended more or less unwillingly, according to the season, with its stiff-backed pews in which we sat aching, counting the pipes in the organ and the balusters in the altar-rail and the dentils in the moulding of the pulpit? Of course you remember it, and the little old lady who sat in a corner ejaculating her hallelujahs and amens with the regularity of a cuckoo-clock, and the solemn precentor who sawed out the time with his hand, and the preacher who took his texts from the Old Testament and rolled the names of the Ten Tribes and their enemies as a sweet morsel under his tongue. The little old lady, you recollect, was valiant in prayer-meeting. She was not afraid to criticize the minister, or to repeat week by week the story of her conversion in her ninth year. Nor did she fail continually to impress upon us boys—facing us sometimes, with uplifted finger—the immanence of him who goeth to and fro in the earth and rageth like a lion, seeking whom he may devour. Ah, those prayer-meetings! Shall we, shall we ever forget them? Or the references to the sinners who sat on the back row (where we always sat)? Or the wailing hymns, or the dismal testimonies, or the waves of dejection that swept over us during the cataloguing of our omissions and commissions?

And there was always a boy! Do you remember him? A boy of our own age, mind you, a boy who ostentatiously arose and, with the decorum of a deacon, dwelt upon his former iniquities and present beatitude. We expected this of an occasional girl, yet the girls never did it; a mumbled text, a flurried word or two, were the extent of their temerity. As for us, it was not our custom to discuss our souls, even among ourselves. It is said that to forget the existence of a stomach is the best symptom of health in that useful organ, and, if the analogy holds, our souls must have been singularly robust. We were bashful about our virtues and vices; we could not fathom the sentiments of Take Time to be Holy; we were in mortal fear that someday somebody might convict us of sin and hale us forthwith into the fold of the elect. Yet here was a boy who flaunted his goodness in our faces. It was evident that he was not normal, that it lay with us as a duty to puncture the bubble of his presumptuousness.

The time came, you remember, very opportunely. On a memorable evening it was announced that this Infant Samuel, as the little old lady called him, was to recite to the congregation the entire Book of Esther from memory. For us, who found it beyond our power to remember a Golden Text of ten words for ten minutes, such a performance was unbelievable. We put our heads together and evolved a plot, dark, yet charming in its simple effectiveness. We decided to make faces at him.

We were expert in the art of face-making, because we had practiced it for weeks upon our sisters who sang in the choir. They had suffered, but were now immune. The grimaces of a Grimaldi could not have ruffled the calm of their scornful features.

We planted ourselves in the front row, and the boy began his recital. In time his preoccupied and lack-lustre eye wandered in our direction and rested upon us. He started, looked away, stammered, recovered, and went bravely on. But we knew that he would look back. We dared not glance at our neighbors, but had faith that each was doing his duty.

Of course he did look back, but why prolong the mournful tale? It is sufficient to say that Esther and Ahasuerus remained unwedded and Haman unhung; and that our victim retired amid the titterings of the judicious and the commiserations of the pious, while we plumed ourselves upon a difficult task laudably accomplished.

I have indulged in this long reminiscence, which probably can be matched in the experience of most of my masculine readers, because it is provocative of thoughts that deserve to be aired. An essay might be written upon the pathos that lies in the spectacle of a boy who is incited to a public display of his goodness; in the docility which is as clay in the hands of deluded adults. That he suffered there can be no doubt—not one half so much under the ordeal of our contriving, which, I hope, cured him, as under the isolation which his dedication to goodness made inevitable. He was a lonely boy, though he may not have realized that he was. That he could ever understand his fellows, or be understood by them, was impossible. He was the victim of the most perverse fate that can afflict a boy: he had been born in the bosom of a family whose piety contained not a grain of the salt of humor, not a particle of the leaven of imagination, not—But I am forgetting. I wish to ask the reader's consideration, not of the victim, but of the tormentors.

Why is it that boys are suspicious of that approximate moral perfection called goodness? Girls find a deep satisfaction in being good—in being neat, in being clean, in being decorous. If they are not these, we call them tomboys, still casting the onus of sinfulness upon the other sex. When we boys confided our exploit to the little girls, we found that they openly defended the boy, though, it must be admitted, they privately admired us, as is the way of their sex. Our fathers, informed by our sisters, and instigated by our mothers, solemnly reproached us, but with a twinkle that would not be hidden. Manifestly, the trail of the serpent was over them, too. They were sorry that they had not sat in the choir.

The meekest of men love to tell how bad they were as boys, hugging their fiction of early depravity with an unregenerate glee. The more innocuous they may be now, the more they love to boast—especially to their wives—of these phantasmal wild oats. The ladies pretend to be shocked at the stories, but are glad to believe them; and so it is not surprising if some men, in their fear of being mistaken for saints, remain boys all their lives.

The pursuit of the ideal is complicated by man's suspicion of goodness, and by woman's curious, but characteristic, indecision whether to espouse perfection or imperfection. Gifted with a natural propensity toward virtue and propriety and neatness and respectability and all the other approximate perfections of life, attaining them with ease and wearing them with grace, she of course values them little enough in man. His foibles interest her more than his virtues. She admires even while she condemns. He, because he is a man, prefers admiration to commendation.

In education, man as a rule inculcates ideals of perfection without pretending to practice them; but woman, with an iron logic which, man's aspersions to the contrary notwithstanding, is characteristic of her, not only points but leads the way. Hence it is that some teachers of her sex have two manners, the human for social occasions, and the divine for the class-room. In the privacy of their homes they have their imperfections; in the class-room they are icily perfect. Their perfectness extends to such details as facial expression and tone of voice. Occasionally a man adopts the duplex character, but with deplorable result. I remember such a one in high school. Those of us who had the good fortune to meet him socially, found that he had his peccadillos of character, manner, and language, but in the school he was a pattern which we despaired of imitating. From his necktie to his reading of Burke's 'Conciliation,' he was without spot or blemish. We did not dare to love him; we gave up all hope of emulation. We nicknamed him Mrs Dawson, and let it go at that.

But women carry this dual character more successfully than men. Whether because they are better actors or because we confuse saintliness with femininity, even as boys we are more ready to forgive it in them. To the little girls, it seems perfectly natural. They catch the idea readily and practice their teachers' precisions and pruderies upon the family. We must admit, too, that in the art of being a pattern, women show a sterner conscientiousness than men. They are not constitutionally so lazy. It requires hard and sustained effort to be a pattern, an inveterate and dogged attention to detail. It is chiefly here that we men fail. The male saints—witness Jerome—had a time of it with their petty temptations, simply because sainthood is largely a matter of detail. Most men are good enough in essentials, but fail in the little things; the little things, of which woman is enamored—too often, the slave. To be perfect gives her a satisfaction that man will never understand; and, prompted by the constitutional laziness aforesaid, he takes refuge in calling goodness womanish.

His institutions, therefore, are good enough in essentials; his political organizations and governments, his bureaus and offices and federations and unions, all are nobly planned, but lack the feminine touch that makes for perfection. His streets are dirty and so are his politics; his laws need dusting; a little sweeping would not hurt his governments; his various organizations would be none the worse for some polishing and weeding and clipping of loose threads and sewing up of rents and various other species of revamping. All these last subtleties are beyond him, just as, be he never so neat, are all the tiny sweetnesses and refinements and knots and bows and satisfying knick-knacks of his wife's person. She is a creature of soupçons and nuances and intuitive niceties. She can endure no compromise with disorder or dirt or decay. Her motes are all beams until they are demolished; she uses a mountain of faith to move a mustard-seed; she cannot see the polished surface for the speck of dust that is on it. In her extreme development she spends her life doing the million and one trifles that man would leave undone.

The trouble is that, not satisfied with all this, she longs to make him perfect, too. Never deterred by the stupendousness of the task, she goes on, century by century, generation by generation, teaching him, preaching to him, marrying him; gently leading him or tyrannously compelling him toward the heaven of her ideal. And here again her gaze is microscopic. In her attention to his foibles she is liable to overlook his sins. She can seldom understand badness in boys, nor can ever see that the boy who is most bad in small matters may be the most good in large. She loves to keep her male offspring lamblike, and tries his docility by making him wear long hair and wide collars and linen and ruffles and lace, never learning but through hard experience that, like the puppy, he takes naturally to mud and feels at ease only close to the soil. When he at last rebels and privily snips off his hair and rends his sashes and furbelows, she weeps, not because of the loss of material, but because of the loss of an ideal.

And who can blame her? It is seldom enough in this world that we can kiss and fondle an ideal, except in dreams.

I have a theory that our school laws should be revised and that we should confide our grammar-school teaching of boys only to women who have been married. My reason is not the one the reader is imagining, however. It is not because she will have had children. No. I do not go so far as that. I merely demand that she shall have had a husband. He is quite sufficient. He is a male. A year's association with him will have softened her fibre, will have aroused in her mind doubts of the perfectibility of mankind. Then, then she will be ready to teach boys.

Yet it must be admitted that every teacher who has managed to remain human is confronted by a dilemma. As a teacher, he is expected to inculcate ideals of perfection, not only in studies, but in deportment; and yet, when he happens to come upon a student who approaches perfection, it is a mournful occasion. The student may be admirable, but he is dull company. It has been suggested that teaching can be a satisfying profession only to very big or very little natures. I suppose that the idea is that the big nature sees the future in the instant, tolerates the present imperfection, dreaming of a distant flawlessness; while the little nature satisfies itself by attaining perfection in trifles.

The average man or woman who has drifted into the profession is saved from despair or insanity by that biological interest in, and curiosity about, humanity, which we call humor. He knows that everlasting concern with perfection in trifles is a belittler of souls; that correcting sentences and paragraphs and Latin and German exercises and algebraic problems and geometrical proofs is poor food for a human mind. On the other hand, instinct tells him that the larger perfection is cold; that it dwells in the rarefied air of the mountain-tops; that it is un-human. To love the derelict student is treason to his profession; yet, as he looks back over the long line of pupils who have passed through his hands, he sees that the ones who remain warm and vivid in his memory are those who fell most short of the very ideals which he tried to inculcate.

Among all the students in a certain school, I have a living recollection of just one, and he was the most imperfect student in it. He refused to study, he refused to behave, he insisted on fighting and bringing snakes to school in his pocket and—I do not exaggerate—standing on his head in the middle of a recitation. He passed most of his days sitting in the headmaster's office, studying demurely when that gentleman was present, and making paper flying-machines when surveillance relaxed. Yet, as I search my heart, I find that my memories of him are pleasant; that I should like to see him again, even at the price of having to recapture his garter-snakes, or of having to turn him right-side-up during a recitation. He was much misunderstood. Some of his teachers, having no faith in my theory of the interestingness of the imperfect, found him a thorn in the flesh, and predicted for him a sudden end by suspension; and there were doubtless times when, in an access of impatience, I longed for the end to come and was ready to officiate at it. He shattered the pedagogic ideal. Try as I would, I was unable to discover in him ideals of any sort, and he refused to adopt any that I offered, however edifying. Yet all the good little boys to whom he administered black eyes with the utmost generosity have faded from my memory and he stands out the brighter for the years that have gone. If he had been good, he, too, would long since have been consigned to the limbo of 'the dream of things that were'. Viewed in the narrow light of class discipline, he was a burden, like the grasshopper; in the broad and genial glow that falls from a humorous philosophy of life, he was a joy, a heart-filling atomy of mischief, a triumphant example of the imperfectness of humanity and the humanness of imperfection.

We can postulate so much of the imperfect thing and so little of the perfect. Flawlessness leaves the weaker imagination so little to take hold of: it is slippery. Even woman, with that inconsistency which makes her adorable, really loves perfection no more than we. Everyone knows that a little girl loves an old doll, or a rag doll, or a one-legged doll, better than the most expensive Parisian wax doll with real hair, and eyes that open and shut. The Parisian beauty has been longed for for months, but now that it has become an entity, it leaves the child cold. If it is so lucky as to lose an arm or some sawdust, there may be hope for it; but so long as it remains new and whole, it can never hope to enter the warmest precincts of the little girl's heart. 'To keep in sight Perfection,' says a contemporary poet, 'is the artist's best delight,' and his bitterest pang that he can do no more than that; yet in another epigram the same poet speaks as follows:

> The thousand painful steps at last are trod,
> At last the temple's difficult door we win.
> Perfect upon his pedestal, the god
> Freezes us hopeless when we enter in.

The little girl is tasting this experience. The contemplation of elastic joints, mechanical eyes, and waxen complexion warmed the cockles of her heart, but the embodiment of these in a palpable doll freezes her hopeless. If the poet, with more imagination, suffers too, and the highest natures—those which we call the transcendental—whiff the sadness that lies in the attainment of the perfect, surely the unimaginative mass of mankind can be excused if they find the inter-lunar regions chilly.

In reckless moments I wonder whether the Greek statues did not suffer more happily at the hands of fate when they lost their arms and heads and legs than we are accustomed to think; whether their dilapidation has not given them a place in our hearts instead of merely in our heads; has not couched them in our love instead of merely pedestaled them in our reverence.

Or, to take an illustration from a lower plane, may it not be that we get a keener pleasure out of eating an imperfect apple? It is neither the best possible apple, which would be perfect, nor the worst possible apple, which would have a kind of negative perfection; it has a worm at the core; but I wonder whether we do not enjoy it more because we have to eat the more carefully to keep from eating him. Besides, he arouses in our mind all sorts of questionings. Why is he there? What kind of worm is he? How did he get in? How would he have got out if we had not ousted him? And—note this—what sort of an apple would it have been if he had taken up his residence elsewhere?

I am rather proud of this little apologue of the apple. For the perfect apple could have roused no queries which the defective apple does not. The same subtle influences went to make both: the same elements, the same forces, the same chemical processes. But the defective apple has in addition to all these—the worm.

There is 'some strangeness' even 'in beauty'. The perfect rhythm is intolerable. We demand chiaroscuro in life as in color. The preciousness of the ointment is the more evident for the fly. 'We love people for their vices,' so the vices do not make them despicable.

If the gods that sit above have a sense of humor, they must find us grown men and women as funny and as sad as we find the boys and girls and dogs. Not knowing the sentiments of the gods, we have to content ourselves with those of the poets and humorists who, we fondly imagine, have in them something of the god-like vision. They look at humanity from above. And they find that the spectacle of humanity trying to be what it cannot be, facing both ways, on the threshold of heaven casting a longing, lingering look behind, is comic and tragic in its very essence; for comedy and tragedy differ chiefly in degree. In the imperfection of humanity lie its tragedy and its humor. Without it, this would be a happier world; but with it, it is a merrier.

EXILE AND POSTMAN

JEAN KENYON MACKENZIE

It used to make me homesick, in our little African clearing, to see the albino woman. She would move about among her brown companions like a flame—and her white body, that flickered in the sun and glimmered in the shade, used to knock at the door of nostalgia. Homesick people always long for a visit, and that albino was so white!

Once, to our neighborhood, where in those days white women did not come, there came a white woman. She did not lodge with us; she lodged with the white officer because she was an officer's wife. We used to wonder if she would call upon us. One of us had a pair of field-glasses, and we used to watch her little figure coming and going about the clearing on the government hill. When one day she was seen to come down into our valley by the zigzag trail, we thought we had a Visit. I cannot tell you how anxious we were, in that little bark house, to make a good appearance—or what fresh disposals were made, with our eyes upon that descent, of our properties. I do not wish to make you too sad, but that white woman did not visit us. She went away. She did not know about us, or about exiles—that they are always dreaming of a Visit.

It seems a hard thing, sometimes, when night closes the doors of all the little trails, that the day has passed without a visitor. It is true of exiles that they have the most unreasonable expectations of the sort, based perhaps upon the migrations of swallows, and not relinquished until the hour of dusk. Yes, then the little trails of the forest are perceived by the mind's eye—which like a cat's eyes sees them better for the dark—to wander away into an infinite distance and a solitude.

Dusk is altogether the most illuminating hour for the exile;

he then knows so exactly where he is; he has a perfectly visual sense of his surroundings. He sees where he is, but how came he to be there? The geography of his circumstance is plain, but not the logic. He who has no other companions than himself suspects this companion, in that hour of dusk, to be a fool. It must be a poor fool, he thinks, who has drifted into such a clearing by such a river!

The forest of the Cameroon is as good a place as any to be homesick; but I will not be saying that the members of my profession—and I am a missionary—are chronic sufferers. Missionaries are, in the main, gay, and for excellent reasons—some of them pagan reasons, for they are little brothers of Antæus; some of them Christian reasons, for they are of the company of successful fishermen. A fisherman with a good catch can defy even the dusk; his string of silver fish is a lantern to his feet.

No, if there were an altar and a service to placate nostalgia it would not be that fisherman who would most attend that service. The path to that altar would be worn brown by the feet of the trader. I think the trader is lonelier than the missionaries are; he is better versed in solitude. He goes into the forest with a backward look; he comes out of the forest sometimes with a secret and a stricken countenance. More than missionaries do, he does. More often than they, he builds out of his lonely horror and the license of solitude a perverse habitation for his soul. Sometimes—and this is very sad—he is afraid. He lingers and lingers on the margin of that green sea of forest.

'The heart,' say the Bulu, 'has gone to hide in the dark.' And this is a Bulu way of saying that the heart is not worn upon the sleeve. Well, upon the sleeve of the white-drill suits that beach-traders wear there is, I will agree, no device of hearts. But those lonely inland traders—those that have traveled ten, twenty, thirty days from their kind—what is that they sometimes seem to wear upon the sleeve of their singlets? And who cares where he wears his heart if there is never a white man's eye to fall upon it! In those little bark huts on the trading posts, where young white men pale with the passing hours, there comes to be a careless fashion in wear, whether of hearts or of collars. In the warm dusk of those little houses, where there is an earthen floor, where there are tin trade-boxes as bright as jockeys' jackets, where there are trade-cloths printed with violent designs, where there is salt fish and cheap scent and tobacco—where all these desirable things may be had for ivory and rubber—there the trader may wear his heart upon his sleeve without shame. None of those brilliant eyes, set in those dark faces, know a white man's heart when they see it. There in his hut is a monotony of brown bodies quick with vehement gestures; there is a tumult of controversy in a tongue he does not know. The sudden glitter of brass ornament is there, and the glitter of brass spears. There are fantastic head-dresses studded with buttons and shells and beads, and scented with the odor of wood-fires. Between those brown bodies and the body of the white man lies the counter. More lies between them than this. There are between them such barriers that the white man is not more lonely when he is alone.

Yet how still it is of an idle day under the thatched leaves of that little house! The sun does its exaggerated violence to the yellow earth of the clearing; the forest hangs its arras over its secret. How far it is, in this place not named on the map, from Manchester! How, when the rain falls, it is other than rainfall on the Clyde! How the pale fruit that hangs high on the ajap tree is not like the apples that ripen in Wishaw!

Do not speak of apples! Nostalgia in her cruel equipment carries a scented phantom apple.

At night there is about that young trader a trouble of drums that never rest. There is the sharp concerted cry of the dancers. There is the concerted wail for the dead. There is about him all the rhythmic beating of the mysterious life of his neighborhood, tormenting him where he lies under his mosquito net. For this he will rise and walk about, the ember of his pipe drifting back and forth in the dark, and his gramophone, roused by himself, making its limited obedient effort.

There is this about a gramophone: it is a thing that speaks the home tongue. I have seen him sitting under the eaves of his little hut, by his little table spread with a checkered cloth, his gramophone beside him, trying, with its tale of the old grouse gunroom, to divert that lonely meal. Now that I think of it, the gramophone is a kind of hero of my little piece—a kind of David with five tunes to do battle with nostalgia. Back in the tent broods Saul, and this poor patient David plays the endless round of five tunes. Until some day there is a javelin in the wall, and a proud black man goes away with a gramophone into the wilderness.

The night sky does more permanent ministry to the homesick, and of all the bright ministers the moon is the most effectual. It is the great reflector of lights; there it comes, swinging up its old path in the sky, and the fires of home are mirrored on its disk. You who read have spread your hands, in your hour of homesickness, to those phantom fires—and other hands are always spread. Some of us were sitting on our heels about a little flame in a new clearing; all of us were alien in that clearing; one of us was white. And the black woman said to the white woman when the moonlight fell upon all those women faces, 'The moon looks upon the villages and upon the home village. We black people, when we sit in the towns of strangers and the moon shines, we say, 'Now by the light of this same moon the people at home dance to the drums!' However far we walk, we look upon the moon and we remember our friends at home.'

Upon another moonlight night, sitting in a forest camp with young black girls for companions, these sang for me a little set of songs—the songs, they told me, of the moon:

'Ah, moné zip, alu a danéya! Ah moné zip!'

('Ah, little gazelle, the night has deepened! Ah, little gazelle!')

This little refrain they sang, clapping their hands ever so lightly, and the meaning of the singing was a warning.

It was a song of the moon, a song for wanderers. And the moon on that remembered night, dragging its net of broken silver cords in among the trees of the forest, caught everywhere the wandering hearts and drew them back on the little rough trails to the home fires. Every night that is a moonlight night there is the casting of that silver net upon far rivers and forests deeper than rivers—wherever aliens make a bed of leaves or sleep on a canvas cot.

On such a night, and caught in such a net, I have met the postman. Yes, on just such a night, when the world appeared as it hangs in space, a crystal globe, and when so observed from a little clearing in an African forest, it was seen to be charted for voyagers, and all its little paths ran readily about the globe to that gilt side which is home. On such a night, and upon such a path, I met the postman.

To hang upon a little wicket gate under the moon at the end of a moon-filled clearing in a breach of the forest—to see the black body of the postman suddenly darken the checkered light upon the path from the west—how to speak of this adventure with moderation! How to speak of postmen at all with moderation! And of those postmen who thread the lonely forests of the world, their loads upon their backs, their rations of salt fish on top of their loads; how to recall their aspects, their monthly or bi-monthly or semi-annual arrivals, the priceless treasures they carry! How speak of these things to men and women who have never followed the little gazelle into those forests where the night has deepened; who have never felt the divinity in postmen!

Imagine that there is a people in this world who let a postman walk up the path unattended, and who wait until he knocks on the door! Who do not shout to their neighbors when they receive a letter, and who receive one every day! These items alone prove the truth of the Bulu proverb that there are tribes and tribes, and customs and customs.

And I will agree that there are, even on the trails of the wilderness, postmen and postmen. There are even, though I hate to dwell upon it, postmen whom I do not trust. Not all postmen have wings upon their heels. The ideal postman does of course fly. He is like:

The bird let loose in eastern skies When hastening fondly home.

He avoids idle wanderers. But they do not all do so. I remember to have been wakened one night in a village by the gossip of two old headmen. They had met before my tent; there in the moonlight they chatted together. All the little life of the village was sleeping; the two old men alone were abroad. They were about the business of the post. It is a pioneer custom in Africa, east and west, that the white man's local letter is franked from town to town. The black man to whom the white man gives his letter carries it to the headman of the next settlement, who carries it in turn to his brother headman down the trail; and so from hand to hand, by day and by night, with a glance from any passing white man, the letter goes forward. Such a letter—carried as the custom is, in a split rod from which there hung, like a flag, a bit of turkey red—changed hands that night before my tent. And now I write it in a white man's book that the postmen loitered.

To stand and chat there in the moonlight with the exile's letter in your hands—how could you do that, you two old heartless headmen? I watched you from my little green tent. It is remembered of you that you so delayed, while in some lonely hamlet under that same moon a white man sickened for a letter. And when one gave the forked stick to the other, it was then too late. If indeed, as you would say, you spoke no more than five words of gossip one to the other, those words were five too many. It is remembered of you, and a thousand nights since when I have waited for the mail, if it were a moonlight night, I have told myself with an extreme self-pity and a bitterness, 'The carrier is gossiping in some clearing.' I have seen in my heart that man with the load of mail upon his back, standing for hours by a friend of his, laughing and asking news one of the other. This conjured vision of two black men holding up the mail is the sad issue of an imagination infected beyond cleansing. You see, I saw them do it.

Some postmen have come in late because their feet were sore. And some, in passing through their home town, have permitted themselves an illness or a marriage. Some have waited, with the mail in their loads, to bury the dead. Such a postman, so given to misadventures and clumsy ill-timed tragedies, was once late to the tune of eleven days. Who remembers what delayed him or what exquisite reasons he gave? And who of us in that little clearing forgets the long hours of that year of days?

Another postman, of an extreme beauty and an extreme speed, arrived before his time. There was a shouting when he came. All the inhabitants of that little settlement of white men called to each other; the four or five of them filled a room of a bark house—those white faces that were growing daily like the face of the Asra, 'bleich und bleicher', were all lit by the flame of the mail. In all that little commonwealth, with its pioneer trades and its pioneer gardens and its pioneer hospital and school and church—in all that settlement all the busy crude wheels of industry slackened and stood still while the white men opened the load of the mail.

'Now they will be reading the books from home!'

And of Ebengé, that young carrier, it is still remembered that he arrived before he was due. 'Ah, Ebengé,' you still say to him from time to time, 'that was a fine walking you walked that walk so long ago when you slept but three nights with the mail!'

Another postman, never to be forgotten by those exiles whom he served, never came at all. This was a boy, too young, you would think, for his great office. The letters in his little pack were from husbands to wives, and they must travel a hundred miles of forest-trail in time of war. Not twenty miles they traveled when the postman, surrounded by black soldiers, was called to deliver. He did not deliver. He could not give the white man's letters to another hand. He said, No, he could not. And for this they killed him. That young body tarried forever upon the trail, witnessing in that interminable delay—as Ebengé had witnessed in his swift coming—to the sacred element in the mail.

Here is the king's touch for the king's evil—the hand of the postman dropping a letter. For this the victims of nostalgia do long service. For this they scribble, in their lonely and various dwellings, their letters. There is a night, in those alien settlements all about the world, that is unlike other nights. It is the night before the mail is closed. The lamp is full of oil that night, and the cup of coffee is at the elbow. On and on, while the stars march, the white man's hand runs upon the page. In villages where there are no street lamps, the white man's window is a lamp all night of the night before the mail. From steamers that are tied to trees among the rushes, in rivers that you do not know, the officer on watch may look all night through such a window at such a man writing, writing a long, long letter—the beating heart of man, articulate in all that heartless darkness.

How quick a seed, you would say, the seed in such a letter! How such a letter must bear, some sixty-, some an hundred-fold! Yet myself I saw this: I saw the harbor-master of Kabinda, a settlement of white men on the west coast of Africa, come aboard the monthly steamer to get the mail. He was an old Portuguese, coffee-colored in his gray linen suit. A long time he had been harbor-master, and many times he had taken the brown bag of mail ashore. This day, when he lifted his bag, he 'hefted' it: the lightness of it in his hand made him smile. Some irony that was the fruit of his long experience of exiles and their letters made that old indifferent man curl the lip. I think that in Kabinda that night there went white men hungry to bed.

I would not like to live in Kabinda, where the postman is so old and so wise. These white postmen know too much; they can count more than ten. And other things they know: they know a thing too sad to tell. Better Ebengé, who ran so swiftly with his load, or little Esam, who thought that for a load of letters some would even dare to die.

AN INDICTMENT OF INTERCOLLEGIATE ATHLETICS

WILLIAM T. FOSTER

I

Intercollegiate athletics provide a costly, injurious, and excessive régime of physical training for a few students, especially those who need it least, instead of inexpensive, healthful, and moderate exercise for all students, especially those who need it most.

Athletics are conducted either for education or for business. The old distinction between amateur and professional athletics is of little use. The real problems of college athletics loom large beside the considerations that define our use of the terms 'professional' and 'amateur'. The aims of athletics reveal the fact that the important distinctions are between athletics conducted for educational purposes and athletics conducted for business purposes.

When athletics are conducted for education the aims are (1) to develop all the students and faculty physically and to maintain health; (2) to promote moderate recreation in the spirit of joy, and as a preparation for study rather than as a substitute for study; and (3) to form habits and inculcate ideals of right living. When athletics are conducted for business, the aims are (1) to win games—to defeat another person or group being the chief end; (2) to make money—as it is impossible otherwise to carry on athletics as business; (3) to attain individual or group fame and notoriety. These three—which are the controlling aims of intercollegiate athletics—are also the aims of horse-racing, prize-fighting and professional baseball.

These two sets of aims are in sharp and almost complete conflict. Roughly speaking, success in attaining the aims of athletics as education is in inverse proportion to success in attaining the aims of athletics as business. Intercollegiate athletics today are for business. The question is pertinent whether schools and colleges should promote athletics as business.

Nearly all that may be said on this subject about colleges applies to secondary schools. The lower schools as a rule tend to imitate the worst features of intercollegiate athletics, much as the young people of fraternities, in their 'social functions,' tend to imitate the empty lives of their elders that fill the weary society columns of the newspapers.

If the objection arises that intercollegiate athletics have educational value, there is no one to deny it. 'Athletics for education' and 'athletics for business' are general terms, used throughout this discussion as already defined. Exceptions there may be: only the main tendencies are here set forth. The whole discussion is based on my personal observations at no less than one hundred universities and colleges in thirty-eight states during the past five years.

The most obvious fact is that our system of intercollegiate athletics, after unbounded opportunity to show what it can do for the health, recreation, and character of all our students, has proved a failure. The ideal of the coach is excessive training of the few: he best attains the business ends for which he is hired by the neglect of those students in greatest need of physical training. Our present system encourages most students to take their athletics by proxy. When we quote with approval the remark of the Duke of Wellington that Waterloo was won on the playing grounds of Eton, we should observe that he did not maintain that Waterloo was won on the grandstands of Eton.

What athletics may achieve without the hindrance of intercollegiate games and business motives is suggested by the experience of Reed College. There the policy of athletics for everybody was adopted five years ago before there were any teachers, students, alumni, or traditions. Last year all but six of the students took part in athletics in the spirit of sport for the sake of health, recreation, and development. Sixty per cent of the men of the college, including the faculty, took part in a schedule of sixteen baseball games. Nearly all the students, men and women alike, played games at least twice a week. There were series of contests in football, baseball, track, tennis, volley-ball, basket-ball, and other out-of-door sports. All of this, according to the report of the athletic association, cost the students an average of sixteen cents apiece. No money for coaches and trainers; no money for badges, banners, cups, and other trinkets; no money for training-tables and railroad fares; no money for grandstands, rallies, brass bands, and advertising. Fortunately, it is the unnecessary expenses that heap up the burdens—the cost of athletics as business. The economical policy is athletics for everybody—athletics for education.

II

Opposed to the three educational aims are the aims of athletics as business—winning games, making money, and getting advertised.

Almost invariably the arguments of students in favor of intercollegiate games stress the business aims and ignore all others. Win games! Increase the gate-receipts! Advertise the college! These are the usual slogans. Thus the editors of one college paper reprimand the faculty for even hesitating to approve a trip of fifteen hundred miles for a single game of football:

'Contrary to the expectations of the students, the matter of the Occidental football game for next fall has not been acted upon as yet. That such an important matter as this has not received attention so far from the Faculty is unfortunate. While it is generally believed that the Faculty will act favorably in regard to letting the game be scheduled, it is understood that some opposition has developed on the ground that such a long trip would keep the football men away from their classes too long a time.

'From every point of view, there seems no reason why the game should not be played. To state any of the arguments in favor of the offer is unnecessary. Everyone knows what it would mean to football next fall, the greater interest it would mean to the game, the incentive it would prove to every football man to work to become one of the seventeen men to take the trip, the advertising it would give to the college, and, perhaps most important, the drawing card it would be to bring new athletes to the college in the fall. These points and others are too well known to need pointing out and too evident to need proof.'

This is a typical football argument. It attempts to prove the necessity of the proposed trip by showing that it would tend to perpetuate the thing the value of which is under dispute.

In like vein the students of Cornell complain because the faculty did not grant an additional holiday in connection with the Pennsylvania football game. It is the familiar cry: 'Support the team! Win games! Advertise the college!'

'Our friends, the professors, will perforce hold forth in their accustomed cells from eight till one of that fair morning. The benches, no doubt, will derive great benefit therefrom...

'We want the football team to have as much support as possible. The Faculty should want the football team to have as much support as possible. The Faculty should foster true Cornell spirit whenever it can honestly do so, and intercollegiate athletics is the greatest single thing that unites the different colleges into Cornell University. A victory over Penn would mean a lot for Cornell.'

After all, how important is this end for which such sacrifices are made? To hear the yelling of twenty thousand spectators, one might suppose this aim to be the only one of great importance in the life of the university. Yet who wins, who loses, is a matter of but momentary concern to any except a score or two of participants; whereas, if there is one thing that should characterize a university, it is its cheerful sacrifice of temporary for permanent gains—in Dr Eliot's fine phrase, its devotion to the durable satisfactions of life.

The making of money, through intercollegiate athletics,

continues a curse, not only to institutions, but as well to individual players. Only childlike innocence or willful blindness need prevent American colleges from perceiving that the rules which aim to maintain athletics on what is called an 'amateur' basis, by forbidding players to receive pay in money, are worse than useless, for while failing to prevent men from playing for pay, they breed deceit and hypocrisy. There are many ways of paying players for their services. Only one of these, and that the most honorable, is condemned.

There are many subterranean passages leading to every preparatory school notable for its athletes. By such routes, coaches, over-zealous alumni, and other 'friends' of a college, reach the schoolboy athlete with offers beyond the scope of eligibility rules. Sometimes payments are made expressly for services as half-back, or short-stop, or hurdler, and no receipts taken, the pay continuing as long as the player helps to win games. Sometimes payments take a more insidious and more demoralizing form. The star athlete is appointed steward of a college clubhouse on ample pay, his duties being to sign checks once a month. Or his college expenses are paid in return for the labor of opening the chapel door, or ringing the bell, or turning out the lights.

Athletes may be paid for their services in other ways that escape the notice of the most conscientious faculties and athletic associations. But there are hundreds of boys who know that they are paid to win games and keep silent; they are hired both as athletes and as hypocrites.

The sporting editor of one of the leading daily papers said recently, 'It is well known that the Northwest colleges are at present simply outbidding one another in their desire to get the best athletes. Money is used like water. It is a mystery where they get it, but they do.'

So common is the practice of paying athletes that they sometimes apply to various colleges for bids. While I was acting as Registrar of Bowdoin College, I received a letter from a man asking how much we would guarantee to pay him for pitching on the college nine. I found out later that he had registered at one college, pitched a game for his class team, left his trunk at a second college awaiting their terms, and finally accepted the offer of a third college, where he played 'amateur' baseball for four years before joining one of the big league professional teams.

At the athletic rallies of a New England college, a loyal alumnus is often cheered for bringing so many star athletes to the college. Officially, the college does not know that he hires men to play on the college teams. And what is to prevent a graduate of the college or any other person from hiring athletes? All but futile are the rules governing professionalism. Is it not a worthy act to enable a boy to go to college? And shall he be denied such aid because he happens to be an athlete? No eligibility committee knows of all these benefactors or even has the right to question their motives. But the objectionable motives themselves can be eliminated by one act—the abolition of intercollegiate athletics. With the subordination of winning games as the chief end in athletics, falls also the money-making aim and its attendant evils.

All the serious evils of college athletics centre about the gate-receipts, the grandstand, and the paid coach. Yet the aim of nearly every college appears to be to fasten these evils upon the institution by means of a costly concrete stadium or bowl, and by means of more and more money for coaches. When the alumni come forward to 'support their team', they usually make matters worse. Typical of their attitude is a letter signed in Philadelphia last fall by some thirty graduates of a small college:

'The team has just closed the most disastrous season in its history... The alumni will coöperate cheerfully with the undergraduates in increasing the football levy. It only remains, then, to initiate a campaign for procuring the money... We must depart from our time-worn precedents and give more money for the coaches! Alumni are tired of reading the accounts of useless defeats!'

The extent to which interest in athletics is deadened by paid coaches was shown last spring, when a track team from one university, after traveling over two hundred and fifty miles—at the expense of the student body—to compete with the team of another institution, took off their running shoes and went home because the coaches could not agree on the number of men who should participate in the games. Could there be a more abject sacrifice of the educational purposes of athletics? Consider the spectacle. A glorious afternoon in spring, a perfect playground, complete equipment in readiness, two score of eager youth in need of the health and recreation that come from sport pursued in the fine spirit of sport. Could anything keep them from playing? Nothing but the spirit of modern American intercollegiate athletics and the embodiment of that spirit, the paid coach, who knows that there is but one crime that he can commit—that of losing a contest.

The athletic policy of many an institution is determined by a commercial aim, the supposed needs of advertising, much as the utterances of many a newspaper are dictated by the business manager. But does the advertising gained through intercollegiate athletics injure or aid a college? At one railroad station I was greeted by a real-estate agent who offered to sell me 'on easy terms a lot in the most beautiful and rapidly growing city in America.' (Thus do I safely cover its identity.) Among the attractions, he mentioned the local college. He was proud of it; he said it had the best baseball team in the state. Apart from that he had not an intelligent idea about the institution, or any desire for ideas. The only building he had visited was the grandstand. He could not name a member of the faculty or a course of instruction. College advertising which gets no further than this is paid for at exorbitant rates.

The people of Tacoma discovered recently that college athletics conducted as a business are too costly. They brought college students 1400 miles to play a football game at Tacoma on Thanksgiving Day for the benefit of the Belgian refugees. The charitable object of the game was widely advertised and there was a large attendance. After they had paid the expenses of the 'amateur' teams, the coaches, and the advertising, they announced that there was nothing left for the Belgians.

A writer in the *North American Review* tries to justify the time spent by college boys in managing athletic teams on the plea that it is good training for business. He gives testimony to this effect from a graduate of two years' standing 'engaged in the wholesale coal business in one of the large New York towns.' Following the usual custom, this young graduate returns to his college and gives the admiring undergraduates the benefit of his wisdom, lest they be corrupted by the quaint notions of impractical professors. He has them guess what part of his college work has proved of greatest use; then he assures them that his best training came as manager of the baseball team. Such is the mature judgment of the coal-dealer. And such is the advice of alumni which makes undergraduates resolve anew not to allow their studies to interfere with their college education. But some people raise the question why a boy should be maintained in college for four years, at a great cost to society and to his parents, in order that he may gain a little business experience when he could gain so much more by earning his living.

The conflicts frequently arising between faculties and students over questions of intercollegiate athletics are the natural outcome of the independent control of a powerful agency with three chief aims—winning games, making money, and getting advertised—which are antagonistic to the chief legitimate ambitions of a university faculty. No self-respecting head of a department of psychology would tolerate the presence in the university of persons working in his field, in no way subject to him and with aims subversive of those of the department. No professor of physical education should tolerate a similar condition in his department. It is one of the hopeful signs in America that several of the men best qualified to conduct athletics as education have declined to consider university positions, unless they could have control of students, teams, coaches, alumni committees, grandstands, fields, finances, and everything else necessary to rescue athletics from the clutches of commercialism.

I have read a letter from one of the ablest teachers in America, declining to accept a certain university position under the usual conditions, but outlining a plan whereby, as the real head of the department of physical education, he might begin a new chapter in the history of American athletics. His plan was rejected, not because it had any defects as a system of education, but solely because it would cause a probable decline in victories, gate-receipts, and newspaper space. That university continued the traditional dual contest of coaches and physical directors with their conflicting ideals. Recently I received a letter from the professor of physical education who did accept the position, himself one of the ablest athletes among its graduates, declaring that he would no longer attempt the impossible, in an institution which deliberately prostituted athletics for commercial ends.

We hear much about the value of intercollegiate games for the 'tired business man' who needs to get out of doors and watch a sport that will make him forget his troubles. It is true that for him a game of baseball may be a therapeutic spectacle. The question is whether institutions of learning should conduct their athletics—or any other department—for the benefit of spectators. Doubtless university courses in history could provide recreation for the general public and make money, if instruction were given wholly by means of motion-pictures. But such courses would hardly satisfy the needs of all students. Is it less important that departments of physical education should be conducted primarily for all students rather than for spectators? We do not insist that banks, railroads, factories, department stores, and legislatures jeopardize their main functions in order to provide recreation for the tired business men. Universities are institutions of equal importance to society, in so far as they attend to their main purposes. Athletics for the benefit of the grandstand must be conducted as business; athletics for the benefit of students must be conducted as education.

III

It is when we rightly estimate the possibilities of athletics as education that the present tyranny of athletics as business becomes intolerable. Is it not an anomaly that those in charge of higher institutions of learning should leave athletic activities, which are of such great potential educational value for all students, chiefly under the control of students, alumni, coaches, newspapers, and spectators? Usually the coach is engaged by the students, paid for by the students, and responsible only to them. He is not a member of the faculty or responsible to the faculty. The faculty have charge of the college as an educational institution; athletics is for business and therefore separately controlled. Why not abandon faculty direction of Latin? Students, alumni, and newspapers are as well qualified to elect a professor of Latin and administer the department in the interests of education, as they are to elect coaches and administer athletics in the interests of education.

A few of the more notable coaches of the country are aware of the possibilities of athletics controlled by the faculty for educational purposes. Mr Courtney, the Cornell coach, spoke to the point when he said:

'If athletics are not a good thing, they ought to be abolished. If they are a good thing for the boys, it would seem to me wise for the university to take over and control absolutely every branch of sport; do away with this boy management; stop this foolish squandering of money, and see that the athletics of the University are run in a rational way.'

Next to the physical development and the maintenance of the health of all the students and teachers of an institution, the main purpose of athletics as education is to provide recreation as a preparation for study rather than as a substitute for study. But, intercollegiate athletics having won and retained unquestioned supremacy in our colleges, students do not tolerate the idea of a conflicting interest.

Even the nights preceding the great contests must be free from the interference of intellectual concerns. An editorial in one of our college weeklies makes this point clear. If a member of the faculty ventured to put the matter so extremely, he would be charged with exaggeration. But in this paper the students naïvely present their conviction that even the most signal opportunities for enjoying literature must be sacrificed by the entire student body in order that they may get together and yell in preparation for their function of sitting in the grandstand. In this case the conflicting interest appeared in no less a person than Alfred Noyes. For a geographically isolated community to hear the poet was an opportunity of a college lifetime. Yet the students wrote as follows:

THE RALLY vs NOYES

'Returning alumni this year were somewhat surprised to find the Hall used for a lecture on the eve of our great gridiron struggle, and some were very much disappointed. The student body was only partially reconciled to the situation and was represented in great part by Freshmen [who were required to attend].'

The relative importance of intercollegiate athletics and other college affairs, in the minds of students, is indicated by student publications. There is no more tangible scale for measuring the interests of college youth than the papers which they edit for their own satisfaction, unrestrained by the faculty.

Let us take two of the worthiest colleges as examples. The *Bowdoin College Orient*, a weekly publication, is typical. For the first nine weeks of the academic year 1914-15, the *Orient* gave 450 inches to intercollegiate athletics. For the same period, it devoted six inches to art, ten inches to social service, thirteen inches to music, and twelve inches to debating. Judging from this free expression, the students rate the interests of intercollegiate athletics nearly three times as high as the combined interests of art, music, religion, philosophy, social service, literature, debating, the curriculum, and the faculty. Second in importance to intercollegiate athletics, valued at 450 inches, are dances and fraternities, valued at 78 inches.

Another possible measure of the student's interest is found in *Harvard of Today from an Undergraduate Point of View*, published in 1913 by the *Harvard Federation of Territorial Clubs*. The book gives to athletics ten pages; to the clubs, six pages; to debating, five lines—and that student activity requires sustained thinking and is most closely correlated with the curriculum. The faculty escapes without mention. 'From an undergraduate point of view' the faculty appears to be an incumbrance upon the joys of college life.

These publications appear to be fair representatives of their class. It is probable, furthermore, that the relative attention given by the student papers to intellectual interests is a criterion of the conversation of students.

Not long ago, I spent some time with the graduate students at an Eastern university. Their conversation at dinner gave no evidence of common intellectual interests. They appeared to talk of little but football games.

On a visit to a Southern state university, I found the women's dormitory in confusion. The matron excused the noise and disorder on the ground that a big football game was pending and it seemed impossible for the girls to think of anything else.

'The big game comes tomorrow?' I asked.

'Oh, no, next week,' she said.

Last spring, at a large university on the Pacific Coast, I met one young woman of the freshman class who had already been to thirty-one dances that year. At a state university of the Middle West, I found that the students had decided to have their big football game on Friday instead of Saturday, in order to wrench one more day from the loose grip of the curriculum. When the faculty protested, the students painted on the walls, 'Friday is a holiday'—and it was.

Intellectual enthusiasm is rare in American colleges, and is likely to be rarer still if social and athletic affairs continue to overshadow all other interests. Their dominance has given many a college faculty its characteristic attitude in matters of government. They assume that boys and girls will come to college for anything but studies. They tell new students just how many lectures in each course they may escape. A penalty of unsatisfactory work is the obligation to attend all the meetings on their schedule, and the usual reward for faithful conduct is the privilege of 'cutting' more lectures without a summons from the dean. Always the aim of students appears to be to escape as much as possible of the college life provided by the faculty, in order to indulge in more of the college life provided by themselves. Their inventive powers are marvelous; they bring forth an endless procession of devices for evading the opportunities for the sake of which (according to old-fashioned notions) students seek admission to college. The complacent acceptance of this condition by college faculties—the pervasive assumption that students have no genuine intellectual enthusiasm—tends to stagnation. In the realm of thought some appear to have discovered the secret of petrified motion.

The pronounced tendencies in higher education aggravate the disease. Feeble palliatives are resorted to from time to time—the baseball schedule in one college, after six hours of debate by the faculty, was cut down from twenty-four games to twenty-two—but the bold and necessary surgeon seldom gets in his good work. When he does operate, he is hung in effigy or elected President of the United States.

Concerning the policy of no intercollegiate games at Clark College, President Sanford says: 'Our experience with this plan has been absolutely satisfactory and no change of policy would be considered. Doubtless some of the less intellectually serious among the students might like to see intercollegiate sports introduced. It is generally understood that in a three-year college there is not time for such extras.' The faculty appear to be unanimously in favor of no intercollegiate games, since the course at Clark College takes only three years. Intercollegiate contests appear to be ruled out chiefly on the ground that, in a three-year course, students cannot afford to waste time. But why is it worse for a young man to waste parts of three years of his student life than to waste parts of four years of it?

The educational effect of our exaggerated emphasis on intercollegiate athletics is shown in the attitude of alumni. It is difficult to arouse the interest of a large proportion of graduates in anything else. At one of the best of our small colleges, in the Mississippi Valley, I saw a massive concrete grandstand. This valiant emulation of the Harvard stadium seemed to me to typify the indifference of alumni to the crying needs of their alma mater. For these graduates who contributed costly concrete seats, to be used by the student body in lieu of exercise, showed no concern over the fact that the college was worrying along with scientific laboratories inferior to those of the majority of modern high schools. 'What could I do?' the president asked. 'They would give the stadium, and they would not give the laboratories.'

IV

There have been numerous attempts to prove that intercollegiate athletics are not detrimental to scholarship by showing that athletes receive higher marks than other students. Such arguments are beside the point. Though we take no account of the weak-kneed indulgence to athletes in institutions where winning games is the dominant interest, and of the special coaching in their studies provided for them because they are on the teams, we must take account of the fact that wherever the student body regards playing on intercollegiate teams as the supreme expression of loyalty, the men of greatest physical and mental strength are more likely than the others to go out for the teams, and these are the very men of whom we rightly expect greatest proficiency in scholarship. That they do not as a group show notable leadership in intellectual activities seems due to the excessive physical training which, at certain seasons, they substitute for study.

But this is not the main point. A large college might be willing to sacrifice the scholarship of a score of students, if that were all. The chief charge against intercollegiate athletics is their demoralizing effect on the scholarship of the entire institution. The weaklings who have not grit enough to stand up on the gridiron and be tackled talk interminably about the latest game and the chances of winning the next one. They spend their hours in cheering the football hero, and their money in betting on him. The man of highest achievement in scholarship they either ignore or condemn with unpleasant epithets.

Further hindrances to scholarship are found in the periodic absences of the teams. It is said that athletes are required to make up the work they miss during their trips, but is not this one of the naïve ways whereby faculties deceive themselves? They are faced with this dilemma. Either the work of a given week in their courses is so substantial, and their own contribution to the work so great, that students cannot possibly miss it, and 'make it up' while meeting the equally great demands of the following week, or else the work of all the students is so easy that the athletes on a week's absence do not miss much. What actually happens, year in and year out, is that the standards of scholarship of the entire institution are lowered to meet the exigencies of intercollegiate athletics.

To what an illogical position we are driven by our fetish worship of college 'amateur athletics'! We especially provide the summer vacation as a period for play and recreation, and as a time when a majority of students must earn a part of the expenses of the college year. For these purposes we suspend all classes. Yet the student who uses this vacation to play ball and thereby earn some money must either lie about it or be condemned to outer darkness. There are no intercollegiate athletics for him; he has become a 'professional'. It matters not how fine his ideals of sport may be, how strong his character, or how high his scholarship. These considerations are ignored. The honors all go to the athlete who neglects his studies in order to make games his supreme interest during that part of the twelve months which is specifically set apart for studies.

Far more sensible would be an arrangement whereby, if we

must have intercollegiate athletics at all, the games could be scheduled in vacation periods, and a part of the gate-receipts, if we must have them at all, could be used for the necessary living expenses of worthy students, instead of being squandered, as much of that money is squandered today. That this will seem a preposterous plan to those who are caught in the maelstrom of the present collegiate system need not surprise us. An accurate record of the history of intercollegiate athletics shows that, year in and year out, the arrangements desired by students are those that interfere most seriously with study during the days especially intended for study.

The maelstrom of college athletics! That would not seem too strong a term if we could view the age in which we live in right perspective—an age so unbalanced nervously that it demands perpetual excitement. We have fallen into a vicious circle: the excesses of excitement create a pathological nervous condition which craves greater excesses. The advertisement of a head-on collision of two locomotives is said to have drawn the largest crowd in the history of modern 'sport'; next in attractiveness is an intercollegiate football game. It is unfortunate that our universities, which should serve as balancing forces—which should inculcate the ideal of sport as a counterpoise to an overwrought civilization—are actually making conditions worse through cultivating, by means of athletics as a business, that passion for excitement which makes sustained thinking impossible and which is elsewhere kept at fever heat by prize-fights, bullfights, and blood-curdling motion pictures.

V

But even if intercollegiate games are detrimental to the interests of scholarship, is not the college spirit they create worth all they cost? Perhaps so. A university is more than a curriculum and a campus. It is more than the most elaborate student annual can depict. Even in Carlyle's day, it was more than he called it: a true university was never a mere 'collection of books'. It is the spirit that giveth life, and 'college spirit' is certainly a name to conjure with. The first question is what we mean by college spirit. A student may throw his hat in the air, grab a megaphone, give 'three long rahs', go through the gymnastics of a cheer-leader—putting the most ingenious mechanical toys to shame—and yet leave some doubt whether he has adequately defined college spirit.

What is this college spirit that hovers over the paid coach and his grandstand—this 'indefinable something', as one writer calls it, 'which is fanned into a bright flame by intercollegiate athletics'? Shall we judge the spirit by its manifestations in an institution famed above all else for its winning teams and its college spirit? In such an institution, not long ago, every student was cudgeled or cajoled into 'supporting the team', and many a callow youth acted as though he thought he had reached the heights of self-sacrifice when he sat for hours on the grandstand, watching practice, puffing innumerable cigarettes, and laying up a stock of canned enthusiasm for the big game. A student who would not support his team by betting on it was regarded as deficient in spirit. Every intercollegiate game was the occasion of general neglect of college courses. If the game was at a neighboring city, the class-rooms were half empty for two days; but the bar-rooms of that city were not empty, and worse places regularly doubled their rates on the night of a big game. Some of the most enthusiastic supporters of the team went to jail for disturbing the peace. If the contest took place at home, returning alumni filled the fraternity houses and celebrated with general drunkenness. 'An indefinable something'—consisting of college property and that of private citizens—was 'fanned into a bright flame' in celebration of the victory. Following this came the spectacle of young men parading the streets in nightshirts. For residents of the town who did not enjoy this particular kind of spirit, the night was made hideous by the noises of revelry. All this and much more was tolerated for years on the assumption that students, imbued with college spirit, should not be subjected to the laws of decent living that govern those members of civilized communities who have not had the advantages of a higher education. The most serious difficulties between faculties and students and between students and the police, the country over, for the past twenty years, have arisen in connection with displays of 'college spirit' after the 'big game'. Any college and any community might cheerfully sacrifice this kind of college spirit.

But some men mean by college spirit something finer than lawlessness, dissipation, and rowdyism. They mean the loyalty to an institution which makes a student guard its good name by being manly and courteous in conduct at all times and in all places. They mean the sense of responsibility which aids a student in forming habits of temperance and industry. They mean that eagerness to make a grateful use of his opportunities which leads a student to keep his own body fit, through moderate athletics, and a physical training that knows no season—is never broken. By college spirit some men mean this and far more: they mean that loyalty to a college which rivets a man to the severest tasks of scholarship, through which he gains intellectual power and enthusiasm, without which no graduate is an entire credit to any college; and finally they mean that vision of an ideal life beyond Commencement which shows a man that only through the rigid subordination of transient and trivial pleasures can he hope to become the only great victory a university ever wins—a trained, devoted, and inspired alumnus, working for the welfare of mankind. There is no evidence that the intercollegiate athletics of today inculcate in many men this kind of college spirit.

Have I exaggerated the evils of intercollegiate athletics? Possibly I have. Exceptions should be cited here and there. But I am convinced that college faculties agree with me in my main contentions. My impression is that at least three fourths of the teachers I have met the country over believe that the American college would better serve its highest purposes, if intercollegiate athletics were no more. At a recent dinner of ten deans and presidents, they declared, one by one, in confidence, that they would abolish intercollegiate athletics if they could withstand the pressure of students and alumni.

Is it therefore necessary for all institutions to give up intercollegiate athletics permanently? Probably not. Let our colleges first adopt whatever measures may be necessary to make athletics yield their educational values to all students and teachers. If intercollegiate athletics can then be conducted as incidental and contributory to the main purposes of athletics, well and good. But first of all the question must be decisively settled, which aims are to dominate—those of business or those of education. And it will be difficult for a college already in the clutches of commercialism to retain the system and at the same time cultivate a spirit antagonistic to it. Probably the quicker and surer way would be to suspend all intercollegiate athletics for a college generation by agreement of groups of colleges—during which period every effort should be made to establish the tradition of athletics for education. If an institution could not survive such a period of transition, it is a fair question whether the institution has any reason for survival.

Typically American though our frantic devotion to intercollegiate athletics may be, we shall not long tolerate a system which provides only a costly, injurious, and excessive régime of physical training for a few students, especially those who need it least. The call today is for inexpensive, healthful, and moderate exercise for all students, especially those who need it most. Colleges must sooner or later heed that call: their athletics must be for education, not for business.

CAR-WINDOW BOTANY

LIDA F. BALDWIN

One thinks of the botanist as in silence and solitude wandering by some forest brook, or penetrating into almost impenetrable swamps, or climbing rocky mountain paths, lured on by the hope of finding some rare and curious flower. But I in my own experience have had some of my best finds from the windows of a railway train.

It was with people sitting all around me, and the engine puffing noisily away on an upgrade, that my delighted eyes first fell on the one-flowered pyrola. The railway cutting had been made in the heart of the deep forest, and as the bank settled down, some of the rarer and shyer forest growths, such as ground-pine, arbutus, and pyrola, in the course of years had slipped over the brink of the cutting and were now part way down the bank. Inside the car were tired and grimy faces; just a few feet outside were forest freshness and greenness, and the white blossoms of the pyrola with their delicate flush.

Sometimes there is no bank on either side of the railway, and from the car window one catches glimpses into the edges of forests, or looks down upon swamps and small clear ponds, or gazes across broad level meadows; but more often one's view from the car window is confined to the narrow ditch of water just beyond the road-bed and to the sides of the cutting just beyond the ditch. Even in that confined outlook there are always possibilities; and it was in just such a ditch of water, as our train slowed up on the outskirts of Buffalo, that I saw growing great numbers of what looked like miniature calla lilies. There were the same golden, erect spadix, and the same ivory-white spathe rolled back in the very curve of the spathe of the calla lily; but the flower was not one quarter the size of the calla. As usual my botany was in my handbag; and the temptation to make a quick dash from the train, to try to secure one specimen for analysis, was almost irresistible. But I did resist the temptation; for the bank was quite steep, and I never could have climbed back in time if the train had started while I was trying to secure my flower; and a lonely woman would have been left in the dusk, watching the train bearing her friends vanish in the deepening twilight. But the small white beauties were never forgotten, and years afterwards I found the flower, arum palustris, growing in a swamp not many miles from my old home.

One July day I traveled from Quebec to Portland on the slowest of trains. The road ran for much of the way, first on one side, then on the other, of the Chaudière River, but never far out of sight of its clear brown waters. Fortunately for me, our locomotive used wood for fuel, and consequently every few hours we would stop at some great woodpile in a forest clearing while the trainmen threw a fresh supply of wood into the tender; and some of the passengers took advantage of the stop to make short explorations into the forest. About mid-day, as we were riding slowly along, I began to notice a pink-purple flower that was new to me, growing here and there in rather marshy places. Shortly after I had first seen the flower the added slowness of the train showed that we were coming to another woodpile. The instant the train stopped I was out of the cars, over the low rail fence, and picking my way carefully from grassy hummock to grassy hummock; and soon I had found a specimen. Upon analysis it proved to be calopogon, familiar to all New Englanders from childhood, but new to my Ohio eyes.

I have never made any formal herbarium, and the only botanical record I have ever kept consists of the date and place of my first seeing the flower written opposite its scientific name in the margin of the pages of my old school-girl's copy of Gray's Botany. But that is the only record one needs to whom all the flowers one knows are either old friends or new acquaintances—in either case distinct individuals. Often, as I have been turning the pages of the old botany in a bit of analyzing, I have stopped at the page on which is written, opposite the scientific name of the calopogon, 'Saint Henry's, Canada, July 11, 1884'; and across the more than twenty years that lie between, I smell once more the balsam of the Canadian forest, and see the amber-brown waters of the Chaudière River, and hear the shouts of the trainmen as they throw the great sticks of wood up to the tender; and giving color to all this mental picture is the pink-purple blossom of the calopogon.

But all trains do not have the accommodating habit of stopping for wood just after you have seen a strange flower; in that case, all that you can do is, take the best mental landmarks you can, and then at the first opportunity go back for your specimen. One summer I was going down on the express from Philadelphia to Cape May. As you near the coast the road runs through very level country, and between the railway and the pine wood lies a strip of marshy ground about forty feet wide. Each year, as I go back to the sea-coast, I watch eagerly for my first sight of the two characteristic flowers of the Jersey coast, the swamp mallow and the sabbatia. On this particular morning I had already seen many of the great mallows with their rose-pink flowers, so like those of the hollyhock that not even the most careless eye can fail to notice the family resemblance; and I had welcomed them as a sure sign of the fast-nearing seashore.

Now, with my face, as usual, close to the window, I was watching the sparse marsh-grass most narrowly to see if I could detect amidst it the pink star-shaped flower of the sabbatia. Suddenly the marsh-grass was set thick with spikes of yellow flowers, just rising above the level of the grass. There was only that one hurried look as the train went by; but from that look I felt almost certain of two things: the first was that I had never seen that flower before, and the second, that it must be close of kin to an old flower friend of mine, the white fringed-orchis.

Then and there I determined to get that flower, and the first thing was to make sure of its location. At first this seemed almost hopeless, since for miles back we had had that narrow strip of marsh-grass flanked by the unchanging pine woods; but in a few minutes our road passed under another railway; here was one landmark, and in a couple of minutes more we went past a way-station slowly enough for me to read the name on the board; now I knew that I could find my plant. The next day we took one of the local trains from Cape May, got off at the station whose name I had read, and started down the track. After a walk of a mile we passed under that other railroad; and about two miles farther down the track I saw again the yellow spikes of the flowers barely o'ertopping the grass.

It had been a hot July morning with a sultry land breeze blowing, and as we walked the three miles down the unshaded track, we had weariedly and unavailingly slapped at mosquitoes at every step. All of these discomforts together had not daunted my courage; but the swarms of mosquitoes that arose buzzing at my first step into the marsh-grass made me draw back to the comparative security of the railway track, with the feeling that no flower could repay one for facing those swarms. A second look at the yellow flowers growing not thirty feet away gave me fresh courage and I started again. I was as quick as possible; but when I was back once more on the track, this time with my hands full of the flowers, face and hands and arms were one mass of blotches from the mosquito bites.

Upon analysis the flower proved to be the yellow fringed-orchis, the handsomest species of its genus, and the one most closely allied to the white fringed-orchis. Our train had been running about forty miles an hour; I had never even known that there was a yellow orchid, but in that one quick glance from the express train the unmistakable family look of the orchis had shown.

Success and pleasure in car-window botany depend not so much on a scientific knowledge of structural details as on the ability of the eye to recognize at a glance the characteristic effect produced by a mass of details. It is this ability which enables you to be sure that you recognize the faces of old flower friends in the hurried glance cast from the window; which enables you to tell with certainty gray-blue clump of houstonias from gray-blue clump of hepaticas, wind-swept bank of purplish phlox from wind-swept bank of wild geranium; and it is that same ability to recognize the characteristic effect produced by a group of structural details which enables one to place without analysis the new flower in the right family.

I have always been secretly very proud of the certainty with which at the first sight of the yellow flower I felt that it was an orchis, but all my feeling in connection with it is not that of pleasure. Certain flowers always recall to me certain sounds; in most cases the sound associated with a flower is the one heard at the time at which I first saw the flower; and to this day, with the thought of the yellow fringed-orchis is inseparably joined that most persistent and irritating of sounds, the buzzing of the mosquito.

But the true history of a car-window botanist is not always a record of successful achievement, of the triumphant finding of his flower; he also has his haunting disappointments, his glimpses of strange flowers which he is never afterwards able to place. One July day, riding through northern New Hampshire, I saw just over the fence at the edge of the woods a tall plant—evidently some kind of a lily. It bore a single dark orange-red flower, which did not droop as do the flowers of the meadow lily, but stood stiffly erect. I have never seen that lily since; though never does a July come, especially if it is to be spent in a new place, that I do not think, 'Maybe this year I shall find my lily.' Perhaps, after all, such experiences are not to be classed with the disappointments either of life or of car-window botany—is it not rather true that to both they give zest and expectancy?

The charm of such botanizing is not alone in finding or in hoping to find some new flower: even more enduring is the pleasure that comes from the recognition of the faces of old friends in new surroundings. An April day's journey was made one long pleasure; for the swamplike ditch just below the road-bed shone golden with the intense yellow of the marsh-marigold, an old friend from my earliest childhood; and when the railway ran half-way up a hillside, I spied, amid the dead leaves of last year, the little clumps of the clustering blue hepaticas, and recognized even in those fleeting glances the singularly starry effect produced by the numerous white stamens; and as the train crossed over the creeks, that flow over rocky bottoms from out the hemlock woods, I saw in the opening up of the creek bed the June-berry trees in showers of white bloom, looking doubly white against the dark green of the hemlocks, just as I had seen them the day before in the hemlock woods of Mill Creek at my own home.

One of the keenest pleasures of the railway botanist comes from his enjoyment of the massed color of great quantities of flowers of the same kind. One morning our train was running along through the level Jersey country; it was at that wretched hour of the morning when you have just taken your place in someone else's seat while the porter is getting your own ready, and you have that all-over miserable feeling that comes from a night's ride in a stuffy sleeper. In an instant all discomfort was forgotten in the sight of a wide salt meadow which seemed one mass of the pink swamp-mallows. The gray morning mist was turned silvery white by the rising sun, and giving color to it all were the wide stretches of the flowers. It was all one shimmering mass of misty silvery-gray, sunlight radiance, and rose-color as delicate as that of the lining of some seashells.

Once again, this time on one of our home roads near Pittsburg, I felt the beauty of the color of great masses of flowers. The railway runs along about half-way up the bluffs by the side of the Beaver River; as we rounded a curve, the steep bank above me turned suddenly intensely red with the vivid color of the scarlet campion. Only those who notice most closely have any idea how rare a color in our wild flowers any shade of true red is. Nearly all the flowers that are commonly spoken of as red are in reality purplish pink or reddish lilac. Indeed I know only two wild flowers whose color is a true red. One of these is the cardinal lobelia, whose petals are of the darkest, clearest, most velvety red; and the other flower is the scarlet campion. The color of this latter is true scarlet, and the river bluff that June morning fairly glowed with its bloom. It is Holmes who compares the color of the cardinal flower to that of drops of blood new fallen from a wounded eagle's breast; but any true comparison for the color of this other flower must be founded on life, and on life when it is at its fullest of strength and of enjoyment.

Even the most ardent of car-window botanists will not claim that the only place from which the beauty of the color of flowers in mass can be appreciated is the window of a railway train. To all there come memories of fitful spring days when in long country drives they have seen partly worn-out meadows and barren hillsides turned to the softest blue-gray mist by the delicate color of countless blossoms of houstonia. And as they drove slowly along the partly dried, muddy roads of mid-April the effect of every varying phase of the spring weather on the massed color sank slowly into their consciousness. They had time to notice how blue was the color-mist lying on the sheltered meadows in the sunshine, and how coldly gray it grew as it crept up the hillsides across which the chill spring wind was blowing.

And if one lives in a country where there are chestnut ridges, one looks forward through all the spring to that one week of late June and earliest July when the chestnut trees will be in bloom. The long staminate flowers of the chestnut are a soft cream-yellow with a greenish tint; and on the ridges where the trees grow in abundance the great irregular masses of their blossoming tops do not stand out against their background of the dark green foliage of midsummer, but blend softly with it, giving to all such an indescribable effect of lightness and airiness that the whole wooded ridge seems not to be fastened securely to the earth, but to be floating cloud-like above it. During that one week of the chestnut-blossoming one stops at door or at window in the midst of the early morning work to watch for the moment when the first rays of the rising sun, falling on the cream-yellow of the chestnut tops, turn them into their own deep gold; and at the restful close of day one lingers on the doorstep through the long June twilight till their blossoming tops can no longer be distinguished from the dark foliage of the other trees in the gathering darkness.

All one's life long the pictures of old meadow lands gray-blue with the mist of the houstonias are recalled by the alternate glinting sunshine and bleak gloom of an April day; and the blossoming chestnut woods form the background to many recollections of the old home life. But these pictures which have become a part of one's inmost consciousness are scarcely more dear than that one, seen for a few moments, of the low-lying Jersey meadows flushing rose-pink with the mallows in the misty morning sunshine; or than that other 'vision of scarce a moment,' the river bluff scarlet with the flowers of the campion, seen from the windows of a railway train.

STUDIES IN SOLITUDE

FANNIE STEARNS GIFFORD

I

She was never lonely, she told herself. The solitude of her little old white house, sitting retired from the village street among its lilac trees and syringas did not frighten or depress her. She could spend a whole day of rain there, seeing no one but the grocer's boy, the big gray cat, and occasional stooped hurrying figures out in the wet street and could come down into evening calmly, busied with her enforced or chosen duties and thoughts. A cloud seemed to wrap her round in many folds of seclusion till the common world of hurry and friction and loud or secret loves and hates was dim to her eyes and ears. Street sounds and whistles of trains at the cross-roads were muffled echoes; but the ticking of the tall clock, the throbbing of rain on a tin roof, the infrequent wind banging at a loose window, the cat's creepy tread on the stairs, grew rhythmic and insistent.

Yet she was not lonely. She never stopped to brood, listening long to perilous voices. She denied even to certain pieces of furniture, books, or ornaments, their passive right to conjure up the spectre of her solitude. If a room seemed too vibrant with unseen presences, she would enter it and drive out the quivering mystery with some brisk petty business of sweeping, of shifting a picture, or rearranging a book-shelf. Often she whistled softly about her work, although there were moments when as if by an instinct she would stop short and glance over her shoulder, to see nothing, and after that to be still.

So the day would shift from gray dawn to gray dusk; and she had not allowed herself to think that she might have cause for loneliness, there in the quiet house behind its dripping lilac trees.

Only in the evenings did the clock and the rain become too loud and real. Then, as she sat with a pleasant book or broidery in the yellow lamplit circle of her sitting-room, warm and quaint in its accumulation of color—old gay reds, greens, blues, tumbled together by generations of fond house-holders, and now subdued into harmony by years and the low light—she would find herself all at once rigid as an ice-image, yet alert as a coiled serpent; listening, listening—for what? For a quick step on the flags before the door? For a long jangling peal at the bell? For a voice in the hall, or a sick querulous summons from the downstairs chamber, or the scraping of a chair from above? No, she knew that she had no cause to wait for these things. There was only the rain, the clock, sleek Diogenes purring on the white fox-skin, the lamp wick fretting a little to itself, and once in a while, out in the dark street, the splash and clatter of wheels, the faint wet whisper of feet that always passed her gate.

So, with a self-scorning smile and a drawing of her hand across her eyes, she would take up again the book or needle-work, and stop abruptly that rigid listening for sounds which never came. Long since, on her first solitary night in the old house, she had vowed to herself that she would not be sad, or strange, no matter what tricks her heart and mind might play her. She would not fear memory and anticipation, but would compel them to be her servants, to keep their distance. She had been young then, and had not quite believed in her solitude. Now that she knew it through and through, she was still aware that to look too far back or too far forward would equally undo her. On these rainy nights of withdrawal, her trial-times were still upon her. If she failed now, if one shudder or one tear escaped her, she was lost forever; and the white house would drive her out, into a world where she could no more choose her own way of being alone.

But she was not lonely, she repeated; and to prove it, her mind would indulge in a fantasia of loneliness. The book would slip from her hand, and she, gazing half-hypnotized into shadowy corners, visited all the solitary people over the wide world. It pleased her to imagine homesick officers in stifling Indian bungalows; young men and girls, fresh come to the City, wandering forlorn through the glare of streets, or idling under their meagre lodging-house gas-jets; light-keepers on desolate sand-dunes and rock-ledges, climbing at night twisted iron steps to tend the eternal lamp; night-watchmen pacing deserted yards and mill-corridors; sailors in the dead watch; poets and prophets trying passionately to capture the wild visions which leaped across their darkness; and most of all, many women sitting as she did in warm quaint rooms, near village streets, hearing the clock tick and the rain throb.

It pleased her, to travel so on light unhindered wing. Almost it seemed as if her soul left her body, and fared out to knock against every lonely window and to keep dumb company round every solitary lamp. And she felt that she was one of an endless army, marching straightforwardly and silently out upon their lives, stripped of the disguises that kindred and close friendship invent, and making, in return for the silence of their hearts and the smiling of their lips, only one demand of all that encountered them.

That demand she never shaped, of her own will. But when she had sat a long time, dreaming, and had at length roused herself to make fast doors and windows, had shut the cat in the kitchen, taken her hand-lamp and gone up the broad stairs to bed—then, in the gay chintz-hung security of her own chamber, her throat would fashion involuntarily those words that her heart and lips refused to let themselves speak.

'It is all right enough,' her throat would say for her, as she turned down the counterpane, untied her shoes, and wound her watch. 'I am quite all safe and right. But—no one must ask me—if I am lonely. No one must ever ask me that.'

II

It had appeared presently that her house was haunted, though not by ghostly terrors. For herself, she had only felt, at times, the vaguely imagined intimation of some presence other than her own in the quiet rooms. But she had no surer knowledge of her dimly harbored guests until a friend, wearied out with the love and care of over-many babies, came to her for rest; and after two days of grateful idleness in her sunny window, asked suddenly, 'Miriam, whose are the Voices?'

'What voices?' Miriam parried; and Lucy described them: happy, laughing voices, as of young people playing and gossiping together. 'I have heard them so often when I was lying alone and you were out, or off somewhere. I almost asked a dozen times who was talking. They are always downstairs, or across the hall, or under the window; and they are such happy voices: young voices—oh, very sweet and glad.'

Miriam smiled and stroked her friend's nervous fingers. Lucy had always heard and seen more than other people did, and now that she was so tired, no doubt her worn-out fancy befooled her lightly. They talked it over together. Lucy, smiling at herself, none the less insisted: there were Voices in the house.

'Some time you'll hear them too,' she nodded. 'They're not sad or dreadful or gloomy; oh, no! They're just young and glad. I love to hear them.'

And another evening, when Miriam came into the sitting-room after an errand down the street, Lucy greeted her eagerly, saying,

'It was music this time. Oh, I've heard such music! I almost went to see if someone wasn't playing. It was like a harp, I think, with a violin and piano: it was very beautiful. I thought someone must be playing, until it came to me that of course it was the Young People. It was happy music, just as the Voices are so happy. Miriam, there are young people somehow in your house.'

It became a sort of gentle pleasant joke between them, while Lucy stayed on. 'Have you heard them today?' Miriam would ask; and sometimes Lucy replied, 'No; they must have gone off on a picnic; it was such a good day'; or 'Yes; they were here while you were out this afternoon. I don't see why you don't hear them.'

And Miriam would shake her head. 'I never hear and see Things, you know. They are your Voices, Lucy; they are your babies grown-up who are talking to you even here in my old-maid house.'

But Lucy denied it. 'No, Miriam, I never heard them anywhere else. They belong to you and your house, and they mean something good, and sweet, and coming, not gone by. They're not ghosts.'

And when at last Miriam kissed her good-bye at the train, Lucy was saying, 'I'm glad to think of you, there in your nice sunny house, with the Voices, and the Music. Good-bye, dear.'

As Miriam sat alone that evening, she wondered about those young happy presences. She wished that she could hear them laugh and sing and play; not merely feel them blindly stirring about her. She sat, deep in reverie, smiling at Lucy's merry yet honest insistence upon her quaint little hallucination—at herself for more than half believing it.

'It is better that I never hear them,' she concluded at last, rather soberly. 'I couldn't live alone this way if I heard them. It is all well enough for Lucy, with her husband and her houseful of babies, to hear things like that; granting that she truly did, dear mysterious Lucy!—But if I heard them—if I heard them—' she glanced about the room as if she half expected to see a gay face above the piano, a bright head bending by the lamp—'it would mean that I was going a little bit mad: yes, just a little bit mad, for all that they are sweet, young voices.'

She shivered, stood up quickly, and went over to the long mirror. 'Miriam,' she whispered, looking into the shadowy face that met hers, 'Lucy said those were young voices, coming voices, not gone by. But you know, Miriam, that if they are, they belong to someone else who may live in this house: to someone else, I tell you, not to you at all. Don't be a fool. You've been quite sensible so far: don't spoil it all now. Do you hear? You mustn't even wish to hear those Voices, or that lovely harp-music. Now you understand.'

Months later she saw her friend again. 'How are the Voices?' Lucy asked gayly, across the laughing baby who pulled at her necktie and snatched down her curls.

'I never hear them,' Miriam answered, almost shortly. 'You

know, don't you—"to him that hath shall be given"?—Please may I hold the baby?'

III

Yet often, when she had spent a part of the day or evening away from home, she had a curious expectation of returning to find her house not empty and silent, but with something alive in it to greet her. She did not think of the people who had been her own in the different days so far past, nor of her living friends, nor of the young presences whose laughter Lucy had insisted upon hearing. It seemed to her simply that there was more life and motion and personality in her waiting house, than just Diogenes crouching on the front porch, and the kettle steaming to itself on the back of the stove.

One winter evening she walked late down the village street. The moon rode high and white. Every frosty breath shone, every step creaked and crackled in the snow. Through the thin leafless maple-trunks and lilac-boughs she could see her house plainly: the snowy roof, glittering to the moon, the low eaves, ragged with silver icicles, and the four yellow windows of the hall and sitting-room, which she had lighted against her late return.

She had a definite sense of expectancy. She was going back to something, to somebody—and found herself hurrying almost joyfully. But with her hand on the gate, she stopped, and stared at the house as if it were strange to her. An icy little stream flowed suddenly round her heart. For a second, all the world—the moon, the village, the house, and her own inner secret universe—staggered and reeled and shook. But as suddenly, everything grew calm and still again. The frightful chill melted from her blood; the moon watched her with the same high virgin regard, and the yellow windows beckoned her home.

She went slowly up the path and into the warm silent hall.

In that moment at the gate, she had realized that it was only Herself to whom she was going back. Herself, who made those windows bright, who piled the logs on the hearth that now she could light and sit by, dreaming. It was Herself, would be running down the stairs to greet her, and fetching an apple from the pantry, and listening to her story of the evening's doings.

It seemed to her almost as if she had become two individuals. One of her went out into the village and the world. The other stayed always in the little white house. She would always be waiting to greet her home.

That was all. Now that she understood it, it did not concern her any more.

She was becoming a good hermit, she commented; but noticed, with the detachment that had grown upon her, that she was not going to remember that shuddering moment at the gate. She blew the fire high, thinking, 'After all, there is nobody but Myself who understands me much,' and was amused at her simple egotism.

IV

But secretly she knew her most perilous enemy. It was not sadness, or selfishness, or the Voices, or the odd wilderness of a determined recluse. It was Eternity.

There was no telling when Eternity might claim her. Sometimes she awoke at dawn, and went down into the dewy garden to work among the roses and iris and pansy plants, with the birds all singing and the sun dancing like a great wise morning star. The day wore on, as she digged and transplanted and clipped and watered, till, weary a little, she went into the house and took up the endless bit of sewing, or some story or poem to finish. And all at once, in spite of the sun, the earth-smell, the brisk village-sounds beyond her garden-fence, she knew that her anchor dragged—she had slipped her moorings in the safe harbor of Time, and was drifting off, off into Eternity.

Then she cared nothing for rose-bugs, or iris-roots, or stockings to darn, or stories to read. She thought of Love, and Sin, and Death; of nations at war and her friends' souls in joy or agony, of God Himself—and they were all as nothing. She saw the flickering garden, she heard the song-sparrow and the clucking hen, she felt her own scrubbed and earth-stained fingers and her beating heart, but these were not necessary to her. She was terribly remote; terribly careless and still and proud; for she was in Eternity.

'What does it all matter?' she would murmur. 'What if they drink and steal and sin and die? or love and lose and win and die too? And what of me? What of me?—We are all in Eternity. God Himself is in Eternity.'

But she kept the peril close. None of the neighbors, who hailed her on the street or gossiped on the vine-hung porch, ever noticed that often, as she talked, she would clasp her hands with a sudden fierce little gesture, as if she were holding tight to some strong arm, and that in her heart she was whispering, even while the swift crooked smile danced across her lips, 'O God, make me remember! Make me remember! We're in Time, now: not in Eternity yet: not in Eternity yet!'

THE GREEK GENIUS

JOHN JAY CHAPMAN

The teasing perfection of Greek Literature will perhaps excite the world long after modern literature is forgotten. Shakespeare may come to his end and lie down among the Egyptians, but Homer will endure forever. We hate to imagine such an outcome as this, because, while we love Shakespeare, we regard the Greek classics merely with an overwhelmed astonishment. But the fact is that Homer floats in the central stream of History, Shakespeare in an eddy. There is, too, a real difference between ancient and modern art, and the enduring power may be on the side of antiquity.

The classics will always be the playthings of humanity, because they are types of perfection, like crystals. They are pure intellect, like demonstrations in geometry. Within their own limitations they are examples of miracle; and the modern world has nothing to show that resembles them in the least. As no builder has built like the Greeks, so no writer has written like the Greeks. In edge, in delicacy, in proportion, in accuracy of effect, they are as marble to our sandstone. The perfection of the Greek vehicle is what attacks the mind of the modern man and gives him dreams.

What relation these dreams bear to Greek feeling it is impossible to say—probably a very remote and grotesque relation. The scholars who devote their enormous energies to a life-and-death struggle to understand the Greeks always arrive at states of mind which are peculiarly modern. The same thing may be said of the severest types of Biblical scholar. J. B. Strauss, for instance, gave his life to the study of Christ, and, as a result, has left an admirable picture of the German mind of 1850. Goethe, who was on his guard if ever a man could be, was still a little deceived in thinking that the classic spirit could be recovered.

He left imitations of Greek literature which are admirable in themselves, and rank among his most characteristic works, yet which bear small resemblance to the originals. The same may be said of Milton and of Racine. The Greeks seem to have used their material, their myths and ideas, with such supernal intellect that they leave this material untouched for the next comer. Their gods persist, their mythology is yours and mine. We accept the toys—the whole baby-house which has come down to us: we walk in and build our own dramas with their blocks.

What a man thinks of influences him, though he chance to know little about it; and the power which the ancient world has exerted over the modern has not been shown in proportion to the knowledge or scholarship of the modern thinker, but in proportion to his natural force. The Greek tradition, the Greek idea became an element in all subsequent life; and one can no more dig it out and isolate it than one can dig out or isolate a property of the blood. We do not know exactly how much we owe to the Greeks. Keats was inspired by the very idea of them. They were an obsession to Dante, who knew not the language. Their achievements have been pressing in upon the mind of Europe, and enveloping it with an atmospheric appeal, ever since the Dark Ages.

Of late years we have come to think of all subjects as mere departments of science, and we are almost ready to hand over Greece to the specialist. We assume that scholars will work out the history of art. But it is not the right of the learned and scholarly only, to be influenced by the Greeks, but also of those persons who know no Greek. Greek influence is too universal an inheritance to be entrusted to scholars, and the specialist is the very last man who can understand it. In order to obtain a diagnosis of Greek influence one would have to seek out a sort of specialist on Humanity-at-large.

I

Since we cannot find any inspired teacher to lay before us the secrets of Greek influence, the next best thing would be to go directly to the Greeks themselves, and to study their works freshly, almost innocently. But to do this is not easy. The very Greek texts themselves have been established through modern research, and the footnotes are the essence of modernity.

The rushing modern world passes like an express train; as it goes, it holds up a mirror to the classic world—a mirror ever changing and ever false. For upon the face of the mirror rests the lens of fleeting fashion. We can no more walk straight to the Greeks than we can walk straight to the moon. In America the natural road to the classics lies through the introductions of German and English scholarship. We are met, as it were, on the threshold of Greece by guides who address us confidently in two very dissimilar modern idioms, and who overwhelm us with complacent and voluble instructions. According to these men we have nothing to do but listen to them, if we would understand Greece.

Before entering upon the subject of Greece, let us cast a preliminary and disillusioning glance upon our two guides, the German and the Briton. Let us look once at each of them with an intelligent curiosity, so that we may understand what manner of men they are, and can make allowances in receiving the valuable and voluble assistance which they keep whispering into our ears throughout the tour. The guides are indispensable; but this need not prevent us from studying their temperaments. If it be true that modern scholarship acts as a lens through which the classics are to be viewed, we can never hope to get rid of all the distortions; but we may make scientific allowances, and may correct results. We may consider certain social laws of refraction—for example, spectacles, beer, sausages. We may regard the variations of the compass due to certain local customs, namely, the Anglican communion, school honor, Pears' soap. In all this we sin not, but pursue intellectual methods.

The case of Germany illustrates the laws of refraction very pleasantly. The extraordinary lenses which were made there in the nineteenth century are famous now, and will remain as curiosities hereafter. During the last century, Learning won the day in Germany to an extent never before known in history. It became an unwritten law of the land that none but learned men should be allowed to play with pebbles. If a man had been through the mill of the Doctorate, however, he received a certificate as a dreamer. The passion which mankind has for using its imagination could thus be gratified only by men who had been brilliant scholars. The result was a race of monsters, of whom Nietzsche is the greatest.

The early social life of these men was contracted. They learned all they knew while sitting on a bench. The classroom was their road to glory. They were aware that they could not be allowed to go out and play in the open until they had learned their lessons thoroughly; they therefore became prize boys. When the great freedom was at last conferred upon them, they roamed through Greek mythology, and all other mythologies, and erected labyrinths in which the passions of childhood may be seen gamboling with the discoveries of adult miseducation. The gravity with which the pundits treated each other extended to the rest of the world, because, in the first place, they were more learned than anyone else, and in the second, many of them were men of genius. The 'finds' of modern archæology have passed through the hands of these men, and have received from them the labels of current classification.

After all, these pundits resemble their predecessors in learning. Scholarship is always a specialized matter, and it must be learned as we learn a game. Scholarship always wears the parade of finality, and yet suffers changes like the moon. These particular scholars are merely scholars. Their errors are only the errors of scholarship, due, for the most part, to extravagance and ambition. A new idea about Hellas meant a new reputation. In default of such an idea a man's career is manquée; he is not an intellectual. After discounting ambition, we have left still another cause for distrusting the labors of the German professors. This distrust arises from a peep into the social surroundings of the caste. Here is a great authority on the open-air life of the Greeks: he knows all about Hellenic sport. Here is another who understands the brilliant social life of Attica: he has written the best book upon Athenian conversation and the market-place. Here is still a third: he has reconstructed Greek religion: at last we know! All these miracles of learning have been accomplished in the library—without athletics, without conversation, without religion.

When I think of Greek civilization—of the swarming, thieving, clever, gleaming-eyed Greeks, of the Bay of Salamis, and of the Hermes of Praxiteles—and then cast my eyes on the Greatest Authority, my guide, my Teuton master, with his barbarian babble and his ham-bone and his self-importance, I begin to wonder whether I cannot somehow get rid of the man and leave him behind. Alas, we cannot do that; we can only remember his traits.

Our British mentors, who flank the German scholars as we move gently forward toward Greek feeling, form so complete a contrast to the Teutons that we hardly believe that both kinds can represent genuine scholarship. The Britons are gentlemen, afternoon callers, who eat small cakes, row on the Thames, and are all for morality. They are men of letters. They write in prose and in verse, and belong to the æsthetic fraternity. They, like the Teutons, are attached to institutions of learning, namely, to Oxford and Cambridge. They resemble the Germans, however, in but a single trait—the conviction that they understand Greece.

The thesis of the British belle-lettrists, to which they devote their energies, might be stated thus: British culture includes Greek culture. They are very modern, very English, very sentimental, these British scholars. While the German Doctors use Greek as a stalking-horse for Teutonic psychology, these English gentlemen use it as a dressmaker's model upon which they exhibit home-made English lyrics and British stock morality. The lesson which Browning sees in *Alcestis* is the same that he gave us in 'James Lee's Wife'. Browning's appeal is always the appeal to robust feeling as the salvation of the world. Gilbert Murray, on the other hand, sheds a sad, clinging, Tennysonian morality over Dionysus. Jowett is happy to announce that Plato is theologically sound, and gives him a ticket-of-leave to walk anywhere in England. Swinburne clings to that belief in sentiment which marks the Victorian era, but Swinburne finds the key to life in unrestraint instead of in restraint.

There is a whole school of limp Grecism in England, which has grown up out of Keats's *Grecian Urn*, and which is now buttressed with philosophy and adorned with scholarship; and no doubt it does bear some sort of relation to Greece and to Greek life. But this Anglican Grecism has the quality which all modern British art exhibits—the very quality which the Greeks could not abide—it is tinged with excess. The Briton likes strong flavors. He likes them in his tea, in his port wine, in his concert-hall songs, in his pictures of home and farm life. He likes something unmistakable, something with a smack that lets you know that the thing has arrived. In his literature he is the same. Dickens, Carlyle, Tennyson lay it on thick with sentiment. Keats drips with aromatic poetry, which has a wonder and a beauty of its own—and whose striking quality is excess. The scented, wholesale sweetness of the modern æsthetic school in England goes home to its admirers because it is easy art. Once enjoy a bit of it and you never forget it. It is always the same, the 'old reliable', the Oxford brand, the true, safe, British, patriotic, moral, noble school of verse; which exhibits the manners and feelings of a gentleman, and has success written in every trait of its physiognomy.

How this school of poetry invaded Greece is part of the history of British expansion in the nineteenth century. In the Victorian era the Englishman brought cricket and morning prayers into South Africa. Robert Browning established himself and his carpet-bag in comfortable lodgings on the Acropolis—which he spells with a K to show his intimate acquaintance with recent research. It must be confessed that Robert Browning's view of Greece never pleased, even in England. It was too obviously R. B. over again. It was Pippa and Bishop Blougram with a few pomegranate seeds and unexpected orthographies thrown in. The Encyclopædia Britannica is against it, and suggests, wittily enough, that one can hardly agree with Browning that Heracles got drunk for the purpose of keeping up other people's spirits.

So, also, Edward FitzGerald was never taken seriously by the English; but this was for another reason. His translations are the best transcriptions from the Greek ever done by this British school; but FitzGerald never took himself seriously. I believe that if he had only been ambitious, and had belonged to the academic classes—like Jowett for instance—he could have got Oxford behind him, and we should all have been obliged to regard him as a great apostle of Hellenism. But he was a poor-spirited sort of man, and never worked up his lead.

Matthew Arnold, on the other hand, began the serious profession of being a Grecian. He took it up when there was nothing in it, and he developed a little sect of his own, out of which later came Swinburne and Gilbert Murray, each of whom is the true British article. While Swinburne is by far the greater poet, Murray is by far the more important of the two from the ethnological point of view. Murray was the first man to talk boldly about God, and to introduce his name into all Greek myths, using it as a fair translation of any Greek adjective. There is a danger in this boldness. The reader's attention becomes hypnotized with wondering in what manner God is to be introduced into the next verse. The reader becomes so concerned about Mr Murray's religious obsessions that he forgets the Greek altogether and remembers only Shakespeare's hostess in her distress over the dying Falstaff: 'Now I, to comfort him, bid him 'a should not think of God—I hoped there was no need to trouble himself with any such thoughts yet.'

Murray and Arnold are twins in ethical endeavor. I think that it was Arnold who first told the British that Greece was noted for melancholy and for longings. He told them that chastity, temperance, nudity, and a wealth of moral rhetoric marked the young man of the Periclean period. Even good old Dean Plumptre has put this young man into his prefaces. Swinburne added the hymeneal note—the poetic nature-view—of which the following may serve as an example:

And the trees in their season brought forth and were kindled anew By the warmth of the mixture of marriage, the child-bearing dew.

There is hardly a page in Swinburne's Hellenizing verse that does not blossom with Hymen. The passages would be well suited for use in the public schools of today where sex-knowledge in its poetic aspects is beginning to be judiciously introduced.

This contribution of Swinburne's—the hymeneal touch—and Murray's discovery that the word God could be introduced with effect anywhere, went like wildfire over England. They are characteristic of the latest phase of Anglo-Grecism.

Gilbert Murray has, in late years, had the field to himself. He stands as the head and front of Greek culture in England. It is he, more than anyone else, who is the figure-head of dramatic poetry in England today; and, as such, his influence must be met, and, as it were, passed through, by the American student who is studying the Greek classics.

II

The Greek genius is so different from the modern English genius that they cannot understand each other. How shall we come to see this clearly? The matter is difficult in the extreme; because we are all soaked in modern feeling, and in America we are all drenched in British influence. The desire of Britain to annex ancient Greece, the deep-felt need that the English writers and poets of the nineteenth century have shown to edge and nudge nearer to Greek feeling, is familiar to all of us. Swinburne expresses his Hellenic longings by his hymeneal strains, Matthew Arnold by sweetness and light, Gilbert Murray by sweetness and pathos—and all through the divine right of Victorian expansion. It has been a profoundly unconscious development in all these men. They have instinctively and innocently attached their little oil-can to the coattails of Euripides and of the other great Attic writers. They have not been interested in Greek for its own sake. They have been interested in the exploitations of Greece for the purpose of British consumption.

Some people will contend that none of the writers of this school are, properly speaking, professional scholars. Others will contend that professional scholarship is tolerable only because it tends to promote cultivation of a non-professional kind. For instance, Jowett was never regarded as a scholar by the darkest-dyed Oxford experts, and Jebb of Cambridge is undoubtedly regarded as an amateur in Germany, because he descends to making translations. The severest classicist is able to talk only about texts. He is too great to do anything else. And yet, properly speaking, these men are all scholars. Murray represents popular scholarship to a degree which would have shocked Matthew Arnold, just as Arnold himself would have been poison to Nauck—Nauck the author of the text of Euripides.

But they are all scholars, and Murray, who is an Australian, and who rose into University prominence on the wings of University Extension, and through his lyric gift rather than through his learning, belongs to Oxford by race and by nature, as well as by adoption. The outsider ought not to confuse him with the whole of Oxford, and the whole of Oxford ought not to disown him after making him the head and front of its Hellenism so far as the world at large can judge. Murray, as St Paul would say, is not the inner Oxford; but Murray is the outer Oxford which the inner Oxford cannot too eagerly sniff at or condemn; because he is no accident, but a true-bred Oxonian of the Imperial epoch.

The tendency of universities has ever been to breed cliques and secret societies, to produce embroideries and start hothouses of specialized feeling. They do well in doing this: it is all they can do. We should look upon them as great furnaces of culture, largely social in their influence, which warm and nourish the general temperament of a nation. Would that in America we had a local school of classic cultivation half as interesting as this Oxford Movement—quaint and non-intellectual as it is! It is alive and it is national. While most absurd from the point of view of universal culture, it is most satisfactory from the domestic point of view—as indeed everything in England is. If in America we ever develop any true universities, they will have faults of their own. Their defects will be of a new strain, no doubt, and will reflect our national shortcomings. These thoughts but teach us that we cannot use other people's eyes or other people's eye-glasses. We have still to grind the lenses through which we shall, in our turn, observe the classics.

III

Ancient religion is of all subjects in the world the most difficult. Every religion, even at the time it was in progress, was always completely misunderstood, and the misconceptions have increased with the ages. They multiply with every monument that is unearthed. If the Eleusinian mysteries were going at full blast today, so that we could attend them, as we do the play at Oberammergau, their interpretation would still present difficulties. Mommsen and Rhode would disagree. But ten thousand years from now, when nothing survives except a line out of St John's Gospel and a tablet stating that Fischer played the part of Christ for three successive decades, many authoritative books will be written about Oberammergau, and reputations will be made over it. Anything which we approach as religion becomes a nightmare of suggestion, and hales us hither and thither with thoughts beyond the reaches of the soul.

The *Alcestis* and the *Bacchantes* are, in this paper, approached with the idea that they are plays. This seems not to have been done often enough with Greek plays. They are regarded as examples of the sublime, as forms of philosophic thought, as moral essays, as poems, even as illustrations of dramatic law, and they are unquestionably all of these things. But they were primarily plays—intended to pass the time and exhilarate the emotions. They came into being as plays, and their form and make-up can best be understood by a study of the dramatic business in them. They become poems and philosophy incidentally, and afterwards:

they were born as plays. A playwright is always an entertainer, and unless his desire to hold his audience overpoweringly predominates, he will never be a success. It is probable that even with Æschylus—who stands hors ligne as the only playwright in history who was really in earnest about morality—we should have to confess that his passion as a dramatic artist came first. He held his audiences by strokes of tremendous dramatic novelty. Both the stage traditions and the plays themselves bear this out. The fact is that it is not easy to keep people sitting in a theatre; and unless the idea of holding their attention predominates with the author, they will walk out, and he will not be able to deliver the rest of his story.

In the grosser forms of dramatic amusement—for example, where a bicycle acrobat is followed by a comic song—we are not compelled to find philosophic depth of idea in the sequence. But in dealing with works of great and refined dramatic genius like The Tempest, or the *Bacchantes*, where the emotions played upon are subtly interwoven, there will always be found certain minds which remain unsatisfied with the work of art itself, but must have it explained. Even Beethoven's Sonatas have been supplied with philosophic addenda—statements of their meaning. We know how much Shakespeare's intentions used to puzzle the Germans. Men feel that somewhere at the back of their own consciousness there is a philosophy or a religion with which the arts have some relation. In so far as these affinities are touched upon in a manner that leaves them mysteries, we have good criticism; but when people dogmatize about them, we have bad criticism. In the meantime the great artist goes his way. His own problems are enough for him.

The early critics were puzzled to classify the Alcestis, and no wonder, for it contains many varieties of dramatic writing. For this very reason it is a good play to take as a sample of Greek spirit and Greek workmanship. It is a little Greek cosmos, and it happens to depict a side of Greek thought which is sympathetic to modern sentiment, so that we seem to be at home in its atmosphere. The *Alcestis* is thought to be in a class by itself. And yet, indeed, under close examination, every Greek play falls into a class by itself (there are only about forty-five of them in all), and the maker of each was probably more concerned at the time with the dramatic experiment upon which he found himself launched than he was with any formal classification which posterity might assign to his play.

In the *Alcestis* Euripides made one of the best plays in the world, full of true pathos, full of jovial humor, both of which sometimes verge upon the burlesque. The happy ending is understood from the start, and none of the grief is painful. Alcestis herself is the good-wife of Greek household myth, who is ready to die for her husband. To this play the bourgeois takes his half-grown family. He rejoices when he hears that it is to be given. The absurdities of the fairy-tale are accepted simply. Heracles has his club, Death his sword, Apollo his lyre. The women wail, Admetus whines; there is buffoonery, there are tears, there is wit, there is conventional wrangling, and that word-chopping so dear to the Mediterranean theatre, which exists in all classic drama and survives in the Punch and Judy show of today. And there is the charming return of Heracles with the veiled lady whom he presents to Admetus as a slave for safe keeping, whom Admetus refuses to receive for conventional reasons, but whom every child in the audience feels to be the real Alcestis, even before Heracles unveils her and gives her back into her husband's bosom with speeches on both sides that are like the closing music of a dream.

The audience disperses at the close, feeling that it has spent a happy hour. No sonata of Mozart is more completely beautiful than the Alcestis. No comedy of Shakespeare approaches it in perfection. The merit of the piece lies, not in any special idea it conveys, but entirely in the manner in which everything is carried out.

IV

It is clear at a glance that the *Alcestis* belongs to an epoch of extreme sophistication. Everything has been thought out and polished; every ornament is a poem. If a character has to give five words of explanation or of prayer, it is done in silver. The tone is all the tone of cultivated society, the appeal is an appeal to the refined, casuistical intelligence. The smile of Voltaire is all through Greek literature; and it was not until the age of Louis XIV, or the Regency, that the modern world was again to know a refinement and a sophistication which recall the Greek work. Now, in one word, this subtlety which pleases us in matters of sentiment is the very thing that separates us from the Greek upon the profoundest questions of philosophy. Where religious or metaphysical truth is touched upon, either Greek sophistication carries us off our feet with a rapture which has no true relation to the subject, or else we are offended by it. We do not understand sophistication. The Greek has pushed aesthetic analysis further than the modern can bear. We follow well enough through the light issues, but when the deeper questions are reached we lose our footing. At this point the modern cries out in applause, 'Religion, philosophy, pure feeling, the soul!' He cries out, 'Mystic cult, Asiatic influence, Nature worship—deep things over there!' Or else he cries, 'What amazing cruelty, what cynicism!' And yet it is none of these things, but only the artistic perfection of the work which is moving us. We are the victims of clever stage-management.

The cruder intelligence is ever compelled to regard the man of complex mind as a priest or as a demon. The child, for instance, asks about the character in a story, 'But is he a good man or a bad man, papa?' The child must have a moral explanation of anything which is beyond his æsthetic comprehension. So also does the modern intelligence question the Greek.

The matter is complicated by yet another element, namely stage convention. Our modern stage is so different from the classic stage that we are bad judges of the Greek playwright's intentions. The quarrels which arise as to allegorical or secondary meanings in a work of art are generally connected with some unfamiliar feature of its setting. A great light is thrown upon any work of art when we show how its form came into being, and thus explain its primary meaning. Such an exposition of the primary or apparent meaning is often sufficient to put all secondary meanings out of court. For instance: It is, as we know, the Germans who have found in Shakespeare a coherent philosophic intention. They think that he wrote plays for the purpose of stating metaphysical truths. The Englishman does not believe this, because the Englishman is familiar with that old English stage work. He knows its traditions, its preoccupation with story-telling, its mundane character, its obliviousness to the sort of thing that Germany has in mind. The Englishman knows the conventions of his own stage, and this protects him from finding mares' nests in Shakespeare. Again, Shakespeare's sonnets used to be a favorite field for mystical exegesis, until Sir Sidney Lee explained their form by reference to the sixteenth-century sonnet literature of the continent. This put to flight many theories.

In other words, the appeal to convention is the first duty of the scholar. But, unfortunately, in regard to the conventions of the Classic Stage, the moderns are all in the dark. Nothing like that stage exists today. We are obliged to make guesses as to its intentions, its humor, its relation to philosophy. If the classics had only possessed a cabinet-sized drama, like our own, we might have been at home there. But this giant-talk, this megaphone-and-buskin method, offers us a problem in dynamics which staggers the imagination. All we can do is to tread lightly and guess without dogmatizing. The typical Athenian, Euripides, was so much deeper-dyed in skepticism than any one since that day, that really no one has ever lived who could cross-question him—let alone expound the meanings of his plays. In reading Euripides, we find ourselves, at moments, ready to classify him as a satirist, and at other moments as a man of feeling. Of course he was both. Sometimes he seems like a religious man, and again, like a charlatan. Of course he was neither. He was a playwright.

V

The *Bacchantes*, like every other Greek play, is the result, first, of the legend, second, of the theatre. There is always some cutting and hacking, due to the difficulty of getting the legend into the building. Legends differ as to their dramatic possibilities, and the incidents which are to be put on the stage must be selected by the poet. The site of the play must be fixed. Above all, a Chorus must be arranged for.

The choosing of a Chorus is indeed one of the main problems of the tragedian. If he can hit on a natural sort of Chorus he is a made man. In the *Alcestis* we saw that the whole background of grief and wailing was one source of the charm of the play. Not only are the tragic parts deepened, but the gayer scenes are set off by this feature. If the fable provides no natural and obvious Chorus, the playwright must bring his Chorus on the stage by stretching the imagination of the audience. He employs a group of servants or of friends of the hero; if the play is a marine piece, he uses sailors. The whole atmosphere of his play depends upon the happiness of his choice.

In the *Agamemnon* 'the old men left-at-home' form the Chorus. There is enough dramatic power in this one idea to carry a play. It is so natural: the old men are on the spot; they are interested; they are the essence of the story, and yet external to it. These old men are, indeed, the archetype of all choruses—a collection of by-standers, a sort of little dummy audience, intended to steer the great, real audience into a comprehension of the play.

The Greek dramatist found this very useful machine, the Chorus, at his elbow; but he was, on the other hand, greatly controlled by it. It had ways of its own: it inherited dramatic necessities. The element of convention and of theatrical usage is so very predominant in the handling of Greek choruses by the poets, that we have in chorus-work something that may be regarded almost as a constant quality. By studying choruses one can arrive at an idea of the craft of Greek play-writing—one can even separate the conventional from the personal to some extent.

The Greek Chorus has no mind of its own; it merely gives echo to the last dramatic thought. It goes forward and back, contradicts itself, sympathizes with all parties or none, and lives in a limbo. Its real function is to represent the slow-minded man in the audience. It does what he does, it interjects questions and doubts, it delays the plot and indulges in the proper emotions during the pauses. These functions are quite limited, and were completely understood in Greek times; so much so, that in the typical stock tragedy of the Æschylean school certain saws, maxims, and reflections appear over and over again. One of them, of course, was, 'See how the will of the gods works out in unexpected ways.' Another, 'Let us be pious, and reverence something that is perhaps behind the gods themselves.' Another, 'This is all very extraordinary: let us hope for the best.' Another, 'Our feelings about right and wrong must somehow be divine; traditional morality, traditional piety, are somehow right.'

Precisely the same reflections are often put in the mouths of the subordinate characters, and for precisely the same purpose. 'Oh, may the quiet life be mine! Give me neither poverty nor riches: for the destinies of the great are ever uncertain.' 'Temptation leads to insolence, and insolence to destruction'; and so forth. Such reflections serve the same purpose, by whomever they are uttered. They underscore the moral of the story and assure the spectator that he has not missed the point.

As religious tragedy broadened into political and romantic tragedy, the Chorus gained a certain freedom in what might be called its interjectional duty—its duty, that is to say, of helping the plot along by proper questions, and so forth. It gained also a Protean freedom in its emotional interpretations during pauses. The playwrights apparently discovered that by the use of music and dancing, the most subtle and delicate, nay, the most whimsical varieties of lyrical mood could be conveyed to great audiences. In spite of this license, however, the old duties of the Chorus as guardians of conservative morality remained unchanged; and the stock phrases of exhortation and warning remained de rigueur in the expectation of the audience. Their meaning had become so well known that, by the time of Æschylus, they were expressed in algebraic terms.

No man could today unravel a Chorus of Æschylus if only one such Chorus existed. The truncated phrases and elliptical thoughts are clear, to us, because we have learned their meaning through reiteration, and because they always mean the same thing. The poet has a license to provide the Chorus with dark sayings—dark in form, but simple in import. It was, indeed, his duty to give these phrases an oracular character. In the course of time such phrases became the terror of the copyists. Obscure passages became corrupt in process of transcription; and thus we have inherited a whole class of choral wisdom which we understand well enough (just as the top gallery understood it well enough) to help us in our enjoyment of the play. The obscurity, and perhaps even some part of what we call 'corruption', are here a part of the stage convention.

Now with regard to the *Bacchantes*—the scheme of having Mænads for a Chorus gave splendid promise of scenic effect; and the fact that, as a logical consequence, these ladies would have to give utterance to the usual maxims of piety, mixed in with the rhapsodies of their professional madness, did not daunt Euripides. He simply makes the Chorus do the usual chorus work, without burdening his mind about character-drawing. Thus the Mænads, at moments when they are not pretending to be Mænads, and are not singing, 'Away to the mountains, O the foot of the stag,' and so on, are obliged to turn the other cheek, and pretend to be interested by-standers—old gaffers, wagging their beards, and quoting the book of Proverbs. The transition from one mood to the other is done in a stroke of lightning, and seems to be independent of the music. That is, it seems to make no difference, so long as the musical schemes are filled out, whether the ladies are singing, 'On with the dance, let joy be unconfined!' or, 'True wisdom differs from sophistry, and consists in avoiding subjects that are beyond mortal comprehension.' All such discrepancies would, no doubt, have been explained if we possessed the music; but the music is lost. It seems, at any rate, certain that the grand public was not expected to understand the word-for-word meaning of choruses; hence their license to be obscure. We get the same impression from the jibes of Aristophanes, whose ridicule of the pompous obscurity of Æschylus makes us suspect that the audiences could not follow the grammar in the lofty parts of the tragedy. They accepted the drum-roll of horror, and understood the larger grammar of tragedy, much as we are now forced to do in reading the plays.

It would seem that by following the technique of tragedy, and by giving no thought to small absurdities, Euripides got a double effect out of his Mænads and no one observed that anything was wrong. In one place he resorts to a dramatic device, which was perhaps well known in his day, namely, the 'conversion' of a bystander. After the First Messenger has given the great description of Dionysus's doings in the mountains, the Chorus, or one of them, with overpowering yet controlled emotion, steps forward and says, 'I tremble to speak free words in the presence of my King; yet nevertheless be it said: Dionysus is no less a god than the greatest of them!' This reference to the duty of a subject is probably copied from a case where the Chorus was made up of local bystanders. In the mouth of a Mænad the proclamation is logically ridiculous; yet so strange are the laws of what 'goes' on the stage that it may have been effective even here.

Some of the choruses in the *Bacchantes* are miracles of poetic beauty, of savage passion, of liquid power. It is hard to say exactly what they are, but they are wonderful. And behind all, there gleams from the whole play a sophistication as deep as the Ægean.

VI

There is one thing that we should never do in dealing with anything Greek. We should not take a scrap of the Greek mind and keep on examining it until we find a familiar thought in it. No bit of Greek art is to be viewed as a thing in itself. It is always a fragment, and gets its value from the whole. Every bit of carved stone picked up in Athens is a piece of architecture; so is every speech in a play, every phrase in a dialogue. You must go back and bring in the whole Theatre or the whole Academy, and put back the fragment in its place by means of ladders, before you can guess at its meaning. The inordinate significance that seems to gleam from every broken toy of Greece, results from this very quality—that the object is a part of something else. Just because the thing has no meaning by itself, it implies so much. Somehow it drags the whole life of the Greek nation before you. The favorite Greek maxim, 'Avoid excess,' does the same. It keeps telling you to remember yesterday and tomorrow; to remember the palæstra and the market-place; above all to remember that the very opposite of what you say is also true. Wherever you are, and whatever doing, you must remember the rest of the Greek world.

It is no wonder that the Greeks could not adopt the standards and contrivances of other nations, while their own standards and contrivances resulted from such refined and perpetual balancing and shaving of values. This refinement has become part of their daily life; and whether one examines a drinking cup or a dialogue or a lyric, and whether the thing be from the age of Homer or from the age of Alexander, the fragment always gives us a glimpse into the same Greek world. The foundation of this world seems to be the Myth; and as the world grew it developed in terms of Myth. The Greek mind had only one background. Athletics and Statuary, Epic and Drama, Religion and Art, Skepticism and Science expressed themselves through the same myths. In this lies the fascination of Greece for us. What a complete cosmos it is! And how different from any other civilization! Modern life, like modern language, is a monstrous amalgam, a conglomeration and mess of idioms from every age and every clime. The classic Greek hangs together like a wreath. It has been developed rapidly, during a few hundred years, and has an inner harmony like the temple. Language and temple—each was an apparition; each is, in its own way, perfect.

Consider wherein Rome differed from Greece. The life of the Romans was a patchwork, like our own. Their religion was formal, their art imported, their literature imitative, their aims were practical, their interests unimaginative. All social needs were controlled by political considerations. This sounds almost like a description of modern life; and it explains why the Romans are so close to us. Cicero, Horace, Cæsar, Antony, are moderns. But Alcibiades, Socrates, Pericles, and the rest take their stand in Greek fable. Like Pisistratus, Solon and Lycurgus, they melt into legend and belong to the realms of the imagination.

No other people ever bore the same relation to their arts that the Greeks bore; and in this lies their charm. When the Alexandrine critics began to classify poetry and to discuss perfection, they never even mentioned the Roman poetry, although all of the greatest of it was in existence. Why is this? It is because no Roman poem is a poem at all from the Greek point of view. It is too individual, too clever, and, generally, too political. Besides, it is not in Greek. The nearest modern equivalent to the development of the whole Greek world of art is to be found in German contrapuntal music. No one except a German has ever written a true sonata or a symphony, in the true polyphonic German style. There are tours de force done by other nationalities; but the natural idiom of this music is Teutonic.

I am not condemning the Latins, or the moderns. Indeed, there is in Horace something nobler and more humane than in all Olympus. The Greeks, moreover, seem in their civic incompetence like children, when contrasted with the Romans or with the moderns. But in power of utterance, within their own crafts, the Greeks are unapproachable. Let us now speak of matters of which we know very little.

The statues on the Parthenon stand in a region where direct criticism cannot reach them, but which trigonometry may, to some extent, determine. Their beauty probably results from an artistic knowledge so refined, a sophistication so exact, that, as we gaze, we lose the process and see only results. A Greek architect could have told you just what lines of analysis must be followed in order to get these effects in grouping and in relief. It is all, no doubt, built up out of tonic and dominant—but the manual of counter-point has been lost. As the tragic poet fills the stage with the legend, so the sculptor fills the metope with the legend. Both are closely following artistic usage: each is merely telling the old story with new refinement. And whether we gaze at the actors on the stage or at the figures in the metope, whether we study a lyric or listen to a dialogue, we are in communion with the same genius, the same legend. The thing which moves and delights us is a unity.

This Genius is not hard to understand. Anyone can understand it. That is the proof of its greatness. As Boccaccio said of Dante, not learning but good wits are needed to appreciate him. One cannot safely look toward the mind of the modern scholar for an understanding of the Greek mind, because the modern scholar is a specialist—a thing the Greek abhors. If a scholar today knows the acoustics of the Greek stage, that is thought to be a large enough province for him. He is not allowed to be an authority on the scenery. In the modern scholar's mind everything is in cubby-holes; and everybody today wants to become an authority. Every one, moreover, is very serious today; and it does not do to be too serious about Greek things, because the very genius of Greece has in it a touch of irony, which combines with our seriousness to make a heavy, indigestible paste. The Greek will always laugh at you if he can, and the only hope is to keep him at arm's length, and deal with him in the spirit of social life, of the world, of the beau monde, and of large conversation. His chief merit is to stimulate this spirit. The less we dogmatize about his works and ways, the freer will the world be of secondary, second-rate commentaries. The more we study his works and ways, the fuller will the world become of intellectual force.

The Greek classics are a great help in tearing open those strong envelopes in which the cultivation of the world is constantly getting glued up. They helped Europe to cut free from theocratic tyranny in the late Middle Ages. They held the Western world together after the fall of the Papacy. They gave us modern literature: indeed, if one considers all that comes from Greece, one can hardly imagine what the world would have been like without her. The lamps of Greek thought are still burning in marble and in letters. The complete little microcosm of that Greek society hangs forever in the great macrocosm of the moving world, and sheds rays which dissolve prejudice, making men thoughtful, rational, and gay. The greatest intellects are ever the most powerfully affected by it; but no one escapes. Nor can the world ever lose this benign influence, which must, so far as philosophy can imagine, qualify human life forever.

IN PRAISE OF OLD LADIES

LUCY MARTIN DONNELLY

It is everywhere the custom, in life, in literature, to celebrate the young girl; to praise her pink cheeks, her shining hair, her innocence, her gayeties—her muslins, even, and blue ribbons. She has become in these latter days a proverb, a type—la jeune fille. Yet, to the discreet observer how gaudy is her charm, how showy and unsubstantial, and of the day only, when matched with graces like those of the truly incomparable old lady! It is an antique convention that hurries off old age with decrepitude and care and quavering palsy. And it may be that the old gentleman is unamiable; that, his days of strenuousness fairly over, he becomes crabbed, a lover of snuff, and unpoetical. But the old lady is a creature of another quality. The refinements of age only enhance the femininity of her charm; to her, whimsicalities, delicate occupations, the fine lines that etch themselves expressively across her brow and about her mouth, are all vastly becoming. With what ineffable grace, moreover, she pronounces certain words in the elegant fashion of an age ago! How softly the old Indian shawls she wears fall about her shoulders! What strange, unlikely stories she tells of the beginning of the century!

I am indeed no novice to her charms. I have been victim to the enchantments of a long line of old ladies from my earliest years upward. When my frocks were still short and I still suffered under the ignominy of pinafores, I remember very well following a friend of my grandmother's about, and fetching big books for her. She was an exceedingly learned old lady, I take it; indeed, my grandmother always spoke of her as strong-minded, wherefore I am sometimes led to doubt whether she would so unreservedly have pleased my maturer taste. But in those early days my devotion impelled me even to the point of learning the alphabets of the curious languages she read. What constituted her peculiar, her romantic charm, however, was the fact that she had traveled in many far-away countries. I always understood it was their strange suns that had turned her skin the yellow color of old parchment, and stopped the whitening of her hair at a grizzly gray. This particular ugly gray I admired along with the rest: it suggested worldly sophistication and a cosmopolitan experience, as did no less her deep voice and blue-veined hands, and her habit of taking a vigorous walk in the morning, before breakfast. Her daughter, she told me, was named Aurore. How I wished that I myself had been favored with such a name!

My grandmother was very different—much prettier and gentler, no doubt; but her daughters bore such stiff, old-fashioned names as Anne and Emeline, and she herself had seldom left New England, and took only a short walk in the sun at noonday, under a tiny black silk parasol. At other times she sat beside her worktable, which had legs of twisted mahogany, and a crimson silk bag hanging down from the middle in a way I never understood. Out of this she occasionally brought scraps of faded old brocades—pink and green they would be, with a rare yellow, or a blue still a little gay; and now and then, when the winter evenings until my bedtime were long, she even found bright-colored beads in a small drawer at the side. Although she had been 'a proficient' in music as a girl, I think she knew no language save English. Emerson she read chiefly; the prayers of Theodore Parker; black volumes of sermons by William Ellery Channing; and sometimes, to me, in a very soft voice, Whittier's poems. In the late afternoons she was accustomed to play at solitaire, letting me sit at a corner of the table to look on. Not infrequently, when excited by the odds against which we were fighting, I forgot to hold up my head, and my long brown curls, falling down among the cards, threw them into disarray, and obliged me to sit at a penitential distance. My grandmother did not choose to be interrupted. But all the games in turn she invariably won by a deft rearrangement of the cards when she saw them going wrong. 'With one's self, you know, my dear,' she would say, judiciously distributing diamonds among the spades—'with one's self it is quite understood.'

Since the days of my grandmother and her friends I have known a hundred other old ladies, if none more charming. There are, I dare say, persons who, in going about the world, meet people of other sorts: actors, perhaps, or ladies of fashion, or diplomatists—first of all, I fancy, to be desired—or spiritualists, or musicians. Personally, I never fall in with anyone except old ladies. In a railway train, for example, I am sure to find myself opposite or beside one, and of late years they have generally had birds with them.

The first I remember—with a bird, that is—was in a German railway carriage going from Berlin to Hanover. At least, my destination was Hanover; the old lady herself was on her way home to Düsseldorf. She had been visiting her nephews and nieces in Berlin; she had a great many of them, she told me. From her fingers, covered with old pearl and diamond rings, I gathered that she was very rich; and from the bouquets of many colors, ranged in the luggage-rack above her head, that the nephews and nieces were trying to persuade her to leave them her fortune. She wore, nevertheless, an air of extreme detachment, holding her long netted silk purse—through whose meshes the Prussian gold gleamed—tightly clasped between two fat fingers. Altogether she was a very portly and regal-looking person, and gave you the impression of being dressed in black velvet, though in point of fact I do not think that she was. But her mantle was fringed heavily several times about, and her hat—for she wore a hat with a brim that dropped slightly, discreetly, all around—was also bordered by a black fringe that just cleared her faded eyebrows and her black beady eyes. She had a gouty foot, too—she was quite complete—that rested on a little folding stool she had brought with her; and she rang imperiously for the guard. When he came she ordered coffee, bullying the cream-faced Teuton into bringing a double portion of sugar to feed her bird, a little green creature, disposed among the flowers above her head. It was with a good deal of difficulty that she struggled up to reach him, but to have him handed down would, she said, excite him unnecessarily. 'Mein Männchen, mein Männchen,' she murmured in a deep, tender tone, as she fed him each successive crumb. After feasting the bird she turned her attention to me, and asking to see the book that I was absorbed in, she kept it until we arrived at Hanover. I had evidently read too much in trains, she remarked, alluding to my eye-glasses. Americans, she knew, were very foolish. Then she asked me the price of everything in the States, and of my traveling bag in particular, and quarreled with me as to the number of marks in a dollar. 'You'll find that I am right,' she assured me, as I was squeezing myself and the brown leather bag she admired out of the narrow door of the German coupé. 'You'll find there are six marks in every dollar. Auf wiedersehen, Fräulein.'

The last of my old ladies with birds I met only a month or two ago, on the way from London down to Southsea—the one place in all the world, I suppose, whither a thin spinster, accompanied by a ragged-tailed bird named Tip, should be traveling. She was, of course, very different from the German dowager; not so far on in years, and, as I indicated, exaggeratedly thin; shy, furthermore, and dressed in a worn black-silk gown, with a lace collar at her throat drawn together by a hair brooch. And she spoke only from time to time, to inquire if we must change carriages at Woking; meanwhile looking a little greedily from Tip to the seedcakes in the hands of three English schoolgirls, who, with shortish frocks and longish hair hanging over their shoulders, sat in a row on my side of the carriage, and scattered crumbs enough to have fattened a family of partridges.

Old ladies at sea, though there without the embellishments of flowers and birds, I have found no less attractive than on land. I fell in with a party of them in the early summer, on their way to Carlsbad to drink the waters; with the exception, that is, of two or three whose destination was Kissingen, and who disbelieved altogether, I learned when we were a few days out from New York, in the rheumatism of the Carlsbad-bound ladies. Carlsbad, they assured me—punctuating their remarks with sniffs of their smelling-bottles as I tucked cushions behind their poor backs—Carlsbad was all fine clothes and frivolity and band music (than which surely nothing has a more wicked sound), and was by no means the place a person really ill would dream of retiring to for her health's sake.

But it matters very little whether I travel in trains or in ships, or whether I rest quietly at home, my companions are rarely of my own age. If I am asked out to luncheon to meet the wife of a melancholy doubtful poet who died young, and on my way to the house in question dwell, not unnaturally, on her youthful tragic grief, on my arrival I find myself confronted by a fat, kindly old lady, crowned with a large black-beaded bonnet that shows a bunch of purple flowers above either ear. If I go to visit some beautiful house secluded in the country, it is an old lady who stands on the threshold. I remember such a mansion, built in Tudor times, and topped with chimneys calculated to make you sigh your soul away in longing; it had once been the dower house of an English queen, and in front of it two peacocks paraded proudly all day long. Others, I knew, went to admire it, and were entertained by the granddaughter, or at least by the middle-aged daughter, of its mistress. Not so on the sunny morning of my visit. Lady W—— herself was working among the flowers in her garden, and herself showed me back to the cascade and the tulip tree, stepping over the lawn with the spirit of a girl, and apologizing with a girl's vanity, too, for her garden hat and gloves.

She was the very flower and mirror of all the old ladies I have ever known; conscious, if you will, of her charm, and all the more charming for that. She led me into the drawing room—she knew she held my heart in her hand—to see her portrait, which, though painted by a celebrated artist, made her look very like any other old lady in velvet and a bonnet and furs. Her great gayety, her beautiful eyes, the sweet curving lines about her mouth, were all forgotten. 'I don't know,' she said to me a little stiffly, as she paused before it, and for a moment glanced across to her maternal grandmother done by Reynolds, with pink cheeks, and with a pink rose in her hand instead of a muff, 'I don't know, my dear, whether it is like or not, but certainly it is a very odd picture.'

More delightful though each one be than the last, it is but reasonable that the wealth of my experience among old ladies should have led me to certain discriminations. Old ladies, I am prepared to say, divide themselves into two classes: the thin, namely, and the fat. Nor is this discrimination so artificial as it may appear. Another equally expressive, equally conclusive, could not be made. And of the two—but this is a matter of prejudice—I prefer the thin, as having commonly more wit, more liveliness, brighter eyes, and a taste for anecdote generally wanting, I think it only right to say, in the fatter, kindlier class. My point of view is possibly ultra-modern, but what will you? La grande dame, so called, vanished with the days and ideals of Louis XIV. At the end of two centuries or so she is rarely to be met with. I have known her only once in all her traditional fairness, but then she was of the essence of perfection. She gave one the impression of having never for a moment been out of the great world; of having lived, though in New York, perpetually with princes—'les princes du sang, les princes étrangers, les grands-seigneurs façon de princes'. But what is my ungraceful pen that it should hazard a description of her, or attempt the splendor of her white hair and her white hands! Her graciousness, her elegance, her worldliness, are not to be compassed by a sentence.

Among modern old ladies, of whom I speak somewhat less diffidently, I affect the more frivolous sort. My own feeling is, very strictly, that in old age the world of affairs should be left behind, and one's hours passed pleasantly among pleasant things. Age should be impulsive, light-hearted—brilliant, if you will; it should fill its days with flowers and music and embroidery; it should drive in low carriages behind plump ponies; it should write a pretty, pointed, epistolary hand, and read nothing heavier than memoirs. Intellectuality may be all very well in youth, but in an old lady anything beyond a delicate pedantry is unlovely. I like old ladies with decided opinions, with a gift for repartee and some skill in the passions. Curiosities, strange modesties—I knew of an old lady who brought her grandsons up never to look into a butcher's shop, deeming it indecorous, even indecent—fantastic economies, eccentricities of various sorts, are delightful. And of all these things the insipidity and jejuneness of youth perforce know nothing. The very pattern of young girls is bound by a strait-lacing conventionality. Formalities, anxieties, uncertainties, sit upon her sleeve. She has no alternative, innocent creature, save to order her days and lay her plans in behalf of a charming old ladyhood.

A MEMORY OF OLD GENTLEMEN

SHARLOT M. HALL

I have always shared the preference of the poet Swinburne for very old people and very little children, and, as it has happened, nearly all of my old people have been of that sex to which Shakespeare refers as coming eventually to the 'lean and slippered pantaloon'.

It began when I was a particularly roly-poly little girl of four, with brown braids carried through the back of my sunbonnet and tied fast in its strings, that the unwelcome shadow of that blue gingham might never be absent.

In compensation, I suppose, there was an equally roly-poly old gentleman who used to toss me up in the long swing under the big oak trees, singing in rhythm to my swaying self the chorus of a then popular song:

Swinging in the lane; swinging in the lane; Sweetest girl I ever met was swinging in the lane.

The great, bending branches spread a canopy befitting a Druid temple, and the new little leaves, like crumpled bronze velvet, brushed my face as I held fast to the ropes, all a-tremble with the spirit of adventure and a little fear that the earth was so very far away, and was tossed up till I could peep into the nest out of which my pet blue jay had tumbled a week before. One of his brothers sat, a disconsolate fluff of faded blue feathers, on the edge of the nest, and the parent birds squalled noisy protest at the sturdy, red-stockinged legs invading their domestic privacy.

The oaks and the swing and the old gentleman were the first milestones on my way to Grown-Up Land. When my round fat arm had no longer to reach straight up to clasp my pudgy fingers around the thumb of my friend; when after many trials I caught the ropes and lifted myself without help to the wide board swing-seat; then I was truly 'big', and trotted off to demand that a new mark should take the place of the one that had lately shown my height on the smooth gray trunk of my favorite tree. Smooth, for those wonderful oaks, centuries old, and each many feet in girth, had been repeatedly stripped of their bark as high as a man could reach; and now, as if tired of renewing the ever stolen coat, contented themselves with a thin, scarlike covering. Since their sapling days, perhaps, slender, conical tepees of buffalo skins had nestled in their shade, and number-less brown babies had swung 'Rock-a-bye baby in a tree-top' from their limbs.

There was a broad hearth of stones between the spreading roots of one where buffalo steaks had been broiled, and where other children had roasted the plump ripe acorns as I was fond of doing.

The buffalo robes for the tepees and deerskins for the gayly wrought moccasins had been tanned with the bark stripped from those very trees under which I played and swung. In the little grove behind my beloved trees, and bordered by the tiny creek where I waded and fished with a bent pin for small flat sunfish as bright as living sunbeams, were bare poles still standing in a circle, lashed together at their tops with strips of bark or thongs of raw-hide.

There were wild cherries in the grove, good in blossom and better in fruit, puckery-sweet wild plums, and a great black-walnut tree dear to myself and the squirrels; and here the spirit of adventure thrilled me again, for my fancy saw dusky faces behind every bush, and the feathery cherry blossoms were always nodding eagle feathers on the head of the warrior just waiting to seize me.

A good deal of this was due to my old friend who had just come from the East, a far-away, mysterious Somewhere to me, and who, I am inclined to think, secretly shared my dread of these brown people in whose home we were interlopers. But some of it came from the tales to which I listened after I was tucked away in my trundle-bed on winter nights, and the men gathered around the fire to talk of Indian raids and hunting and trapping adventures.

Not a few of my old gentlemen at this time were gray-bearded scouts and hunters, with great caps of fur and long rifles that seemed to tower above my head as far as the oaks. Children were rare novelties to those men of the plains, and I was passed from shoulder to shoulder, delighted with tales of bear and buffalo, and fingering with awed hands the beaded shot-pouches and belts of embroidered buckskin, but feeling all the while almost as far above earth as when I swung over the blue jay's nest. Then we moved away, and my next old gentleman was the very antithesis of the first. Small and thin and morose, with a bitterness that almost hid the sadness in his face. A misanthrope, a miser, an atheist, said his neighbors; but, in truth, only a man over whom hung the shadow of a tragedy that had darkened his life. Sometimes for days his mind 'traveled a crooked road', as he said, and then he would wander alone in the hills, or shut himself up with his books; and no smoke came out of the chimney, and no answer was given to curious people who knocked at the door. Most children feared him, but I did not; that and my love of books made the bond between us. He lent me quaint old histories and philosophies, full of big words that sounded very fine as he rolled them off in a sonorous voice. I learned to know Swedenborg from Kant, and Kant from Comte, and was in a fair way to become a philosopher myself when again we moved—so far that we both knew the parting was final.

With fingers still pudgy I crocheted him a pair of marvelous green 'wristers' as a farewell gift, and he brought me a thick red volume, De Foe's *History of the Devil*, with pictures that made my brown braids rise up visibly every time I looked at them, and a single German silver teaspoon, which he said was to form the nucleus of my wedding silver.

Years later some book thief of abnormal tastes robbed me of the treasured De Foe, but the spoon still reposes in solitary state, untroubled by additions, and most unlikely ever to serve the end for which my old friend designed it.

My last word of him was in an ill-scrawled, childish letter from a schoolmate: 'Mr Cushion is dead; the doctor gave him some medicine and he died.' I was old enough to have a certain gladness mingle with my regret. The shadow was lifted; there were no more crooked roads to travel; my old friend was at rest.

It was my next old gentleman who introduced me to Shakespeare and the 'lean and slippered pantaloon'. A wicked sense of the appropriateness of the quotation flashed into my mind as he read it; I wondered, in fact, if the Bard of Avon had been shuffling around in dressing-gown and carpet slippers when it was written. Yet this untidy old man, who loved Shakespeare, reveled in Shelley, and wrote heroic verse and Greek dramas by the sackful, had, they told me, been a brilliant soldier, the pick and pride of his regiment, the model in dress and deportment of all the fresh recruits. Surely the irony of fate is something more than rhetoric.

If he wrote in lighter vein, he had lived in tragedy; between The Skylark and Under the Greenwood Tree we had glimpses of bloody battlefield, of disease-reeking, famine-scourged Southern prisons, of narrow escapes, and men hunted like wild beasts.

Very proud was my old friend when my own blundering thoughts first shaped themselves in verse; I doubt if Hamlet on his first appearance received such an ovation. And then one night the sacks of manuscript were packed, the little trunk strapped, and the daylight train bore away, we never knew whither, one who left word to no one, but three books—the battered Shakespeare, Shelley minus his cover, and a first edition of Whittier—to a little girl.

No word has come out of the silence, but when I am making air castles I like to think that some summer night I shall visit the Parthenon and find my old friend writing Greek dramas in the moonlight.

After that my old gentlemen began to come in pairs and trios, so that they seldom threw such a clearly focused memory. The one whom I loved best was not really the best known; we were both too shy to realize in time how much we might have been to each other. He was a gentle, quiet, courtly man; I remember that I always involuntarily looked for the pages holding up my court train of velvet and ermine when he bowed to me: a scholarly man, whom one would have taken for some gifted professor or polished diplomat: and he was in fact an Indian scout, known the length of the West for his courage and fidelity and unshakable honor. He would have stood with his life to a promise given the blackest renegade that ever harried his trail.

I knew in a vague way that his was a name in history; but we were always too busy with Sir Edwin Arnold and the Vedas and Mahatmas to talk of that. I can see him now throwing back the silver hair from a face as fine as some old marble Jove, and repeating the Sanskrit tales or the lines he loved best:

'Such as thou shalt see not self-subduing do no deed of good, In youth or age, in household or in wood: It needs not man should pass by th' Orders Four To come to Virtue; doing right is more Than to be twice born: therefore wise men say Easy and excellent is Virtue's way.'

Fit words for him who subdued himself with such gentle patience to years of blindness; never saying 'Is the sun shining?' but 'How beautiful the hills are in the sunshine!' It was always daylight in his soul, till he slept at last in the sunniest corner of his beloved hills.

There are many dear old gentlemen still; indeed, now that I think of it, I have known but one young man at all intimately, and him I have not met face to face. Homer and Odysseus have been such satisfying friends to me that I have not missed Paris and Adonis. The flavor of old wine has been too long on my lips for me to change now, and I shall be well content to have it said of me at last: 'Here lieth one who had the friendship of old men and little children's love.'

VIOLA'S LOVERS: A STUDY IN THE NEW MORALITY

RICHARD BOWLAND KIMBALL

I sometimes think that our relations with our children, or our pets, are successful because we expect nothing in return. Yet, after all, the relations are reciprocal; and I have been thinking today of some of the things I have got from an old dog who has been in our family for years and years. I have learned several spiritual truths from her, and I have learned them more thoroughly, perhaps, because she never had the slightest idea that she was teaching me anything. Dogs, of course, show various characteristics—some are snobs, others take naturally to a low life, others again are aristocratic and reticent and self-controlled; but I have never known a dog yet that you could describe as exactly a moralist.

Viola came to us out of the primeval woods with an effect of apparitional beauty. Rather a poetic name for a dog, perhaps; but there was such a union of grace and timidity, such a charm of silken draperies and russet ruff and tail almost sweeping the ground, that we were irresistibly reminded of a Viola we had seen recently. It was as if the dog said mutely, 'What should I do in Illyria?'

She had evidently been through a terrible experience. A broken rope was around her neck; she was as gaunt as a wolf; her eyes were almost iridescent with terror, like the wonderful eyes of some hysteriacs.

Imprison her soft hand and let her rave, And feed deep, deep upon her peerless eyes!

We did not adopt Viola; she adopted us. She followed us to the tent where we were spending the summer, and there she stayed with us, to remain on guard when we were away, to welcome us on our return with such a show of abject gratitude. I think a male dog could not have shown such a union of love and fear; her spirit had evidently been broken; it became our task to lure her confidence back again—and here began my own education. If I spoke with—well, decision to my wife, poor Viola slunk to the ground. She thought the tone was meant for her. I would never claim to be a model husband, but I did learn from Viola, theoretically at least, that one can have good manners even in the privacy of the family circle.

More rapidly than we could have expected Viola's terrors left her, and she resumed the normal canine outlook on life-like humans I have known who have managed to counteract the false starts of their early childhood—obsessions regarding dark closets, snakes, or an avenging Deity.

I am not going to dwell on the intelligence Viola manifested after she had freed herself from fear. All dogs are wonderful, even when they are not intelligent. The most stupid dog I know mopes around the house and refuses to eat whenever his master is away, thus evincing an emotional sensibility more valuable than the smartness of the most Frenchified of poodles that ever trod the vaudeville stage. Unlike a collie of my acquaintance, Viola did not keep the woodbox replenished; nor had she a vocabulary of several hundred words, like another collie that I know. Still, she had an aptitude to learn spelling. When it was inadvisable to take her out for a walk, we spelled the words, vainly trying to conceal the fact from her, as we would from a child; and often, to this day, people stop me on the road, and ask if I am the owner of the dog that knows how to spell.

What I want to dwell on is my own education rather than Viola's, and this began in earnest after we had moved to the real country, and lived in a little farmhouse without any farm. Viola was a lovely ornament to the dooryard; but it seemed a pity that there were no flocks or herds to evoke her ministering care. We didn't even keep chickens; we were ostensibly in the country to cultivate thoughts—such as they were—and while Viola might be said to inspire thoughts, they hardly gave her the necessary exercise. A collie should have a run of ten miles every day, and it was pathetic to see Viola lying in the doorway, ears erect, eyes eager, watching, waiting, hoping for something to happen. I should not be surprised if her very eagerness attracted the thing she longed for.

Our next-door neighbor, a man fully as fond of dogs as myself, was early attracted to her. He had recently lost his own dog, and asked if he might borrow Viola to help him catch his chickens, and if she might accompany him on the long drive he took every day through the countryside. With perfect good will, and in utter innocence, I consented. Little did I dream, as they say in the novels, of what lay before me.

I had an idea that Viola would understand that she was merely loaned for these expeditions; that she would come back from them with undiminished loyalty, grateful to me for having given her a chance for exercise. But our friendly neighbor had a very taking way with dogs. Aside from the wonderful trips, which were enough to turn the head of any collie, he knew how to talk dog-language better than I did. He knew how to pinch a dog's ear in the most seductive manner. With him, doggishness was both an art and a science.

There was nothing lovelier than the sight of Viola rounding up the chickens, shepherding them into their houses, holding down a recalcitrant pullet with her paw, or bringing in her mouth a dowager hen to her foster-father. If I had the gift of a sculptor and wished to carve a personification of pride, I think I should depict Viola bringing in a chicken—her tail aloft, like a plume of triumph, her eyes shining, stepping over imaginary obstacles like a high-manège horse with an air of dignity that was really ludicrous. If an unlucky chicken got away from her, away she went across meadows, and over walls, her beautiful voice vibrating through the landscape, sometimes breaking to an octave higher in her excitement.

It was fun to see her scour ahead of the wagon when her new

master took her out to help him pick up eggs. It was charming to see her come home sitting on the seat beside him, tired but still eager, looking to right and left, sniffing the air, learning all sorts of smell secrets which are closed forever to our supposedly superior human consciousness. Is it any wonder that it was necessary for me to go next door to get her, and that she followed me along the path with a certain droopy air that was hardly flattering?

There is not much in the literary life that would interest an outdoor dog. I felt somewhat like a dry-as-dust professor married to a young and attractive wife who is being taken to all the routs and parties throughout the neighborhood by a disgustingly youthful and handsome cavalier. I know nothing quite so shriveling to the soul as jealousy, nor anything so hard to fight against. I reasoned that Viola's expeditions were doing her good, that I ought to be grateful for them, and I repeated the antediluvian fallacy that my jealousy was only indicative of my love. Nothing that I could say to myself made any difference; and if I were in danger of forgetting how I felt, there were plenty of other persons to remind me.

'Well,' said the fisherman, 'I guess you don't know whether that dog is yours or Lysander's!' And my most intimate friend remarked genially, 'If I had a dog, I'd want it to be my dog, or I wouldn't want to have any.'

It was bad enough to bear the sympathy of the community; it was worse to witness the triumph of my rival. Often, after I had brought home the drooping Viola, Lysander would follow after her. Instantly she revived like flowers in water. She smiled, she was even coquettish. They began a lengthy conversation I could not understand—little sounds from him, little grunts from her. If, by any chance, through a belated sense of duty, she happened to remain beside my chair, he surreptitiously snapped his fingers and made little sucking sounds that he fancied were inaudible, and then she sidled over to his chair.

If jealously is an index of one's love, it is strange that, the more jealous I became of Lysander, the less I loved Viola. 'Well, let her stay with him,' I said to myself. 'I guess he won't object to having me pay for the license.'

She did stay; she sometimes stayed all night; and few things in my life have been more humiliating than my visits to get her. Lysander was glad to see me—oh my, yes! He welcomed me with a crooked sardonic smile that I understood thoroughly. Viola knew just as well as he did why I had come, and pretended to take an interest in the wallpaper. As we walked home along the path, I scolded her, and she slunk to the ground and asked my pardon. Was there anything in her life that could make her conscious of any evil? Of course not. Without realizing it, I was exercising a sort of spiritual coercion over her. I was really condemning her for what was a true expression of collie life; but she accepted my suggestion of evil. I have often wondered since, how many persons in the human realm are suffering from a sense of sin as false as hers was. Of course, I did not philosophize the situation at the time. I simply felt disquietude when I was with her. This disquietude increased rapidly until I apparently disliked her; and I suppose that in my feeling for her there was actually an element of hate.

'Very well,' I said to myself in effect, 'there are better dogs in the world than ever were licensed. The next one I get, I'll keep for my very own.'

I had now reached my low spot—a centre of indifference; and if this were fiction, the reader might expect an ever-increasing objective crescendo from this point onward, culminating in a stirring climax. Possibly Viola would rescue me from a burning building, thus showing that she really loved me, after all. Unfortunately I am dealing with facts of a rather intangible nature. I have noticed that in life coffee and pistols for two are not called for so often as in literature. We pass the time of day with an acquaintance, discuss the play, and what not, little dreaming that behind that smiling exterior a spiritual crisis may be taking place.

My crisis was rather interesting because it seemed almost physical. Not so much in the subconscious brain ganglia as in the sympathetic nerve-centres, the process was taking place—the reverse process of what had taken place during my period of jealousy. I could almost hear a spiritual clicking going on inside me, as if I were composed of children's blocks which had become disarranged and were being replaced in a symmetrical pattern. One by one, the filaments of possession were being broken—that sense which in its grossest terms is really a sort of fatuous pride. Say what we will, most of us feel that we deserve praise and tribute for having selected so attractive a wife, for having begotten such charming children. Having no longer any more of a proprietary interest in Viola than I had in the wild flowers, or the sea, or sky, I got a fresh eye on her. I could not help admiring her, and I could not help admiring her for herself alone. Having no longer any taint of possession, it was impossible for me to impose my will on her, so I adopted unconsciously the courtesy one shows to someone else's wife.

'Well, Viola,' I would say, 'do you want to come home tonight? You don't have to.'

She would look up and listen, cock her ears, consider the matter. Sometimes she would decide to stay with Lysander, and sometimes, strangely enough, she would decide to go home with me. If she came, she came happily, because she was exercising the prerogative of an independent creature. Her sense of sin or shame left her; and somehow we were all gainers, Lysander, Viola, and myself. He no longer snapped his fingers or made little sucking noises. These had been psychical reactions from my jealous emanations when we were struggling for Viola's favor; but we were now united in doing what we could to make her happy; and our friendship, which had suffered previously, in this new office became confirmed. What expansive talks we had about her! How he rushed over to tell me the latest example of her wisdom or affection; and when one expects nothing from a dog, it is rather pleasant to feel suddenly, while struggling with a sentence, a damp delightful nose inside your hand.

Sometimes I fancy that Viola, in forming her friendship for Lysander, had a prevision; for the time came when we had to leave her, and in whose hands could it be better to leave her than Lysander's and his wife's?

Most dog stories end with the death of the dog, but I can assure the reader that Viola is still very much alive. Not agile any longer, she has become a privileged parlor guest, for the stairs are too much for her. Sometimes she even finds it impossible to bury a bone, and then she goes through the pantomime of burying it. She knows that we know that she has not really done it. Her assumption of achievement is ludicrous. Who says dogs have not a sense of humor?

She is beautiful as old ladies are beautiful. If she wore a lace stomacher, she would make a magnificent Rembrandt—rich browns, tawny gold, and, in the heart of the picture, the spirit of her personality as mellow and pervasive as a flame.

I don't see Viola often nowadays, but what I gained by renouncing a purely personal interest in her has extended itself somehow beyond what we know as the realm of time and space. This sounds rather esoteric, but what I mean is that I am very happy whenever I think of her, whether I am with her or not. I feel very near her though we are separated by a hundred miles; and I should not be surprised if, in the muffled 'Woof! Woof!' of her dreams, she often lives again what I happen to be thinking of at the moment—wonderful runs with Teddy, the cocker spaniel, or the homeric combat with the woodchuck beside Simon Brook.

As I sit thinking of Viola, there happens to come into my mind, by one of those odd associations that have so little logic in them, an apparently trivial incident that took place a day or so ago. A couple of little girls stopped me on Arlington Street, Boston, and asked the way to Marlboro Street. It chanced that I was going to Marlboro Street myself, and I offered to conduct them there, but they were walking in the leisurely way of children, taking in everything on the way, and I soon outstripped them. At the corner of Marlboro Street, however, I turned and waved to them to indicate that this was the street they wanted, and they waved back to show that they understood.

That was apparently the end of the incident; but two or three blocks up Marlboro Street, something impelled me to turn. The children had found the street, they were following safely, they were evidently watching me; for as soon as I turned, they waved again. As I went up the steps of the house where I had an appointment, I looked back for the third time. The children, now become almost fairy-like figures, were still watching me. Up went their hands and up went mine, and across the long length of city street, we waved in greeting and farewell.

I do not know why the incident should have seemed to contain an element of real beauty. I was reminded of George E. Woodberry's poem in which a somewhat similar incident is celebrated. A boy, you remember, while playing, ran heedlessly into the poet, and the poem ends:

> It was only the clinging touch
> Of a child in a city street;
> It hath made the whole day sweet.

What struck me even more than the beauty of my adventure was the quality of permanence that it seemed to wear. In my under-consciousness, there was something immortal about it. Can it be possible that our casual relations, where love is—our relations with children, or with strangers whom we shall never see again, or with the lower animals whose span of life is necessarily very limited—can it be possible that these relations are less ephemeral than we think? Would it be too much to hope that the relation between Viola and myself is a small but permanent addition to the store of worth-while things?

HAUNTED LIVES

LAURA SPENCER PORTOR

I

It is my increasing belief, to which the careful observation and study of years give strength, that all lives may be said to be haunted in greater or less degree by certain recurrent thoughts or influences or impressions or realizations, which, visiting and revisiting the chambers of the mind, probably from earliest years, come at last to dwell persistently with us, returning again and again like the French ghostly revenants, making free to haunt those long-closed rooms of the memory where once, it may be, they moved in the full daylight of consciousness and realization, as delights or dreads, joys or terrors of the soul.

'Two ideas,' says Pater, in writing of Leonardo, 'were especially fixed in him, as reflexes of things that touched his brain in childhood beyond the measure of other impressions—the smiling of women, and the motion of great waters.' And later on, 'He became above all a painter of portraits; faces of a modeling more skillful than has been seen before or since, embodied with a reality which almost amounts to illusion on dark air. To take a character as it was, and delicately sound its stops, suited one so curious in observation, curious in invention.'

So we seem to see Leonardo possessed always by the interest and beauty and meaning of faces, fascinated by the individuality, the infinite variety, the delicately interpretative meanings of them; reminiscent of the charm of them; visited by a hundred recurrent lovelinesses of them; preoccupied by their mystery; and above all, it seems, haunted and summoned by the lovely and enigmatic smiling of women.

To recognize this is to know much of Leonardo and his work;

and even if we read no more of Pater's memorable essay, he has succeeded in these three sentences in bringing before us some impression of the essential man which is not readily forgotten, and has admitted us as it were to a partial knowledge of that great and diverse mind.

But all this is rare, very rare in biography. We write biography, for the most part, as we write history—with a leaning toward dates and successions of events.

M. Taine in the introduction to his *History of English Literature* makes a strong protest, it will be remembered, against this method of writing history. He cites Carlyle's *Cromwell* and Sainte-Beuve's *Port Royal* as examples of the opposite and more modern method. In these event and happening are given but secondary place; in these it is always rather the subtle underlying causes which are touched on with particular insistence. It is the tragedy of the soul of *Cromwell* which is so memorably recorded by Carlyle; and by Sainte-Beuve it is the intricate psychology of an entire institution which is laid bare.

It is according to this method, Taine argues, not only that history should be written, but also that we should study the literature of any nation. He then proceeds through his several volumes to his memorable consideration of English literature, dwelling repeatedly on the psychology of the English people as it manifests itself in their literature. He calls attention again and again to certain recurring ideas or ideals which manifest themselves persistently in this particular race, which haunt it almost as an individual is haunted by certain not always definite, yet strongly formative influences.

All this is not very new in substance, yet in application it belongs distinctly to modern times. It falls in with the spirit of research and inquiry so active in the past half century, and announces as with prophetic voice—for it was written as much as fifty years ago—the psychology of nations, of which we only lately begin to speak with real seriousness.

We have long admitted, it is true, a certain psychology of

eras—a kind of 'soul' of certain times, or 'spirit' of certain ages, manifesting itself diversely in diverse periods. And, quite as the name of an individual not alone summons to the mind that individual and no other, but connotes a particular personality, so such wide phrases as 'The Elizabethan Age', 'The Renaissance', 'The Homeric Age', the 'Age of Chivalry' do not alone designate certain ages, but in each case connote some essential quality which went to render that particular age memorable and significant. This quality is found to be in every instance dependent upon some idea or ideal which, drawing its power often from unremarked and not always discoverable sources, moulds and fashions the thought and motives of the times.

So the art, the science, the religion, the philosophy of any given age, all these do but flower from causes that have their roots deep under the surface; and he who would acquaint himself with any notable period must study, not so much the outward and obvious facts and happenings of that period, as the hidden and subtle forces lying beneath all these.

But if the true history of a people cannot be given, or the true spirit of an era be revealed by a mere citing of events, however important or carefully chosen, what shall be said of the futility of studying that infinitely more delicate thing, the history of a human soul, by method of index and compilation? Yet that is precisely what much of our accepted and well-credited biography amount to, and we have little of what might be called the more modern method. One looks in vain in the average Lives of great men for any careful consideration or analysis of the remote causes or springs of personality.

Certain biographical facts are, it would seem, expected and provided. These facts the average biographer sets out in a perfectly conventional order, somewhat as the host of the conventional inn—I hope I may be forgiven the comparison—sets out the usual table d'hôte in certain courses time-honored and anticipated. If the biographer is a well-known man—if this be at the sign of Chesterton, or Colvin, or Birrell, or Gosse—then there will be added, without extra cost, the sprightly light wine of easy style.

In a well-known biography of Hawthorne we have for chapter titles the following: 'Early Years'; 'Early Manhood'; 'Early Writings'; 'Brook Farm and Concord'; 'The Three American Novels'; 'England and Italy'; 'Last Years'.

In an equally well-known life of Keats—and in lieu of something better it is perhaps the least unsatisfactory of them all—we have, among other page and chapter headings: 'Leigh Hunt'; 'Determination to Publish'; 'Poems of 1817'; 'Margate'; 'Winter at Hampstead'; 'Doubts of Success'; 'Northern Tour'; 'Absorption in Love and Poetry'; 'Haydon and Money Difficulties'; 'The Odes'; 'The Plays'; 'Recast of Hyperion'; 'Last Days and Death'. It is true that there comes a whole chapter at the very last, under the promising title, 'Character and Genius'; but reading it hopefully, one finds but talk of 'self-control', 'sweetness of disposition', 'sympathy', 'good sense', 'honor', 'manliness'—with a somewhat hackneyed reference to the Greek purity and the mediæval richness of imagery which characterize Keat's poetry, and a few words concerning his influence on a later age.

Now, considering the vivid and marvelous personality of the man, if these be not the bare bones and laboratory skeletons of biography, then I do not know bare bones or skeletons when I have sight of them.

No one questions that these are helpful if one is studying anatomy; that they may even be admitted as necessary to an understanding of that timely temple of abode in which the fiery spirit for a while took up its residence; but to call this a 'life' of the man, which gives so little knowledge of his spirit's habits of living!

If I turn to a little volume of Shelley on my table, where only eighteen small pages out of five hundred and ninety-two are devoted, as it happens, to the same subject, and only at that to the closing incident of Keats's career—his untimely death—I find him spoken of in somewhat more adequate fashion.

I shall not quote the words metred out in verse, as they stand in the volume, but shall ask to be allowed to set them down as if they were mere running prose, as follows:

For he is gone where all things wise and fair descend.

So much for the sense of shining and resplendent peace that comes with the going of so large a spirit! But let us read on. It is Urania now who is addressed concerning the poet:

Thy youngest dearest one has perished; thy extreme hope, the loveliest and the last. The bloom whose petals, nipt before they blew, died in the promise of the fruit, is waste; the broken lily lies—the storm is overpast. The quick Dreams, the passion-winged ministers of thought, who were his flocks, whom near the living streams of his young spirit he fed, and whom he taught the love which was its music, wander not, wander no more... And one with trembling hand clasps his cold head, and fans him with her moonlight wings, and cries: 'Our love, our hope, our sorrow is not dead; see on the silken fringe of his faint eyes, like dew upon a sleeping flower, there lies a tear some Dream has loosened from his brain.' And others came—Desires and Adorations, Winged Persuasions, and Veiled Destinies, Splendors and Glooms and glimmering Incarnations of hopes and fears and twilight Phantasies...all he had loved and moulded into thought from shape, and hue and odor and sweet sound, lamented Adonaïs... He is made one with Nature; there is heard his voice in all her music, from the moan of thunder to the song of night's sweet bird; he is a presence to be felt and known in darkness and in light, from herb and stone, spreading itself where'er that Power may move which has withdrawn his being to its own; he is a portion of the loveliness which once he made more lovely; he is gathered to the kings of thoughts who waged contention with their times' decay, and of the past are all that cannot pass away.

And this further, this little bit about the poet's grave:

Here pause, these graves are all too young as yet, to have outgrown the sorrow which consigned its charge to each; and if the seal is set, here, on one fountain of a mourning mind, break it not thou!... From the world's bitter wind seek shelter in the shadows of the tomb. What Adonaïs is, why fear we to become?

It will be objected that this is not biography at all, but poetry, and very famous poetry at that. I am aware, full aware of it. I have only to remark that, since there is a beating upon the gates and the starved people demand bread and there is none, 'Why then, let them eat cake!' There is perhaps more pure essence of biography in lines like these, which purport not to be biography at all, than in any pompous three-volume *Life*, which comes decked in scarlet, and heralded by the trumpet-blasts of publishers well versed in the psychology of advertising.

Or take all these supreme lines away and leave me but that one by the same hand, 'The soul of Adonaïs like a star,' and I am not sure that I am not richer by that, than by many biographical chapters.

II

It has always seemed to me that the best possible biographer, even including the immortal Boswell, would have been Horatio. Ophelia might have been better still had she kept her poor senses. Even having lost them, she seems to do no less than draw back a shimmering veil from the soul and life of Hamlet in the few remarks she makes concerning him: 'Where is the beauteous majesty of Denmark?'

Horatio, never having dreamed, certainly, of writing an account of Hamlet's life at all, yet seems to set forth in his few words more of Hamlet than is to be found in all the commentaries. What is there not revealed in his 'Here, sweet lord, at your service,' and his 'O my dear lord!'

There is further evidence of his qualification, of course, in Hamlet's unforgettable words concerning him:

Horatio, thou art e'en as just a man
As e'r my conversation coped withal.

and at the very last—

> 'Horatio, I am dead,
> Thou livest; report me and my cause aright
> To the unsatisfied.

But that which fits Horatio more than all, it seems to me, to bring report to others concerning the life, the motives and character of his 'sweet lord', is that he had long been aware of those fearful and familiar hauntings of his lord's mind—hauntings which, for the purposes of the play, must be dramatized into the very form of a ghost, but which were in reality something far subtler still, and less bodied. It was of these delicate and awful visitings that Horatio was, more than the rest, aware and sensitively expectant.

It is such an eagerness, such an expectancy, and such an ability as well, I take it, that are needed by him who would understand the life of any great man and would hope to interpret it to others. He who would give us an adequate study of any life whatsoever must, it would seem, reckon on and investigate those subtle hauntings of mind and spirit of which the biographers have as yet, apparently, taken so little account, having left such investigations to be followed, and that only along somewhat morbid lines, by the psychiatrists and psycho-analysts.

For these, it is true, have recognized clearly that there are such hauntings, though they do not call them such. It is recognized by them that there is frequently an unconscious retention by the mind, and a repression within the unconscious self, of former striking and formative experiences. Freud and his followers tell us that an unpleasant or shocking experience, long dead to the conscious memory, may nevertheless return to haunt and newly shock and distress us when consciousness sleeps. In dreams it is, they tell us, that morbid fears or hateful repressions or unlawful desires of all kinds return to move where they will, unhindered and invulnerable. In whatever scientific or psychologic terms we speak of these things, it all sounds very ghostlike, and the more so when one recalls that these haunting manifestations vanish at the awaking to consciousness, as ghosts at the crowing of the cock; then, be it ghost or old repression, 'the extravagant and erring spirit hies to his confines' once more.

The avowed task of the Freud school is the anticipation, the expectation, and at last the careful analysis of these morbid hauntings, these repressions and forbidden desires. It is the self-appointed task of the psycho-analyst to watch for these things, to recognize them, speak with them, and examine into their meanings and purposes, as Hamlet with the ghost of his father on the battlements of Elsinore. All this has been looked upon—rightly, no doubt—as epoch-making in the history of psychology, and more especially as it applies to the study and treatment of nervous and mental disorders.

But to deal only with the morbid hauntings of the mind is to look upon the gloom and night of things only. For, by the same token, it would seem there must be other presences not morbid; other haunting influences, not dreadful, but lovely. There must be without doubt many an exquisite or startling experience or impression, long since passed over into the world of our dead memories—perhaps the frail beauty of flower or leaf, some unearthly delicacy of laced moonlight on the floor of the forest, the spaciousness of dawn, the beauty of women, the kindly clinging touch of hands—some impression which found in us, in early youth it may be, a congenial abode, and returning to us again and again (never in the full daylight of consciousness, but in a dim and twilight fashion, in some delicate haunting form 'as the air invulnerable'), obtains at last a ghostly possession of some chamber of the mind, holds from there a kind of subtle occupancy of our thoughts, in time a sort of dominion over our personalities, and even at last, it must be, exerts a definite influence upon our characters.

For it is precisely the exact and delicate response to such subtle visitings, whether it be a visiting of fear and dread or of beauty and delight, which, expressing itself in the individual's manner of living and taste for life, we call personality; which, manifesting itself in his art, we call style; which, exhibiting itself in his purpose and action, we call character.

It is in this sense, then, that the lives of all of us, and very especially the lives of the great, may, without fantastical imagery, be said to be haunted. And if this be true, then it is obvious that, without reference to such hauntings, no so-called 'lives' or biographies of great men can be complete.

III

It seems likely that the new criticism must more and more take into account these delicate and psychological reckonings; but meanwhile how shall we, the unelect, seeking unacademically among the lives of the great, become aware of these subtle influences which forever haunt the characters and the works of great men? How shall we put ourselves sensitively in touch with that which is so essentially characteristic; with those mysterious influences of personality which, working together, make, for instance, a poem of Arnold's a poem of Arnold's unmistakably, and a painting of Raphael's so much his own that we are wont to speak of it as 'a Raphael'?

Again I turn to Horatio. There must first of all be in us, I believe, a deep love of the men whom we would know—'O my sweet lord!' There must be on our part all that loyal and watchful friendship which would make any hearsay or report concerning them a matter of interest to us; further, there must be that full intimate companionship to be had, not by hearsay at all, but only by living day after day with these men and their works; and lastly, there must be in us a sensitiveness to spiritual and haunting presences in their lives—a patient and sensitive watching as it were upon the battlements of Elsinore.

If we turn from Leonardo, as Pater presents him to us, to another notable and equally strong type—to Isaiah; if we ignore all those facts usually insisted upon in biography; if we dismiss as less important the kings and rulers of his age and the dramatic yet negligible circumstances of his times; and if we give our attention rather to the subtle predilections and preoccupations of this great mind, we find Isaiah visited again and again, haunted unceasingly it would seem, by certain effects and meanings, and lovelinesses and memories of light.

Again and again we see him sensitive to its manifestations. Here and there throughout his writings we find him noting and delighting in its return, greeting it with relief and rejoicing, as after a long night's watching; calling to his people passionately to arise and waken from the darkness of their sins, holding up his own streaming torch, as it were, across their night, in shining prophecy of the better luminary already on the way, which was to be the light of the world.

'Arise! Shine!' he cries, 'for thy light is come and the glory of the Lord is risen upon thee... The People that walked in darkness have seen a great light; they that dwell in the land of the shadow of death, upon them hath the light shined... Then shall thy light break forth as the morning... And the Gentiles shall come to thy light, and kings to the brightness of thy rising... The Lord shall be to thee an everlasting light, and thy God thy glory... The sun shall no more go down, neither shall thy moon withdraw herself.'

His mention also of trees and their boughs and roots and branches is even more frequent still. Here, likewise, 'two ideas' seem 'especially fixed in him as reflexes of things that touched his brain in childhood beyond the measure of other impressions'.

When we study Dante carefully and watch with him also, we find him to have been, hardly less than Isaiah, haunted by the same loveliness, the beauty and meaning of light. For him not less, light would seem to have had a most insistent and spiritual appeal. Far too many to quote are his innumerable exact and sensitive descriptions of it, his careful and repeated observations of its gradations and delicate alterations. Memorably, too, he has it in mind in speaking of Saint Francis of Assisi, that sun of righteousness risen out of the mediæval night. 'Call it not Assisi,' he cries; 'if you would truthfully name it, call it the East because of the sun that rose there.'

Likewise, one who watches patiently and devotedly with Homer cannot but become sensible at last how his mind entertains constantly the thought and moving beauty of the various air. Perpetually, it must have been, he was haunted by the freshness and loveliness of it as it moved across the Ægean and the windy isles of Greece. Pure and awful, in the semblance of the blue-eyed Athena, it was the air which passed among his Greek hosts at eventide, or went stirringly among the serried ranks, reviving with a touch the old spirit in them; or in the tent of Achilles took him by the yellow hair, and directed him, a spirit and a presence.

Again and again throughout the Iliad and the Odyssey, the sensitive and watchful will note this persistency and preoccupation, this recurrent observation of the air in its manifold behaviors, as of something dear or memorable, from the swirling, snatching Harpies to the clean-breathed morning; from the sullen sultriness of Achilles's wrath—a stubborn heat that will not stir—to the swift flight of windy arrows cleansing the banquet-hall of Ithaca. So too, that divinity to whom he paid his most constant homage was Athena, goddess of knowledge and of the air, who exquisitely typified, not alone wisdom, but, as almost one with wisdom, the most moving and yielding of the elements.

How well by these things have we come to know Homer—who yet know not by seven chances even so much as the city of his birth! The bare facts of biography seem poor when compared with these preferences, these preoccupations and predilections of the very man himself.

So, too, though we knew little else about him, it were possible to take the full measure of St Francis of Assisi by his haunting persistent love of brotherhood. Nothing else in all his deeds and words is half so strong. One even comes to believe that his devotion to his beloved Lady Poverty was—doubtless unknown to himself—rendered solely because it made him one of a larger fraternity and brother to a greater number of men. The fire that burned and seared him was his brother, even as was the beneficent luminary that warmed him. From his triumphant salutation to his radiant 'brother the sun,' on down to the delicate and gentle admonishings of his 'little brothers' the birds and fishes, the thought of an unlimited and unfettered fraternity perpetually dominates his loving spirit.

In like manner I have noted in my many readings of Matthew Arnold that his mind seems to have responded with a peculiar sensitiveness, and been often subject to the sound and meaning of moving waters, and to the high destiny of stars. It would seem that 'the unplumbed, salt, estranging sea' came in time to have a definite power over him in the ordering of his images and even in the determining of his philosophies; that rivers flowing silver under the sun, or, unguessed, in subterranean chambers, became to him interpretative of life itself, and their course and channel and ultimate end a promise to his soul. It is not alone in his poetry that one finds the 'incognizable sea', and hears so frequently of its coasts and beaches and sands and watery wastes and isles; of voyages and charts; the 'swinging waters and the clustered pier'; the ebbing and flowing of tides; and the still stars: one comes upon these in his prose not less, very especially and memorably in his 'Study of Poetry'.

It may be argued that these might be mere favorite figures and symbols; but it is hardly thinkable, after a careful study of them, that they are not rather haunting influences and impressions having long a familiar access to the chambers of his mind, now taking him with his forsaken Merman:

Down, down, down!
Down to the depths of the sea!

or with the Neckan beside the green Baltic, pointing out the sounding deeps, and the starry poles, and interpreting life's meanings by them.

So too, to pass but lightly from one to another, we can hardly read Chaucer devotedly without at length becoming aware how this poet seems to have been haunted by the idea of the freshness and loveliness of the day's awaking; his very heroes and heroines again and again seeming to partake of it, and to be like dawn themselves upon the hills.

Up rose the sun and up rose Emilie.

The 'yonge squire' too, of 'twenty yere of age'—

> Embrouded was he, as it were a mede
> All full of fresshe floures, white and red.
> Singing he was, or floyting all the day.
> He was as fresshe as is the moneth of May.

In his most delicate descriptions one feels the presence as of a breaking light, and the birds seem forever to sing in his green coverts.

It is the dawn and early morning of the year not less which is dear to him—and which he has chosen, perhaps by an election not wholly his own, as the season in which to order and assemble his famous pilgrimage.

> When that Aprille with his schowres swoote
> The drought of Marche hath pierced to the roote

◆

Then longen folke to gon on pilgrimages.

And so, out into the dawn of the year they go, making an immortal morning of it.

IV

Two more lives suggest themselves as especially rich in the testimony they bring of haunting influences which permanently moulded them—those of Keats and Rossetti.

It is well known how completely the early life of Rossetti came under the influence of the Florence of the Middle Ages, and how from the very beginning there fell athwart his life and across his very name the shadow of her greatest son. It is doubtful whether we gain as much knowledge of him by a study of the modern times in which he lived, as by turning our attention to the history and ideals of the Florence of the time of Dante and Lorenzo de' Medici.

'It has been said,' writes Pater, 'that all the great Florentines were preoccupied with death. *Outre-tombe! Outre-tombe*! is the burden of their thoughts, from Dante to Savonarola. Even the gay and licentious Boccaccio gives a keener edge to his stories by putting them in the mouths of a party of people who had taken refuge from the danger of death by plague, in a country house. It was to this inherited sentiment, this practical decision that to be preoccupied with the thought of death was in itself dignifying and a note of high quality, that the seriousness of the great Florentines of the fifteenth century was partly due; and it was reinforced in them by the actual sorrows of their times.'

A careful study of Rossetti reveals him also, like them, early and profoundly preoccupied with death. The richly lighted chambers of his mind are in their dark moments visited repeatedly by its pity and its melancholy. Space does not admit of citing here the many evidences; but if ever a mind was visited, preoccupied, and at last mastered by a strong idea, a dominant persuasion, the mind of Dante Gabriel Rossetti was so haunted—so dominated—by the idea of death.

When we turn to Keats's life and writings, they offer examples hardly less notable. For as Rossetti was haunted by the idea of death, so Keats would seem from the first to have been preoccupied by the idea of beauty. By his own memorable confession he had worshiped the spirit of it in all things; he has not the slightest feeling of humility, he says, toward anything in existence with three exceptions only: The Eternal Being, the Memory of Great Men, and the Principle of Beauty.

There is further and ample evidence throughout his writings that he was perpetually possessed by certain definite forms of beauty: by the beauty of mead and moon, the wash of waters at their priestly task, the splendor of the night's starred face; but very especially and more often, it would seem, was he haunted by that most intimate and tangible of all lovelinesses—the loveliness of flowers.

There is constant reference to them, a constant recurring delight in them. Their influence again and again visited him and pervaded his most delicate observations. The memory of flowers again and again laid a detaining hand upon him, and must have ministered to him unrecorded in how many a night hour, mindful, reminiscential, with what gentle ministerings!

They bloom in his lines everywhere, familiar as the name of the beloved on the lips. It will be recalled that they stand among those things of beauty which he names with so much devotion as 'joys forever'; 'daffodils, with the green world they live in' shedding an ethereal sunlight across the more sombre beauty of 'the dooms we have imagined for the mighty dead'.

So, too, 'hushed cool rooted flowers, fragrant-eyed', touch his memory with an ever-freshening sensibility. The greatest pleasure he has experienced in life, he tells us, is in watching the growth of flowers; and to him—as Hazlitt recalls—Hebrew poetry was faulty because it made so little mention of them; and for the converse reason, it would seem likely, Chaucer and Spenser were forever his delight.

What he specially longs for now, he writes—he has been ill, and is within a year of his death—is 'the simple flowers of Spring'.

In the same letter we get a glimpse of certain early personal associations not fully followed, which would seem to lend an added loveliness to flowers which he had always found in themselves so lovely.

'How astonishingly,' he writes, '...does the chance of leaving the world impress a sense of its natural beauties upon us! Like poor Falstaff, though I do not "babble", I think of green fields; I muse with the greatest affection on every flower I have known from my infancy—their shapes and colors are as new to me as if I had just created them with a superhuman fancy. It is because they are connected with the most thoughtless and happiest moments of our lives. I have seen foreign flowers in hothouses, of the most beautiful nature, but I do not care a straw for them. The simple flowers of our Spring are what I want to see again!'

He did see them once again, and then no more.

In the account of his drive to Rome, he who reads sympathetically must enjoy most, it seems to me, as doubtless Keats did, the autumn flowers which Severn gathered for him by the way and put into his remembering hand.

Lying quiet at the last, as Severn tells us, with his hand clasped on the white carnelian Fanny Brawne had given him, when all other presences seemed to have departed from him—Love and Ambition having for the last time visited him—and when life itself, with her hand already on the latch, stood ready to depart, there lingered yet awhile beside him that old sense of loveliness that had so often, even from earliest infancy, visited and haunted his spirit—the loveliness and friendliness of flowers. Already, in some vision of his spirit, he was laid down in their green world he knew so well and loved. 'I feel,' he said, 'the flowers growing over me'.

V

The observations I have suggested are here touched on but lightly, and in passing. I have made no profound study of them, or of the infinitely subtle psychology which, without doubt, underlies such hauntings of the spirit. I have but known these men from childhood and from early youth: have watched with them in many watchings. If there be one boast left me when I also shall go down into the darkness to which they have so long lent splendor, it may well be that these I have loved and have cherished with a whole heart, and would have served them if I could, than Horatio not less eager: 'Here, sweet lord, at your service.'

But be all that as it may, I am yet persuaded that it is by some such means as I have here touched on that all biography of the better sort must in time be written. Turn where we will among the great, we find facts of date and birth and schooling and death and all outward circumstance to have been the lesser factors. All these Time at last—the only lastingly considerable biographer—rejects and throws away. That which Time retains as precious and imperishable is rather some fine essence of the spirit, some essential personality built up and moulded by preferences, predilections, and prepossessions of a most highly spiritual order. The loves, the desires, the dear delights of men; the returning dreams, the recurrent longings that will not be gainsaid; the dead and long-lost dreamings that revisit the glimpses of our moon—these are indeed the spirits of us, and our immortalities.

Nor is it only as aids to a more just analysis of the great that these infinitely subtle influences may be considered. Plus on *connait de langues plus on est de personnes*. If the knowledge of another language gives one another life, as it were—makes of one yet another person—what may not be said to be added unto us by the knowledge—not the mere speculation, but the intimate knowledge—of another soul, and that soul one of the great ones of the earth?

This can be had only by an intimate companionship, not with the mere flagrant facts, but with the spiritual visitings, the dear desires and predilections, which haunt all rich lives significantly, perpetually, even as they haunt life itself.

For life is but an infinitely ancient abode, haunted by recurring presences surpassingly spiritual; as he knows who has seen death pass in and out of the ancient chambers in the night watches, or who has heard the autumn rains how reminiscent in patient woodlands, or who has been aware of lovely springs long-gone keeping tryst at certain seasons with the evening star in the twilight, or has felt them stealing back, ghostly and exquisite, when the April crescent hangs thoughtful and remote above dark apple-boughs.

In life as in lives, the presences move dark and dread or shining and lovely; and in the lives of the great as in life itself the shining and lovely would seem to be the more constant visitants. It is not to be forgotten that, though Banquo knocks his fearful summons, and the murdered Dane speaks with hollow mouthings, yet drifting forms dance no less gayly and delicately on midsummer nights in woodsy hollows by the moon.

It is noteworthy and remarkable that even those among the great whose lives have been sombre with tragedy have been visited—indeed they often more than others—by recurring influences of a most haunting beauty, like Beethoven, who with ears dull yet heard high symphonies, and Milton, who with sight closed to all outward loveliness saw yet in the darkened chambers a vision as of squadrons of bright-harnessed angels ranged in order serviceable, and knew the pastures and the silent woods to be full of sweet voices and light steps:

Oh, friend, I hear the tread of nimble feet, Hasting this way!

It is of all such haunting and recurrent presences, be they dread or lovely, that he who most knows life is most aware, and that he who would know the lives of great men must be most sensitively observant. These are the things that must be watched for faithfully and with a whole heart and a single devotion: 'Here, sweet lord, at your service!' Leaving all prejudice or interest of our own, it is for us, in studying the lives of great men, to make their affair ours as wholly as may be; and to forget ourselves in a knowledge so much more dearly to be desired.

And by no means, I believe, may this be done so surely as by a patient study of those high elections, those persistent hauntings of mind and spirit which have influenced and, it may be, in so large a measure directed the lives of all great men; giving their mind its bent, their personality its leanings; often guiding, it must be, their motives, and suggesting their high behaviors; laying upon them, as the ghost upon Hamlet, purposes and duties thence never to be avoided, inevitably to be discharged; lending to their speech its lovely and broidered figures, or to the work of the hand its so memorable distinctions, and to all their activities that which we call 'characteristic'—something particularly and peculiarly their own; some chosen and essential and precious manner of expression which, mortal though they be, lives on, surviving them; and which is not to be found elsewhere in its kind or measure throughout all the rich and inexhaustible ages.

THE ACROPOLIS AND GOLGOTHA

ANNE C. E. ALLINSON

The following letters contain a true record of a mind's journey.

ATHENS, May 1, 1914

My Dear Friend:

We drove in from Eleusis this afternoon, once more breathlessly watching the Acropolis offer its white and golden marbles to adornment by the setting sun. Our Greek winter is drawing to an end and this was our good-bye visit to the Mysteries. How clear and lucid the beauty of the place seemed today, from the brightness of the sea and the firm modeling of the mountains to the bloom of the placated earth! Demeter and Persephone were evidently together in safety, the mystery of the unseen forgotten in the palpable joy of life restored.

    On our way back we stopped, of course, at the Convent of Daphne, to make ourselves tea in the sunlit courtyard, and to take one more look at the Byzantine mosaics. I confess that this time they seemed to me quaint bits of the wreckage of mediævalism cast upon the shore of Hellenism. If the mediæval part of Christianity is as inextricable as you say it is, then I will grant you that 'Christian thought' is an outworn system compared with the immortal mind of Greece. As we crossed the bridge over the Cephisus, the Parthenon, which is far more mutilated than the little convent, once more sent abroad from broken colonnades and crumbling pediments the impression that some perennial spirit and undying vitality had, indeed, as Plutarch once suggested, mingled in its very composition. The Shrine of Wisdom seemed to take up and weld together all the mysticism and all the rationalism of the world.

Was it really ten years ago that I wrote to you after such another journey along the Sacred Way? And ten more still since I last saw you at the little station of Eleusis? You were going back to Patras to take ship for Italy, and we—and those others—had ended an afternoon spent among the ruins by speculating on those great nights of Demeter, Mystical, holy.

I remember how sure you were that the wilder ideas in the Mysteries, which allowed for the redeeming death of gods and over-stated immortality, were but vagrants in the ordered area of Greek reason and sanity. Somebody older and wiser than I began to appeal to Plato on behalf of Greek transcendentalism, but you retorted that he was only the most disorderly vagabond of them all. Then your train clattered into the toy station, and you held my hand for a moment and said with a kind smile, 'Au revoir, petite savante, icibas.'

But we never have seen each other again and probably never shall. Only an odd accident, you know, led to the annual letters which have spun the leisurely web of intimacy between two travelers so disparate in age and in nationality. You said that the differences in our experience, speech and traditions were lost in our common pilgrimage to Greece. My youth reminded you of the youth of Hellas, your age embodied for me her store of wisdom.

It is your book which has set me on the trail of these old memories. For when we began our letters you said that, since we knew little of each other's objective lives, we should have to concern ourselves with inner impressions; and now your printed opinions open up the question how the years have treated us in this matter of subjective experience. For one thing, automatically they have made me your equal. When we met, you, at forty-five, had experienced middle age. At sixty-five you are but confirming its revelation. You have yet to come to the fresh experience of old age. So that now, when I am forty-five, I may for a time talk with you eye to eye.

Your twenty years, unless you have misled me, have held no transforming experiences. Joys have but grown more dear and familiar. Sorrows, of a shattering kind, have let you alone. Your work prospers, your fame is assured, your children have grown up to be well in body and mind. All your fruit is ripening in the tranquil sunshine. My years, on the other hand, sweeping me out of the twenties into the forties, have been packed with fresh happenings to heart and head and will. Disaster has been left out of the brew, but almost everything else I have tasted. Perhaps this difference between us—unless it is one of sex—explains why you, in the books you have written lately, deal with philosophies and religions as if they sprang, Athena-like, out of the intellect, while to me they seem the issue of a normal union: if they are begotten of thought they are brought forth in anguish by experience.

In this last book you are interested in Hellenism and Christianity as forms—or attributes—of 'civilization'. I cannot forget that each of them means the way in which men and women have managed and are managing their diurnal round. You remember, don't you, the delightful story of Plato lecturing one day in the Academy on the Absolute Good, and his audience drifting away from him—except one man who was Aristotle? I have often wondered about the different things the other men did that day after they had run away from the Idea! At any rate the complex was as 'Hellenic' as the conversation of the philosophers.

And when one turns to Christianity—why, the very philosopher who first intellectualized a Way and a Life had himself been born anew of the intensely personal experience of sin and repentance. Do you know Frederic Myers's Saint Paul?—ah! there was a 'Greek scholar' who understood a Christian!

> So shall all speech of now and of to-morrow,
> All he hath shown me or shall show me yet,
> Spring from an infinite and tender sorrow,
> Burst from a burning passion of regret.

You, reading history, would be willing to obliterate Christianity and restore Hellenism as a universal ideal. I would rather see them united in each separate life.

Before I explain what I mean by this I must beguile you by some agreement with you in your criticism of 'cardinal' Christian doctrines! You are right, I think, in objecting to the emphasis laid by the church upon a future life. But you seem to me unnecessarily disturbed by a theory. Christians, like the followers of many other faiths, do 'believe' in immortality. In fact, I suspect that only specifically intellectual people actually disbelieve in it—and, with all respect to yourself, I must add that the opinion of intellectuals on the destiny of the spirit fails to hold my attention! The authority of the spiritually gifted—including both Socrates and St Francis—is overwhelmingly on the side of the soul being immortal. But does that make any more difference in the life of the flesh today than in the time of Alcibiades? Mediæval Christians certainly went mad over heaven and hell; but who now neglects Demeter's green earth for apocalyptic visions? You are depressed by a shadow cast from the printed page. Stop reading and look about at your friends! They are not too startled by the white radiance of eternity to install the latest electric lights!

As to your horror over the Christian 'adoration of suffering', that seems to me better founded in view of the historic and continued insistence upon the cross as a symbol. I agree with you. I can scarcely express the revulsion which I feel in picture galleries before the endless succession of crucifixions and tortured saints. Until we conquer disease or discard violence there will be physical suffering in the world. But it is a thing to fight against, not to worship. For man to have painted and carved as beautiful a racked body seems to me an insult to the God who made straight limbs and fair flesh, and a strange betrayal of the Galilean who wished to heal the suffering of others as long as he lived, and only accepted it for himself as an incidental necessity at the end. He had no mediæval disregard for the flesh. The agony in Gethsemane consisted in facing the obligation to offer up a body and a life which were very precious to him. The glory consisted in the sacrifice, not in the temporary torture to which it led. Love, not suffering, is the core of Christianity. A truer symbol than the defeated body on the cross would be the same body strong and beneficent among men.

Here the Periclean sculptor would have done better for us than the mediæval painter. But only here. Neither he nor any of his contemporaries could have understood Gethsemane. Their greatness consisted in their selection, out of the prodigal abundance which lies before man, of noble possessions. They were far superior to the Puritans in that they retained art with morals, and they were equally superior to the modern Romanticists in that they picked and chose only such beauty as they believed could be amalgamated with character. Their inferiority to the Christians lay in their failure to hold their treasures in trust for humanity.

And now I come back to my argument against you. We who boast of being the 'heirs of the ages' need not be as limited as you imply. The modern man or woman can combine the Greek ideal of self-development with the Christian ideal of self-dedication. In reality, I am not arguing, but asserting. I know that this union is possible by the only evidence which is admissible—the evidence of a life. I have known for many years one person who unites in a normal experience your grandiose abstractions of Christianity and Hellenism. This person is my mother. Do not take her sex as an obstacle. She is a better example than some famous man might be, because her character is not obscured by public achievement. She has none of the limitations of a profession or career, or of some unique strain of genius. What she is creates careers or feeds genius. She is the most complete human being I have ever known, and yet her wholeness is a presage of what we all might become. It is to a life like this that you ought to go when you take stock of the philosophies of the world!

My mother's external fortune, judged by Greek standards, is good—too good, of course, for a woman. She has received from fate much that would have satisfied a Greek man: the consciousness of citizenship in a proud and prospering nation; health, long life, an active mind, and enough money to live tastefully; and, finally, satisfactory children (if I may be permitted to say this) and the approval of her fellow citizens. The Greek estimate of the importance of such approval springs, I suppose, from intense feeling for the communal life. No Greek man could be mentally less confined to the walls of a house than is my mother, and an Athenian voter could scarcely have served his polis more completely than she serves our little town. The only difference here between her and a Periclean citizen is that she is perplexed and shy rather than expectant and gratified when evidences of public approval are forced upon her.

In natural endowment, also, my mother is singularly Greek, because she possesses diverse qualities harmoniously welded into one whole. We are conscious of no contradictions in her, and yet she is both sane and imaginative, sensitive and practical, dominating and gentle.

Finally, in her conscious activities she is Greek. There is, for example, her moral insistence upon form and beauty. If you could live in her house for a day you would see Hellenism as a diurnal practice. Her taste is flawless; everything she touches turns to beauty and to a tranquillizing order and simplicity. She selects a vase or a baking dish with the æsthetic fastidiousness which beset the artists and artisans of Athens.

And, furthermore, she is Greek in her perennial enthusiasm for fresh knowledge. Her enjoyment of life seems to me intense because she is never tired of exploring the world through every kind of human achievement. She has the curiosity of the Hellenic mind. The Athenian men who were like her made it worthwhile for other men to be scientists and philosophers and poets.

And yet my mother is a Christian. You see what I believe she has and is. Well, all of this she takes in her two hands and offers daily. Of course, she believes in immortality, but she never talks about the future life, and I have told you of her vigorous interest in this one. Of course, too, she has known many sorrows—who has not at seventy?—but she has consistently concealed pain and suffering instead of enthroning them. Her Christianity is compounded of Love. As it streams out from her it is the creative, regenerating passion for humanity which transcended the reasoned goodwill of the pagan philosophers and transcends the materialistic serviceableness of the modern humanitarians. In the noblest pagan literature there is no emotion at all resembling that which suffuses the New Testament. In this emotion my mother lives and moves and has her being.

I snap my fingers at Nietzscheism when I realize that she is the strongest personality in my little world. She dies daily for us, but we live her way! No superman could impose his will more effectively than this Christian in whom power and sacrifice are one. God is love. If all history tried to make me a skeptic my mother's nature would keep me a believer.

> Whoso hath felt the spirit of the Highest
> Cannot confound nor doubt him nor deny;
> Yea with one voice, O world, tho' thou deniest,
> Stand thou on that side, for on this am I.

I have spoken of my mother's health and energy. Just lately these have flagged a little, and I came away this time with some misgivings, and only for my husband's sake. But her letters have quite reassured me. Lately she wrote, 'I am daily thankful that nothing prevented you from spending this winter on the Acropolis. In thinking of you I can't manage to dislodge you from the hill long enough to eat and sleep.'

She knows me! We have traveled all over the country this year, but always come back to Athens and the Attic plain as to the heart of Greece. We went to Egypt in midwinter, and on our return hurried almost from the ship to the Parthenon. It had snowed lightly and the whitened summits of Pentelicon and Hymettus and Parnes lay in sharp relief under the brilliant sky. A Greek friend of mine, looking at these fleshless mountains, said proudly, 'It is not every one who dares show her bones.' Attica needs no softening mist, no glamorous moonlight, no romantic obscuration. Her beauty is born of light and her teaching is light. In Egypt man was mocked by the desert. Small wonder the Christian saints hid themselves there to punish their poor bodies! Here man seeks the sun and stands erect in his dignity. Mediævalism, I grant you, must make way for this immortal humanism. The 'mystery of suffering' is an invention of distorted minds. Stripped of disguise, suffering is merely an evil to be done away with by Love. This, I take it, is the message of the Acropolis to the Christian.

We are leaving next week for a month in London, and then home. May Fortune multiply your royalties and Athena inspire another book!

Faithfully yours.

P.S. The American mail is just in. A letter from a neighbor in my native town says that no one in my mother's house will disobey her order that I am not to be sent for, but that I am greatly needed. It is possible that she will not live until I can reach her. We shall sail for New York day after to-morrow. My world begins to crumble.

PINELANDS, MAINE, April 20, 1915

My Dear Friend:

As I begin this letter there flashes into my mind the last sentence which I wrote to you a year ago from Greece—that my little world was crumbling. And since then how your own world has been shattered, and the universe almost set reeling in its course! I remember how I talked on in that letter about areas of experience, blocking you off into twenty-year periods! I thought then that only the years would carry us into new seas. But in twelve months you have been swept from the moorings of your middle life. France is again facing the enemy as she did in your boyhood, but now your sons are risking lives more precious than your own. Your wife and daughters are nursing the wounded and the stricken. You, 'too old to fight'—and so in a flash set forward into old age—are nevertheless finding your pen tipped with passion instead of with philosophy. One of your lyrics is being sung in the trenches. You are no longer an intellectualist, but a voice of France. And thousands upon thousands of other men and women are experiencing a similar metamorphosis. Who knows what new philosophies and religions will be born?

I have been wondering whether you would still call Plato an intruder and vagabond in Hellenism. Greek thought changed under the shock to Athenian civilization caused by the Peloponnesian War. By this abstraction do we mean anything else than that Plato and other men had brought home to them the transitoriness of prosperity, the helplessness of morals, learning, and art before a recrudescence of primitive violence, and the limitations of humanism? The material stage in those days was small—little states wage a little war—but in view of her spiritual importance the suffering of Athens was a world-experience of the first magnitude. Possibly Plato seems to you now less a vagrant than a pilot.

For certainly our 'new religion,' if we bring one to birth, cannot be composed of truths wholly unknown before. Some of our new creative energy will go into stripping the veil from the face of that Reality which men at one time and another have beheld. I find it easy to believe this because through an intensive personal experience of my own I have been brought to perceive a truth which is two thousand years old. Last year I argued about Christianity, choosing this part, discarding that. This year I have knelt and touched the hem of the seamless robe. The experience would be too intimate and sacred to reveal were it not bound up with your own. Let me tell you about it. It is the only way in which I can talk with you about your sons who are facing death and suffering.

I wrote you that I was called home from Athens by my mother's illness. She died last month. During the intervening months revelation after revelation came to me. My mother had grown worse rapidly and at first I was shocked to my innermost heart by the change in her. All her strength seemed turned to weakness. Her rich and varied life had shrunk to the hushed quiet of a sick-room. Her tranquil face had become haggard. Her eager intellect had slipped away from her. There was nothing left of the beautiful Hellenism of her life. A Periclean Greek would now have seen in her only an illustration of the shadow lurking within the sunshine, the tragedy of bodily weakness and old age and death.

And since she no longer had riches to offer, what had become of her Christianity? The question could not frame itself, for I was caught and lifted out of my despair by the swift impression that about my frail mother there glowed a radiance which outshone the sunlight of her active years. The dayspring from on high had but put to flight the lesser stars. Everyone who could see her was conscious of it. One of her nurses said to me, 'She is so different from the weak people I've seen before. I feel so warm, somehow, when I'm with her.'

A further revelation was that my mother was done with life and with us. She was exquisite in her treatment of us, managing in receiving still to be the giver. One day she said to me, unforgettably, 'You are making pain and sickness very beautiful.' But that inward eagerness of hers which had led me to believe that she had the Greek feeling for this world was now turned toward a new and vaster world. She had exhausted the experiences of this life—marriage and children, work and achievement, knowledge and beauty, joy and sorrow. In seeing this I saw too how far short they fall of the potentialities of an immortal soul. With her energy and imagination she had drained every drop out of them, but now she tossed them aside for some new wine.

The only time she ever spoke to me of the death which I was sure she knew was drawing close, she did it lightly, with that humor which was a part of her sanity. The doctors had just left her room after consulting about some new form of her sickness, and she turned to me with a smile and said, 'Don't repair me too often! I shall never get free if I don't get worse.' But she told a friend of her own age that nobody could imagine how eager she was to be gone. 'I can hardly wait,' she said, 'to find out about it all. The only thing that troubles me is that the others will be sorry.' I am not sorry. Since she wanted eternity without my grief, she shall have it.

In the last few months Nature did us one of her not uncommon services. Much of my mother's physical strength came back to her, as if at the end the body was determined to be a fit mate for the soul it had so long accompanied. She could move about once more in her little polis. During my last visit at home I was enchanted by a sweet and bubbling gayety which seemed to flow from some hidden spring of contentment. A week later she died swiftly, before I could reach her. All our friends talked to me of the light in her face during that week, and an old bedridden Irish servant, telling me of a visit from her, exclaimed, 'I kept thinking that she was just like a bride, dressed so beautifully and looking so happy.' The Christian figure of the soul and God! The old Celtic eyes had seen the truth. Of such substance was my mother's faith in a future life. It was, indeed, the evidence of things unseen! I perceived the fresh heart of Christianity in a belief so aged that it had built the pyramids centuries before it set up the temples at Eleusis. Never again shall I be found chattering while the great trumpet blasts for immortality echo down the ages.

But before my mother's death another veil had been lifted for me. Behind it I found the meaning of the cross. The experience will hardly bear words. It was very simple, the issue of intimate daily living, but it transformed one human mind as Bible and church, history and art had never done. On the day it happened to me I was open to no impressions from without. The weather was severe in our northern town whose normal beauty is not un-Greek in its austerity and lucidity. A stormy east wind drove dark clouds across the sky, and our firs and pine trees loomed black and forbidding. I turned from the window to the soft loveliness of my mother's room. There my heart and mind were closed to all abstract thought and large emotions, for the nurse was away and I was absorbed in the details of thermometer and medicines. My whole being was centred in the hope that I might make my mother comfortable during those hours. With inexpressible tenderness I began to bathe her, doing for her in her frailty at the end of life what she had so often done for me in mine at the beginning. Then it was that my eyes were opened. You know what a Greek would have seen in a body worn with age, emaciated by sickness, bearing many marks of suffering. But I beheld in it the central beauty of the world. If the noblest of the marble Aphrodites had stood in the room I should have recoiled from her in horror. I knew that my mother's sickness was due to her prodigal waste, for us, of her natural strength. Her flesh had been spent for us—for me. In a sudden supreme moment I was at one with the disciples, passionately loving the friend who had given his body to be broken for them; at one with the mad Christian iconoclasts, shattering heathen statues; at one with the mediæval artists, painting and carving the crucified Christ.

Later I came to see that only in that hour had I grasped the significance of my mother's life. At first I had thought of her suffering as subordinate to her love, an incident among her sacrifices. Now I know it to be a sacramental reality, preëxistent in all her earlier beneficence and at the end the earnest of her immortality.

Later still I realized what had happened. In an obscure individual hour had been reënacted an experience which once befell the world. The antique order was swept away by a tidal wave of emotion, and in its place was left a new life and thought and art. Mediævalism, which had offended me in history, issued from the feeling of men and women as unknown as myself, married to the expression of thinkers, poets and artists. In understanding, at last, the feeling, I came to understand the way in which it was expressed.

When the Christian world, recovering its balance by means of the Renaissance, once more accepted the worth of antiquity, it refused to surrender the new treasure which it had gained in its temporary recoil from humanism. Popes on the throne retained the symbol which had comforted slaves in the Catacombs. The same cross survived the Reformation and persists, plastically and verbally, as the sign of modern Christianity. Until lately this paradox was as strange, in its way, as that of a Borgian posing as Vicar of the Crucified. Last year I saw all kinds of people trying to obliterate suffering: the intellectuals were denying its efficacy, the humanitarians its necessity, the Christian Scientists its reality. In our various modern forms of speech we were addressing prayers to Hygeia, enshrined on the Acropolis.

> Then, with terrible suddenness, the roar of guns
> interrupted us.
> Clouds and darkness
> Closed upon Camelot.

Some one light in the encircling gloom we must have, if we are to work our way out into a renewal of civilization. Are we to discover it by still another paradox, in the very mystery of suffering which we have been denying? If one of your sons (which God forbid!) should be brought home mutilated, you would not choose to remember him in his young strength and beauty, because he would seem more beautiful to you stretched upon his cross. You would not rest in your agony, or in your fierce anger that such things are possible in the world. You would pass from these to the conviction that his suffering for France made his humanity divine. I do not pretend to understand the matter. I only know it to be true. Even the Greeks presaged it at Eleusis, but they forgot it as they turned homeward. For us it still lies beyond reason, but is beginning to be clearer than the axioms of reason. The mystery of suffering is more lucid than the fact of well-being.

My friend, may we not look upon this as the answer of Golgotha to the Acropolis?

Faithfully yours.

THE BAPTIZING OF THE BABY

ELIZABETH TAYLOR

The Baby arrived in a howling nor'easter. The fields were white with driving snow, the sea was white with the spindrift of gale-lashed waves, when the little procession filed into the parsonage courtyard. There were a father, five godfathers, two godmothers, and a few non-official friends. No baby was visible, but a muffled gurgle betrayed her presence. One of the godfathers, a fine young Viking of a lad, had a woman's dress-skirt buttoned around his neck and hanging down in front. Within its warm folds was the Baby.

The Baby's age was but four weeks, and this her first journey into the outside world. Custom has decreed that a Faroe Island baby must not pass its parents' threshold until it goes to the Pastor to be received into the Church, and so made secure from the Powers of Darkness. Having once left its home, it cannot return with the sacred rite unperformed.

Imagine, then, the dismay that fell upon the Baby's escorts when they learned that the Pastor had gone to the capital, several days before, on important church business. To Thorshavn! Only seven miles away, by sea, to be sure, but, with that gale, it might as well be seventy. What to do now? The Baby could not be taken back unbaptized. And there was the baptismal feast all arranged: sweet soup, hung mutton, potatoes, coffee, little cakes, with card-playing in the afternoon, and rice-porridge and sandwiches in the evening. The Baby's mother was putting the sweet soup over the fire when they left that morning. Five miles by fjord they had come; then, as the gale increased, and they neared the open sea, they had 'set up' on land, and trudged the remaining three miles through deep snow.

'Oh, well,' sighed the father, 'we may as well "take it with quiet". The women-folk are too weary, anyhow, to go through those drifts again. We had better send one man home to explain matters, while the rest of us visit our friends. The storm may lessen at any time, so we can go to Thorshavn and bring home the Pastor.'

But—the Baby—And here the 'Pastorinde' was called upon to advise. Yes the Pastorinde did know of a newly-arrived baby in the village, and she doubted not that its mother would kindly permit the stranger-baby to share and share alike with her own.

I, too, was 'weather-fast'. From Thorshavn I had come, twelve days before, to 'hold Jule' at the parsonage, intending to return two days after Christmas. Then came this long storm. There was no going to Thorshavn by sea; but in a roundabout way, by fjord and fjeld, it might be done in a case of necessity, such as this church-meeting that the Pastor must attend.

The foreman of the eight-man boat, however, flatly refused to take me. 'The Herr Pastor,' he explained patiently, 'has strong legs. He can jump and stand fast in surf, climb cliffs, and go through deep snow. But it is no journey for women-folk in high winter-time.'

So I was left behind when the Pastor went to Thorshavn.

One must start before daylight these short winter days to enable the boats to return before dark. For eight days I had been living as much packed up as possible, sleeping lightly, waking in the blackness of morning at the sound of voices in the kitchen below. Groping to the head of the stairway, I could hear the decision of the foreman: 'Not possible today, Fru Pastorinde. There is ribbingur i sjónum (dangerous sea) outside.' And back I would creep shivering, sure of one day more in the parsonage.

'What is the Baby's name to be?' I asked one of the godfathers, as we chanced to meet the next day. An embarrassed silence was followed by an abrupt change of subject, and I felt that I had made a faux pas. Later, I was told that a baby's name must never be asked, never be told, before baptism. I knew, already, some bits of babylore. For instance, if a child cries while it is being baptized, it will have a good voice and sing well at the ballad dances. The water must never be allowed to run down into the baby's eyes, or it will have 'second sight'. This is not a happy gift, and I notice that the godmother holding the child, tilts it at the right moment so that the water flows back over the forehead. I know, too, that the man who carries a baby-boy to and from the church goes as fast as possible, so that the boy will be strong at the oar, sure-footed on the fjelds.

All this, you observe, for the boy baby. No such trouble is taken for a mere girl. But, for both alike, there is this precaution: never leave a child alone before it is baptized. Until then it falls easily into the power of evil spirits, and is in danger of being carried away by Hulderfolk. These underground creatures are not 'the little people', or the Brownies. In size and appearance they resemble human beings. They have boats and go to the fishery; they have cows, sheep (that are always gray), dogs (large black hounds that often have a light on the end of their tails); but one thing the Hulderfolk lack and that is souls. If, however, they can take away a Faroe baby and substitute one of their own, and it is baptized, then that child will have a soul.

I know a peasant woman whose daughter died in childbirth not long ago, leaving her baby to her mother's care. The father of the baby was fishing in Iceland, and the old woman lived alone in her little cottage. I went to see her, and during my visit, she wished to show me some articles in another part of the house. Wherever we went she took the cradle with her. I understood the reason and said to her:

'But, Sanna, living by yourself as you do, are you not obliged sometimes to leave the baby alone?'

'Yes, Fróken,' she replied sadly, 'several times I have had to leave him just for a few minutes. But I put the Psalm-book under his pillow, I mark him with the sign of the Cross, and I run my best!'

Another story I have heard lately is about a Hulderchild on Videró. A peasant and his wife had a baby-boy, a good happy healthy child, who never cried or made trouble. One day the mother had to leave him alone a little while. When she returned she found the baby crying and fretting. Its face seemed changed, somehow, and yet she could not say that it was not their child. From that time it cried night and day until the parents were worn out, and they took it to the Pastor to ask his advice. Now the Pastor 'knew more than his Paternoster', as the saying is; that is, he had studied Black Art. He examined the child and said he feared it was a bytte (changeling). 'Now,' said he, 'go home and build a great brewing fire in the fire-place. In each of the four corners put a limpet-shell filled with milk. Then hide yourselves, so you can see and hear the child, but it will not know you are there. If it says or does anything that shows it is a Hulderchild, then you may hope to get your own baby back again.'

The parents followed carefully the Pastor's instructions, and, trembling with anxiety, awaited the result. As the fire roared and crackled, the child stirred uneasily and stopped crying. Then it raised itself on its elbow and watched the fire and the four limpet-shells that were sizzling away in the corners. Then they heard the child laugh scornfully, and saw it point at the limpets. 'Huh!' it exclaimed, 'how can a child be expected to thrive in a house where they have such things for kettles! They should just see the great kettles—the great brewing-pots—in the house of my father, Buin!'

The Hulderchild had betrayed itself! That night there was no crying, the parents slept in peace and woke to find their own good happy baby in the cradle.

What are the cradle-songs this Baby will hear in the cabin where she first saw the gray light of December? Verses from the old Kingos Psalm-book, ballads of the Long Serpent and King Olaf, of Queen Dagmar's death, the Whale Song, stories from the Iceland Sagas and the Nibelungenlied. Little verses, too, Mother Goosey jingles; one that is sung in Norwegian to babies in all the Scandinavian lands:

Row, row to the fishing ground,

> How many fishes have you found?
> One for Father,
> One for Mother,
> One for Sister,
> One for Brother,
> One for him that drew the nets,
> One for my little Baby.

Here is a little Faroe verse:

> Down comes the Puffin to the sea,
> With his head carried high.
> 'Little Gray-titlark, lend me thy boat?'
> 'Small is my boat, short are my legs—
> But come thee on board;'
> And the oars rattle in the oarlocks.

When the Baby grows a little bigger, she will not be taught that 'the Bossy-cow says, "Mo-o-o", the Pussy-cat says, "Me-ow". No, she will learn what the birds say:

> The Puffin says, 'Ur-r! UR-R! UR-R!'_
> The Raven says, 'Kronk! KRONK! KRONK!'_
> The Crow says, 'Kra! KRA! KRA!'_
> The Eider-duck says, 'Ah-oo! AH-OO! AH-OO!'_
> The Wheatear says, 'Tck! TCK! TCK! None so pretty as I!'_

and so on through a long list of the birds of fjeld and sea.

Summer and winter the birds will be the Baby's neighbors. From her father's cabin she can hear the eider-ducks cooing softly as they rise and fall just beyond the white crest of the breakers. Starlings bubble and chortle on the grassy house-roof; from the dark cliffs sounds the raven's clarion cry, and there are always seagulls near. With spring come all the sea-fowl to the bird-cliffs, and curlew, golden plover, and Arctic jaegers, 'plaintive creatures that pity themselves on moorlands'. All through the long dark winter the wren and titlark sing cheerfully. The 'mouse's brother' the Baby will call the Faroe wren, and she will know one fact of which grave scientists are ignorant, that the 'mouse's brother' and the titlark sing a bird-translation of a verse from the old Kingos Psalm-book. She will know, too, how the eider-duck won her down, the story of the naughty shag and the Apostle Peter, why the cormorant has no tongue, and that the great black-backed gull once struck our Lord upon the Cross and thenceforth bore a blood-red spot on his bill. Well can the Baby say in the words of the Kalevala, 'The birds of Heaven, the waves of the sea, have spoken and sung to me; the music of many waters has been my master.'

Few will the Baby's pleasures be. She will never have a Christmas tree, nor hang up her stocking, nor have other presents than a pair of mittens or a woollen kerchief for her head. The day before Christmas she will help her mother to scrub everything that can be scrubbed, indoors and out, working far into 'Jóla-Natt', so that all shall be sweet and clean for the birthday of our Lord. And next morning, in the sod-roofed church where never was a fire made, she will sit with her mother on the women's side, waiting meekly after service until the last man and the last boy have left their seats. She will dance lightly on the sea-rocks, her fair hair blowing in the wind, retreating as the big waves crash down, and singing something which sounds like '*Ala kan eje taka mej*!' (The wave cannot catch me!) She sings it to the same little tune I sang as a child when dancing back and forth across the danger-line of Taffy's land, mocking the rushes of an agile Taffy.

From seven to fourteen years she will go to school two weeks out of every six (the schoolmaster must be shared between three hamlets), and when fourteen years old, she will be confirmed, if she has learned enough Danish to pass the examinations and to say the prayers and creed. On that morning of confirmation she will turn up her hair, and wear a dress skirt that will flap about her little heels. And that afternoon there will be chocolate and cakes in her father's cabin, with friends coming and going.

She will know suspense and fear and sickening dread when

'the boats are out', and the great gales burst without warning. From every hamlet the sea has taken many; not one home has been spared. She cannot escape the common lot; of grief she shall have her share.

◆

Three days of storm passed and the Baby was not thriving. She needed her mother, and a consultation was held, the old sea-dogs of the hamlet advising. The gale was surely lessening, and with nine picked men, eight to row and one to steer, it could and should be done. The passage was to be made to Thorshavn to bring the Pastor home. So off they went in the early morning.

I was in my room, upstairs, about eleven o'clock, when I noticed that the roar of the wind and the creaking and groaning of the timbers overhead had ceased. I went to the window in time to see a great mass of snow gathered up from the ground and hurled against the house. In that short pause the wind had changed, and now blew from the west with redoubled fury. I hurried downstairs, and one glance at the Pastorinde's face confirmed my fears. She knew only too well where the returning boat was at that hour: far out, off the worst place on the coast, in fierce sea-currents, and in the full sweep of this new off-shore gale. The men were in dire peril. Many boats the Pastorinde had known to 'go away' in such a storm, after hours of desperate struggle to hold the boat in place and make some headway toward land. Then, as strength failed, there would be a slipping seaward, faster and faster, till men and boat went under, overwhelmed by a mighty cross-sea—'the drowning wave'.

Hour after hour went by; the Pastorinde paced the rooms, pale and silent. Under the shelter of walls and boat-houses were groups of men looking seaward. At last a shout, and men pointing; out in a smother of flying foam a dark spot had been seen, then lost, then seen again far away under the cliffs of distant Stromö. The boat was slowly making its way to a point due west, where it could blow in with the gale. All the men and boys who could stand on their legs were down in the surf to meet it, and with a rush the boat was borne up on land.

All was ready in the parsonage. The rug in the dining-room rolled up, hot coffee made, food on the table; and the Pastorinde was standing in the doorway as the men toiled feebly up, their clothes streaming with sea-water. Nine men only! Where was the tenth—where was the Pastor? And, all together, the tale was told. The Pastor, they had found, was not in Thorshavn; two days ago the Danish gun-boat had carried him off to Trangisvaag on some church affair, and nothing had been seen of him since. Higher and higher rose the voices, trembling with the irritation and unreasoning anger of utter exhaustion. The storm had struck them at the worst place; for four hours they had struggled just to hold their own, and were drifting seaward, when a short lull came, and with hope renewed they fought again and at last reached the sheltering cliffs of Stromö. Their eyes were wild and glassy, their hair matted, their hands swollen and bleeding from straining at the oars. The Pastorinde—wise woman—wasted no words of sympathy: she poured coffee, hot fragrant coffee with plenty of cream in it. The men drank and the talking quieted to grateful mumbles, and the cups were filled again, while their clothes dripped sea-water and the floor was all afloat.

Two mornings later, before dawn, I heard a knock on my door, and the Pastorinde's voice calling, 'The storm has ceased and they are going to take the Baby to Thorshavn, to be baptized by the Thorshavn pastor. They will take you, too, if you can be ready in half an hour.'

We were ready, all the baptismal party, plus myself and the borrowed 'maternal font'. One of the men came for me with a lantern, and I clutched his strong hand and slipped and slid over the icy rocks. Lights flared here and there, and land, sea, and sky were all one blackness; only a faint gray line showed where the sea was breaking. The surf was still high, covering the usual landing-place. One by one, we women were carried to a group of rocks that rose above the surf. Beyond, the boat was pitching and tossing, two men in the rowing-seats keeping the high sharp prow pointing toward the land. It was no easy matter to get on board, but we stood not upon the order of our going but jumped at once. At one moment I was on top of two godmothers, the next moment five godfathers scrambled over me to their places at the oars. Muffled shrieks arose and ejaculations:

'*Ak Gud bevare os!*'

'*Ak Herre Jesu!*' The boat swept out into the darkness, and we women-folk picked ourselves up and sorted ourselves out.

It was bitterly cold, and it rained—oh, how it rained! But we didn't care, we were going to Thorshavn at last, and there was a good sea. The change of wind, the down-pour, had flattened the broken surges. Only the great ground-swells swept landward, rank on rank, crashing along the coast. We mounted slowly to their summits and glided down the outer slopes with the motion of a bird in flight. Gayly rose the talk in the boat, and there was a lighting of little pipes, one at a time, so that the rowing need not be hindered. Now a faint yellow gleam on the southern horizon beyond the down-dropping veils of mist; then, dimly seen, the snow-crowned heights of Naalsö rising eighteen hundred feet from the sea. The danger-point on Stromö passed, and then in the distance twinkling lights, and a breath from shore bearing the fragrance of peat-smoke.—'So he bringeth them to their desired haven.'

Out on the fjord the Danish gun-boat rose and fell, and on the wet shore-rocks was a lonely figure gazing out to sea, like the pictures of Napoleon on Elba. It had a familiar look—it was—yes, it was the Pastor!

They laid hands on the Pastor, as though they expected him to vanish from their sight. The Baby would be baptized then and there. Scant time was given to the godmothers to change their shoes, skirts, and stockings, and to prink.

Clang, Clang! Clang! rang the church-bell in treble staccato notes. There was a clattering of pattens in the stony lanes as children hurried to the Baptism. The Pastor, a dignified priestly figure in his long black robes and Elizabethan ruff, left the Thorshavn parsonage, passed through the side gate to the church-portal, and the bell-ringing died away.

◆

I was down at the landing an hour later to say 'farvel' to the Pastor and the baptismal party. And as the boat left shore I turned away to my little cabin-home with a sigh of relief. The Baby—Karin Marin Malene Elsebet Jakobina Jakobson—was baptized.

WORRIES OF A WINTER WALK

WILLIAM DEAN HOWELLS

The other winter, as I was taking a morning walk down to the East River, I came upon a bit of our motley life, a fact of our piebald civilization, which has perplexed me from time to time, ever since, and which I wish now to leave with the reader, for his or her more thoughtful consideration.

I

The morning was extremely cold. It professed to be sunny, and there was really some sort of hard glitter in the air, which, so far from being tempered by this effulgence, seemed all the stonier for it. Blasts of frigid wind swept the streets, and buffeted each other in a fury of resentment when they met around the corners. Although I was passing through a populous tenement-house quarter, my way was not hindered by the sports of the tenement-house children, who commonly crowd one from the sidewalks; no frowzy head looked out over the fire-escapes; there were no peddlers' carts or voices in the road-way; not above three or four shawl-hooded women cowered out of the little shops with small purchases in their hands; not so many tiny girls with jugs opened the doors of the beer saloons. The butchers' windows were painted with patterns of frost, through which I could dimly see the frozen meats hanging like hideous stalactites from the roof. When I came to the river, I ached in sympathy with the shipping painfully atilt on the rocklike surface of the brine, which broke against the piers, and sprayed itself over them like showers of powdered quartz.

But it was before I reached this final point that I received into my consciousness the moments of the human comedy which have been an increasing burden to it. Within a block of the river

I met a child so small that at first I almost refused to take any account of her, until she appealed to my sense of humor by her amusing disproportion to the pail which she was lugging in front of her with both of her little mittened hands. I am scrupulous about mittens, though I was tempted to write of her little naked hands, red with the pitiless cold. This would have been more effective, but it would not have been true, and the truth obliges me to own that she had a stout, warm-looking knit jacket on. The pail-which was half her height and twice her bulk-was filled to overflowing with small pieces of coal and coke, and if it had not been for this I might have taken her for a child of the better classes, she was so comfortably clad. But in that case she would have had to be fifteen or sixteen years old, in order to be doing so efficiently and responsibly the work which, as the child of the worse classes, she was actually doing at five or six. We must, indeed, allow that the early self-helpfulness of such children is very remarkable, and all the more so because they grow up into men and women so stupid that, according to the theories of all polite economists, they have to have their discontent with their conditions put into their heads by malevolent agitators.

From time to time this tiny creature put down her heavy burden to rest; it was, of course, only relatively heavy; a man would have made nothing of it. From time to time she was forced to stop and pick up the bits of coke that tumbled from her heaping pail. She could not consent to lose one of them, and at last, when she found she could not make all of them stay on the heap, she thriftily tucked them into the pockets of her jacket, and trudged sturdily on till she met a boy some years older, who planted himself in her path and stood looking at her, with his hands in his pockets. I do not say he was a bad boy, but I could see in his furtive eye that she was a sore temptation to him. The chance to have fun with her by upsetting her bucket, and scattering her coke about till she cried with vexation, was one which might not often present itself, and I do not know what made him forego it, but I know that he did, and that he finally passed her, as I have seen a young dog pass a little cat, after having stopped it, and thoughtfully considered worrying it.

I turned to watch the child out of sight, and when I faced about towards the river again I received the second instalment of my present perplexity. A cart, heavily laden with coke, drove out of the coal-yard which I now perceived I had come to, and after this cart followed two brisk old women, snugly clothed and tightly tucked in against the cold like the child, who vied with each other in catching up the lumps of coke that were jolted from the load, and filling their aprons with them; such old women, so hale, so spry, so tough and tireless, with the withered apples red in their cheeks, I have not often seen. They may have been about sixty years, or sixty-five, the time of life when most women are grandmothers and are relegated on their merits to the cushioned seats of their children's homes, softly silk-gowned and lace-capped, dear visions of lilac and lavender, to be loved and petted by their grandchildren. The fancy can hardly put such sweet ladies in the place of those nimble beldams, who hopped about there in the wind-swept street, plucking up their day's supply of firing from the involuntary bounty of the cart. Even the attempt is unseemly, and whether mine is at best but a feeble fancy, not bred to strenuous feats of any kind, it fails to bring them before me in that figure. I cannot imagine ladies doing that kind of thing; I can only imagine women who had lived hard and worked hard all their lives doing it; who had begun to fight with want from their cradles, like that little one with the pail, and must fight without ceasing to their graves. But I am not unreasonable; I understand and I understood what I saw to be one of the things that must be, for the perfectly good and sufficient reason that they always have been; and at the moment I got what pleasure I could out of the stolid indifference of the cart-driver, who never looked about him at the scene which interested me, but jolted onward, leaving a trail of pungent odors from his pipe in the freezing eddies of the air behind him.

II

It is still not at all, or not so much, the fact that troubles me; it is what to do with the fact. The question began with me almost at once, or at least as soon as I faced about and began to walk homeward with the wind at my back. I was then so much more comfortable that the aesthetic instinct thawed out in me, and I found myself wondering what use I could make of what I had seen in the way of my trade. Should I have something very pathetic, like the old grandmother going out day after day to pick up coke for her sick daughter's freezing orphans till she fell sick herself? What should I do with the family in that case? They could not be left at that point, and I promptly imagined a granddaughter, a girl of about eighteen, very pretty and rather proud, a sort of belle in her humble neighborhood, who should take her grandmother's place. I decided that I should have her Italian, because I knew something of Italians, and could manage that nationality best, and I should call her Maddalena; either Maddalena or Marina; Marina would be more Venetian, and I saw that I must make her Venetian. Here I was on safe ground, and at once the love-interest appeared to help me out. By virtue of the law of contrasts; it appeared to me in the person of a Scandinavian lover, tall, silent, blond, whom I at once felt I could do, from my acquaintance with Scandinavian lovers in Norwegian novels. His name was Janssen, a good, distinctive Scandinavian name; I do not know but it is Swedish; and I thought he might very well be a Swede; I could imagine his manner from that of a Swedish waitress we once had.

Janssen—Jan Janssen, say-drove the coke-cart which Marina's grandmother used to follow out of the coke-yard, to pick up the bits of coke as they were jolted from it, and he had often noticed her with deep indifference. At first he noticed Marina—or Nina, as I soon saw I must call her—with the same unconcern; for in her grandmother's hood and jacket and check apron, with her head held shamefacedly downward, she looked exactly like the old woman. I thought I would have Nina make her self-sacrifice rebelliously, as a girl like her would be apt to do, and follow the cokecart with tears. This would catch Janssen's notice, and he would wonder, perhaps with a little pang, what the old woman was crying about, and then he would see that it was not the old woman. He would see that it was Nina, and he would be in love with her at once, for she would not only be very pretty, but he would know that she was good, if she were willing to help her family in that way.

He would respect the girl, in his dull, sluggish, Northern way. He would do nothing to betray himself. But little by little he would begin to befriend her. He would carelessly overload his cart before he left the yard, so that the coke would fall from it more lavishly; and not only this, but if he saw a stone or a piece of coal in the street he would drive over it, so that more coke would be jolted from his load.

Nina would get to watching for him. She must not notice him much at first, except as the driver of the overladen, carelessly driven cart. But after several mornings she must see that he is very strong and handsome. Then, after several mornings more, their eyes must meet, her vivid black eyes, with the tears of rage and shame in them, and his cold blue eyes. This must be the climax; and just at this point I gave my fancy a rest, while I went into a drugstore at the corner of Avenue B to get my hands warm.

They were abominably cold, even in my pockets, and I had suffered past several places trying to think of an excuse to go in. I now asked the druggist if he had something which I felt pretty sure he had not, and this put him in the wrong, so that when we fell into talk he was very polite. We agreed admirably about the hard times, and he gave way respectfully when I doubted his opinion that the winters were getting milder. I made him reflect that there was no reason for this, and that it was probably an illusion from that deeper impression which all experiences made on us in the past, when we were younger; I ought to say that he was an elderly man, too. I said I fancied such a morning as this was not very mild for people that had no fires, and this brought me back again to Janssen and Marina, by way of the coke-cart. The thought of them rapt me so far from the druggist that I listened to his answer with a glazing eye, and did not know what he said. My hands had now got warm, and I bade him good-morning with a parting regret, which he civilly shared, that he had not the thing I had not wanted, and I pushed out again into the cold, which I found not so bad as before.

My hero and heroine were waiting for me there, and I saw that to be truly modern, to be at once realistic and mystical, to have both delicacy and strength, I must not let them get further acquainted with each other. The affair must simply go on from day to day, till one morning Jan must note that it was again the grandmother and no longer the girl who was following his cart. She must be very weak from a long sickness—I was not sure whether to have it the grippe or not, but I decided upon that provisionally and she must totter after Janssen, so that he must get down after a while to speak to her under pretence of arranging the tail-board of his cart, or something of that kind; I did not care for the detail. They should get into talk in the broken English which was the only language they could have in common, and she should burst into tears, and tell him that now Nina was sick; I imagined making this very simple, but very touching, and I really made it so touching that it brought the lump into my own throat, and I knew it would be effective with the reader. Then I had Jan get back upon his cart, and drive stolidly on again, and the old woman limp feebly after.

There should not be any more, I decided, except that one very cold morning, like that; Jan should be driving through that street, and should be passing the door of the tenement house where Nina had lived, just as a little procession should be issuing from it. The fact must be told in brief sentences, with a total absence of emotionality. The last touch must be Jan's cart turning the street corner with Jan's figure sharply silhouetted against the clear, cold morning light. Nothing more.

But it was at this point that another notion came into my mind, so antic, so impish, so fiendish, that if there were still any Evil One, in a world which gets on so poorly without him, I should attribute it to his suggestion; and this was that the procession which Jan saw issuing from the tenement-house door was not a funeral procession, as the reader will have rashly fancied, but a wedding procession, with Nina at the head of it, quite well again, and going to be married to the little brown youth with ear-rings who had long had her heart.

With a truly perverse instinct, I saw how strong this might be made, at the fond reader's expense, to be sure, and how much more pathetic, in such a case, the silhouetted figure on the coke-cart would really be. I should, of course, make it perfectly plain that no one was to blame, and that the whole affair had been so tacit on Jan's part that Nina might very well have known nothing of his feeling for her. Perhaps at the very end I might subtly insinuate that it was possible he might have had no such feeling towards her as the reader had been led to imagine.

III

The question as to which ending I ought to have given my romance is what has ever since remained to perplex me, and it is what has prevented my ever writing it. Here is material of the best sort lying useless on my hands, which, if I could only make up my mind, might be wrought into a short story as affecting as any that wring our hearts in fiction; and I think I could get something fairly unintelligible out of the broken English of Jan and Nina's grandmother, and certainly something novel. All that I can do now, however, is to put the case before the reader, and let him decide for himself how it should end.

The mere humanist, I suppose, might say, that I am rightly served for having regarded the fact I had witnessed as material for fiction at all; that I had no business to bewitch it with my miserable art; that I ought to have spoken to that little child and those poor old women, and tried to learn something of their lives from them, that I might offer my knowledge again for the instruction of those whose lives are easy and happy in the indifference which ignorance breeds in us. I own there is something in this, but then, on the other hand, I have heard it urged by nice people that they do not want to know about such squalid lives, that it is offensive and out of taste to be always bringing them in, and that we ought to be writing about good society, and especially creating grandes dames for their amusement. This sort of people could say to the humanist that he ought to be glad there are coke-carts for fuel to fall off from for the lower classes, and that here was no case for sentiment; for if one is to be interested in such things at all, it must be aesthetically, though even this is deplorable in the presence of fiction already overloaded with low life, and so poor in grades dames as ours.